iPhone® & iPad™
Game Development
FOR
DUMMIES®

**by Neal Goldstein, Paris Buttfield-Addison,
and Jon Manning**

WILEY

Wiley Publishing, Inc.

iPhone® & iPad™ Game Development For Dummies®

Published by
Wiley Publishing, Inc.
111 River Street
Hoboken, NJ 07030-5774

www.wiley.com

WILEY

About the Authors

Neal Goldstein is a recognized leader in making state-of-the-art, cutting-edge technologies practical for commercial and enterprise development. He was one of the first technologists to work with commercial developers at firms such as Apple Computer, Lucasfilm, and Microsoft to develop commercial applications using object-based programming technologies. He was a pioneer in moving that approach into the corporate world for developers at Liberty Mutual Insurance, USWest (now Verizon), National Car Rental, EDS, and Continental Airlines, showing them how object-oriented programming could solve enterprise-wide problems. His book (with Jeff Alger) on object-oriented development, *Developing Object-Oriented Software for the Macintosh* (Addison Wesley), introduced the idea of scenarios and patterns to developers. He was an early advocate of the Microsoft .NET framework, and he successfully introduced it into many enterprises, including Charles Schwab. He was one of the earliest developers of Service Oriented Architecture (SOA), and as Senior Vice President of Advanced Technology and the Chief Architect at Charles Schwab, he built an integrated SOA solution that spanned the enterprise, from desktop PCs to servers to complex network mainframes. (He holds three patents as a result.) As one of IBM's largest customers, he introduced the folks at IBM to SOA at the enterprise level and encouraged them to head in that direction.

He is currently passionate about the real value mobile devices can provide and has eight applications in the App Store. These include a series of *Travel Photo Guides* (http://travelphotoguides.com) developed with his partners at mobilefortytwo and a *Digital Field Guides* series (http://lp.wileypub.com/DestinationDFGiPhoneApp) developed in partnership with John Wiley & Sons. He also has a cool little, free app — *Expense Calendar* — that allows you to keep track of things like expenses, mileage, and time by adding them to your calendar.

Along with those apps, he has written several books on iPhone programming, including *iPhone Application Development For Dummies* (both editions) and *Objective-C For Dummies,* and he coauthored (with Tony Bove) *iPhone Application Development All-In-One For Dummies* and *iPad Application Development For Dummies.* He is also the coauthor (with Jon Manning and Paris Buttfield-Addison) of a forthcoming book on using the Unity platform for game development.

Because you can never tell what he'll be up to next, check regularly at his Web site: www.nealgoldstein.com. You can also check out his Facebook page at www.facebook.com/nealgoldsteinbooks and follow him on Twitter at www.twitter.com/nealgoldstein.

Jon Manning has a collection of careers, which he swaps out as necessary: He's co-founder of Secret Lab (the world's most dangerous mobile games startup), a Senior Software Engineer at Meebo, Inc. (where he builds mobile apps that reach a stupidly huge number of people), and a Graduate Researcher in Human-Computer Interaction at the University of Tasmania in Australia (a land of computers and kangaroos). When he isn't working on apps or books, he's working on adding more letters to the end of his name. He spends nowhere near enough time around cats. You can find Jon online at `www.desplesda.net` and on Twitter at `www.twitter.com/desplesda`.

Paris Buttfield-Addison wears many hats: He's co-founder of Secret Lab (`www.secretlab.com.au`), author, educator, and Product Manager (Mobile) at Meebo, Inc., one of the Web's fastest growing consumer Internet companies (`www.meebo.com`). Paris has degrees in HCI, computer science, and medieval and modern history. He enjoys designing, producing, and building awesome experiences for mobile devices. Through some miracle of time management, he is also a Graduate Researcher in information management at the University of Tasmania, Australia. You can find Paris on the Web at `www.paris.id.au` and on Twitter at `www.twitter.com/parisba`.

Dedication

Neal Goldstein: To my children Evan and Sarah, and all my personal and artist friends who have kept me centered on the (real) world outside of writing and technology. But most of all, to my wife Linda, who is everything that I ever hoped for and more than I deserve. Yes, Sam . . . the light at the end of the tunnel is not a freight train.

Jon Manning: To my family, for introducing me to this whole "computers" thing.

Paris Buttfield-Addison: To my mother and father, for all the usual things — everything.

Authors' Acknowledgments

There is no better acquisitions editor than Katie Feltman, who did a superb job of keeping us on track and doing whatever she needed to do to us to stay focused on writing. Linda Morris did a great job in the early stages of the project, and project editor Pat O'Brien made sure all the parts were pulled together. Also thanks to copy editor Jen Riggs and technical editor Erick Tejkowski for helping us make things clearer. Thanks again to our agent Carole Jelen for her continued work and support in putting together these projects.

Publisher's Acknowledgments

We're proud of this book; please send us your comments at http://dummies.custhelp.com. For other comments, please contact our Customer Care Department within the U.S. at 877-762-2974, outside the U.S. at 317-572-3993, or fax 317-572-4002.

Some of the people who helped bring this book to market include the following:

Acquisitions, Editorial, and Media Development

Project Editor: Pat O'Brien

Acquisitions Editor: Katie Feltman

Copy Editor: Jen Riggs

Technical Editor: Erick Tejkowski

Editorial Manager: Kevin Kirschner

Media Development Assistant Project Manager: Jenny Swisher

Media Development Associate Producers: Josh Frank, Marilyn Hummel, Douglas Kuhn, and Shawn Patrick

Editorial Assistant: Amanda Graham

Sr. Editorial Assistant: Cherie Case

Cartoons: Rich Tennant (www.the5thwave.com)

Composition Services

Project Coordinator: Sheree Montgomery

Layout and Graphics: Timothy C. Detrick, Joyce Haughey, Andrea Hornberger

Proofreaders: Laura Albert, Shannon Ramsey

Indexer: BIM Indexing & Proofreading Services

Publishing and Editorial for Technology Dummies

Richard Swadley, Vice President and Executive Group Publisher

Andy Cummings, Vice President and Publisher

Mary Bednarek, Executive Acquisitions Director

Mary C. Corder, Editorial Director

Publishing for Consumer Dummies

Diane Graves Steele, Vice President and Publisher

Composition Services

Debbie Stailey, Director of Composition Services

Contents at a Glance

Table of Contents

Introduction

*O*n September 1, 2010, Steve Jobs took the stage in San Francisco to announce the latest and greatest iPod. During his speech, he gloated an astonishing statistic that Apple has 50 percent of the mobile gaming market; he followed up with the even more astonishing statistic that the iPod touch alone outsells both Nintendo's mobile products and Sony's mobile products — combined.

We don't really need to say any more than that to convince you that developing games for Apple's mobile platforms is worthwhile! We probably will though.

As you continue to explore the iOS as a gaming platform, you'll be amazed at the possibilities for simple, quick attention-grabbing games that last for mere moments of time. The iPhone and iPad are, in addition to being useful and powerful mobile computers, the most interesting gaming devices in recent memory. The combination of powerful hardware, a decent display, permanent Internet connectivity, and an enormous user base (120 million iOS devices as of late 2010) makes it possible to create a class of games for mobile users that were once possible only on desktop PCs. But not only that — Apple's App Store provides a direct sales and distribution channel to potential users that really can't be beaten.

The iPhone and iPad, and iOS in general, are game changers for the world of game development. Never before has it been so easy for an individual, or a small group, to build a game that can be distributed to the world. One of the hallmarks of a great iOS game is that it leverages the unique hardware and operating system (iOS) that Apple produces for an extremely polished and consistent, yet unique, experience. The iOS Software Development Kit (SDK), which you use to develop iOS games, includes tools such as OpenGL ES, which makes the type of 3D graphics that would've never been possible on a mobile device, dare we say it, simple. The frameworks supplied in the SDK are especially rich and mature. All you really have to do is add your game's user interface and game play mechanics to the framework, and then *poof* . . . an instant game. Well, sort of — but we help you through the patches that are a bit more challenging, as we guide you along the way to making an awesome game.

If you're familiar with older versions of the SDK, you're in for a pleasant surprise: SDK version 4.1, which includes Xcode 3.2.3, is a lot, lot better and easier to use. This book is based on iOS 4.1 for iPhone and iOS 3.2 for iPad (the latest versions at the time of writing) and Xcode 3.2.3.

If this seems too good to be true, well, okay, it *is,* sort of. What's really hard, after you figure out the language and framework, is how to create a program structure for an iOS. Although there are lots of resources, the problem is exactly that: There are *lots* of resources — as in *thousands* of pages of documentation! You may get through a small fraction of the documentation before you just can't take it anymore and plunge right into coding. Naturally enough, you'll have a few false starts and blind alleys until you find your way, but we predict that after reading this book, it's (pretty much) smooth sailing.

About This Book

iPhone & iPad Game Development For Dummies is a beginner's guide to developing games for the iPhone, iPod touch, and iPad, which all run Apple's iOS. And not only do you *not* need any iPad (or iPhone) development experience to get started, but you also don't need any Macintosh development experience either. We expect you to come as a blank slate, ready to be filled with useful information and new ways to do things.

The iOS devices allow you to build truly innovative, simple, and clever games that can reach a wider audience than was ever possible for independently developed games in the past. And because you can also start small and create fun, simple games that entertain the player, it's relatively easy to transform yourself from "you know nothing" into a game developer who, though not (yet) a superstar, can still crank out quite a respectable game.

The iPhone and iPad devices can be home to some pretty fancy games as well — so we take you on a journey through building not just a simple game but also a souped up version for the iPad that uses OpenGL ES (a 3D graphics system that we cover in Chapter 22) so that you know the ropes for developing your own game.

This book distills the hundreds (or even thousands) of pages of Apple documentation, not to mention our own game and app development experiences, into only what's necessary to start developing real, fun games. But this is no recipe book that leaves it up to you to put it all together; rather, we take you through the frameworks and iOS architecture in a way that gives you a solid foundation in how games really work on the iPhone, iPad, and iPod touch. This book acts as a roadmap to expand your knowledge as you need to.

This book is a multiple-course banquet, intended to make you feel satisfied (and really full) at the end.

Conventions Used in This Book

This book guides you through the process of building iOS games. Throughout, you use the provided iOS framework classes for iOS (and create new ones, of course) and code them using the Objective-C programming language.

Code examples in this book appear in a monofont so they stand out a bit better. That means the code you see looks like this:

```
#import <UIKit/ UIKit.h>
```

Objective-C is based on C, which (we want to remind you) *is* case-sensitive, so please enter the code that appears in this book *exactly* as it appears in the text. This book also uses the standard Objective-C naming conventions — for example, class names always start with a capital letter, and the names of methods and instance variables always start with a lowercase letter.

All URLs in this book appear in a monofont as well:

```
www.nealgoldstein.com
```

If you're ever uncertain about anything in the code, you can always look at the source code on the Internet at `www.nealgoldstein.com` or `www.traffic.secretlab.com.au`. (You can grab the same material from the *For Dummies* Web site at `www.dummies.com/go/PONIES`.) From time to time, we provide updates for the code there and post other things you might find useful. Neal also offers insights about everything from developing apps to the future of mobile devices and applications at `www.nealgoldstein.com`. Secret Lab also posts articles and notes on game design and development at `www.secretlab.com.au`.

Foolish Assumptions

To begin creating your iOS games, you need an Intel-based Macintosh computer with the latest version of the Mac OS on it. (No, you can't program iPhone applications on the iPad!) You also need to download the iOS SDK — which is free — but you have to become a Registered iOS Developer before you can do that. (Don't worry; we show you how in Chapter 2.) And, oh yeah, you need an iPhone or iPod touch (or an iPad if that's your target device). You don't run your game on them right away — you use the Simulator that Apple provides with the iOS SDK during the initial stages of development — but at some point, you need to test your application on a real, live iOS device.

This book assumes that you have some programming knowledge and that you have at least a passing acquaintance with object-oriented programming, using some variant of the C language (such as C++, C#, or even Objective-C). If not, we point out some resources that can help you get up to speed (including Neal's book, *Objective-C For Dummies*). The examples in this book focus on the frameworks that come with the SDK; the code is pretty simple (usually) and straightforward. (We don't use this book as a platform to dazzle you with fancy coding techniques.)

This book also assumes that you're familiar with the iPhone and iPad, and that you've at least explored Apple's included applications to get a good working sense of the iOS look, feel, and style. Browse the App Store to see the kinds of games available there, and maybe even download a few free ones (as if we could stop you).

How This Book Is Organized

iPhone & iPad Game Development For Dummies has five main parts, which we explain in more detail in the following sections.

Part I: Getting Started

Part I introduces you to the iOS game development world. You find out what makes a great iOS game, and how to exploit the iPhone, iPod touch, and iPad's best features to create a compelling and fun gaming experience. You also discover how to sign up for the iOS Developer Program and become an official developer so that you can distribute your games through the App Store. You also explore the components of the iOS SDK, such as Xcode (the Apple development environment) and Interface Builder.

Part II: Traffic, The Game

In this part, you find out how iPhone games work, and we explain how to use the frameworks that form the raw material of any iOS app to assemble the user interface of our example game, *Traffic,* and to move things around on the screen. We also reveal design patterns that you need to adopt to make use of the iOS SDK. Part II also describes how to debug your games, provision your work for testing on real devices (and for distribution to the App Store), and play music and sounds.

Part III: The Social Aspects

Part III is deceptively short but intensely illuminating. These four chapters describe integrating more social technologies with your game, including Apple's Game Kit framework for wireless networking among people on multiple devices, Facebook for posting social updates, and external display support for making your game have more of a party atmosphere.

Part IV: The iPad

With the basics behind you and a good understanding of the iPhone game architecture under your belt, it's time to talk about money and the iPad. In this part, we discuss Apple's iAd for generating revenue through the sale of advertising displayed in your game. Part IV also covers the theoretical and practical aspects of upsizing your game to the world of high-resolution and technologies introduced with the iPhone 4 and the iPad, such as gesture recognizers. We dip a toe in the world of OpenGL ES (Apple's fast 3D graphics library) and speed up the world of *Traffic* with some new effects and features for the iPad version.

Part V: The Part of Tens

Part V consists of some tips to help you avoid figuring out everything the hard way. We talk about some key differences to consider when designing games for the iPad and iPhone, discuss some marketing tips to help get you on the road to App Store success, and showcase our ten favorite games to be inspired by.

Icons Used in This Book

This icon indicates a useful point that you shouldn't skip.

This icon represents a friendly reminder. We describe a vital point here that you should keep in mind while proceeding through a particular section of the chapter.

This icon signifies that the accompanying explanation may be informative (dare we say, interesting?), but it isn't essential to understanding game development. Feel free to skip past these tidbits if you want.

This icon alerts you to potential problems that you may encounter along the way. Read and obey these blurbs to avoid trouble.

Where to Go from Here

Dive into the exciting world of iOS game development! If you're nervous, take heart: The iOS is still so new and such rich territory for developers to mine, that no company or individual has a lock on innovating with it. Your idea just might be the exciting game that everyone's waiting for.

Don't forget to check out our Web sites at www.nealgoldstein.com, www.secretlab.com.au, and www.traffic.secretlab.com.au or www.dummies.com/go/iphoneipadgameprogramming.

Now, get ready to have some fun building games!

Part I
Getting Started

The 5th Wave   By Rich Tennant

"Yes, I have experience with nonprofit organizations. I created an iPad game called "Deep Sea Oil Drilling Adventure.""

In this part . . .

You say you want a revolution? Well, here's the plan: This part explains what you need to know to get started on the Great iOS Game Design and Development Trek. After reading this part, you can evaluate your idea for an iOS game application, see how it stacks up, and figure out what you have to do to transform it into something that knocks your users' socks off.

You have to register as an Apple developer if you want to get the Software Development Kit (SDK) and all the other goodies that Apple provides for developers — and of course, that means agreeing to a confidentiality agreement. And if you actually want to run your application on a real iOS device, you have to join the iOS Developer Program. This part gets you through these processes and introduces you to the SDK. Here's a breakdown of the chapters in this part:

- ✔ Chapter 1 describes the features of iOS devices and the elements that make a great game. You find out how to exploit the platform's features and embrace its limitations. You also discover how to design with both while keeping user expectations in mind.

- ✔ Chapter 2 gets you into the Apple developer village. You find out how to register as a developer, join the program, explore the developer center on the Web, and download the SDK.

- ✔ Chapter 3 goes into more detail about the SDK itself. You find out all about Xcode and Interface Builder, how to start a game project from a template, how to build and run a game, and how to customize Xcode to your liking.

Chapter 1

Building Great iOS Games

*J*ust as you find with any type of app, the range of games available for the iPhone (and iPad) is huge. They range from games that are expected to be chart busters from the beginning (the games produced by giant studios, such as Electronic Arts) to games made by individuals in their spare time that become huge hits (for example, *Trism* and *Flight Control*).

So, as a soon-to-be iPhone and iPad game creator, you need to find your slot in the range of games. As the authors of this book, we help you do that. In this chapter, we tell you how to get into the game developer mindset, determine what makes a good game, initiate a game concept, and then design the game to fully develop that concept.

When we started writing this book, we spent a lot of time figuring out the best way to showcase iOS game development. After much deliberation, we decided to showcase a complete game, dubbed *Traffic,* from start to finish. The alternative was to merely show you how to build pieces that could be useful in the development of a game. Instead, we chose to build a commercial-quality game step by step, demonstrating all the concepts and knowledge you need to build an amazing, real game of your own.

Enjoy!

iPhone, iPads, iDon'tKnows

The *iPad,* Apple's new computer, is fresh out of the factories and being bought by the millions. The iPad has been (somewhat unfairly) described as a "giant iPhone," which is inaccurate from a user experience point of view but rather accurate from a technical point of view.

Both the iPad and the iPhone run the same operating system — *iOS.* This means that 95 percent of the skills you pick up by reading this book apply to the iPad as much as they do to the iPhone. When we talk about iOS, or iOS

devices, we're talking about the iPhone, the iPod touch, and the iPad.

Because these devices are so similar, whenever we refer to development on the iPhone, we also talk about development on the iPad as well.

Parts I, II, and III of this book discuss the development of the game for both the iPhone and the iPad. Part IV has more focus on the iPad and discusses the changes that you need to make so your game is the best it can be on the iPad.

Figuring Out What a User Wants from an iPhone Game

Think about a typical weekday — it's 8 a.m., and you're waiting for your train. You're bored. You've already checked your e-mail more times than is healthy, you've checked Twitter and told the world that your train is late, and you've checked the latest news headlines in your favorite news application. And you're still bored.

If only you had a game to pass the time! If you're using an iPhone, you probably do. You take your iPhone out of your pocket and touch the icon of your current favorite game to ease your boredom for a moment. Sixty seconds later, your bus arrives. You instantly snap out of the pocket-sized game world you were absorbed in, push your iPhone's Home button, and get on the bus.

On the train, you take a seat and pull your iPhone back out. Touching the icon of your favorite game again, you ease right back into play at exactly the same point you left off before you got on the train. Ten minutes later, your train pulls up at your stop, and you hit the Home button, pop the iPhone into your pocket, and head into work.

Why does all this matter? This scenario reflects the way most people play the best of the games available on the iPhone. They want to be able to listen to their music while they play, and they don't want the game to demand so much of them that they'll miss their train, or worse.

People play their iPhone games in potentially loud, bright, and distracting environments while they wait for something else to happen or while they talk to people. They play them for a minute or two before switching to something else, and they expect their iPhone to know what they were up to when they finally come back to the game.

Establishing a Game Developer Mindset

Why develop iPhone and iPad games? Because you can. Because it's time. And most of all, because it's fun! Developing a game that can potentially reach an audience in the millions is a hugely rewarding experience no matter how you look at it. Here's what makes developing games so much fun:

- ✓ **iOS games are usually small and conceptually simple to understand.** As with iPhone apps, a single developer, or maybe one with a partner and some graphics support, can do them. You don't need an enormous team with hordes of people, managers, and paperwork to create something rich and compelling. You have the power to create something that can reach millions, and you can do it from your own home.

- ✓ **Games on the iPhone and iPad are focused and clean.** The games get straight to the point of what makes them fun and help the users to dive in and out with ease. They're simple but not simplistic. This makes the design and implementation much easier and faster.

- ✓ **The popularity of the iOS platforms (that is, the iPhone and the iPad) makes getting your work into the hands of users easier than ever.** Getting your game onto a mobile device used to mean negotiating a deal with a publisher; these days, it's as simple as signing up online with Apple.

Before we talk about how to design your games, it's worth pointing out the single most valuable piece of advice one iOS game developer can give another: *Play other people's games!*

The more you play iOS games, the better you understand them. The better you understand them, the better your own games become. When you play, if you try to determine how the game actually works, you often strike inspiration. Many games appear simple on the surface, but if you delve deeper beneath the interface by paying closer attention to how you interact with the game and what the game presents to you in return, you reveal much hidden complexity in the way the game is constructed.

Discovering how others have built their games while you play them is the best way (other than reading this book) to develop your game building skills and gain a better understanding of what makes a great game tick.

Noting the Features of Good Games

Figure 1-1 shows the final version of the *Traffic* game you develop throughout this book. The concept for this game came to us after we noticed the popularity of simple puzzle games, line-drawing games, and solid (but simple), smartly presented game designs in the App Store.

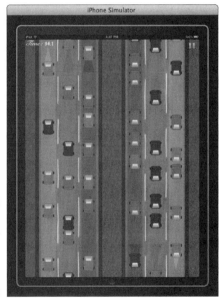

Figure 1-1:
The *Traffic* game you build in this book.

How complex is the *Traffic* game? Not very. After you figure out how the game works in your head, and on paper, the actual programming doesn't take very long. Developing *Traffic* took us a little more than two months, working on and off.

Good iOS games share characteristics with good iOS applications of any kind. Before you jump in and design and build your game, make sure that you recognize these characteristics and incorporate them in your creation. We don't use *all* these characteristics in the *Traffic* game because it doesn't make any sense to simply cram ideas and features into a game in the spirit of embracing a platform. Judicious picking and choosing is essential to building a great game. In the next sections, we go over some of the most important.

Device-guided design

One of the keys to creating a great iOS application is to take advantage of the functionality that the device offers. In the case of a new platform (such as the iPhone 4 and the iPad), capitalizing on the new possibilities is especially important — especially when the application is a game!

Games are often expected to push the limits of a platform. When your game can easily incorporate new iOS (or hardware) functionality, new frontiers of game design and innovation open before you. These elements of iOS functionality — and how they relate to games — are as follows:

- **Accessing the Internet:** Allowing your games to offer users the ability to post their high scores to social networking sites, such as Facebook, or quickly and easily download new levels or content packs for your games is not just a good idea, it's essential. Word of your game spreads faster as users share their scores and favorite levels via their Facebook or Twitter pages. Your users also feel more connected and invested in your game because they're sharing it with their friends! By providing access to extra content stored online, your game's initial download size can also be made quite small.

  We cover making your game into a social beast in Chapter 16.

- **Detecting the location of the user:** Using the iPhone's built-in location services, you can determine the device's current location or even be notified when that location changes. In the context of gaming, location has a variety of potential uses — though many of them aren't obvious. For example, you could create a location-based game in which the player's location influences the game.

  Pac-Manhattan, a 2004 research project into location-aware games, had players running around the streets of New York carrying bulky GPS devices and re-creating a game of the arcade classic *Pac-Man.* Six years later, you have all the power of that hardware in your users' pockets.

- **Tracking motion and orientation:** The iPhone and iPad contain three accelerometers and a compass (and the iPhone 4 adds a gyroscope), which help you detect very small changes in movement. You can use these features to detect when the user turns the device from vertical to horizontal. In the case of iPhone games, you're probably more interested in subtle movements, such as tilting.

  Cro-Mag Rally, by Pangea Software, features a unique racing experience in which the user holds the iPhone like a steering wheel and turns it to drive the car. There are also a number of dexterity-based games in which the player must roll a ball around an obstacle course, such as *Super Monkey Ball* and *Labyrinth. Traffic* makes use of the accelerometer to detect the user shaking the device; you can read about how to add the feature to the game in Chapter 25.

✔ **Tracking multiple screen touches:** Because people use their fingers, rather than a mouse, to select and manipulate objects on the iPhone screen, take advantage of the fact that people have more than one finger! The iPhone can detect up to five individual fingers on the screen at any one time and lets you determine when people perform gestures with their fingers on the screen. The iPad can detect up to 11 individual touches on the screen simultaneously. (That's ten fingers plus your nose! We checked, using Jon's nose.)

In games, gestures allow your players to have a very fluid and natural source of input to your game world. Flicking, pinching, and scrolling are very natural-feeling things to do in the iOS. If your game takes advantage of them, your users will notice, and they'll already know how to perform the most basic inputs to your game without needing a tutorial.

✔ **Playing audio and video:** The iOS makes playing and including audio and video in your application easy. You can play sound effects or take advantage of the multichannel audio and mixing capabilities available. You can also play back many standard movie file formats, configure the aspect ratio, and specify whether the controls are displayed.

Of course, no game would be complete without a solid set of sound effects and a catchy theme tune! The iOS makes it easy to add these things as well as tweak the more complex and optional aspects of them, should the need arise.

✔ **Accessing the user's music library:** The iOS also makes gaining access to your user's songs, audio books, and audio podcasts very simple. You don't have to restrict your users to your game's theme music, but can allow them to pick and choose a custom playlist from their own library (or even assemble an entirely new playlist on the fly). This deceptively simple offering can help make your users feel more at home while playing your game and often entices them back to play more.

✔ **Accessing simple, ad hoc, location-based networking:** Specifically designed with games in mind, Apple's Game Kit allows you to create ad hoc Bluetooth networks among multiple iOS devices without the need for relatively complex Bluetooth pairing. This means your games can provide users with a very simple-to-activate multiplayer functionality, with the only requirement that they must be in proximity to another iPhone or iPad user running your game.

Incorporating the fun

Games need to be fun. When developing any game, examine several core principles of making the playing experience fun. There isn't a secret formula for games, but instilling and maximizing fun makes a better game for your users:

✔ **Happy players feel in control.** A lot of the fun in computer games is found in the pleasure of taking and manipulating the game world.

- In *first-person shooter games* (combat-based games in which you have direct control over the way you move and the direction you look in), this manipulation takes the form of running around and shooting things. The player has control over what lives or dies in the game world but needs to be mindful of the dangers present in that world.

- In *strategy games,* the player manipulates the world by sending units out to do battle, but also needs to be mindful of how and where to allocate these resources.

In either case, a good game gives the players the feeling of control by reacting quickly to their input in a way that reflects what the player wants.

✔ **Happy players get surprised.** A game that's exactly the same every time has no replay value. A game in which you can anticipate enemy behavior after only a few seconds gets boring very fast. And so, another important component of a good game's fun factor is the amount that it surprises the player.

An acceptable definition of fun itself could be *pleasure with surprises.*

By combining the pleasure of being in control with an element of random chance, you can ensure that your game is neither too predictable nor too random.

✔ **Happy players find patterns.** As people play a good game, certain patterns of behavior emerge in the way they play. For example, in first-person shooters, the best players sidestep around corners, rather than turn around them, because sidestepping means that they can immediately aim and shoot at any threat around the corner. Clever game developers notice these patterns of play and find ways to improve the player's experience of them.

Designing a Good Game

Although jumping straight into code and getting down to building a game is exciting, clear and concise design is incredibly important in game development (perhaps even more so than it is to application development). Designing a game is a very rewarding experience. Although the frameworks and tools provided by Apple's iOS *Software Development Kit (SDK)* are vital to the process of building an iPhone or iPad game, knowing what you're going to build before you touch the SDK is just as vital.

Beginning with an idea

Game designs don't just spring into existence, fully formed. *Game design* is an organic process involving writing, reading, examining, rewriting, and updating. Go through the process of constructing an idea several times before you settle upon one.

A game concept starts to feel complete when it has the following:

✔ A description of the basic mechanics of the idea (how the game should play out and the basic actions that the player takes while playing)

✔ A basic story describing the motivation for the game play

✔ A flow (a basic game play description)

✔ Conceptual notes on graphics, feel, and audio

✔ Some examples of typical user interactions

So, how do you get these elements of your game concept in place? Well, the process somewhat depends on your game, and we can't really give you a blanket solution that works every time. But we can walk you through the steps of defining the elements as we did for the *Traffic* game. This process offers an understanding of the design decisions required and one method for arriving at them.

Making the idea fun, feasible, and unique

The idea for *Traffic* came from staring at the traffic passing and thinking, "That would make a fun game . . ." Of course, an iPhone game based on realistic simulation of traffic patterns wouldn't be too fun or accessible, so we had to pare down the idea to something that would work on the device. Line-drawing games have shown great longevity as popular titles at the App Store, so we approached the *Traffic* design with the idea that it'd be a line-drawing game.

In *line-drawing games,* the player sees an overall view of a scene and uses the iPhone's touchscreen to score points by drawing lines from one object to another (or a *goal* object). The genre has exploded in popularity, and you find many different variations on the general idea. Some great examples of line-drawing games that carry off the concept well are *Flight Control*, by Firemint, and *Harbor Master*, by Imangi Studios.

We didn't want *Traffic* to be just another line-drawing game, so we brainstormed further — striking upon the idea of a three-lane traffic system with different colored cars. As shown in Figure 1-2, the idea evolved over time, starting at a line-drawing game and ending at a traffic-swiping game. (We discuss how we evolved the game for the iPad in Chapter 19.)

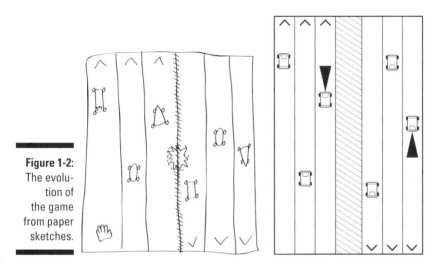

Figure 1-2: The evolution of the game from paper sketches.

Evolving the Game

No game idea comes fully formed, and it's important to try several approaches to a game concept before you commit your time to actual development. To do this, you must reduce the cost of throwing away ideas. And you'll throw away plenty of ideas. Trust us on that. One of the cheapest ways to try out ideas is to do so on paper.

Prototyping on paper

You may laugh, but drawing your game on paper (as shown in Figure 1-2) is one of the most important things you can do to make sure you're building a truly great game. So, how do you draw your game without feeling like a fool? And how do you make sure what you're drawing is useful?

To effectively prototype your game on paper, you need a few things; all are very cheap and easy to acquire. Here's the list.

✔ Lots of pencils, of various grades

✔ Some paper

✔ Some friends to "play" your paper game

✔ Patience, a good idea, and a sense of humor

After you collect what you need, sit down and think about the flow of your game. Think about even the most mundane things, such as menus and the game's launch. Here's the paper-prototyping process that you use to design the game flow, its mechanics, and its look and feel:

1. **Think about your game as a series of interconnected boxes of functionality and then draw those boxes and connections.**

   Start at the highest level you can go and distill the representation to the basic set of game functions you need to implement.

   As shown in Figure 1-3, making decisions about the flow of your game early is important.

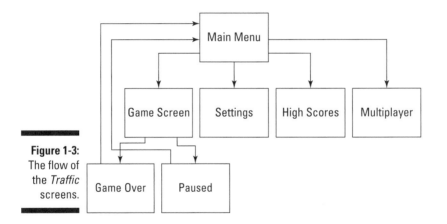

Figure 1-3:
The flow of the *Traffic* screens.

2. **Draw the game board, and then add lines and arrows to show how objects move onscreen, as shown in Figure 1-4.**

   The simple act of drawing how game objects move and how they react to the user helps solidify how you see the game. These movements and reactions are the *game mechanics*. When designing your game's mechanics, consider how to keep the players busy without causing undue frustration.

   In general, giving the players the ability to do more means that the game maintains the player's interest. This is critical for games because if the player gets bored at any stage, the Home button is inches away from her fingers. Your game needs to be fun, intuitive, and exciting from the moment you launch the application.

Traffic iPad vs. iPhone

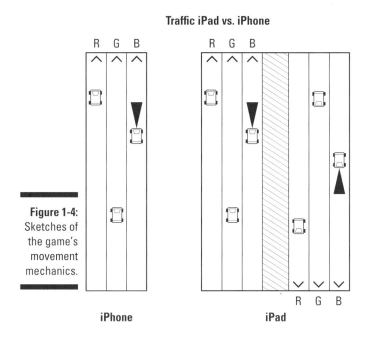

Figure 1-4: Sketches of the game's movement mechanics.

iPhone   iPad

3. **Add the elements of style, color, and smaller graphical details that establish the look and feel for your game.**

Figure 1-5 shows the finished visual prototype of the game's main menu.

Ask yourself questions like the following, and create your look and feel accordingly. Do you want your game to look:

- Simple or complex?

- Realistic or cartoony?

- Serious or funny?

- Bright and cheerful, or dark and brooding?

Consider the amount of development time you have to invest (making the game art look realistic takes a large amount of time). Additionally, players expect things that look realistic to behave in realistic ways (which also takes time to code). In most games, the game designer is forced to make a trade-off over realism and fun, and we suggest that you err on the side of fun.

See the sidebar, "Moving through *Traffic*," nearby in this chapter, for some of the thought process we used to design the mechanics and look and feel for the *Traffic* game.

Moving through *Traffic*

The process of prototyping your game on paper gives you a great opportunity to think through how you want the game to work before you commit anything to code. Here are some of the thoughts we had while designing *Traffic:*

- Originally, we saw the game mechanics as being a choice among cars driving forward, cars turning, and the player directing traffic. However, this simply wasn't fun enough — more than half the cars didn't need to do anything to win points.

- There wasn't enough to indicate which cars should go where. We thought about adding blinking indicator lights on the cars but didn't feel that these would be visible enough.

- By adapting the game into three lanes going forward, we could have more cars onscreen at once without overloading the player in terms of the possibility of having them crash. This, in turn, allowed the player to concentrate on managing more cars.

- We decided on a simple, brightly colored theme and designed every aspect of the game's look around that. The buttons would be reminiscent of traffic lights, the cars would be seen from the top-down, and we'd keep the amount of clutter onscreen to a minimum.

Figure 1-5:
The initial prototype of the main menu.

Distilling the ingredients of fun

There's no secret formula, ingredient, or blueprint for making your games fun. The hints and tips in this section help, but ultimately the only way to make a game fun is to tweak it until it's right.

Most players find games fun if they feel in control, can establish some patterns of play, and find that they're occasionally surprised by some element of the game. When you design a game, think through how to accomplish these characteristics of fun.

Giving a player control

When designing a game experience, figure out what the player controls. If an aspect of the game isn't controlled by the player, ask yourself whether the player could control it, even indirectly — and if he can't, would the game work without it?

Giving the player control can be a complex process and can take a lot of development time to fully implement. However, you can "cheat" in a couple ways and still have the player feel like she controls more than she actually does. For example, in the role-playing game *Mass Effect,* players can choose the flow of conversations by selecting the next line that they wish to say. However, having every conversation branch into every choice is simply too many options for the game developers to cover, but reducing the number of choices reduces the amount of control that they wanted the players to have.

The solution that the *Mass Effect* developers chose is quite elegant and simple: Instead of showing the exact line that the player's character would say, the game shows the intent of the next line. When the player chooses an intent, the line that their character would speak would be close to, but not quite, the text that the player chose.

The upshot of all this was that the developers could re-use lines of dialogue for different intents shown onscreen. By creating the illusion of choice, the player feels more involved; but in reality, the game developers didn't have to do any more work than they needed to.

Surprising a player

One simple way to add surprise is by adding random events to your game design. The venerable game *Missile Command* has a very simple rule set: Missiles fall from the sky, and the player must shoot them down. The fun comes from the random speed and direction that missiles fall. Players don't have infinite ammunition and can't afford to recklessly shoot everywhere, in hopes of getting every missile at once. The challenge (and surprise for the player) becomes anticipating where and how the missiles fall.

Encouraging patterns of play

Play your game (and have others play it) enough that you can pick out patterns of play. Then build responses to these patterns by adding a slight tilt to the screen, highlighting screen areas, adding subtle animations, and so on to make the player feel like his character is more involved in the game action. The effect is subtle but noticeable, and the game plays better for it.

A great example of one of these patterns is a side-scrolling game based on jump mechanics (think *Super Mario Brothers*, by Nintendo). After a certain amount of time playing, people become used to timing jumps as well as combining running and jumping. Observe this when you test your game with others; you can reward skilled jumping and running combinations, and work out new ways to test these skills.

If your game is so eclectic that your players can't find any patterns to improve their game with, take that as a signal that you need to add a little more structure to the game.

Applying Sid Meier's Rule of Halves

A lot of games rely on the finely tuned parameters, such as the speed of cars, the strengths of enemies, and the amount of ammo in your gun. These parameters often need to be just right — if they're not, the game feels wrong in difficult-to-define ways.

When trying to tune a game, the logical choice is to make small changes until it's right. Unfortunately, that's not possible when hundreds of factors are involved in a game — it'd simply take too much time. Thankfully, there's a solution.

Sid Meier, the legendary developer of such classics as *Civilization,* has a simple rule for tuning a game's parameters. If a parameter doesn't feel just right, either double it or cut it in half. If a car moves too fast, reduce its speed by half. If the gun feels too weak, double the amount of damage it does.

The point isn't that these new values are magically correct; in fact, you're likely to overshoot by a wide margin. The point is to narrow down the range of things to check. If your car is now too slow, change its speed to somewhere between its old speed and the speed it is now. Repeat this process until your parameters feel right.

Sid's rule of halves is quite a bit faster than the alternative, which can often involve plugging random numbers into your game code and seeing what works best; in fact, the math nerds among us will notice that it turns the time needed to figure out the best value from a linear equation to a logarithmic one. There's no arguing with science, kids.

Get your game out to other people: Show it to your friends, show it to strangers, and eventually, you need to bite the bullet and ship it. You won't find better feedback than from a paying customer's reaction; he won't pull his punches if he doesn't have fun with it.

What's Next

We're sure that you're raring to go now and just can't wait to download the SDK from the iPhone developer portal. That's exactly what each and every one of us did — when we first started development, we were ultra-keen and dived right into the code. Only later did we figure out that we needed to spend a little more time upfront understanding how games and applications work in the iOS environment.

We ask you to be patient! In Chapter 2, we explain what goes on behind the screen, and then, we promise, it's time to play in *Traffic*.

To make sure you're ready, head on over to the Web site at `http://traffic.secretlab.com.au` or `www.dummies.com/go/iphoneipad gameprogramming`. When you're there, click the big button that says "Download Resources". You'll get a zip file containing the imagery, audio, and other elements you'll need to build *Traffic*. Keep it safe and easily accessible, since we'll be referring to it a lot. The site also contains the latest version of each code listing, so if you get lost or just want to copy and paste the code instead of retyping it, make sure you grab that, too.

Chapter 2

Becoming an iPhone Developer

In This Chapter

▶ Registering as a developer

▶ Exploring the iPhone Dev Center

▶ Installing the SDK

▶ Joining the Developer Program

*I*f you want to develop games for the iPhone and iPad, you have to get involved with (yet another) major corporation and its policies and procedures. Say hello to the iPhone Developer Program. Although Apple's iOS Software Development Kit (SDK) is free, you have to register as an iOS developer first. That gives you access to all the documentation and other resources found on the iPhone Dev Center Web site. This whole ritual transforms you into a Registered iPhone Developer.

Becoming a Registered Developer is free, but there's a catch: If you actually want to run your application on your iPhone or iPad, as opposed to only on the Simulator that comes with the SDK, you have to join the Developer Program. Fortunately, membership in the iPhone Developer Program costs only $99 per year, and you have no choice if you want your application to see the light of day on the iPhone.

In this chapter, we lead you through the process of becoming a Registered Developer, signing onto — and then exploring — the iPhone Dev Center Web site, downloading the SDK so you can use it, and then (finally) joining the Developer Program.

What you see when you go through this process may be slightly different from what you see here. Don't panic. Apple changes the site from time to time. By the time you get this book in your hands, the Web sites will have been updated, and you'll see iOS SDK 4.1 (or whatever the current version of the SDK is) plastered all over the Web site.

Becoming a Registered iPhone Developer

Just having to become a Registered Developer annoys some people. What's worse, the process itself can be a bit confusing as well. Fear not! Follow these steps, and we get you safely to the end of the road. (If you've registered already, skip to the next section, "Exploring the iPhone Dev Center," where we show what the iPhone Dev Center has available as well as how to download the SDK.) Here's how to register:

1. **Point your browser to `http://developer.apple.com/iphone`.**

   This URL takes you to a page similar to the one shown in Figure 2-1. Apple changes this site occasionally, so when you get there, it may look a little different than the figure. You may be tempted by some of the links but hold off. You can't go far until you log in as a Registered Developer.

2. **Click the Register link in the top-right corner of the screen.**

   A page appears explaining why you should become a Registered iPhone Developer.

3. **Click the Get Started button in the top left area of the screen.**

   A page appears asking whether you want to create or use an existing Apple ID.

Figure 2-1:
The iPhone
Dev Center.

You can use your current Apple ID (the same one you use for iTunes or any other Apple Web site) or create a new Apple ID and then log in. We recommend creating a new Apple ID to use specifically for your game development endeavors. This means you can better work with others in the future, without sharing your personal iTunes account.

- *If you want to use a new Apple ID or if you don't have an Apple ID,* select Create an Apple ID and then click the Continue button. The page, as shown in Figure 2-2, appears.

- *If you already have an Apple ID you want to use,* select Use an Existing Apple ID and then click the Continue button. Log in with your Apple ID and password on the screen that appears. That takes you to Step 4 with some of your information already filled out.

4. Fill out the personal profile form and then click the Continue button.

If you have an Apple ID, most of the form is already filled out.

You must fill in the country code in the Phone field. For example, if you live in the United States, the country code is 1; for Australians, the country code is 61; and so on.

5. Complete the professional profile form and then click the Continue button.

On this form, you're asked some basic business questions. After you click the Continue button, you're taken to a page that asks you to agree to the Registered iPhone Developer Agreement.

Figure 2-2:
Creating an
Apple ID.

6. **Select the confirmation that you have read and agree to be bound by the agreement, and that you're of legal age; then, click the I Agree button.**

   If you just created your Apple ID, you're asked for the verification code that was sent to the e-mail address you supplied when you created your Apple ID.

   If you used your existing Apple ID, skip to Step 8.

7. **In your e-mail program, open the e-mail from Apple and get the verification code, and then enter the verification code where you left off in the iPhone Dev Center and click the Continue button.**

   A page confirming your account is set up and verified appears.

8. **On the page indicating your account is verified, click the Visit Phone Development Center button.**

   You're automatically logged in to the iPhone Dev Center, as shown in Figure 2-3.

You're now officially a Registered iPhone Developer. The next section shows you what you can do with your new status.

Figure 2-3:
Logged in to the iPhone Dev Center.

| iPhone Dev Center | Mac Dev Center | Safari Dev Center |
| Hi, Jonathon Manning | My Profile | Log out |

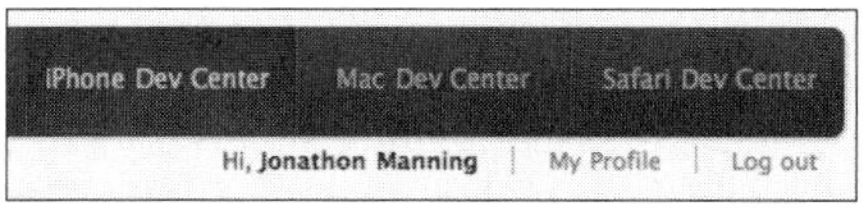

Exploring the iPhone Dev Center

Later in this section, we talk a little bit about some of the resources available to you in the iPhone Dev Center, but for the moment, we focus on what you're *really* after — the iOS SDK 4.1 download that you see when you scroll to the bottom of the iPhone Dev Center page (see Figure 2-4).

Figure 2-4:
The area where you'll download the iOS SDK.

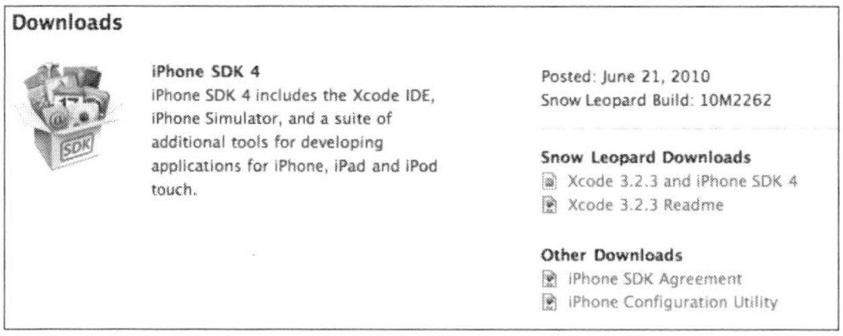

Downloads

iPhone SDK 4
iPhone SDK 4 includes the Xcode IDE, iPhone Simulator, and a suite of additional tools for developing applications for iPhone, iPad and iPod touch.

Posted: June 21, 2010
Snow Leopard Build: 10M2262

Snow Leopard Downloads
Xcode 3.2.3 and iPhone SDK 4
Xcode 3.2.3 Readme

Other Downloads
iPhone SDK Agreement
iPhone Configuration Utility

The history part

We'd be remiss if we didn't make an attempt to explain the differences between the various incarnations of iOS SDK versions. Grab your comfortable sofa, because I'm about to tell you a story. Parts of it may even be true.

Once upon a time, Apple only had one mobile device platform, which it called *iPhone OS.* This ran on both the iPod touch and the iPhone, and later on ran on the iPhone 3G and iPhone 3GS. Things were simple and good. As new features got added to the iPhone OS, the version number increased, until Apple had version 3.1.3 running on every device it had ever made.

Then, Apple secretly developed a tablet, called the iPad. It was developed so secretly that nobody inside Apple apart from the iPad team even knew about it — not even the iPhone OS engineers.

Now, this iPad device was certainly not a phone. You couldn't even treat it like a giant iPod touch, since the bigger screen meant that you need to use it differently (more on this in Chapter 19!). This meant that extra features needed to be added to iPhone OS, but the changes had to be added to a separate version of the OS. The iPad developers called this version 3.2, and this iPhone OS 3.2 only ran on the iPad, and not the iPhone.

When the iPad came out, there were now two different versions of iPhone OS:

- 3.1.3, for hand-held devices
- 3.2, for the iPad

For developers, this meant that there were now effectively two different platforms, with different classes and features available. (Apple later realized the absurdity of calling the OS "iPhone OS," and renamed it *iOS.)*

Later, Apple released iOS 4, which ran on everything *but* the iPad. Apple promised that iOS 4 would run on the iPad by the end of 2010.

The upshot is that there are two different versions of iOS:

- 4, which (currently) runs on the iPhone and iPod touch
- 3.2, which runs on the iPad

Fortunately, the iOS SDK download contains the SDKs for both versions, but you do need to keep in mind the differences between versions and what features and hardware they support!

Note to self: tell more interesting stories in the future.

The SDK includes a host of tools for you to develop your application. Here's a handy list to help you keep them all straight:

- **Xcode:** This refers to Apple's complete development environment, which integrates a code editor, a build system, a graphical debugger, and project management. (We introduce you to the code editor's features in more detail in Chapter 3.)

- **Frameworks:** The iPhone's multiple frameworks make it easy to develop apps that can take advantage of all the device's features. You can think of creating an app as simply adding your application-specific behavior to a framework. The frameworks do all the rest. For example, the UIKit framework provides fundamental code for building your application — the required application behavior, classes for windows, views (including those that display text and Web content), controls, and view controllers. (All the things we cover in Chapter 4, in other words.) The UIKit framework also provides standard interfaces to core location data, the user's contacts and photo library, *accelerometer* (movement sensor) data, and the iPhone's built-in camera.

Building a game, however, is a little more complicated. Although you always use the frameworks, you deal with the development environment in a more raw form than you might be used to if you've developed an app before. We cover the specifics of building a game around Apple's frameworks in Chapter 4.

✔ **Interface Builder:** We use Interface Builder in Chapter 5 to build the basic user interface for the *Traffic* game. But Interface Builder is more than your run-of-the-mill program that builds graphical user interfaces. In Chapter 3, we show you how Xcode and Interface Builder work together to give you ways to build (and automatically create at runtime) the user interface — as well as to create objects that provide the infrastructure for your game.

✔ **iPhone Simulator:** The Simulator allows you to debug your game and do some other basic testing on your Mac by simulating the iPhone and iPad. The Simulator runs most iPhone and iPad apps, but it doesn't support some hardware-dependent features. (We give you a rundown on the Simulator in Chapter 4.) A good game is developed about 40–60 percent between the Simulator and a real device, respectively.

✔ **Instruments:** The Instruments application lets you measure your application while it runs on a device. This app gives you a number of performance metrics, including those to test memory and network use. The Instruments app also works (in a limited way) on the iPhone Simulator, and you can test some aspects of your design there.

The iPhone Simulator doesn't emulate such real-life iPhone and iPad characteristics as CPU speed or memory throughput. If you want to understand how your application performs on the device from a user's perspective, you have to use the actual device.

Looking forward to using the SDK

The tools in the SDK support a development process that most people find comfortable. They allow you to rapidly get the standardized user interface parts of your game up and running to see what the game actually looks like. You can add code a little at a time and then run it after each new addition to see how it works. After the infrastructure of your game works, you then iterate through the game play features, adding logic as needed.

We take you through this incremental process as we develop the *Traffic* game; for now, here's a bird's-eye view of basic iPhone and iPad application development, one step at a time:

1. Start with Xcode.

   Xcode provides several project templates that you can use to get you off to a fast start. (In Chapter 5, you do just that to get your user interface up and running quickly.)

2. Design and create the user interface.

   Interface Builder has graphic-design tools you can use to create your application's user interface. This saves a great deal of time and effort. These tools also reduce the amount of code you have to write by creating resource files that your application can then upload automatically.

   If you don't want to use Interface Builder, you can always build your user interface by scratch, creating each individual piece and linking them all together within your program. Sometimes Interface Builder is the best way to create onscreen elements; sometimes the hands-on approach works better. Game development for the iPhone and iPad strikes an interesting balance between using Interface Builder and hand-coding interface elements because games can't rely entirely on the standardized pieces of user interface that Apple's UIKit framework provides. Games are complex beasts that can sometimes entirely rely on custom drawing routines to create the game environment.

3. Write the code.

   The Xcode editor provides several features that help you write code. We run through these features in Chapter 3.

4. Build and run your game.

   You build your game on your computer and run it in the iPhone Simulator application or (provided you've joined the Developer Program) on your device. When you develop a game, you spend most of your time running your game on real devices, for a number of reasons that we cover in Chapter 13.

5. Test your game.

   You need to test the functionality of your game as well as response time. One crucial thing you need to test for when building a game (as opposed to an app) is fun. We cover how to do this back in Chapter 1.

6. Measure and tune your game's performance.

   After your game is running, make sure that it makes optimal use of resources, such as memory and CPU cycles. Creating an efficient game is arguably even more important than creating an efficient app because hiccups in your game's performance can detract noticeably from potentially fast-paced game play.

7. Do the whole process again until your game is done and then submit the app to the App Store.

Resources on the iPhone Dev Center

You're not left on your own when it comes to the steps list in the preceding section. After all, you have us to help you on the way — as well as a heap of information squirreled away in various corners of the iPhone Dev Center. We find the following resources to be especially helpful:

- **The Getting Started Videos link:** These are relatively light on content, but give you a good introduction to the basics of iOS development.

- **The Getting Started Documents link:** Think of these documents as an introduction to the materials in the iOS Reference Library. These give you an overview of iPhone development and best practices. To get to the Getting Started documents, click on the Guides link on the left of the page. Included is *Learning Objective-C: A Primer.* It is an overview of Objective-C and also includes links to *Object-Oriented Programming with Objective-C* and *The Objective-C 2.0 Programming Language* (the definitive and rather technical guide to the programming language you'll be using to write the game). You'll also find these documents if you search inside Xcode's documentation.

If you've never programmed in the Objective-C language, you can find some basic information in the iPhone Reference Library. But if you want to really figure out Objective-C as quickly (and painlessly) as possible, go get yourself a copy of *Objective-C For Dummies,* by Neal Goldstein (Wiley Publishing, Inc.). That book explains everything you need to know to program in Objective-C, and it assumes you have little or no knowledge of programming (it does a great job — take it from us!).

- **The iOS Reference Library:** This is all the documentation you could ever want (except, of course, the answer to that one question you really need answered at 4 a.m., but that's the way it goes). To be honest, most of this stuff turns out to be really useful *after* you have a good handle on what you're doing.

As you go through this book, an easier way to access some of this documentation is through Xcode's Documentation window, which we show you in Chapter 3.

- **The Coding How-To's link:** This info tends to be a lot more valuable when you already have something of a knowledge base. It covers specific features of the iOS, and tells you how to implement them — it's a great reference, but not a good learning tool.

- **The Sample Code link:** On the one hand, sample code of any kind is always valuable. Most good developers look to these kinds of samples to get started. They take something that closely approximates what they want to do and modify it until it does. When we started iPhone development, no books like this one existed, so much of what we gathered came from looking at the samples and then making some changes to see how things worked. On the other hand, sample code can give you hours of (misguided) pleasure and can be quite the time-waster and task-avoider.

✔ **Apple Developer Forums:** You'll find this link at the top-right of the page when you're signed in to the dev center. We'd be the first to say that developer forums can be very helpful, but we'd also be the first to admit that they are a great way to avoid doing other things, such as working on the next game. As you scroll through the questions people have, be careful about some of the answers you see. No one validates the information people give, so take the answers with a grain of salt. But take heart: Pretty soon, you can answer some of those questions better than them.

You won't see these forums if you're signed in with a free membership. We'll cover how to sign up for the paid membership in the next section of this chapter.

Downloading the SDK

Time to download! Make your way to that bottom part of the iPhone Dev Center — the section that has the iOS SDK 4.1 downloads prominently displayed (refer to Figure 2-4).

Make sure that you're logged in to the Dev Center before you proceed — if you're not logged in, these links might not appear as we've described them. You can log in by clicking the button at the top-right of the page.

By the time you read this book, the SDK may no longer be version 4.1. Download the latest (non-beta, non-prelease) SDK. That way, you get the most stable version to start with. The latest version of the iOS SDK also contains the latest version of the iPad SDK.

In the past, two downloads were available for the iOS SDK — one for Leopard (Mac OS X 10.5), and one for Snow Leopard (Mac OS X 10.6). These days, however, the latest version of the iOS SDK is compatible only for Snow Leopard. For that reason, this book assumes you're using Snow Leopard too!

Underneath the download link is another link to a readme file (Xcode 3.2.4 Read Me). This link leads to a PDF, *About Xcode and the iPhone SDK,* that tells you everything you need to know (and more) about this version of the SDK. Peruse the PDF at your leisure but don't get too hung up if something in it baffles you. We explain the things that you actually need to know.

After perusing *About Xcode and the iPhone SDK,* click the iPhone SDK you want to download. (***Remember:*** The iOS SDK is on the right side of the Downloads section. The download might not be in exactly the same place when you try it, but a download link displays prominently, no matter what.)

After you click the link, you can watch the download in Safari's download window (which is only slightly better than watching paint dry). This could take awhile, so take the time to doodle some game ideas on a piece of paper, like we suggest in Chapter 1.

When the SDK finishes downloading, the iOS SDK window appears onscreen, complete with an installer and various packages tied to the install process. Double-click the iOS SDK installer and follow the installation instructions. After you do all that, you have your very own iPhone SDK on your hard drive.

You become intimately acquainted with the iOS SDK during the course of your project, but for now, you still have one more bit of housekeeping to take care of: joining the official iPhone Developer Program. Read on to see how that works. This is the bit where you need to pony up some cash, so dust off your wallet.

Joining the iPhone Developer Program

The Simulator that comes standard with the iOS SDK is a great tool for figuring out how to program, but it does have some limitations. For instance, the Simulator doesn't support some hardware-dependent features, and when testing, it can't really emulate such everyday iPhone and iPad realities as CPU speed or memory throughput.

Minor annoyances, you might say. And you might be right, if we were developing business apps and not games! Games *really* need to be built and tested on real devices during development, not the poor cousin of an iPhone that the Simulator represents. We cover the reasons behind this in Chapter 3. The real issue, therefore, is that just *registering* as a developer doesn't get you one very important thing — the ability to actually run your application on your iPhone and iPad, much less to distribute your game through Apple's iPhone App Store. (Remember that the App Store is the only way for commercial developers to distribute their games to more than a few people.) To run your app on a real iOS device or get a chance to profile your app in the iPhone App store, you have to enroll in either the Standard or Enterprise version of the iPhone Developer Program. There is much speculation behind the reason for this, but the bottom line is that's simply the way it is. At least (we swiftly note) the program isn't all that expensive.

The approval process used to take awhile, and although it's usually quicker these days, you still can't run your applications on your iPhone or iPad until you're approved. Enroll as early as possible.

Here's how you get enrolled as a Registered iPhone Developer:

1. **Go to `http://developer.apple.com/iphone/program`.**

   The iPhone Developer Program page appears, as shown in Figure 2-5.

2. **Click the Enroll Now button.**

   A new page appears, telling you to choose your program and outlining the details of each developer program, as shown in Figure 2-6.

   The Standard program costs $99. The Enterprise program costs $299 and is designed for companies developing proprietary in-house applications for iPad, iPhone, and iPod touch. To be sure you select the option that meets your needs, give the program details a once-over.

3. **Click the Continue button.**

   You don't actually get to choose Standard or Enterprise yet. But you do get an overview of the process and a chance to log in again with your Apple ID and password.

4. **Log in and click the Continue button.**

   After logging in, you can choose Standard Individual, Standard Company, or Enterprise program. Figure 2-7 shows you the differences among the different options.

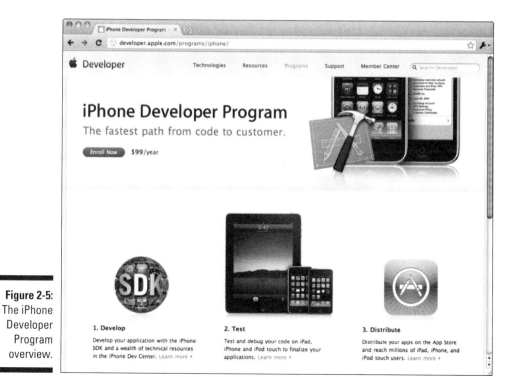

Figure 2-5: The iPhone Developer Program overview.

Complete your personal profile
(All form fields are required)

Create Apple ID

Desired Apple ID:

Password:
(6–32 characters)

Re-enter Password:
(6–32 characters)

Security Information

Birthday: Select Month   Select Day

Security Question:

Answer:

Figure 2-6:
Checking
out program
details.

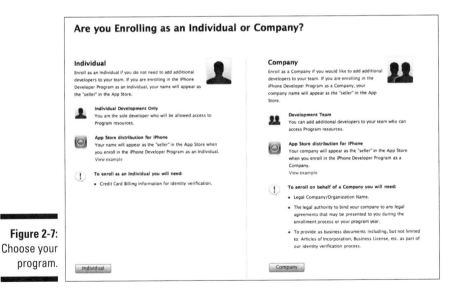

Are you Enrolling as an Individual or Company?

Individual

Enroll as an Individual if you do not need to add additional developers to your team. If you are enrolling in the iPhone Developer Program as an Individual, your name will appear as the "seller" in the App Store.

Individual Development Only
You are the sole developer who will be allowed access to Program resources.

App Store distribution for iPhone
Your name will appear as the "seller" in the App Store when you enroll in the iPhone Developer Program as an Individual.
View example

To enroll as an Individual you will need:
• Credit Card Billing information for identity verification.

Individual

Company

Enroll as a Company if you would like to add additional developers to your team. If you are enrolling in the iPhone Developer Program as a Company, your company name will appear as the "seller" in the App Store.

Development Team
You can add additional developers to your team who can access Program resources.

App Store distribution for iPhone
Your company will appear as the "seller" in the App Store when you enroll in the iPhone Developer Program as a Company.
View example

To enroll on behalf of a Company you will need:
• Legal Company/Organization Name.
• The legal authority to bind your company to any legal agreements that may be presented to you during the enrollment process or your program year.
• To provide us business documents including, but not limited to: Articles of Incorporation, Business License, etc. as part of our identity verification process.

Company

Figure 2-7:
Choose your
program.

5. **Make your choice, and then click the appropriate button (either Individual or Company).**

   The page that appears gives you more information on the option you selected.

6. **Click the Continue button.**

   Depending on the option you selected, you're given the opportunity to pay (if you selected Standard Individual), or you're asked for some more company or enterprise information and then given the chance to pay.

   Although joining as an individual is easier than joining as a company, there are clearly some advantages to enrolling as a company — for example, you can add team members (something which we discuss in connection with the developer portal in Chapter 13).

   When you join as an individual, your real name appears when the user buys (or downloads for free) your application in the App Store. If you're concerned about privacy or if you want to seem "bigger," the extra work invoked in signing up as a company may be worth it for you. That said, there's something to be said for appearing "small;" we cover this, and other marketing techniques, in Chapter 27.

7. **Continue through the process; it is extremely self explanatory from here. All you need to do is provide information when the Web site asks you for it.**

   Eventually, you're accepted in the Developer Program of your choice.

The next time you log in to the iPhone Dev Center, notice that the page has changed somewhat. As a freshly minted official iPhone developer, you see a page like the one shown in Figure 2-8. You have a new iPhone Developer Program Portal link on the right in the iPhone Developer Program section.

iPhone Developer Program

iPhone Provisioning Portal ❯

iTunes Connect ❯

Apple Developer Forums ❯

Developer Support Center ❯

⚠ **Renew Your Program**
Your iPhone Developer Program will expire in **23** days. Don't wait.
Renew your membership now ▸

Figure 2-8: The Developer Program Portal link is available.

If you click the iPhone Developer Program Portal link, you see all sorts of things you can do as a developer, as shown in Figure 2-9.

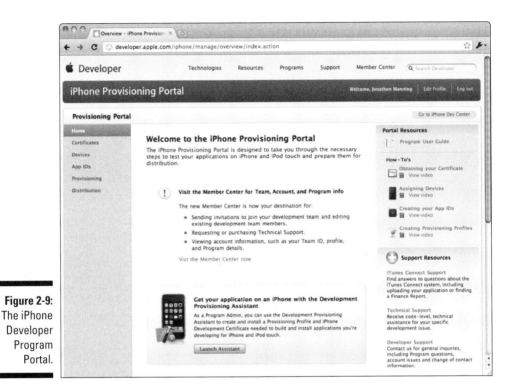

Figure 2-9:
The iPhone
Developer
Program
Portal.

Don't linger too long at the iPhone Developer Program Portal page, simply because it can be really confusing unless you understand the process. Many a day has gone by where one of us has spent a little too long logged in to the portal and ended the week rocking slowly and sobbing in a corner of the room. We explain this portal — which lets you provision your device, run your application on it, and prepare your creation for distribution to the App Store — in Chapter 13.

Getting Ready for the SDK

Don't despair! (Well, feel free to, but snap out of it as quickly as you can.) We know the process is tedious, but it's over now. Going through this was definitely the *second* most annoying part of your journey toward developing software for the iPhone and iPad. The most annoying part is figuring out *provisioning* — the hoops you have to jump through to actually run your application on a real, tangible, existing iPhone. We take you through the provisioning process in Chapter 13, and frankly, getting *that* process explained is worth the price of the book.

In Chapter 3, you use the SDK you just downloaded. We assume that you have some programming knowledge and that you also have some acquaintance with object-oriented programming, with some variant of C, such as C++, C#, and maybe even Objective-C. If those assumptions miss the mark, help us out, okay? Take another look at the "Resources on the iPhone Dev Center" section, earlier in this chapter, for an overview of some of the resources that could help you get up to speed on some programming basics. Or, better yet, (as we already said), get yourself a copy of *Objective-C For Dummies,* by Neal Goldstein.

We also assume that you're familiar with the iPhone (and iPad) itself and that you've explored Apple's included applications to become familiar with the iPhone's look and feel. You should also have racked up a decent credit card bill from buying games in the App Store — it's all in the name of research after all. Remember, now these purchases are a business expense, if you're into that sort of thing!

Chapter 3

Your First Date with the SDK

*B*y the time you're through with this book, you'll probably be sick of hearing it, but the iOS is one of the easiest, most flexible, and potential-filled platforms that you can develop games for. The iPhone is so easy to build things for that it puts the power back in the hands of someone with a good idea, rather than someone with all the money. The iPad is likewise.

One of the things that really got us excited about iOS initially was how easy it was to develop for it. The Software Development Kit (SDK) comes with so many tools, you'd think developing must be really easy. Well, to be honest, developing is *relatively* easy.

In this chapter, we introduce you to the SDK; it's a low-key, get-acquainted kind of affair, sort of a classy, restrained first date. We show you the real nuts-and-bolts stuff in later chapters, when you actually develop a real game.

Developing with the SDK

The SDK supports the kind of development process that's a breath of fresh air after working with some other platforms: You can develop your applications without tying your brain in knots.

The development environment allows you to rapidly get a basic user interface up and running. The idea here is to add your code incrementally — step by step — so you can always step back and see how what you just did affected the Big Picture.

Game development often doesn't *quite* follow this process, but your steps in development generally look something like this:

1. With *Xcode,* Apple's development environment for the OS X operating system, create a project, design the user interface and the game play.

2. Write the code for the interface and game logic.

3. Build and run your game.

4. Test your game (for bugs and for fun).

5. Measure and tune your game's performance (and tweak it for maximum fun).

6. Tweak and test until you're done.

In this chapter, we start at the very beginning, with the very first step, using Xcode. (Starting with Step 1? What a concept! We're trendsetters.) The first step of the first step is to create a project.

Creating Your Project

To develop an iPhone game, you work in an *Xcode project.* So, time to fire up one (which will be pretty basic at this stage). To work in an Xcode project:

1. **Launch Xcode.**

   After you download the SDK (see Chapter 2 if you haven't downloaded it yet), it's a snap to launch Xcode. By default, Xcode downloads to /Developer/Applications, where you can track it down to launch it.

   Here are a few hints to make Xcode handier and more efficient:

   • Drag the icon for the Xcode application all the way to the Dock so you can launch it from there. You use Xcode a lot, so launching it from the Dock makes your life easier.

   • If you're lazy like us, you could also search for Xcode and launch it with *Spotlight,* Apple's built-in Mac OS X-wide search engine.

   • When you first launch Xcode, the welcome screen, as shown in Figure 3-1, appears. The welcome screen is chock-full of links to the Apple Developer Connection and Xcode documentation. You may want to leave this screen up to make it easier to get to those links, but we usually close it. If you don't want to be bothered with the welcome screen in the future, deselect the Show at Launch check box.

2. Close the welcome screen for now, because you don't need it.

Figure 3-1:
The Xcode welcome screen.

3. Choose File⇨New Project from the main menu to create a new project.

You can also just press Shift+⌘+N to create a new project.

However you start a new project, you're greeted by the New Project window, as shown in Figure 3-2. In the New Project window, you get to choose the template you want for your new project. Note that the left-most pane has two sections: one for the iOS and the other for Mac OS X.

4. In the New Project window, click on the Application line under the iOS heading.

The main pane of the New Project window refreshes, revealing several choices, as shown in Figure 3-2. Each of these choices is actually a template that, when chosen, generates some code to get you started.

5. Select Navigation-Based Application line from the choices displayed and then click the Choose button.

A standard save dialog box appears.

When you select a template, a brief description of the template displays underneath the main pane. (Figure 3-2 shows a description of the Navigation-Based Application. You can click some of the other template choices to see how they're described as well. Just be sure to click the Navigation-Based Application template again to get back to it when you're done exploring.)

Figure 3-2:
The New
Project
window.

6. **Enter a name for your new project in the Save As field, choose a Save location (the Desktop works just fine), and then click the Save button.**

7. **Name your project Traffic.**

   You can name your project something else, but pay close attention to changing file and class names elsewhere in the book if you do. The examples throughout this book build on the *Traffic* game project.

   After you click Save, Xcode creates the project and opens the Project window — which looks like Figure 3-3.

Figure 3-3:
The Traffic
Project
window.

Exploring Your Project

To develop an iPhone game, you have to work within the context of an Xcode project. You do most of your work on projects using the Project window very much like the one in Figure 3-3. If you have a nice, large monitor, expand the Project window so you can see everything in it as big as life. (This is another great excuse for the business expense of buying an enormous, swish-looking Apple display. Business expense now, remember?)

Think of the Project window as Command Central for developing your game; it displays and organizes your source files and the other resources needed to build your game.

If you take another peek at Figure 3-3, you see the following elements of the Xcode window for your project:

- **The Groups & Files list:** An outline view of everything in your project, containing all your project's files — source code, frameworks, graphics, and some settings files. You can move files and folders around and add new folders. If you select an item in the Groups & Files list, the contents of the item display in the topmost pane to the right — otherwise known as the Detail view.

  Some of the items in the Groups & Files list are folders whereas others are just icons. Most have a *disclosure triangle* next to them. Clicking the disclosure triangle to the left of a folder expands the folder to show what's in it. Click the triangle again to hide what it contains.

- **The Detail view:** Here you get detailed information about the item you selected in the Groups & Files list.

- **The toolbar:** Here you can find quick access to the most common Xcode commands. You can customize the toolbar by right-clicking it and choosing Customize Toolbar from the contextual menu that appears. You can also choose View➪Customize Toolbar. By default, you'll find the following buttons on the toolbar:

  - *The Build and Run button:* Compiles, links, and launches your application.

  - *The Breakpoints button:* Turns breakpoints on and off and toggles the Build and Run button to Build and Debug. (We explain this in Chapter 10.)

  - *The Tasks button:* Allows you to stop the execution of your program that you've built.

  - *The Info button:* Opens a window that displays information and settings for your project.

TIP

✔ **The status bar:** Look here for messages about your project. For example, when you build your project, Xcode updates the status bar to show where you are in the process — and if the process completed successfully.

✔ **The Favorites bar:** Works like other Favorites bars you're familiar with to let you bookmark places in your project.

This bar isn't displayed by default; to display it onscreen, choose View⇨Layout⇨Show Favorites Bar from the main menu.

✔ **The Text Editor navigation bar:** This navigation bar contains a number of shortcuts, as shown in Figure 3-4. We explain more about them as you use them.

- *The Bookmarks menu:* Create a bookmark by choosing Edit⇨Add to Bookmarks.

- *The Breakpoints menu:* Lists the breakpoints in the current file — we cover breakpoints in Chapter 10.

- *The Class Hierarchy menu:* The superclass of the current class you are working on, the superclass of that superclass (if any), and so on (these show the relationship between each element of your code, which we'll discuss more later). This allows you to browse through the interrelating files of your project, using their relationship to browse.

- *The Included Files menu:* Lists both the files included by the current file and the files that include the current file.

- *The Counterpart button:* This allows you to switch between header and implementation files.

✔ **The Editor view:** Displays a file you've selected, in either the Groups & Files list or Detail view. You can also edit your files here, or you can double-click a file in Groups & Files or Detail view to open the file in a separate window.

To see how the Editor view works, check out Figure 3-5 in which we clicked the disclosure triangle next to the Classes folder in the Groups & Files list and the RootViewController.h class in the Detail view. You can see the code for the class in the Editor view. (We deleted the comments you normally see when the template creates the classes and files for you.)

Figure 3-4:
The Text Editor navigation bar.

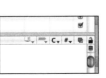

Clicking the Counterpart button switches you from the header (or interface) file to the implementation file, and vice versa:

- Header files define the class's interface by specifying the *class declaration* (what it inherits from), *instance variables* (a variable defined in a class — at runtime, all objects have their own copy), and methods.

- The implementation file contains the code for each method.

Below the Lock icon is the Split View icon that lets you split the Editor view. This icon enables you to look at the interface and implementation files at the same time, or even the code for two different methods in the same or different classes.

If you have any questions about what something does, position the mouse pointer above the icon and then a tooltip pops up to explain it.

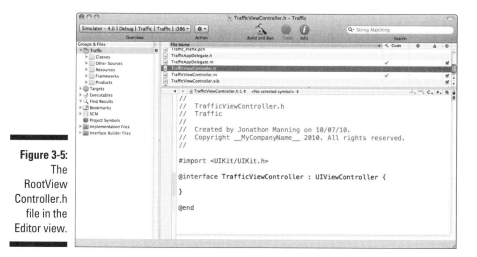

Figure 3-5:
The RootView Controller.h file in the Editor view.

The first item in the Groups & Files list, as shown in Figure 3-5, is Traffic. This is the container that contains all the source elements for your project, including source code, resource files, graphics, and a number of other pieces that we won't mention for now but get into in due course. Your project container has five distinct groups (or folders, if you will) — Classes, Other Sources, Resources, Frameworks, and Products. Here's what gets tossed into each group:

✔ **Classes** is where you should place all your code, although you aren't obliged to. As you can see from Figure 3-5, this project has four distinct source-code files:

- TrafficAppDelegate.h
- TrafficAppDelegate.m
- RootViewController.h
- RootViewController.m

✔ **Other Sources** is where you typically would find the pre-compiled headers of the frameworks you use, such as Traffic_Prefix.pch and main.m, your application's main function.

✔ **Resources** contains files that are used by your program when it's running, such as xib files, property lists (which we explain in Chapters 11 and 12), images and other media files, and even some data files.

Whenever you choose the Navigation-Based Application template (see Figure 3-2), Xcode also creates the following three files for you:

- RootViewController.xib
- MainWindow.xib
- Traffic-Info.plist

xib files contain your interface, which you design in the Interface Builder application. We'll be covering them in this chapter and following chapters. We hope you grow to love xib files as much as we do.

You don't use xib files when building games as much as you do when building apps, because games involve moving around visual elements on screen a lot more than apps usually do.

If you want to find out everything there is to know about xib files and how exciting they can be, pick up a copy of *iPhone Application Development For Dummies,* by Neal Goldstein (Wiley Publishing, Inc.) — we hear the author is a pretty cool chap.

✔ **Frameworks** are code libraries that act a lot like prefab building blocks for your code edifice. (We talk lots about frameworks in Chapter 14, and talk even more about them in Chapter 15.) By choosing the Navigation-Based Application template, you tell Xcode to add the UIKit framework, Foundation.framework, and CoreGraphics.framework to your project because it expects that you need them in this template.

You need quite a few frameworks to build the *Traffic* game. We show you how to add a framework in Chapter 14.

✔ **Products** is a bit different from the previous four items in this list: It's not a source for your application but rather the compiled application itself. The Traffic.app is located here. At this moment in Xcode, this file is listed in red because the file can't be found (which makes sense because you haven't built the game yet).

When a filename appears in red, Xcode can't find the underlying physical file.

If you happen to open the Traffic folder on your Mac, you don't see the folders that appear in the Xcode window. That's because those folders are simply logical groupings that help organize and find what you're looking for; this list of files can grow to be pretty large, even in a moderate-size project.

When you have a lot of files, you have better luck finding things if you create subgroups (or even whole new groups) within the Classes group and/or Resources group. (In Xcode, the words "group" and "folder" are largely interchangeable.) Subgroups are useful if you have different sets of images you want to manage, such as those that might belong to your interface and those that belong to your game graphics. You create subgroups (or new groups) in the Groups & Files list by choosing New Project⇨New Group from the main menu. You then can select a file and drag it to a new group or subgroup.

Building and Running Your Application

It's really a blast to see what you get when you build and run a project that you created using a template from the project creation window. Running the application that your project creates is relatively simple:

1. **Choose Simulator – 4.1 | Debug from the Overview drop-down list in the top-left corner of the Project window to set the active SDK and active build configuration.**

   A *build configuration* tells Xcode the purpose of the built product. You can choose between

   - *Debug,* which has features to help with debugging

   - *Release,* which results in smaller and faster binaries

   We use Debug for most of this book, so we recommend you use Debug now. Debug is useful because it is more forgiving to the development process, and provides us with more helpful information as we go.

   Your build configuration may be chosen already, as shown in Figure 3-6. Here's what that means:

   - When you download an SDK, you actually download *multiple* SDKs — a Simulator SDK and a device SDK for each of the current iOS releases.

   - For this book, we use the Simulator SDK and iOS 4.1 (and iOS 3.2 for iPad, later on). In Chapter 13, we show you how to switch to the device SDK and download your application to a real-world iPhone or iPad. But before you do that, here's one catch: You have to be in the iPhone Developer Program to run your application on a device, even on your very own iPhone. We cover how to join the Developer Program back in Chapter 2.

2. **Choose Build⇨Build and Run from the main menu to build and run the application.**

   You can also press ⌘+Return or click the Build and Run button in the Project window toolbar.

   The status bar in the Project window tells you all about the build progress, the build errors like compiler errors or warnings, and whether the build was successful. Figure 3-6 shows that this was a successful build.

Figure 3-6:
A successful build.

Because you selected Debug for the active build configuration, the Debugger Console may launch for you, as shown in Figure 3-7, depending on your Xcode preferences. We get to them in a second. (We give you the lowdown on debugging in Chapter 10.) If you don't see the console, choose Run⇨Console to display it.

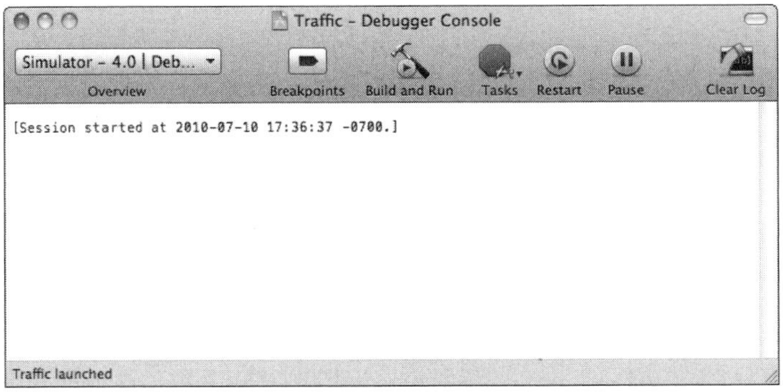

Figure 3-7:
The Debugger Console.

After the Debugger Console launches in the Simulator, your first application looks a lot like Figure 3-8. You see the status bar and a gray window, but that's it. (We know . . . this may look even more insipid than the traditional "Hello World," but we fix that later.) You can also see the Hardware menu, which we explain in the following section.

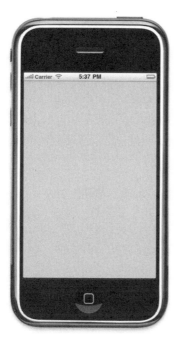

Figure 3-8:
Your first
application.

Working with the iPhone Simulator

When you run your application, Xcode installs it on the iPhone Simulator (or a real iOS device if you specified the device as the active SDK) and launches it. By using the iPhone Simulator's Hardware menu and simulating touches with mouse clicks, the Simulator mimics most of what a user can do on a real iPhone.

The simulator has some limitations that we point out in this chapter, including several features that are present on the real device but missing from the simulator. Always test your program on a real device, since the Simulator isn't enough.

Imitating hardware interaction

Use the iPhone Simulator Hardware menu (refer to Figure 3-8) when you want your device to do the following:

✔ **Change devices:** Choosing a different device from the Hardware⇨Device menu allows you to toggle between simulating an iPhone and an iPad. We discuss this more in Chapter 13.

✔ **Change versions:** Choosing a different OS version from the Hardware⇨ Version menu allows you to test your game in different versions of the iPhone OS. We also discuss this more in Chapter 13.

✔ **Rotate left:** Choosing Hardware⇨Rotate Left rotates the Simulator to the left. This enables you to see the Simulator in Landscape mode.

✔ **Rotate right:** Choosing Hardware⇨Rotate Right rotates the Simulator to the right.

✔ **Use a shake gesture:** Choosing Hardware⇨Shake Gesture simulates shaking the iPhone.

✔ **Go to the home screen:** Choosing Hardware⇨Home does the expected — takes you to the home screen.

✔ **Lock the Simulator (device):** Choosing Hardware⇨Lock locks the Simulator, allowing you to see what happens when the user presses the Lock button at the top of the iPhone.

✔ **Send the running application low-memory warnings:** Choosing Hardware⇨Simulate Memory Warning fakes out your Simulator by sending it a (fake) low-memory warning. We don't cover this, but it is a great feature for seeing how your game may function in the real world.

✔ **Toggle the status bar between its Normal state and its In Call state:** Choose Hardware⇨Toggle In-Call Status Bar to check out how your application functions when the iPhone doesn't answer a call (Normal state) and when it supposedly does answer a call (In Call state).

The status bar becomes taller when you're on a call than when you're not. Choosing the In Call state shows you how things look when your application is launched while the user is on the phone.

✔ **Simulate a hardware keyboard:** Choosing Hardware⇨Simulate Hardware Keyboard tells the simulated device that a hardware (Bluetooth or keyboard dock) keyboard is connected to the device.

Emulating gestures

On a real iPhone or iPad, a *gesture,* such as a tap, drag, or so on, is something you do with your fingers to make something happen in the device. Table 3-1 shows you how to simulate gestures with your mouse and keyboard.

Table 3-1	Gestures in the Simulator
Gesture	*iPhone Action*
Tap	Click the mouse.
Touch and hold	Hold down the mouse button.
Double tap	Double-click the mouse.
Swipe	1. Click where you want to start and hold down the mouse button. 2. Move the mouse in the direction of the swipe and then release the mouse button.
Flick	1. Click where you want to start and hold down the mouse button. 2. Move the mouse quickly in the direction of the flick and then release the mouse button.
Drag	1. Click where you want to start and hold down the mouse button. 2. Move the mouse in the drag direction.
Pinch	1. Move the mouse pointer over the place where you want to start. 2. Hold down the Option key, which makes two circles appear that stand in for your fingers. 3. Hold down the mouse button and move the circles in or out.

Uninstalling applications and resetting your device

Uninstall applications on the Simulator the same way you would on the iPhone or iPad, except use your mouse instead of your finger:

1. **On the home screen, place the pointer over the icon of the application you want to uninstall and hold down the mouse button until the icon wiggles.**

2. **Click the icon's Close button — the little x that appears in the upper-left corner of the application's icon.**

3. **Click the Home button (the one with a little square in it, centered below the screen) to stop the icons wiggling.**

   Once they've stopped wiggling, the application is completely uninstalled.

Recognizing the Simulator's limitations

Running applications in the iPhone Simulator isn't the same thing as running them in the iPhone. Here's why:

✔ **The Simulator uses Mac OS X versions of the low-level system frameworks, instead of the actual frameworks that run on the device.**

✔ **The Simulator uses the Mac hardware and memory.** Your Mac has a lot more memory and processing power than an iPhone, which means that your programs will run a lot faster on the Simulator than they will on the real device. That's why it's critically important to run on real iPhones and iPads, because if you don't, you won't have a good idea of how your game actually runs. To really determine how your application will perform on an honest-to-goodness iPhone device, you have to run it on a real iPhone device. (Lucky for you, we show you how to do that in Chapter 13.)

✔ **Xcode automatically installs applications in the iPhone Simulator when you build your application with the iPhone Simulator SDK (see Figure 3-8, for example).**

✔ **You can't get Xcode to install applications downloaded from the App Store in the iPhone Simulator.** This is because applications from the App Store are built for running on real iOS devices — their internals are completely different to how an app built for the simulator works.

✔ **You can't fake the iPhone Simulator into testing at multiple geographic locations.** The location reported by the CoreLocation framework in the Simulator is fixed at 37.3317° N Latitude and 122.0307° W Longitude. That location just happens to be 1 Infinite Loop, Cupertino, California, 95014. Can you guess which company with a fruit motif lives there?

✔ **The Simulator responds to a maximum of two fingers.** If your game's user interface can respond to touch events involving more than two fingers, test that on an actual device. The actual iPhone device can track 5 fingers on the screen at once, and the iPad can track 11. (Ten fingers plus your nose, perhaps?)

✔ **You can access your computer's accelerometer (if it has one) through the UIKit framework.** Its reading, however, differs from the accelerometer readings on an iPhone (for some technical reasons that we don't get into). We discuss the accelerometer further in Chapter 25.

✔ **OpenGL ES uses renderers on devices that are very slightly different to those it uses in iPhone Simulator.** As a result, a scene on the Simulator and the same scene on a device may not be identical at the pixel level. We cover OpenGL ES in detail in Chapter 22.

You can also move an application icon by pressing down on it until the icons start wiggling, and dragging it around to where you want it to go.

To reset the Simulator to the original factory settings — which also removes all the applications you've installed — choose iPhone Simulator⇨Reset Content and Settings.

Customizing Xcode

Xcode offers options galore. The most important ones for you to consider at this point in your iOS game development careers are to make the debugging console appear when the application is run (which will help you find and fix problems later down the track), and to make Xcode automatically download new documentation as it becomes available — which is important, given how fast iOS development moves!

1. **With Xcode open, choose Xcode⇨Preferences from the main menu and then click the Debugging button in the toolbar.**

   The Xcode Preferences window refreshes to show the various preferences.

2. **In the On Start drop-down list, choose Show Console, as shown in Figure 3-9, and then click the Apply button.**

Figure 3-9:
Always
show the
console.

This automatically opens the Debugger Console after you build your application so that you don't have to open it to see your game's text output.

3. **Click the Building button in the toolbar, as shown in Figure 3-10.**

4. **In the Build Results Window: Open During Builds drop-down list, choose Always, as shown in Figure 3-10, and then click the Apply button.**

   The Build Results window opens (and stays open). Finding and fixing errors is easier this way.

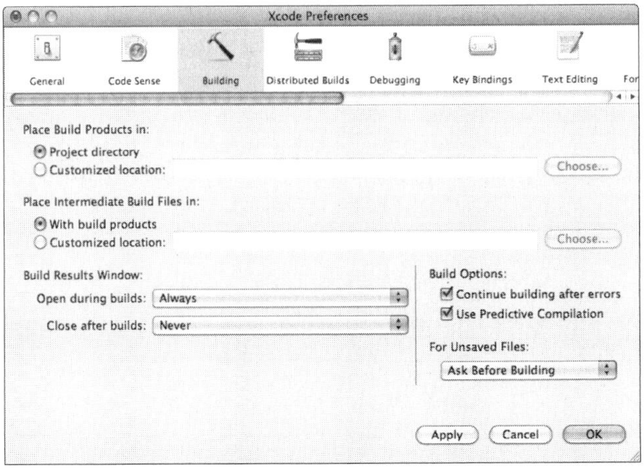

Figure 3-10:
Show
the Build
Results
window.

5. **Click the Documentation button in the toolbar, as shown in Figure 3-11.**

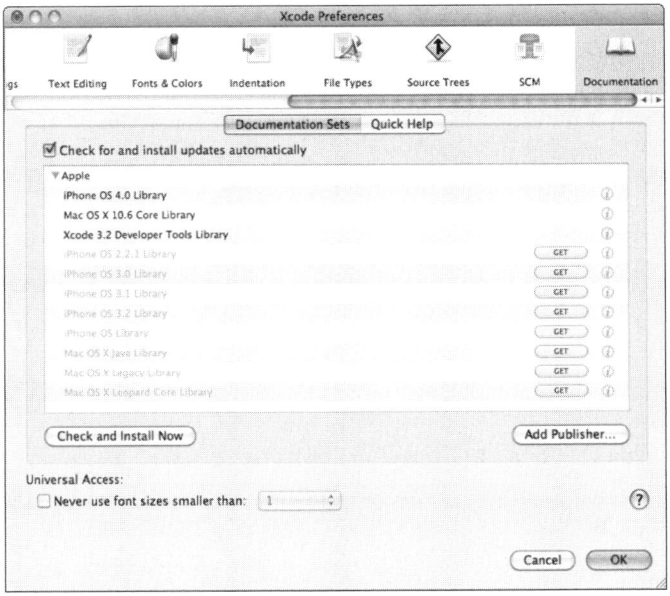

Figure 3-11:
Accessing
the docu-
mentation.

6. **Select the Check For and Install Updates Automatically check box, and then click the Check and Install Now button.**

   Xcode checks that your documentation is up-to-date (this also allows you to load and access other documentation).

7. **Click OK to close the Xcode Preferences window.**

You can also set the tab width and other formatting options in the Indentation section of the Xcode Preferences window. The default is 4.

You can also have the editor show line numbers. If you click the Test Editing button in the Xcode Preferences toolbar, you can select the Show Line Numbers under Display Options check box. We don't do this now, but this is very useful in Chapter 10, when we discuss debugging.

Using Interface Builder

Interface Builder is a great tool for graphically laying out your user interface by using standard iOS user interface components. You can use Interface Builder to design your game's main user interface and then save what you've done as a resource file, which is then loaded into your game at runtime. Then this resource file is used to automatically create the window, all your views and controls, and some of your application's other objects (such as view controllers).

For more on view controllers and other application objects, check out Chapter 4.

For building games, you don't use Interface Builder as much as if you were building apps, but it's critical to the iPhone development process.

If you don't want to use Interface Builder, you can also create your objects programmatically — creating views, view controllers, and even things like buttons and labels in your own application code.

Here's how to build your basic interface with Interface Builder:

1. **In your Project window's Groups & Files list, expand the Resources group.**

2. **Double-click the RootViewController.xib file, as shown in Figure 3-12.**

   Don't make the mistake of opening the MainWindow.xib. You need the RootViewController.xib file.

   TrafficAppDelegate is still in the Editor window; that's okay because you're set to edit the RootViewController.xib file in Interface Builder, not in Xcode's Editor window. That's because double-clicking always opens a file in a new window — this time, the Interface Builder window.

   Windows appear as they were the last time you left them. If this is the first time you've opened Interface Builder, you see three windows that look something like those in Figure 3-13.

   Not surprisingly, the View window looks exactly as it did in the iPhone Simulator window — as blank as a whiteboard wiped clean.

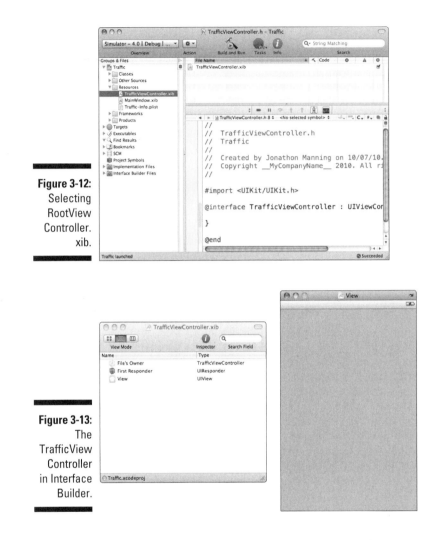

Figure 3-12:
Selecting
RootView
Controller.
xib.

Figure 3-13:
The
TrafficView
Controller
in Interface
Builder.

Interface Builder supports two file types:

- ✔ **nib:** An older format, which stored its contents as incomprehensible binary information.

- ✔ **xib:** A newer format, which stores its contents as clean XML code.

  Functionally, these are both the same — they both are used for storing your application's interface. The iPhone project templates all use xib files.

Although the file extension is now `.xib`, everyone still calls them nib files. *nib* and the corresponding file extension `.xib` are acronyms for NeXT Interface Builder. The Interface Builder application was originally developed at NeXT Computer, whose OpenStep operating system was used as the basis for creating Mac OS X. (Here ends the history lesson!)

The RootViewController.xib window (the far-left window in Figure 3-13) is the nib's main window. This window acts as a Table of Contents for the nib file. With the exception of the first two icons (File's Owner and First Responder), every icon in this window (in this case, there's only one) represents a single instance of an Objective-C class that is created automatically when this nib file loads.

Interface Builder doesn't generate any code that you have to modify or even look at. Instead, it creates freeze-dried Objective-C objects that the nib loading code reconstitutes and turns into real objects at runtime.

If you take a closer look at the three objects in the RootViewController.xib file window — and if you have a pal who knows the iPhone backward and forward — you'd find out the following about each object:

✔ **The file's owner proxy object:** This is the controller object that is responsible for the contents of the nib file. In this case, the file's owner object is actually the RootViewController that was created by Xcode and is the primary object you use to implement the application's functionality. The file's owner isn't created from the nib file; it's created in one of two ways — either from another (previous) nib file or by a programmer who codes it manually.

In Interface Builder, you can create connections between the file's owner and the other interface objects in your nib file.

✔ **First responder proxy object:** This object is the object with which the user is currently interacting. For a view, first responder usually starts as the view controller object. If, for example, the user taps a text field to enter some data, the first responder would then become the text field object.

Although you use the first responder mechanism quite a bit as you build the *Traffic* game, you don't have to do anything to manage it. First Responder is set automatically and is maintained by the UIKit framework.

✔ **View object:** The View icon represents an instance of the UIView class. A UIView object is an area that a user can see and interact with. In this application, you have to deal with only one view.

Take another look at Figure 3-13; notice the other window open besides the main window. Look at the window with View in the title bar. That window is the graphical representation of the View icon. If you close the View window and then double-click the View icon, this window opens again. This is your canvas for creating your user interface: It's where you drag user interface elements, such as buttons and text fields. These objects come from the Library window (the third window you see in Figure 3-14).

Figure 3-14:
The Library
window.

The Library window contains your palette — the stock Cocoa Touch objects that Interface Builder supports. Dragging an item from the Library window to the View window adds an object of that type to the view.

You'll notice that the window shown in Figure 3-13 is shaped like an iPhone screen, which of course won't work too well when running on an iPad. In Chapter 19, we'll be adjusting the game's interface to fit on this larger, differently-shaped screen.

If you happen to close the Library window, whether by accident or by design, choose Tools➪Library to get it to reappear. You can also quickly open it by pressing ⌘-Shift-L.

Part II
Traffic, The Game

The 5th Wave   By Rich Tennant

"Other than this little glitch with the landscape view, I really love my iPhone."

In this part . . .

This part takes our game concept, Traffic, and turns it into a real game for the iPhone. Starting with how apps in general work, we build the user interface, tell you how to move stuff around on the screen, turn the game play into game logic, debug your problems, and provision your iOS devices for distribution and the game itself for submission to the App Store.

And finally, because no game is fun without choice or noises, we discuss how to set and get user preferences as well as how to make your game play sound effects and music at the appropriate junctures.

This part gets you through the grunt work of turning an idea into a game, using the best practices of Apple's iOS SDK. Here's a breakdown of each chapter:

- ✔ Chapter 4 describes how iOS apps, in a general sense, work and gives you the understanding you need for the rest of this part.
- ✔ Chapter 5 lets you get down and dirty with Apple's interface tool, Interface Builder, as you assemble the *Traffic* main menu screens.
- ✔ Chapter 6 gets things moving on the screen!
- ✔ Chapter 7 takes the things that move and injects behavior into them.
- ✔ Chapter 8 discusses the design of the game and how that translates into software architecture to implement the logic.
- ✔ Chapter 9 takes the game logic and implements the game.
- ✔ Chapter 10 shows you how to swat the bugs in your games using the Debugger and Static Analyzer. You find out all about setting breakpoints that stop your app cold in the Simulator so that you can examine the contents of variables and messages to objects.
- ✔ Chapter 11 lets you keep score so your players remain happy and fulfilled.
- ✔ Chapter 12 educates you on the fine art of respecting your user's preferences.
- ✔ Chapter 13 guides you through provisioning your devices to run your game during development, and we even discuss how to set up your game for development and for submission to the App Store.
- ✔ Chapter 14 covers the vitally important aspect of making your game play sound and music.

Chapter 4

How iOS Games Work

*O*ne of the things that makes developing for iOS devices so appealing is the richness of the tools and frameworks provided in Apple's iOS Software Development Kit (SDK) for iPhone and iPad applications. The *frameworks* are especially important; each one is a distinct body of code that actually implements your application's generic functionality — it provides the application's basic way of working, in other words. This is especially true of one framework in particular — the *UIKit framework,* the heart of the standard user interface.

In this chapter, we lead you on a journey through most of the iOS user interface architecture — a mostly static view that explains what the various pieces are, what each does, and how they interact with each other. This lays the groundwork for developing the *Traffic* application's user interface, which you get a chance to tackle in Chapter 5. After we cover the architecture — but before you start major coding — we take you on a similar tour of the iPhone application *runtime environment* — the dynamic view of all the pieces working together when, for example, the user launches your application or touches a button onscreen — and how the various high-level components of your app fit together.

Using Frameworks

A framework is designed to easily integrate any of the code that gives your application its specific functionality — the code that runs your game or delivers the information that your user wants, for example. Frameworks are therefore similar to software libraries but with an added twist. Frameworks also implement a program's flow of control, unlike in a software library, where it's dictated by the programmer. This means that instead of the programmer deciding in what order things happen — what messages are sent to what objects and in what order when an application launches, or what messages are sent to what objects in what order when a user touches a button onscreen — all that is already a part of the framework and doesn't need to be specified by the programmer.

When you use a framework, you give your application a ready-made set of basic functions; you've told it, "Here's how to act like an application." With the framework in place, all you need to do is add the application's specific functionality you want — the content, the controls, and the views that enable the user to access and use that content — to the frameworks.

The frameworks and the iOS provide some complex functionality, such as

- ✔ Launching the application and displaying a window onscreen

- ✔ Displaying controls onscreen and responding to a user action — changing a toggle switch, for example, or scrolling a view, such as the list of your contacts

- ✔ Accessing sites on the Internet, not just through a browser but from within your own program

- ✔ Managing user preferences

- ✔ Playing sounds and movies

- ✔ Drawing fast 3D graphics

- ✔ Connecting two iOS devices wirelessly for multiplayer games

- ✔ Playing audio from the user's iPod library

Some developers talk in terms of *using a framework*. We think about the matter differently: You don't use frameworks so much as they "use" you. You provide the functions that the framework accesses; it needs your code to become an application that does something other than start, display a blank window, and then end. This perspective makes figuring out how to work with a framework much easier. (For one thing, this approach lets the programmer know where he's essential.)

If this seems too good to be true, well, okay, it is — all that complexity (and convenience) comes at a cost. Getting your head around the whole thing and knowing exactly where (and how) to add your application's functionality to that supplied by the framework can be really difficult. That's where *design patterns* come in. Understanding the design patterns behind the frameworks gives you a way of thinking about a framework, especially UIKit, that doesn't make your head explode.

Using Design Patterns

A major theme of iOS development is that, when it comes to iPhone app development, the UIKit framework does a lot of the heavy lifting for you. That's all well and good, but it's a little more complicated than that: The framework is designed around certain programming paradigms, or *design patterns.* The design pattern is a model that your own code must be consistent with. **Remember:** Although the UIKit framework does a lot of heavy lifting when drawing an interface, it doesn't help you as much when you're building a game.

To understand how to take best advantage of the power of the framework — or (better put) how the framework objects want to use *you* best — you need to understand design patterns. If you don't understand them — or if you try to work around them because you're sure you have a "better" way of doing things — it actually makes your job much more difficult. (Developing software can be hard enough, so making your job more difficult is definitely something you want to avoid.) Getting a handle on the basic design patterns that the framework uses and expects helps you develop applications that make the best use of the frameworks, which means you need only to do the least amount of work in the shortest amount of time.

The iOS design patterns can help you to understand not only how to structure your code, but also how the framework itself is structured. They describe relationships and interactions between classes or objects, as well as how responsibilities should be distributed amongst classes so the iPhone does what you want it to do.

The common definition of a design pattern is "a solution to a problem in a context." ("Uh, guys, that's not too helpful," we hear you say.) At that level of abstraction, the concept gets fuzzy and ambiguous. Here's how we use the term throughout this book:

> In programming terms, a *design pattern* is a commonly used template that gives you a consistent way to do a particular task.

Here are the six basic design patterns you need to be comfortable with when developing iOS games:

- ✔ Model-View-Controller (MVC)
- ✔ Delegation
- ✔ Target-action
- ✔ Notifications
- ✔ Block model
- ✔ Managed memory model

We start with the MVC design pattern, which is the key to understanding how an iPhone application works. We discuss delegation and target-action later in this chapter in the section "Adding Your Own Application's Behavior." The managed memory model we explain in Chapter 6, and we briefly touch on notifications in Chapter 17.

The sixth basic design pattern — blocks and concurrent programming — enables you to execute tasks concurrently (including, in iOS 4.0 and above, the use of Grand Central Dispatch) and is way beyond the scope of this book.

The Model-View-Controller (MVC) pattern

The iPhone frameworks are *object-oriented.* The easiest way to understand what that really means is to think about a team. The work that needs done is divided and assigned to individual team members (or *objects*). Every member of a team has a job and works with other team members to get things done. What's more, a "good" team member doesn't butt in on what other members do — just as objects in object-oriented programming spend their time taking care of business and not caring what the object in the virtual cubicle next door does.

Object-oriented programming was originally developed to make code more maintainable, reusable, extensible, and understandable (what a concept!) by tucking all the functionality behind well-defined interfaces — the actual details of how something works (as well as its data) is hidden. This makes modifying and extending an application much easier.

Great — so far — but a pesky question still plagues programmers: Exactly how do you decide on the objects and what each one does?

Sometimes the answer to that question is pretty easy — just use the real world as a model (eureka!). In the *Traffic* game that you build throughout this book, Vehicle and Lane are some of the classes we use. But with a generic program structure for your game, how do you decide what the objects should be? That may not be so obvious.

The MVC pattern is a well-established way to group application functions into objects. Variations of it have been around at least since the early days of *Smalltalk,* one of the very first object-oriented languages. The MVC is a high-level pattern — it addresses the architecture of an application and classifies objects according to the general roles they play in an application.

The MVC pattern creates, in effect, a miniature universe for the application, populated with three kinds of objects. The MVC pattern also specifies roles and responsibilities for all three kinds of objects, and specifies the way they're supposed to interact with each other. To make things more concrete (that is, to keep your head from exploding), imagine a big, beautiful, 60-inch flat screen TV. Here's the gist:

- ✔ **Model objects:** These objects together comprise the content "engine" of your application. They contain the application's data and logic — making your application more than just a pretty face. In the *Traffic* game, the model is a list of vehicles and lanes that the game knows about, and knows how to control the behavior of.

  You can think of the *model* (which may be one object or several that interact) as a particular television program. One that, quite frankly, doesn't give a hoot about what TV set it is being shown on (in this case, the vehicles don't particularly care about where they're drawn onscreen, for example).

  In fact, the model shouldn't give a hoot. Even though the model owns its data, the model should have no connection at all to the user interface and should be blissfully ignorant about what's done with its data.

- ✔ **View objects:** These objects display things onscreen and respond to user actions. Pretty much anything you see is a kind of view object — the window and all the controls, for example. Your views know how to display information that it got from the model object, and how to get any input from the user the model may need. But the view itself should know nothing about the model. The view may handle a request to move a vehicle from one lane to another, but it doesn't bother with what that request means. The view may display the different lanes, but it doesn't care about the meaning of the color of those lanes.

  You can think of the *view* as a television screen that doesn't care about what program is showing or what channel you just selected.

  The UIKit framework provides many different kinds of views, as you find out later in this chapter.

If the view knows nothing about the model and the model knows nothing about the view, how do you get data and other notifications to pass from one to the other? To get that conversation started (Model: "I've just updated my data;" View: "Hey, give me something to display," for example), you need the third element in the MVC triumvirate, the *controller*.

✓ **Controller objects:** These objects connect the application's view objects to its model objects. They supply the view objects with what they need to display (getting this data from the model) and also provide the model with user input from the view.

You can think of the *controller* as the circuitry that pulls the show off of the cable and sends it to the screen, or requests a particular pay-per-view show. In the case of games, the controller usually houses the over-arching game logic and code for game play mechanics.

The MVC in action

The *Traffic* game is designed around a collection of cars, which the user taps and drags around the screen, moving in the game. The model contains each car object, which contains information about their destination, speed, and position. You also need a way to show the position of the cars onscreen — in this case, use UIKit classes. Finally, you need a controller to tie together the model and view. (We'll be covering this in Chapters 5, 6, and 7.)

When the user taps a car view to drag it, the controller is updated about its new position and instructs the view to draw it in a different spot onscreen. Additionally, if this causes two cars to crash, the view is told to show the game over screen.

The process, and how it relates to the concept of models, controllers, and views, is illustrated in Figure 4-1.

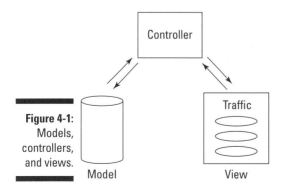

Figure 4-1:
Models,
controllers,
and views.

When you think about your application in terms of model, view, and controller objects, the UIKit framework starts to make sense. The fog also begins to lift from where at least part of your application-specific behavior needs to go. Before we get more into that, however, you need to know a little more about the classes provided to you by the UIKit that implement the MVC design pattern — windows, views, and view controllers.

Working with Windows and Views

After a game launches, it's the only application running on the system with full and complete control of that system — aside from the operating system software. Of course iOS games, for the most part, have only a single window, so you don't find separate document windows to display content. Instead, everything displays in that single window, and your game interface takes over the entire screen. When your game runs, that's all the user does with the iPhone or iPad.

Looking out the window

The single window you see on the iPhone or iPad screen is an instance of the UIWindow class. This window is created at launch time, either programmatically by you or automatically by UIKit loading it from a *nib* file — a special file that contains instant objects that are reconstituted at runtime. (You find out more about nib files in Chapter 7.) You then add views and controls to the window. In general, after the window object is created, you never really have to think about it again.

An iOS window can't be closed or manipulated directly by the user. Your application programmatically manages the window.

Although your application never creates more than one window at a time, the iOS does use additional windows on top of your window. The system status bar is one example. You can also display alerts on top of your window by using the supplied Alert views.

Figure 4-2 shows the window layout on the iPhone for the *Traffic* game.

Admiring the view

In an iOS game world, view objects are responsible for the view functionality in the MVC architecture.

A *view* is a rectangular area onscreen (on top of a window). Throughout this chapter, we often refer to the *Content view* — the view that is placed inside the window, as shown in Figure 4-2.

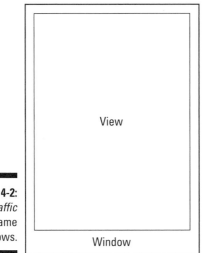

Figure 4-2:
The *Traffic* game windows.

In the UIKit framework, windows are really a special kind of view, but for purposes of this discussion, we talk about views that sit on top of the window.

You need to think about views in two ways. From the user perspective, the views sit on top of each other. From a programming perspective, however, the views that are on top of the windows *visually* are really subviews inside the window view. Keep reading to find out more about views.

What views do

Views are the main way for your application to interact with a user. This interaction happens in two ways:

✔ **Views display content.** For example, views make drawing and animation happen onscreen.

In essence, the view object displays the data from the model object.

✔ **Views handle touch events.** They respond when the user touches a button, for example.

The view hierarchy

Views and subviews create a view hierarchy. You have two ways of looking at a view hierarchy (no pun intended this time) — *visually* (how the user perceives it) and *programmatically* (how you create it). You must be clear about the differences, or you'll find yourself in a state of confusion that resembles Times Square on New Year's Eve.

Looking at a view hierarchy visually, the window is at the base of this hierarchy with a *Content view* (a transparent view that fills the window's Content rectangle) on top of it. The Content view displays information and allows the user to interact with the application, using (preferably standard) user interface items, such as text fields, buttons, toolbars, and tables.

Whenever a view is shown inside another view or window, the view that gets added is a *subview*. A subview is just a view that exists inside another view, which is known as its *superview*. A view can be a subview and a superview at the same time — for example, if you made a view, put it in the content view, and then put another view inside the first.

The view hierarchy is as follows:

- ✔ Views added to the Content view become *subviews* of it.

- ✔ Views added to the Content view become the *superviews* of any views added to them.

- ✔ A view can have one (and only one) superview, and zero or more subviews.

The view hierarchy may seem counterintuitive, but a subview is displayed *on top of* its parent view (that is, on top of its superview). Think about this relationship as containment: A superview *contains* its subviews. Figure 4-3 shows an example of a view hierarchy. The window contains both the status bar at the top, and the white content view. Inside the content view, there are four buttons.

Controls — such as buttons, text fields, and the like — are really view subclasses that become subviews. So are any other display areas you may specify. The view must manage its subviews and resize itself with respect to its superviews. Fortunately, much of what the view must do is coded already for you. The UIKit framework supplies the code that defines view behavior.

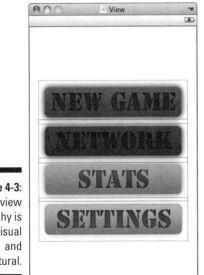

Figure 4-3:
The view
hierarchy is
both visual
and
structural.

The view hierarchy plays a key role in both drawing and event handling. When a window is sent a message to display itself, the window asks its subview to render itself first. If that view has a subview, it asks *its* subview to render itself first, going down the structural hierarchy (or up the visual structure) until the last subview is reached. This subview then renders itself and returns to its caller, which renders itself, and so on.

You create or modify a view hierarchy whenever you add a view to another view, either programmatically or with the help of Interface Builder. The UIKit framework automatically handles all the relationships associated with the view hierarchy.

Exploring the kinds of views you use

The UIView class defines the basic properties of a view, and you may be able to use it as is — you take it a little further in the *Traffic* game by simply customizing some controls.

The framework also provides you with a number of other views that are subclassed from UIView. These views implement the kinds of things that you need to do on a regular basis.

Use the view objects that are part of the UIKit framework. When you use an object, such as a UISlider or UIButton, your slider or button behaves just like a slider or button in any other iPhone application. This enables the consistency in appearance and behavior across applications that users expect.

Container views

Container views are a technical (Apple) term for Content views that do more than just lie onscreen and display your controls and other content. The UIScrollView class, for example, adds scrolling without you doing any work.

UITableView inherits this scrolling capability from UIScrollView and adds the ability to display lists and respond to the selections of an item in that list; think of the Contacts application (and a host of others). UITableView is one of the primary navigation views on the iPhone; table views aren't used much in games, and they don't grace you with their presence again in this book.

Another Container view, the UIToolbar class, contains button-like controls — and you find those everywhere on the iPhone. In Mail, for example, you touch an icon in the bottom toolbar to respond to an e-mail. You don't use these either because games aren't boring.

Controls

Controls are the fingertip-friendly graphics extensively used in a typical application's user interface. Controls are actually subclasses of the *UIControl superclass,* a subclass of the UIView class. They include touchable items, such as buttons, sliders, and switches as well as text fields in which you enter data.

Controls make heavy use of the Target-Action design pattern, which we get to soon. (We talk more about controls and how they fit into the Target-Action pattern later in this chapter, in the section "Adding Your Own Application's Behavior.")

Display views

Think of *Display views* as controls that look good but don't really do anything except, well, look good. These include UIImageView, UILabel (which you use in Chapter 9 to display parts of the *Traffic* interface), UIProgressView, and UIActivityIndicatorView.

Text and Web views

Text and *Web views* provide a way to display formatted text in your application. The UITextView class supports the display and editing of multiple lines of text in a scrollable area. The UIWebView class provides a way to display

HTML content. These views can be used as the Content view or can also be used in the same way as a Display view, as a subview of a Content view. UIWebViews is also the primary way to include graphics and formatted text in text Display views.

Alert views and action sheets

Alert views and *action sheets* present a message to the user, along with buttons that allow the user to respond to the message. Alert views and action sheets are similar in function, but look and behave differently. For example, the UIAlertView class displays a blue alert box that pops up onscreen, and the UIActionSheet class displays a box that slides in from the bottom of the screen.

Navigation views

Tab bars and *navigation bars* work in conjunction with view controllers to provide tools to navigate in your application. Normally, you don't need to create a UITabBar or UINavigationBar directly — it's easier to use Interface Builder or configure these views through a tab bar or navigation controller.

The window

A *window* provides a surface for drawing content and is the root container for all other views.

Each application typically has only one window. You make an additional window in Chapter 17, when we talk about external screens; don't worry though, it's pretty simple!

Controlling View Controllers

View controllers implement the controller component of the MVC design pattern. These controller objects contain the code that connects the application's view objects to its model objects. They provide the data to the view. Whenever the view needs to display something, the view controller gets what the view needs from the model. Similarly, view controllers respond to controls in your Content view and may do things like tell the model to update its data (when the user adds or changes text in a text field, for example), compute something (the most recent high scores for the game, say), or change the view being displayed (like changing to the settings screen when the user is on the main menu).

As we describe in "The Target-Action pattern" section later in this chapter, a view controller is often the (target) object that responds to the onscreen controls. The Target-Action mechanism is what enables the view controller to be aware of any changes in the view, which can then transmit to the model or control the behavior of other parts of the application.

Here's how the model-view-controller pattern applies to iOS application interfaces.

1. A message is sent to that view's view controller to handle the request.

2. The view controller's method interacts with a model object.

3. The model object processes the request and updates the data it contains.

4. The model object sends the data back to the view controller.

5. The view controller creates a new view to present the information.

View controllers have other vital iOS responsibilities as well, such as

✔ Managing a set of views — including creating them or flushing them from memory during low-memory situations.

✔ Responding to a change in the device's orientation — say, landscape to portrait — by resizing the managed views to match the new orientation.

✔ Creating *modal* views that require the user to do something (touch the Yes button, for example) before returning to the application.

You'd use a modal view to ensure the user paid attention to the implications of an action (for example, "Are you *sure* you want to clear all your high scores?"). Modal views take control of the entire screen, and force the user to deal with them before they can do anything else. Dialog boxes are an example of a modal view.

View controllers are also typically the objects that serve as delegates and data sources for table views.

In addition to the base UIViewController class, UIKit includes subclasses, such as UITabBarController, UINavigationController, UITableViewController, and UIImagePickerController, to manage the tab bar, navigation bar, and table views as well as to access the camera and photo library.

Even if your game is entirely built with custom graphics, use a view controller just to manage a single view and then auto-rotate it when the device's orientation changes.

Using naming conventions

When creating your own classes, follow standard framework-naming conventions:

🖋 Class names (such as `View`) start with a capital letter.

🖋 The names of methods (such as `viewDidLoad`) start with a lowercase letter.

🖋 The names of instance variables (such as `frame`) start with a lowercase letter.

When you name conventions this way, it makes it easier to understand from the name what something actually is.

Adding Your Own Application's Behavior

Earlier in this chapter (by now, that might seem like a million years ago), we mention two other design patterns used in addition to the Model-View-Controller (MVC) pattern. If you have a photographic memory, you don't need us to tell you that those two patterns are the Delegation pattern and the Target-Action pattern. These patterns, along with the MVC pattern and subclassing, provide the mechanisms for you to add your application-specific behavior to the UIKit (and any other) framework.

The following are ways to add behavior:

🖋 **MVC pattern:** The first way to add behavior is through model objects in the MVC pattern. Model objects contain the data and logic that make, well, your application.

🖋 **Subclassing:** The way people traditionally think about adding behavior to an object-oriented program, if you want to know the truth — is through *subclassing*. With subclassing, create a new subclass that inherits behavior and instance variables from another superclass and then add additional behavior, instance variables, and *properties* (methods used to access the variables stored inside classes) to the mix until you come up with what you want. The idea here is to start with something basic and then add to it — kind of like taking a 1932 Ford and turning it into a hot rod. You'd subclass a view controller class, for example, to respond to controls.

🖋 **Delegation pattern:** The Delegation pattern allows you to customize an object's behavior without subclassing by basically forcing another object to do the first object's work for it. For example, the Delegation design pattern is used at application startup to invoke a method `appli-cationDidFinishLaunching:` that gives you a place to do your application-specific initialization. All you do is add your code to the method.

✔ **Block Object pattern:** You can add behavior by using block objects. The Block Object design pattern is similar to Delegation, but it's more *event driven* in that it allows you to create methods or functions that you can pass to other methods or functions that are executed as needed. For example, you might want to have some code that scrolls the view as necessary when the keyboard appears. You'd pass that to a method that's invoked when the keyboard appears.

✔ **Target-Action pattern:** The Target-Action design pattern allows your application to respond to an event. When a user touches a button, for example, you specify what method should be invoked to respond to the button touch. What's interesting about this pattern is that it also requires subclassing — usually a view controller — to add the code to handle the event.

In the next few sections, we go into a little more detail about the Delegation and Target-Action patterns.

The Delegation pattern

Delegation is a pattern used extensively in iOS development, so much so that you really have to clearly understand it. In fact, we have no problems telling you that, after you understand it, your life will be much easier. Until the light bulb went on for us, we sometimes felt like we were trying to make our way across a busy freeway without being knocked down.

As we say in the preceding section, delegation is a way to customize the behavior of an object without subclassing it. Instead, one object (a framework object) delegates the task of implementing one of its responsibilities to another object. You use a behavior-rich object supplied by the framework as is and put the code for program-specific behavior in a separate (delegate) object. When a request is made of the framework object, the method of the delegate that implements the program-specific behavior is called automatically.

For example, the UIApplication object handles most of the actual work needed to run the application. But, as you soon see, it sends your application delegate the `application;didFinishLaunchingWithOptions:` message to give you an opportunity to restore the game's window and view to where it was when the user previously left off. You can also use this method to create objects that are unique to your game.

When a framework object has been designed to use delegates to implement certain behaviors, the behaviors it requires (or gives you the option to implement) are defined in a protocol. *Protocols* define an interface that the delegate object implements. On the iOS, protocols can be formal or informal, although we concentrate solely on the former because it includes support for things like type checking and runtime checking to see whether an object conforms to the protocol.

In a formal protocol, you usually don't have to implement all the methods; many are declared *optional;* you only have to implement the ones relevant to your application. Before an object attempts to send a message to its delegate, the host object determines whether the delegate implements the method (via a `respondsToSelector:` message) to avoid the embarrassment of branching into nowhere if the method isn't implemented.

You find out much more about delegation and the Delegation pattern when you develop the *Traffic* game in later chapters — you'll be working directly with the UIApplication's delegate in Chapter 11.

The Target-Action pattern

The *Target-Action* pattern lets your game know that a user did something. He may have tapped a button or entered some text, for example. The control — a button, say — sends a message (the *action*) that you specify to the target you have selected to handle that particular action. The receiving object, or the *target,* is usually a view controller object.

If you wanted to start your car from your iPhone (not a bad idea if you have ever lived in some frigid place like Minneapolis), you could display two buttons, Start and Heater. When you tapped Start, you could have used Interface Builder to specify that the target is the CarController object and that the method to invoke is `ignition`. Figure 4-4 shows the Target-Action mechanism in action — buttons are connected to actions, and when they are tapped, the corresponding action code is run. (If you're curious about IBAction and `(id) sender`, don't worry: We explain what they are when we show you how to use the Target-Action pattern in your game.)

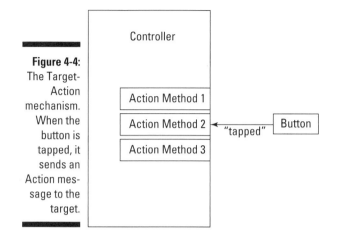

Figure 4-4:
The Target-
Action
mechanism.
When the
button is
tapped, it
sends an
Action mes-
sage to the
target.

The Target-Action mechanism enables you to create a control object and tell it not only what object you want handling the event, but also the message to send. For example, if the user touches a Ring Bell button onscreen, you want to send a Ring Bell message to the view controller. But if the Wave Flag button on the same screen is touched, you want to send the same view controller the Wave Flag message. If you couldn't specify the message, all buttons would have to send the same message. That would then make coding more difficult and more complex because you'd have to identify which button had sent the message and what to do in response, and make changing the user interface more work and more error prone.

As you soon discover when creating your application, you can set a control's action and target through Interface Builder. This allows you to specify what method in which object should respond to a control without writing any code.

You can also change the target and action dynamically by sending the control or its cell `setTarget:` and `setAction:` messages.

For more on Interface Builder, check out Chapter 5.

Moving Ahead with Your Game

Congratulations! You have just gone through the Classic Comics version of hundreds of pages of Apple documentation, reference manuals, and how-to guides.

One of the challenges facing a new developer is to determine which of these mechanisms to use when. (That was certainly the case for us.) To ensure that you have an overall conceptual picture of iOS application architecture, check out the Cheat Sheet for this book, where we give you a summary of which mechanisms are used when. (We wish we'd had this when we developed our games — but at least you do now.) You can find the Cheat Sheet for this book at:

```
www.dummies.com/cheatsheet/iphoneandipadgamedevelopment
```

Well, you still have a bit more to explore — for example, how all these pieces work together at runtime (details, details . . .). But before that piece of the puzzle can make sense, you need to touch, feel, and get inside an application. As part of that process, we do a little demonstrating:

- ✔ We show you how to build a user interface for your game in Chapter 5.

- ✔ We show you how to make that interface really come to life in Chapter 6.

- ✔ We finish the conversation on iOS architecture, when you really start building the game, in Chapters 7 and 8.

When you've had a stroll through those adventures, you'll know everything you need to know about how to create a user interface and add the functionality to make your game do what you promised the user it would do. (How's that for a plan?)

Chapter 5

Building the User Interface

*I*n this chapter, we show you how to build the first screen shown to the user — the main menu — and display it on the iPhone. The user interface is the most crucial part of your game. Even if the game-play concepts that make up your game are the most elegant and entertaining, your game won't fly if your users can't figure out how to interact with your interface!

When you design your game's interface, onscreen real estate is limited on the iPhone (as cool as the screen is, it's still way smaller than a desktop monitor). The main menu is the first thing your user sees when he starts the game; therefore, it needs to look good! The tools you use in this chapter are *Interface Builder,* to design the screen the user sees, and *Xcode,* to set up the behavior of the screens.

When you write an iPhone application, the first thing the user notices about your application isn't the application or how it looks. Applications on the iPhone are presented as a grid of icons, and your application needs to look its best — even when it's not running!

In this chapter, you start by building the interface of the main menu using buttons, and then dress them up with some custom images. This makes your application stand out, which is important: If the user isn't impressed, she may just quit the app and do something else. When that's done, add some extra polish, such as an application icon and a launch screen. We'll come back and revisit this for the iPad in Chapter 19.

Building the Main Screen

To lay out the interface, start Interface Builder, which we show you how to do in the following sections. Figure 5-1 shows what the interface you'll build looks like in the iPhone Simulator, which is a tool that Apple provides that lets you test out your project without having to mess around with putting the application on a real iOS device.

Before you get the final application though, you need to open the project!

Figure 5-1:
How the
Traffic
main menu
looks in the
Simulator
when
finished.

Opening the project

To start working with the project, open it:

1. **Launch Xcode.**

   You can find Xcode in /Developer/Applications. If you added the Xcode icon to the Dock (see Chapter 4), you can launch Xcode from there.

2. Open the Traffic project.

If you haven't created the project yet, you should head back to Chapter 3 to get started!

a. Choose File⇨Open.

The Open dialog appears.

b. Navigate to (and open) the Traffic project you created in Chapter 3.

The Traffic Project window appears onscreen.

Creating the first screen

After you open the project, create the files that describe the first screen that users see when they start your app. We show you how to build the first screen by using Interface Builder and manipulating .xib files. Follow these steps:

1. In the Groups & Files panel (on the left side of the Project window you open in the preceding section), click the triangle next to the Resources folder to expand it, as shown in Figure 5-2.

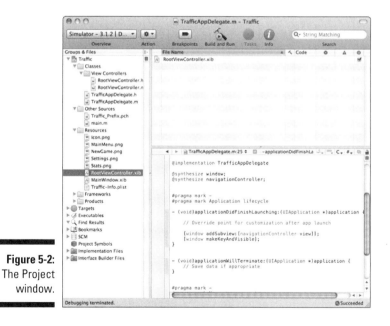

Figure 5-2:
The Project window.

2. In the expanded Resources folder, double-click the RootViewController. xib file to open the Root View Controller in Interface Builder.

If you've never run Interface Builder before, you see something that looks like Figure 5-3; however, if you've already explored Interface Builder, you see the windows as you last left them.

For the rest of these steps, you'll be working in Interface Builder to construct the interface.

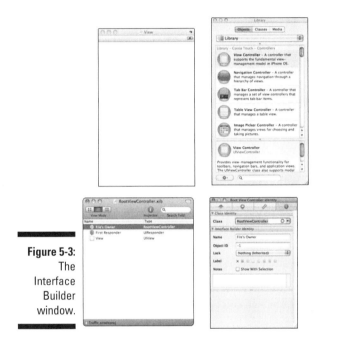

Figure 5-3: The Interface Builder window.

3. Check whether the Library window (at the top right in Figure 5-3) is open already; if it isn't, choose Tools⇨Library to open it.

Alternatively, press ⌘+Shift+L to open the Library window.

4. Click the Objects tab at the top of the Library window and choose Library in the drop-down list, if not selected already.

The Library has all the components you can use to build a vanilla iPhone user interface. These include all the visible controls you see on a standard iPhone screen, such as labels, buttons, and text fields, and non-visible objects you need to create the plumbing to support the screen that the user will interact with.

RootViewController.xib is a file that is created by Xcode when you create the project from the "Navigation-based application" template (as you did in Chapter 3).

Because you created the application using the Navigation-Based Application template, the RootViewController will contain a Table View. This is the wrong kind of view that we want to use, because for this project you'll need to work with plain Views, which act as plain canvases.

5. **Select the Table View from the Document Window, and press Delete to remove it. Then, drag a View from the Library window into the Document window. Finally, select the File's Owner in the Document window, hold down the Control key, and drag from the File's Owner to the View. Choose "view" from the list that appears.**

Once you've done this, the file contains a View window. All you have to do here is add the static text, images, and other elements that make up your main menu. To do that, you just drag the controls you need from the Library window into your View window. Dragging any of these objects to the View window from the Library window means that those objects will appear when your application is loaded.

6. **Type** button **into the search box at the bottom of the Library window, as shown in Figure 5-4.**

The Library filters the available controls to objects named *button.* You're interested in the UIButton object.

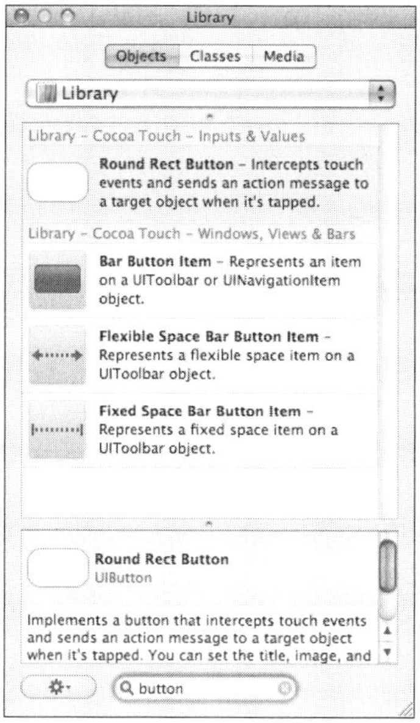

Figure 5-4:
The filtered Library, showing button-like objects.

7. **Click and drag a UIButton from the Library into the View window three times.**

   This adds three buttons to the view.

8. **Drag the buttons around to lay them out, as shown in Figure 5-5.**

   The precise positioning doesn't matter a great deal, but in this book we make the assumption that the buttons are laid out in the order of "New Game", "Stats," and "Settings." This becomes semi-important in Chapter 6, when we add animation to these buttons.

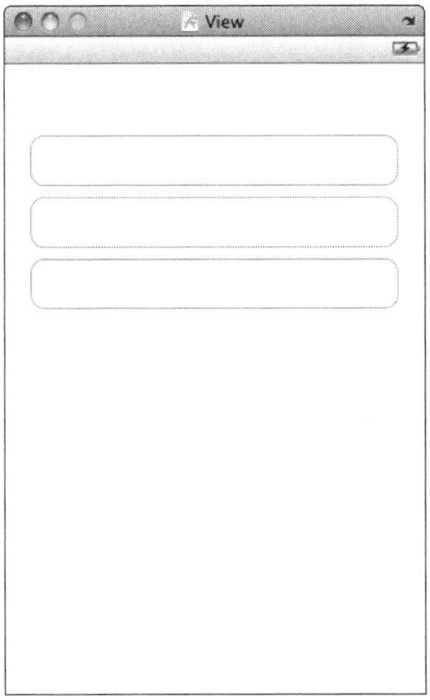

Figure 5-5:
Lay out the buttons.

Interface Builder provides handy guides to help you align the buttons properly. If you don't see the guides, choose Layout⇨Snap to Guides to turn them on.

9. **Make sure that the Inspector window is open; if it isn't, choose Tools⇨Inspector to open it.**

   Alternatively, press ⌘+Shift+I.

   The Inspector window allows you to see (or *inspect*) the various settings and options of each item in your view. Every single item you work with can be manipulated with the Inspector window, which is also known as *your new best friend*. Expect to work with the Inspector window a lot!

10. **Click the Attributes tab (it's the left tab at the top of the Inspector window), as shown in Figure 5-6.**

    Alternatively, press ⌘+1.

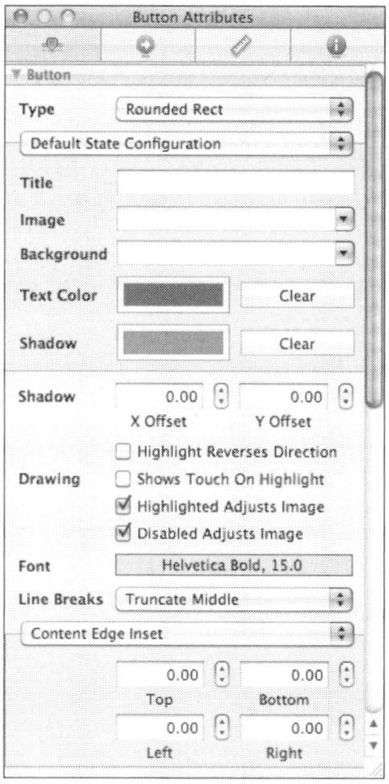

Figure 5-6:
The Button
Attributes
pane of the
Inspector
window.

11. **Select the top-most button that you added to the View window.**

    The Inspector window changes to show information about that button.

12. **Type** New Game **into the Title field and press Return to change the button's name that appears on the main menu.**

    The button in the View window updates to include the new label.

13. **Repeat Steps 11 and 12 for the other two buttons, but name them Stats and Settings, respectively.**

    The results look like Figure 5-7.

14. **Choose File⇨Save or press ⌘+S to save the interface file.**

The last step is to make the blue navigation bar go away. Navigation bars appear at the top of many applications to indicate to the user what screen they're on, as well as to provide a button for letting them return to the previous screen. We don't need that.

We're going to open up the .xib file that controls whether the bar appears. We're also going to change the RootViewController.h and RootViewController.m files to not try to use a Table View (which, as you might remember, we removed earlier in the chapter).

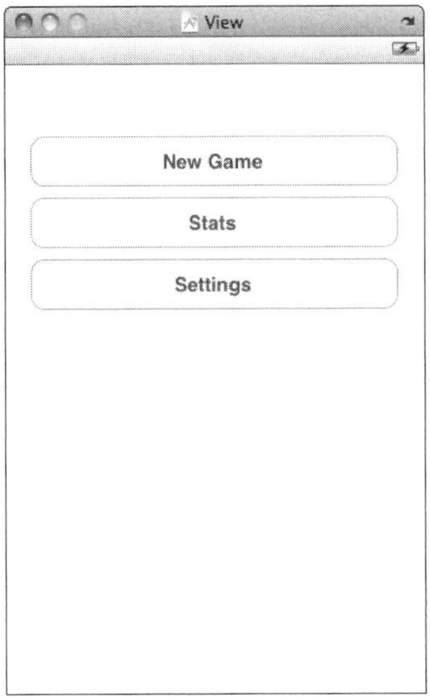

Figure 5-7:
Three
labeled but-
tons in the
View
window.

1. **In Xcode, double-click on MainWindow.xib to open it in Interface Builder.**

2. **Click on the Navigation Controller object in the document window to select it.**

3. **Open the Attributes Inspector window by pressing ⌘+1.**

4. **Uncheck the "Shows Navigation Bar" check box at the top of the Attributes Inspector. Save the file by pressing ⌘+S.**

5. **You're done with Interface Builder for now. Go back to Xcode and click the Build and Run button.**

   Select all of the text, and replace it with the following code:

   ```
   #import "RootViewController.h"
   @implementation RootViewController
   @end
   ```

   Once you've done that, open RootViewController.h, select all of the text, and replace it with the following code:

   ```
   #import <UIKit/UIKit.h>
   @interface RootViewController : UIViewController {
   }
   @end
   ```

   Finally, press the Build and Go button at the top of the window.

   The iPhone Simulator launches, showing your application in all its button-based glory, as shown in Figure 5-8.

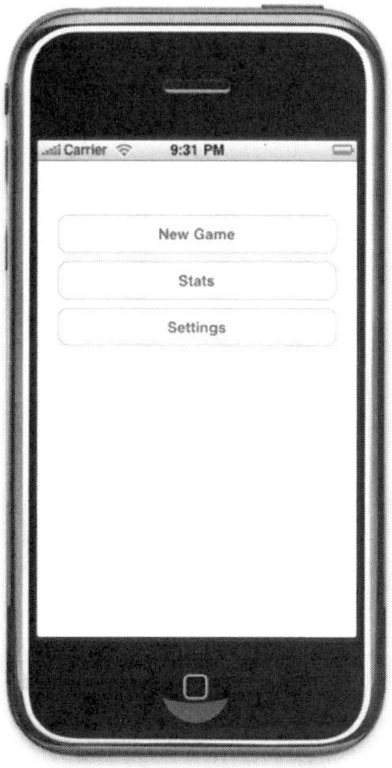

Figure 5-8:
The appli-
cation in
the iPhone
Simulator.

Making the buttons look fancy

A game is all about spit and polish — your players really want to have some-thing interesting to interact with, and it's up to you to deliver an interesting experience. One of the ways that you can do this is to make what they inter-act with visually appealing. To that end, you want to make these buttons look fantastic, and you want to add a background image to the main screen to spiff up things a bit.

Adding images to the buttons

To make the buttons look nice, you'll first need to add the necessary image files to the application, and then apply them to the buttons you've added.

1. **If the application is open, press the Home button at the bottom of the iPhone Simulator to quit the application. Make sure that Xcode is open.**

2. **To add images to the project, open the Images folder (included in the collection of resources you downloaded in Chapter 1), and then click and drag MainMenu.png, NewGame.png, Stats.png, and Settings.png from the Images folder into the Resources group in Xcode, as shown in Figure 5-9.**

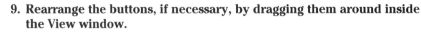

You'll be working a lot with the resources in this collection. Make sure you have it easily accessible as you read through this book!

3. Select the Copy Items into Destination Group's Folder (If Needed) check box and then set the "Reference Type" drop-down list to "Default".

Xcode and Interface Builder now know about the images.

4. Open RootViewController.xib in Interface Builder, and select the New Game button in the View window.

For this example, change the New Game button's style from the white, rounded rectangle (which, to be honest, looks kind of ugly) to your custom image.

5. Click the Attributes tab in the Inspector window. Choose Custom from the Type drop-down list near the top of the window.

The rounded rectangle behind the button disappears.

6. Type NewGame.png **into the Image field or choose NewGame.png from the Image drop-down list.**

Select all the text in the Title field and delete it — you don't need a text label for this button.

Don't worry; the button looks a little strange — the image appears, but its sides are cut off.

7. While you still have the New Game button selected, choose Layout⇨ Size to Fit to size the New Game button.

Alternatively, press ⌘+= (equals sign).

The button changes to the right shape, showing all the image.

8. Repeat Steps 4–7 for the other two buttons; however, apply the Stats. png image to the Stats button and the Settings.png image to the Settings button.

Make all the buttons the right size with Size to Fit (⌘+=).

9. Rearrange the buttons, if necessary, by dragging them around inside the View window.

The view looks like Figure 5-10.

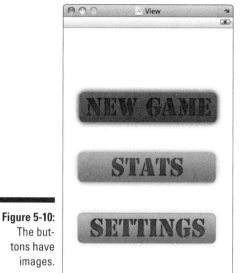

Figure 5-10:
The buttons have images.

By default, custom image buttons on iOS automatically adjust the image when the user interacts with the button or when the button becomes disabled. When the user taps the button, it becomes darker; if the button ever is disabled, it becomes semi-transparent.

Adding a background image

Once the buttons have their pretty images, you'll need to add the background image for the main menu. To do this, follow these steps:

1. **Open the RootViewController.xib file in Interface Builder. Type image into the Library's search box.**

   This filters the controls to image-related options. You want UIImageView. Drag one out into the View window, on top of the buttons you prepared in the previous section.

2. **Set the Image of your new Image View to MainMenu.png.**

   Select the Image View, and open the Attributes Inspector by pressing ⌘+1. Type in "MainMenu.png" in the Image field that appears at the top of the Inspector window.

   The image view changes to display a portion of the image; use the Size to Fit option to make it take up the proper amount of space, by selecting it and pressing ⌘+= (see Step 7 in the preceding section).

The background image obscures the buttons — this is okay because you move it to the background in a moment.

3. **Drag the image to fit in the center of the View window with no white gaps on any of the edges.**

4. **Choose Layout➪Send to Back to send the background image to the back of the view, behind the buttons.**

   The menu buttons appear on top of the background.

5. **Save the file by choosing File➪Save, go back to your project in Xcode, and run it.**

   Your application appears, showing the fancy buttons and spiffy background, as shown in Figure 5-11.

Figure 5-11:
The finished application, with fancy graphics.

Adding Icons and Launch Screens

In this section, we show you how to add the icon and launch screen to the application. The iPhone transforms the icon, as shown in Figure 5-12. Icons on iOS follow a fairly simple standard — square, and encoded as PNG images. The clever thing about iOS is that it automatically gives the images you provide rounded corners, a slight bevel, and a shiny gloss to make the icon fit with Apple's built-in applications.

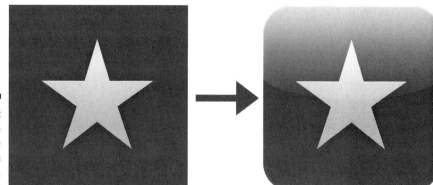

Figure 5-12:
How the
iPhone
transforms
icons.

Your icon actually needs to be two different files — one for the high-resolution iPhone 4, and one for all other iPhone devices. The lower-resolution icon needs to be in a file called Icon.png, and it needs to be 57 pixels wide and 57 pixels high. The high-resolution icon needs to be in a file called Icon@2x.png, and it needs to be 114 pixels wide and 114 pixels high.

On the iPad, you'll need another icon yet again. Icons for the iPad need to be stored in a file called Icon-iPad.png, and they need to be 72 pixels wide, and 72 pixels high.

Simple, no?

Icons are important because they're the first piece of your game that most users see; they need to be enticing, attractive, and representative of the overall theme of your game.

A launch screen is just as important as a good icon because the launch screen tricks the user into thinking that your application launches faster than it actually does (see the nearby sidebar "Why your game needs a launch screen," in this chapter). If your launch screen shows the first screen of your application, minus the controls that the user can tap, the application looks like it's launched a lot quicker than it actually has. This is a subtle technique used to make the iPhone feel faster overall. We use this technique in the provided launch screen image, which you find in the resources you could download in Chapter 1.

Adding the icon

Adding an icon to your project is a very simple process — in fact, most of the work is in designing the image itself! Follow these steps to add the icon to the application:

1. **Find the Icon.png image in the project resources you downloaded in Chapter 1.**

2. **Click and drag the Icon.png image into your project in Xcode.**

3. **Select the "Copy Items into Destination Group's Folder (If Needed)" check box and set the "Reference Type" drop-down list to "Default".**

   Don't rename the file: It must be Icon.png (see the previous section for details.) By default, iOS looks for a file with this filename.

4. **Run the application by clicking the Build and Run button in Xcode.**

   The application launches in the Simulator, but you're more interested in what happens when it's closed.

5. **Close the application by clicking the Home button at the bottom of the iPhone Simulator.**

   Behold: Your icon appears on the home screen, as shown in Figure 5-13!

Figure 5-13:
The iPhone's home screen with your application's icon.

TIP

Why your game needs a launch screen

The iPhone is actually quite a small and relatively slow computing device; it has only a fraction of the memory of the Mac you're using to develop on, and it can't run more than one third-party application at a time.

This isn't to say that the iPhone is underpowered; in fact, it's quite a mighty device for its size. However, sometimes you have to compensate for bits when its performance isn't the greatest. One such bit is in launching applications. To launch an application, the iPhone needs to load quite a bit of data into memory:

✔ The program

✔ Any resources it needs to run

✔ Any *frameworks,* or chunks of code needed to run the program

Loading this data can take some time. To hide this delay, iPhone applications can display a *launch screen* that's shown the instant the user taps the application's icon. This tricks the user into thinking that the application has launched already, when in fact, it's still getting off the ground. When the application finishes launching, the launch screen is replaced by your application. If you guessed that the iPad would be significantly more powerful, just because it's bigger — well, think again. Everything about speed applies to the iPad as well.

A little bit of magic happens here. By default, Xcode assumes that your icon's image is Icon.png. In the following section, you do a similar trick with the application's launch screen.

Adding the launch screen

Time to create a *launch screen,* which is a picture that displays while the application launches. This screen disappears after your program finishes loading and makes your application look like it loads faster than it actually does.

To maximize this illusion of speed and to give the user the best experience, your launch screen needs to look like the application has almost (but not quite) finished launching: The user needs to see every aspect of the application except components that they can interact with, such as buttons. That way when your application's view replaces the launch screen, it simply looks like the buttons have newly appeared, which is much less of a change than simply having the entire application pop into view at once.

For this example, the game's launch screen is simply a background image of the main menu. When the application finishes loading, the user sees the buttons appear.

By default, Xcode assumes that your launch screen is a Default.png image. You find the Default.png image in the project resources you downloaded in Chapter 1. Here's how to add it:

1. **Click and drag the Default.png image into your Resources group in Xcode.**

   Use the same settings as when you imported files in the last section, and don't rename the file.

2. **Select the "Copy Items into Destination Group's Folder (If Needed)" check box and set the "Reference Type" drop-down list to "Default".**

   Don't rename the file! It must be Default.png, because that's the name of the file that iOS will look for when it launches the application.

3. **Run the application by clicking the Build and Run button.**

   As you watch the Simulator open the application, note how the application appears to launch faster. Also notice that the only thing that changes onscreen when the application finishes launching is the addition of the buttons.

Congratulations! Your application is a hyper-advanced interactive program from the world of tomorrow! There's one last step to do in this chapter, before we start building up more features.

Renaming the view controller

Currently, the view controller that shows the main menu is called "RootViewController." This is the name used by Xcode when the application was created, but it isn't terribly descriptive. We're going to rename it to "MainMenuViewController."

To do this, we're going to use a tool that's built into Xcode that's designed for this sort of code-level rearranging. It's called the Refactor tool.

There are two steps involved here: renaming the code files, and renaming the interface files.

Follow these steps to rename the file.

1. **Open RootViewController.h in Xcode. Click inside the word "RootViewController." Press ⌘-Shift-J to open the Refactor tool.**

2. **Type "MainMenuViewController" in the window that appears. Click "Preview", and Xcode will figure out what it needs to do to rename the file. Once it's done, the "Preview" button will change to "Apply". Click it.**

Once you've done these steps, the view controller files will be renamed to MainMenuViewController.m and MainMenuViewController.h. The only exception will be RootViewController.xib, which Xcode doesn't rename. You'll need to do this change manually — Xcode tries to be as cautious as it can.

1. **Right-click on RootViewController.xib in the Groups and Files list, and choose "Rename." Name the file "MainMenuViewController.xib".**

2. **Double-click on MainWindow.xib to open it in Interface Builder. Double-click on the Navigation Controller object in the document window to open it.**

3. **Click on the View that appears. Open the Attributes Inspector by pressing ⌘+1.**

4. **In the "NIB Name" field in the Attributes Inspector, replace "RootViewController" with "MainMenuViewController".**

5. **Save the file.**

Once these steps are done, you're now ready to expand on the feature set of the application!

Chapter 6

Making Objects Appear and Move

*I*n this chapter, we show you how to work with that amazing screen that's built into every iOS device — iPhones, iPod touches, and iPads. Apple machines have always been strongly focused on the visual look of the software, and the iPhone is definitely no exception. Huge chunks of the documentation are devoted to how to effectively use the many tools that Apple provides to help make your applications as easy to build as possible. This chapter is all about knowing how the applications all work under the hood so you can take the most advantage of the features and tools available to you.

In addition to showing you how to draw graphics onscreen, we take a look at one of the youngest features to arrive in the world of OS X, mobile or otherwise: Core Animation. *Core Animation* is a set of application programming interfaces (APIs) that makes it easier to create motion and animation in your interfaces. Core Animation is responsible for the fluid movement that you see on every iOS device, and it's simple to code.

Drawing with Views

Turn on your iPhone and take a look at its screen. Everything you can see on your iPhone is drawn by a *view* — a piece of code that's responsible for telling the iOS how a certain piece of the screen is supposed to look. When you're building your own custom interface, this is worthwhile knowledge.

Useful graphics structures

CGRect is a *C structure:* It contains only data and doesn't have any methods; you can't send messages to a C structure like you can with Objective-C classes. Also note that when you talk about CGRect (or any other structure), you don't include the asterisk (*) after the name.

CGRect is used to describe a rectangle. This is how it's laid out:

```
struct CGRect {
    CGPoint origin;
    CGSize size;
};
```

CGRect is nothing but a CGPoint that describes the position of the top-left corner of the rectangle, and a CGSize that describes, well, its size.

When working with CGRects, you don't deal with CGPoint and CGSize directly, but knowing about them is useful, and the CGRect structure isn't much use without them. Here's what CGPoint and CGSize look like:

```
struct CGPoint {
    CGFloat x;
    CGFloat y;
};

struct CGSize {
    CGFloat width;
    CGFloat height;
};
```

A CGFloat is just a floating point number, such as 4.325. Floating point numbers are used for storing decimal numbers.

With CGRect, you can refer to the values that directly define the rectangle. For example, if you want to make a rectangle 10.5 pixels wide, write

```
myRect.size.width = 10.5;
```

And if you want to set the rectangle to be 55 pixels away from the left of its container, write

```
myRect.origin.x = 55;
```

Views are objects that inherit from the UIView class. Every control and image you place in your views is a class that descends from this great, almighty class, and you might expect that its sheer power and flexibility would be daunting. Not really: Drawing your own custom content is as simple as overriding one method: drawRect:.

When you override the drawRect: method, you override the point where the Cocoa Touch framework expects you to jump in and provide some direction on what to show. The drawRect: method looks like the following code; if you spend a lot of time writing custom views, you need to become very familiar with it:

```
- (void)drawRect:(CGRect)rect
```

When `drawRect:` is called, everything is set up already for you to do your drawing. All you have to do is issue the instructions to draw lines, shapes, and colors onscreen.

The `drawRect:` method takes only one parameter — a CGRect. For more detailed information on what CGRect is, see the sidebar "Useful graphics structures" elsewhere in this chapter. This CGRect describes the area in which you're expected to do your drawing. The rectangle is the bounds of the view — only stuff that you draw within this rectangle appears in your view.

Bounds is one of those keywords in iPhone graphics that needs to be explained a little bit before we can talk about it like grownups. Raise your hand if you've ever heard of a Cartesian coordinate system. Hey, nicely done! A *Cartesian coordinate system* is a way of laying out a grid of points so that each point gets a unique pair of numbers. Points in the same row share the same x-coordinate, and points in the same column share the same y-coordinate.

This approach to computer graphics has worked extremely well over the years, and it's no surprise that it's also made its way into iOS. In iOS, the zero-coordinate, or the point that is (0,0) on the grid, is at the top left of the screen, as shown in Figure 6-1.

Figure 6-1:
A side-by-side comparison of a conceptual grid and the grid that exists on your iPhone.

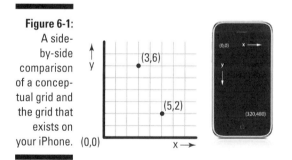

Figure 6-2 is a real world example of grids on the iPhone. Remember how everything on the screen has an associated view? This is a simple interface that we threw together in Interface Builder to show you where the views are. You can easily work out how the grid system works on your screen; there's a grid point for every glowing dot on the device. But did you know that every view on the screen has its own coordinate system? It's true!

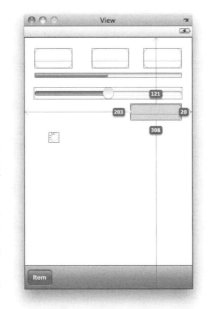

Figure 6-2:
Controls on
the iPhone
screen,
with boxes
showing the
outlines of
their views.

You can refer to a point inside a view in either of two ways: relative to its frame, or relative to its bounds:

✔ A view's *frame* is its size and position relative to its *super view* (the view that contains this view). Position (0,0) in the frame refers to the top-left corner of the view's super view.

✔ A view's *bounds* is its size and position relative to its *own* view. Position (0,0) in the bounds refers to the top-left corner of the view.

Composing a complex view and painting it entirely with bounds coordinates is easy, and you don't have to worry about existing in a larger space and interacting with lots of views.

How Drawing Works on iOS

Drawing on iOS needs to be very efficient. Remember, the iPhone is a rather underpowered device, and the software needs to be able to squeeze every last drop of juice out of it to get that famous iPhone taste.

The best way to optimize code is to make it do less work. (Actually, that's really important and takes most people lots of time to figure out properly, so we'll say it again, louder: *The best way to optimize code is to make it do less work.*) An example of this principle in action is speeding up drawing. The best way to draw faster is to draw less — show fewer objects onscreen at once and update the objects only when necessary, keeping changes to a minimum. And that's exactly what the iPhone does: It draws things as few times as it absolutely has to and then takes a hands-off approach unless you really need something new to display. That's where the idea of setting a view to be displayed comes in.

When you create and add a view to the screen, iOS tells the view to draw its contents (by calling `drawRect:`) and displays whatever comes out of that method onscreen. The iOS then stores that picture in memory. Whenever the view's position or visibility changes — say, for instance, another view comes over the top of your view — the view doesn't have to repaint because the drawing system remembers what your view looks like and makes it reappear as soon as the obstruction moves.

Sometimes it's important to let the drawing system know that you actually want to repaint the entire thing. This can happen when you have new data to display onscreen; perhaps your label has new text in it, and the user needs to be shown what it is.

When you want to tell the iOS to redraw your content, send your view the `setNeedsDisplay:` message:

```
[myView setNeedsDisplay:YES];
```

The clever thing about using the setNeedsDisplay system is that you give the drawing system time to deal with things in its own way. In the past, if you wanted to draw something, you had to tell the graphics systems to prepare a drawing context, be ready for you to send your pixels, and generally be prepared to organize your entire code around when and where you needed to make the pretty happen.

The setNeedsDisplay system, on the other hand, is rather elegant: After your program checks for and deals with events, such as touch input, it looks for all views that need displays and then draws them. Cocoa Touch uses this system, too, so you have a little less control over when the drawing actually happens, but that's a small price to pay for speed.

Keeping all this in mind, it's time to display the objects that make up the game. You need a place to put them all, and that's where the TrafficViewController comes in. We delve into that in the following section.

Building the Traffic View Controller

A *view controller* is an object that's responsible for being the intermediary between your application and the view that's displayed onscreen. The view controller "owns" the view: No other object in the application is allowed to manipulate it, and to get things to happen onscreen, the other objects in your app must tell the view controller to do it for them. This means that you have a very clean separation between the higher-level concepts (such as cars, scores, and timing) in your game and the lower-level implementation details (such as bitmaps, opacity, and screen positions).

Cocoa Touch is built around view controllers. Ever used an application that lets you tap a control, which causes a new screen to slide in from the side? You just saw a view controller appear. View controllers allow the application to be divided into manageable chunks.

View controllers can also be managed by other view controllers. The sliding-in effect is controlled by the *navigation view controller*, a special subclass of view controllers that maintains a virtual "stack" of other view controllers. The view controller at the top of the stack shows onscreen:

- ✔ When you want to show another view controller, push it onto the stack, and the navigation view controller takes care of the animation for you (if you want one).

- ✔ When you want to go back to the previous screen, pop off the top of the stack, and the navigation controller takes care of the animation.

In this way, navigation controllers are very well-suited to *hierarchical information display* in which the user starts at one screen, visits another, comes back, and explores the application using the first screen as the hub for the application. The fact that the user can always tap the back button makes it very difficult for her to get lost in your app. The structure of the *Traffic* game you're building is also hierarchical.

View controllers also provide a way to easily move among different screens in your application. Because the game play section of the application is one of those screens, it makes sense to create a new view controller that manages the action.

Before you add the code for this view controller, though, it's worth taking a look at something that you write quite a bit in all the classes you make: properties.

Properties

An interesting fact about Objective-C is that all *instance* variables — variables that exist inside your classes — are considered private, and you can't directly access them from other classes. In the past, this meant that every time you wanted to expose a variable to other classes, you had to write a setter method and a getter method for that variable.

Setter methods are methods that take a value and set a variable to that value. *Getter* methods are methods that return a value for a variable. Sounds simple, right? (Now imagine writing setter and getter methods for a class with 20 instance variables!)

People got sick of writing so many methods, so Apple introduced properties in *Objective-C 2.0,* which is the language you use to write iOS applications. *Properties* allow you to simply state that a variable should be accessed by other classes, as well as allow you to specify *how* they should be accessed.

Here's an example of a property — the relevant code is in bold. This is a header file for an example class.

```
@interface MyClass : NSObject {
  NSString* name;
  NSURL* url;
  int counter;
}

@property (nonatomic, retain) NSString* name;
@property (nonatomic, retain) NSURL* url;
@property (assign) int counter;

@end
```

Because the `@property` lines exist in the header file, they're included into classes that use this class. Therefore, other classes know about the property and can use it.

Property declarations begin with `@property`, and they contain setter information, followed by the type and name of the property. To explain what setter information is, you first need to understand how properties are synthesized.

For every property that you declare in your header, you must also synthesize it in your implementation file. Here's the implementation file for the preceding example class.

```
#import "MyClass.h"

@implementation MyClass
@synthesize name,url,counter;
@end
```

When you tell the compiler to synthesize a property, it looks at the type of the property and its name, and then creates both the setter and getter methods for you.

You can specify what the setter method actually does by changing the setter information. To understand why you might need multiple types of setters, remember how memory is managed for Objective-C objects — if an object wants to keep a reference to another object and keep it from going out of memory, it needs to *retain* it. Sometimes, though, you might want to make a *copy* of an object, rather than retain the original object. Finally, you might have a property that isn't an object at all (as is in the case of that `int` property), so retaining doesn't make sense.

That's where the setter information comes in. By declaring a property to be `retain`, `assign`, or `copy`, you're telling the compiler what sort of setter to make.

Additionally, for retained setters, it's often a good idea to declare the properties as *nonatomic* — this disables a couple tests that prevent the setter from being run by multiple threads at once (which is something a bit beyond the scope of the book).

Actions and outlets

In earlier chapters, you designed a very nice interface, but interfaces need to be able to work with your application's code in order to drive behavior in your game. When writing iOS applications, this is achieved by adding *actions* and *outlets* to classes you write.

Actions

When a button is tapped, it's generally expected that it causes something to happen. (If nothing happens, the user probably thinks your app is broken or incomplete!)

To make the connection between a button being tapped and code being run, you need to do two things: Write the code that should run when the button is tapped (known as an *action*), and then connect the action to an *event* (such as a button being tapped).

Writing an action is easy. They're just methods in Objective-C that follow a specific pattern, which looks like this:

```
- (IBAction) actionMethodName:(id)sender {
    // action code goes here, and will be run when the
         connected event happens
}
```

The key parts are the fact that the method returns an IBAction and takes a single parameter — an id, which represents the object that triggered the action to be run.

After you write the method, you need some way to connect the method to your interface. This is where Interface Builder steps in. Interface Builder doesn't just build the interface of your application, it also reads your code, looking for keywords like IBAction, which it uses to figure out the existence of things like actions. If Interface Builder sees a method that returns IBAction, it allows you to connect an interface to that method.

When the user actually taps the button (or other control that you've connected to the action), the code you've written is run. Also, remember that `sender` parameter that the method has? When the method is run, that parameter is the control that the user interacted with (such as the button object that was tapped).

Outlets

Actions let your code respond to the user working with your interface, but often you want to work the other way around — in many cases, you need your code to change aspects of the interface.

In Objective-C, the only way to work with an object is to have a variable that refers to it. "But, gloriously wise and surprisingly inexpensive *For Dummies* book," you cry, "I designed my interface entirely in Interface Builder! How can my code have these variables?"

Fear not, for this exciting tome is here to answer your questions.

To get your code to work with objects that are set up in Interface Builder, do two things: Create an *outlet variable* and then connect the control in Interface Builder to that outlet. As you can see, it's a very similar process to setting up actions. Outlet variables are just regular, old variables in your class, but they have a very specific format to them.

Here's an example of an outlet variable that refers to a button.

```
IBOutlet UIButton* myButton;
```

As you can see, the code looks just like a variable declaration, but with IBOutlet stuck on the front. IBOutlet is included for Interface Builder's benefit — when it goes through your code looking for IBAction methods, it also looks for IBOutlet variables. Interface Builder then lets you connect those outlets to the controls and objects that exist in your interface.

After you connect a control to an outlet variable, you can use that variable to refer to that object in your code. So, if you want to make the sample myButton button vanish from the screen (by changing its `hidden` property), do this:

```
myButton.hidden = YES;
```

Just like any other variable!

Setting up the animations

Take a look at MainWindow.xib, which you find in the Resources folder in your project. The file contains two main views: the window itself and a navigation controller.

In this chapter, you build just the two screens (the main menu and the game itself), but later, you add more screens, such as settings and high scores. A navigation controller makes it simple to, well, navigate among these various screens.

To build a playing field, you need to create the new view controller that displays the game and then do some basic setup that makes it look like a proper game play board. After you do that, make the main menu show this new view controller when the New Game button is tapped. You do this shortly by adding the code for the new files that will be needed.

Listings 6-1 and 6-2 contain the code for the TrafficViewController files. Listings 6-3 and 6-4 contain some changes you'll need to make to MainMenuViewController. Following those, you see instructions on what to do with them.

Listing 6-1:   TrafficViewController.h

```
#import <UIKit/UIKit.h>

@interface TrafficViewController : UIViewController {

}

@end
```

Listing 6-2:   TrafficViewController.m

```
#import "TrafficViewController.h"

@implementation TrafficViewController

@end
```

Listing 6-3:   MainMenuViewController.h

```
#import <UIKit/UIKit.h>
@interface MainMenuViewController : UIViewController {
}
-(IBAction) newGame:(id)sender;
-(IBAction) showStats:(id)sender;
-(IBAction) showSettings:(id)sender;
@end
```

Listing 6-4:   MainMenuViewController.

```
#import "MainMenuViewController.h"
#import "TrafficAppDelegate.h"
#import "TrafficViewController.h"

@implementation MainMenuViewController

-(IBAction) newGame:(id)sender {
  TrafficViewController* traffic = [[TrafficViewController
          alloc] initWithNibName:@"TrafficViewController"
          bundle:nil];

  [self.navigationController pushViewController:traffic
          animated:NO];

}

-(IBAction) showStats:(id)sender {
}

-(IBAction) showSettings:(id)sender {
}

@end
```

To write the code that adds the new screen to the game:

1. **Add the new TrafficViewController files to the project.**

   See Listings 6-1 and 6-2 for the content of the files. You don't need to add any new code yet; the files are quite sparse to start, but you'll fill them with code soon.

a. Press ⌘+N to create a new UIViewController subclass and call it TrafficViewController.

b. Make sure that UITableViewController subclass is off and With XIB for User Interface is on — these are the check boxes that appear in the middle of the dialog.

2. **While you're working with the files in the project, add the file Road. png to the project.**

You find this file in the collection of resources for this book. We provide instructions on how to get these in Chapter 1.

3. **Add the background image to the new view controller as a UIImageView:**

a. Open TrafficViewController.xib in Interface Builder by double-clicking the file in Xcode.

b. Drag in a UIImageView from the Library window and make it the same size as the view controller's view. Set its image to Road.png by selecting it, opening the Attributes Inspector (by pressing ⌘+1), and choosing Road.png from the Image drop-down list.

4. **In MainMenuViewController.h, add the code that declares the existence of the methods that will be run when the buttons are tapped (see the code in bold in Listing 6-3).**

5. **In MainMenuViewController.m, add the code to display the new TrafficViewController object (listed in bold Listing 6-3) when you tap the New Game button.**

This code creates a new TrafficViewController object and tells it to load the contents of the nib file TrafficViewController. The code then tells the navigation controller to show the new view controller but not to show any animation.

6. **Connect the button to the `newGame:` method.**

a. To do this, select the MainMenuViewController object, and open the Connections Inspector window by pressing ⌘+2.

You see a list of *connections* — actions and outlets that exist in your code that you can connect to your interface.

b. Click and drag from the small circle that appears to the right of `newGame:` in the list to the New Game button.

c. Choose Touch Up Inside in the list that appears.

This list contains the possible events that can be triggered through the user's interaction with the button. The Touch Up Inside event is sent when the user lifts her finger from the screen at the point where the button is. Because this event means that the user has tapped the button, it's the perfect one to connect to the code that responds to a tap.

7. **Run the game and tap the New Game button to make sure everything works properly.**

The main menu disappears and is replaced with the view of the road.

You just set up the foundation for building the rest of the game. Check out the following section to add some cars.

Creating Cars for the Game

Cars in the *Traffic* game you create in this book start out simple and get a little more complex as the game evolves. To start with, you create a simple class that draws the car image. Later, this class decides where the view needs to be onscreen, and eventually, how the instances of this class fit into the rest of the game at large.

Adding an image view subclass

There's no sense in doing more work than you have to. Apple's tools for developing for the iPhone are all about making things easier for the developer, and image display is no exception.

At the visual level, a car in a video game is nothing more than an image. Your cars, therefore, just need to be a view object that displays a car image. In Chapter 7, we show you how to add interaction with the user through touches by extending this new object.

In this section, you add a new subclass to the UIView class. At first, this subclass just shows a picture, but you build upon it to add touch-driven interaction. Listings 6-5 and 6-6 contain the code you need to add to the Vehicle class files.

Vehicle.h, the interface file for the Vehicle class, sets up the class as a subclass of UIView, which allows you to use it to draw to the screen. Vehicle.h also adds a UIImage variable, which stores the actual image that is drawn onscreen. *Vehicle.m* is the implementation of the Vehicle class, which actually shows the image onscreen.

Listing 6-5:   Vehicle.h

```
#import <UIKit/UIKit.h>

@interface Vehicle : UIView {
        UIImage* image;
}

@end
```

Listing 6-6: Vehicle.m

```
#import "Vehicle.h"

@implementation Vehicle

- (id)initWithFrame:(CGRect)frame {
  UIImage* loadedImage = [UIImage imageNamed:@"RedCar.
          png"];

  CGRect rect = CGRectMake(frame.origin.x, frame.origin.y,
          loadedImage.size.width, loadedImage.size.
          height);

  self = [super initWithFrame:rect];
  image = [loadedImage retain];

  self.opaque = NO;
  self.backgroundColor = [UIColor clearColor];

  return self;
}

- (void)drawRect:(CGRect)rect {
  [image drawInRect:rect];
}

- (void)dealloc {
  [image release];
  [super dealloc];
}

@end
```

To start getting these cars onto the screen, follow these steps, which have you adding the necessary files and writing the code that shows the image:

1. **To add the new Vehicle files to the project, create a new Cocoa class by pressing ⌘+N and choosing Objective-C class from the collection of file types that appears.**

2. **Make the class a subclass of UIView by choosing UIView in the drop-down list, which appears in the middle of the window; click Next and then name the class Vehicle when prompted.**

   This creates a new class that implements the `initWithFrame:` and `drawRect:` methods. The code you add in the next couple steps over-rides them, performs the class's setup in the `initWithFrame:` method, and draws the image in `drawRect:`.

3. **While you add new files to your project, add the RedCar.png file to the project's resources as well.**

   You can find this file in the resources collection you downloaded in Chapter 1.

4. **Replace the codes in Vehicle.h and Vehicle.m with the codes in Listings 6-5 and 6-6.**

   Trust us; the codes we provide are better!

A fair bit of stuff goes on in this code, so in the next few sections, we go through each one of the methods and explain what they do.

initWithFrame:

The `initWithFrame:` method is the first message that the Vehicle class ever receives; it sets up the values of the class and gets it ready to be used.

`initWithFrame:` is also interesting because it receives a CGRect (a rectangle structure) that defines the view's working area. The Vehicle class does something a little tricky: Instead of setting itself up with the size it's given, it works out its own size based on an image that it knows it's going to use.

When the `initWithFrame:` method begins, the following happens:

1. The method loads the image.

2. The method creates a brand new CGRect that's at the same *origin,* or position, as the CGRect that was passed to the method as a parameter, but uses the width and height of the loaded image.

3. The class calls the superclass's implementation of `initWithFrame:` with the *new* CGRect.

4. The superclass sets up the view with the dimensions specified by the CGRect, and control returns to your code in the Vehicle class.

   Calling the superclass returns an object, which you assign to the `self` variable (which represents the current object). This is a quirk of Cocoa: The `self` variable — the pointer to the object that runs the current method — isn't valid until you get it from your superclass's initializer.

5. After the `self` pointer has been set up, time for housekeeping:

   • The image that was loaded is stored in the instance variable and retained for later.

- The view is set as *not opaque,* which means that parts of it are transparent (because you want to show things that are underneath the car, such as the road).

- The background color is set to transparent (for the same reason).

6. The initializer does its duty to the rest of the system and returns the `self` pointer.

Whew! After these steps are complete, the view is ready to be added to the screen.

drawRect:

The `drawRect:` method is somewhat basic compared to the initializer. The goal of `drawRect:` is to put a picture in the provided rectangle — and that's just what the code we provide does. Because we kept a reference to the image, you can simply tell the image to draw itself in the drawing rectangle, and that's that.

dealloc

The `dealloc` method is called when the retain count of the object is zero. `dealloc` is called when your object is about to be removed from memory. This method releases any memory that was retained over the lifetime of the object — in the Vehicle class's case, you need to get rid of the image by sending it the `release` message.

Releasing memory is important: If you don't, the system doesn't know whether it's safe to dedicate the storage to other, more productive uses. A *memory leak* occurs when memory isn't released properly; and that memory leak is a pernicious little blighter. If memory isn't released back to the system and no object knows that the memory is in use, the memory can never be accessed by your program until your application quits. Typically, you lose only a few kilobytes at a time, but if you have a memory leak in code that gets called several times over the course of your program, it really adds up. Eventually, you run out of memory, and when you run out of memory, your program crashes. That's why memory leaks are no good.

Adding the car to the view

After the class is set up, create an instance of it and put the instance in the game view. For now, you put the code that creates the new view in the startup methods of the game's view controller.

Follow these steps to create and add a new car to the screen:

1. **Import the Vehicle.h header file at the top of TrafficViewController.m, to let the compiler know about the class that you're using.**

2. **Create and then add the new Vehicle view.**

   Do this in the `viewWillAppear:` method, which is called just before the view is put onscreen, but after all the loading takes place. The code in bold in Listing 6-7 does all this; add the code in Listing 6-7 to TrafficViewController.m.

   This code runs when the view is about to appear onscreen. This code allocates and creates a new Vehicle class, and puts this new Vehicle at the position (150,100) in the view. The code then adds it to the view, letting the world at last see your work!

Listing 6-7:   TrafficViewController.m

```
#import "TrafficViewController.h"

#import "Vehicle.h"

@implementation TrafficViewController

- (void) viewWillAppear:(BOOL)animated {
        // Add a vehicle

        Vehicle* v = [[Vehicle alloc]
        initWithFrame:CGRectMake(150, 100, 0, 0)];
        [self.view addSubview:v];
}

@end
```

The rectangle being passed to the new vehicle has the position of (150,100) but a size of 0 x 0. The size could be anything, really; the `initWithFrame:` builds its own frame rectangle out of the position that it's given and the size of the image it uses.

Go ahead and test the game. When you tap the New Game button, you see a nice, shiny red car sitting on the road. If you don't see the car, check to make sure that the code is correct, and that you added the RedCar.png file to the project. So far, things are doing a lot of sitting there but not much movement. In the following section, you can fix that by making your main menu pop with animation.

Using Core Animation to Animate Buttons

Core Animation is one of those fascinating frameworks that has more power than you might initially think; it's a flexible way of animating different parts of your views, allowing you to make your interface incredibly fluid and responsive. The game needs to grab the player's attention from the first moment, and a great way of doing that is to animate the buttons. In this section, you make the buttons on the main menu pop into existence when the view appears.

To do that, you need to understand how iOS actually draws the objects you put onscreen.

Understanding layers

Every single view that displays onscreen shows the contents of a memory buffer, or a *layer.* You never see the layer itself; instead, the view takes the contents of the layer and redraws it onscreen, taking into account rotation, stretching, and whether other views are on top of it.

In addition to the picture that eventually gets drawn onscreen, layers also have a number of properties that affect how they display. Some of these properties are things you've worked with already, such as the position or frame (see Listing 6-6). Other properties, such as scale, opacity, background color and size, and so on, can be manipulated to make some interesting visual effects.

Core Animation allows you to smoothly transform one property from one state to another. This means that you can, for instance, tell a layer to slide from the top of the screen to the other, while becoming transparent and shrinking. Simple animations are really easy to do in Core Animation. Here's an example of how to make any view fade away:

```
[UIView beginAnimations:@"FadeAnimation" context:nil]
myView.alpha = 0.0;
[UIView commitAnimations];
```

To tell Core Animation to animate any property changes, the first line of code calls `[UIView beginAnimations:context]`. This method takes two properties:

✔ A **string** that represents a name you want to give to the animation.

The name identifies the animation among all others that go on in your app. The name can be anything; it's needed in this method call because every animation that currently affects your views needs a name.

✔ An arbitrary **pointer** to any information you want to associate with the animation that you may want to get access to later.

You can leave the pointer to be set to `nil` in the majority of cases.

After you tell Core Animation that you want the property changes to be animated, change the new properties to the values you want Core Animation to animate them to (that's the second line in the preceding snippet of code). After you give Core Animation its marching orders, `[UIView commitAnmations]` tells Core Animation to actually begin animating. And that's it!

This is actually one of two ways you can control animations. The second is using *blocks* — for more information on these, check out the nearby sidebar, "Blocks in Objective-C."

Simple animations like this are easy to use, but sometimes you want to have more control over the timing or have a more complex animation than a simple linear movement from A to B. You can achieve this with the CAKeyframeAnimation class, which we cover in the next section.

Working with CAKeyframeAnimation

CAKeyframeAnimation allows you to build complex animation and then attach it to more than one layer. Animations are constructed from some of the oldest traditions in animation — *key frames,* which are the main positions that an object is in over the course of an animation.

If you create a CAKeyframeAnimation and provide it with the *key frames* — in Core Animation's case, this means the values of the properties that you want the view to animate between — Core Animation takes care of all the in-between frames that create the illusion of the view moving, as shown in Figure 6-3.

Blocks in Objective-C

One of the newest features that Apple added to iOS 4 is the ability to add blocks to your application's code. A *block* is effectively a method or function that you can store in a variable, and pass around as a parameter. This means that you can write a chunk of code, store it in a block, and then use it at a later point — you don't need to define the code as a method that's attached to a class. You can think of blocks as separate code objects that you can run at any time.

Because blocks are objects, you can also retain them and store them for later use (and reuse). This means that you don't have to spend as much time setting up a complex delegate object because you can simply provide a block that performs the same tasks as the delegate would.

Blocks are a little beyond the scope of this book, so we don't go into a huge amount of detail on how to use them. Instead, we show you how to write that fading animation with blocks.

Instead of wrapping the animation between calls to UIView, create two blocks: one that's run to start the animation and one that's run when the animation is finished.

Here's what the start animation block looks like:

```
void (^animationBlock)(void) = ^ (void) {
  // Make the changes that need to be animated.
  myView.alpha = 0.5;
};
```

As you can see, the only line in the block itself is the one that does the animating — it changes the alpha value of the view to 0.5, making it 50 percent transparent.

The completion block looks quite similar:

```
void (^completionBlock)(BOOL) = ^ (BOOL finished) {
  // This code is run after the animation ends.
  myView.alpha = 1.0;
};
```

The only difference is that this block receives a parameter, indicating whether the block actually completes the animation. In this case, the completion block resets the alpha value back to 1, making the view fully opaque.

After the blocks are set up, make the animation actually run. This happens when you tell iOS to run the animations, using the two previous blocks. The call to make the animations happen looks like this:

```
UIView  animateWithDuration:1.0  animations:animationBlock
completion:completionBlock];
```

Pretty simple! The real power of blocks comes from the fact that you can store them in variables and use them whenever you like. You can even give them to other classes and let them run the code, and they'll run perfectly fine.

The `animateWithDuration:animations:completion:` method has a couple sibling methods that are just variations on the same theme: You can tell iOS to run an animations block without providing a completion block, or you can tell iOS to run an animations block with some additional parameters. For more information on how to use these ludicrously powerful features, look at the Xcode documentation for UIView.

A couple extra notes on blocks: They run only on iOS 4 and above — they don't run on iOS 3.2, which (at the time of writing) is the only version of iOS that the iPad runs. For that reason, we use the older style, non-block methods to control code. However, blocks are the future, and you should definitely read up on how to use them. The best resource for figuring out how to use blocks is *Blocks Programming Topics,* which is included in the Xcode documentation and is also available online at `http://developer.apple.com/iphone/library/ documentation/Cocoa/Conceptual/Blocks`.

Figure 6-3:
A triangle rotating, showing the two key frames in the anima-tion, and some of the in-between frames.

To create the pop effect, the animation progresses like this, from start to finish:

1. The layer is scaled to almost 0 percent of its normal size.

2. The layer grows to be a little bigger than normal size.

3. The layer shrinks back down to normal size, and the animation is done.

This animation feels quite natural and organic because it mimics the elastic feeling of muscle or skin; it stretches a little beyond normal and then relaxes.

In the next section, we show you how to make each of the buttons appear onscreen slightly after each other. This creates a pleasant downward-moving effect onscreen, as each one of the buttons pops out after the other. If you set up this downward-moving effect, the eye is drawn to each button in the list, one after the other.

Making the buttons bounce

Ready to make some things move on your screen? Here's how:

1. Add the QuartzCore.framework to your project:

a. *Right-click the Frameworks folder in your project and then choose Existing Frameworks from the Add menu.*

b. *Select QuartzCore.framework in the list that appears.*

This framework contains the necessary classes used for working with Core Animation.

The next three steps involve adding code to MainMenuViewController.h. Look at Listing 6-8 for the code you need to add, which is in bold.

2. **Let the compiler know about the new framework in your code by importing <QuartzCore/QuartzCore.h> in MainMenuViewController.h.**

3. **Add outlets for each of the buttons in MainMenuViewController.**

Because you work directly with the buttons (and don't just receive actions sent by them), you need variables that let you refer to them.

4. **Add an instance variable to store the CAKeyframeAnimation; call it popAnimation.**

After you complete these steps, MainMenuViewController.h looks like Listing 6-8.

Listing 6-8: MainMenuViewController.h

```
#import <UIKit/UIKit.h>
#import <QuartzCore/QuartzCore.h>

@interface MainMenuViewController : UIViewController {
  IBOutlet UIButton* newGameButton;
  IBOutlet UIButton* statsButton;
  IBOutlet UIButton* settingsButton;

  CAKeyframeAnimation* popAnimation;
}

-(IBAction) newGame:(id)sender;
-(IBAction) showStats:(id)sender;
-(IBAction) showSettings:(id)sender;

@end
```

After you set up the class to store the right information, add the code that prepares the animations. To do so, follow these steps:

1. **Add the following code to MainMenuViewController.m:**

```
@synthesize newGameButton, statsButton,
      settingsButton;
- (void)viewDidLoad {
  [super viewDidLoad];
```

```
popAnimation = [CAKeyframeAnimation
       animationWithKeyPath:@"transform.scale"];

popAnimation.keyTimes = [NSArray arrayWithObjects:
       [NSNumber numberWithFloat:0.0],
       [NSNumber numberWithFloat:0.7], [NSNumber
       numberWithFloat:1.0], nil];
  popAnimation.values = [NSArray arrayWithObjects:
       [NSNumber numberWithFloat:0.01],
       [NSNumber numberWithFloat:1.1], [NSNumber
       numberWithFloat:1.0], nil];

[popAnimation retain];

}
```

This code synthesizes the properties for the button objects, and creates a new key frame animation that modifies the scale of any layer it's attached to. It also sets up appropriate key frames that make the layer grow to 110 percent of its normal size in the first 70 percent of the animation time and then shrink down to 100 percent by the end of the animation. The animation is then retained because you need it later.

Because you're applying what's effectively the same animation to all three buttons, you don't need to duplicate the code. That's why you use only one popAnimation variable — after you've set it up, you don't need to make it again. The only trick is in making each button pop up in a pleasing order.

To that end, you need to make a method that takes a single button as its parameter and sets up the animation on it. You can then call that method three times, rather than writing three times as much code.

2. **Apply the animation to the layers by adding the following method to MainMenuTrafficController.m.**

   This code takes a single view as its parameter and tells it to be visible. It then takes the pop animation that was set up when the view loaded, and applies it to the view's layer, telling it to modify its scale.

   ```
   - (void)popView:(UIView*)view {
   [view setHidden:NO];
   [[view layer] addAnimation:popAnimation
          forKey:@"transform.scale"];
   }
   ```

   Here's one last piece of the puzzle: You need to actually apply the animation to the buttons. You do that when the view appears onscreen.

3. **Set off the animations when the view appears by adding the following method to MainMenuTrafficController.m:**

   ```
   - (void)viewWillAppear:(BOOL)animated {
   [popAnimation setDuration:0.3];
   ```

```
    [newGameButton setHidden:YES];
    [statsButton setHidden:YES];
    [settingsButton setHidden:YES];
    [self performSelector:@selector(popView:)
            withObject:newGameButton afterDelay:0.25];
    [self performSelector:@selector(popView:)
            withObject:statsButton afterDelay:0.3];
    [self performSelector:@selector(popView:)
            withObject:settingsButton afterDelay:0.35];

}
```

This code sets the animation to last 0.3 seconds and then tells all the buttons to become invisible. Then, the popView: method is scheduled to run three times, with each of the three buttons. Feel free to play with the timings!

Here's how the animation works: When the view controller is created, viewDidLoad is called on it. This gives the view controller the opportunity to set up the animation and generally prepare. When the view controller finishes setting up, the code hides all the buttons and schedules them to become visible, one after the other.

The code that makes each button visible starts by making them be *unhidden* (or set up to draw themselves onscreen) so that the animation can actually be seen. The code then applies the pre-prepared animation to the view's layer, and Core Animation does the rest.

 4. **Run the game.**

Watch the menu while the application loads. Each button pops into existence, one after the other.

Congratulations! You've built your own cars, put them on the highway, and made it look easy. If you keep this up, maybe you'll even convince one of us, who shall remain nameless, to get a license.

Chapter 7

The Life Cycle of an iOS Game

▶ Starting with the nib file

▶ Managing interruptions and memory

▶ Responding to touch input and gestures

▶ Moving cars on screen

*T*ake a step back from the code and look at what happens when the user taps your application's icon. In this chapter, we demystify what happens between the application's launch and when the user taps a button in your views. We also look at how memory is managed in iOS, the operating system that runs on all mobile Apple devices, and how touch input is handled and processed inside your application. By the end of this chapter, you'll know how to respond to touch events, and drag cars around onscreen in the *Traffic* game.

Starting with the Main Nib File

When your application launches, every application that runs on Unix-like operating systems, which includes the iOS, starts with the `main()` function. If you look at main.m (found in the Other Sources group in your Xcode project), you find the implementation that *Traffic* uses. Here's the code:

```
int main(int argc, char *argv[]) {
    NSAutoreleasePool * pool = [[NSAutoreleasePool alloc]
            init];
    int retVal = UIApplicationMain(argc, argv, nil, nil);
    [pool release];
    return retVal;
}
```

When the user taps on your application's icon on the home screen, iOS looks inside your application's bundle and opens the Info.plist file. This file describes everything that the OS needs to know about your application, including how to start it. It then finds the binary file that contains your compiled code, and locates the `main` function. This function is called by iOS the instant the application starts. The main goal of `main` is to call `UIApplicationMain`, which is the function that starts the rest of the application.

Initialization

UIApplicationMain is a function that, after it starts, kicks off the main program that will (eventually) stop when the user presses the Home button. But how does this function actually work, and how does the application do useful things for the user?

Buried inside the Info.plist file for the application is a *Main nib file base name* entry. If you open this file, you see that it's set to MainWindow — which, coincidentally, is the name of one of the `.xib` files in the project. (Chapter 3 explains the basics of `.xib`, or *nib,* files.)

This technique loads the application's important objects. The Main nib file base name entry in the Info.plist file is used by UIApplicationMain. UIApplicationMain, as part of the application launching process, loads the nib file specified by the Info.plist file. This nib file contains the freeze-dried app delegate object, along with the window that the application displays all its contents in. While UIApplicationMain starts the application, it creates the main UIApplication object, along with the app delegate.

After the app delegate loads and sets up, the main UIApplication object sends the delegate the `applicationDidFinishLaunching:withOptions:` message. This is your application's opportunity to do any set up that it might need to do.

In the case of *Traffic,* another object loads from the MainWindow nib file — a navigation controller, which in turn loads *another* nib file. This second nib file, in this case, is MainMenuViewController.xib, which you built in Chapter 5. Finally, after everything launches, the main event loop starts. This is where all the action is.

Event processing

An iOS application, after it launches, performs an *event loop* that goes like this:

1. Wait until an interesting event happens.

   The iOS app doesn't do anything until then.

2. When an event happens, deal with it.

3. Go back to Step 1.

The event loop drives all the action in every app you've ever used. Here's a closer look at what the event loop is looking for, and how it makes all the apps on the iPhone and iPad perform useful things:

- ✔ **Events that come from the user:** These events occur the most often and include screen touches and movement detected by the accelerometer (the sensor built into the device that detects motion and gravity).

- ✔ **Events that don't come from the user:** These include things like messages from the operating system and timers that are set up to trigger events for the application.

- ✔ **Events caused as a result of other events:** For example, when the user brings up the keyboard and types, she generates both touch events (because she taps on the virtual keyboard) and text events (because the keyboard sends letters and numbers to your application).

For the application to intelligently react to events, the events need to be delivered to the appropriate parts of the app. In the section "The stages of a touch," later in this chapter, we explain how the iPhone figures out where touch events need to be delivered based on what region of the screen the user taps.

Termination

When the user clicks the Home button (the physical button below the screen), the application is sent into the background. When this happens, the app delegate is sent the `applicationDidEnterBackground:` message, which informs the app delegate that the application is about to stop being the app displayed onscreen. When an app is in the background, it does less — it can't display things onscreen; it isn't guaranteed to be kept running; and it has fewer resources dedicated to it by the system, so it runs slower.

After a period of time, an app that's in the background is sent into a *suspended* state in which the app is still in memory, but it doesn't run any code — it won't react to events and it can't communicate with the user. The app is frozen in carbonite just like Han Solo (although the app *did* shoot first, unlike Han it seems).

If the application's icon is tapped again, the application is brought back from whatever state it's in, whether that's background or suspended. The application delegate then receives the `applicationDidEnterForeground:` message, and the user can then interact with the app once more.

 Applications in the background are never told that they're about to be suspended! This is because the system may need to freeze your program very quickly and can't afford to wait around while your code potentially takes time to sort itself out.

Apps are brought out of suspension only when the user launches the app again. When this happens, the application wakes up, dusts itself off, and is sent back into action right where it left off. Applications aren't told that they're coming out of suspension or that they just left suspension — they simply start again.

Your application may be terminated while it's suspended. If your application is suspended, it's still in memory, which means that it's taking up memory that could be used by other applications. If an app requests more memory from the operating system than is currently available, the system terminates apps in the background, in this order:

1. Suspended applications that are using a lot of memory.

2. Applications running in the background that are using lots of memory.

3. Other suspended applications.

4. Other apps running in the background.

5. If there's *still* not enough memory, the operating system throws up its hands in dismay and terminates the foreground application because it's asked for more memory than the OS can provide.

Figure 7-1 shows the states your application can be in:

✔ **Active:** The application is on the screen and the user is interacting with it.

✔ **Inactive:** The application is still in the foreground, but an interruption (like a phone call or text message) is taking precedence.

✔ **Backgrounded:** The application is no longer on the screen, but will keep running for a short while.

✔ **Suspended:** The application has been frozen, and is not executing any code.

✔ **Terminated:** The application has been completely stopped, and has been removed from memory.

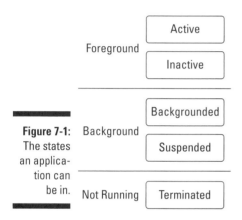

Figure 7-1:
The states
an applica-
tion can
be in.

Considering Other Runtime Issues

In exchange for being given access to the user, your app has to agree to be a good citizen on the iOS platform. If your application hangs, takes too long to launch, or generally misbehaves, it's likely to be terminated without notice by the OS. Additionally, your application needs to accept that it will be occasionally interrupted by things, such as phone calls, text messages, and other events that the OS considers more pressing. You'll learn how to handle these interruptions in the next section.

Responding to interruptions

When your application runs in the *foreground* — it's placed onscreen and interacts with the user — it's in one of two states:

✔ An **active** application responds to touches and gets to show itself onscreen.

✔ An **inactive** application still runs and is onscreen, but it isn't necessarily completely visible to the user and it can't respond to touches.

When an interruption occurs, your app instantly stops being active and becomes inactive. Interruptions take over the screen and need to be dealt with by the user before he can use your app. Examples of interruptions include

- *Phone calls,* which take over the entire screen

- *SMS messages,* which display a dialog on top of your application

When your application receives an interruption, the app delegate is sent the `applicationWillResignActive:` message, which is the application's cue to stop doing processor-heavy work and to pause the game.

The user might choose to accept that incoming phone call or view that incoming SMS message, which sends your application to the background. When that happens, the application delegate receives `applicationDidEnterBackground:`, which is your application's signal that the application is now no longer the one on the screen. If the user dismisses the interruption (for example, if they decline the incoming phone call) then the application delegate receives the `applicationDidBecomeActive:` message.

Managing memory on the iPhone

The iPhone has a limited amount of memory. Lots of which is already taken up by the OS — only so much memory is available for your own application. Unlike most computers, the iPhone doesn't have a *swap file* (which uses its permanent storage as extra memory for applications). Therefore, with no more memory, applications have to quit.

If your application uses too much memory, iOS warns the app by sending the `applicationDidReceiveMemoryWarning:` message to the app delegate. This is your only warning, and your application needs to take steps to reduce its memory usage quickly. If the system continues to run low on memory, iOS terminates the application without notice.

If this happens, the application vanishes from the screen, along with the current progress of the game. In other words, the application appears to crash. The user's game isn't saved, her high scores aren't stored, and your game appears to have a terrible bug — which, from Apple's point of view, it does.

To avoid this, you must reduce the amount of memory needed by your application:

- Avoid loading very large pictures or sounds.

  Keep images under 200K, and sounds under 100K (except for long tracks, like music).

- If you're making a very large game, such as a first-person shooter or racing game, don't load everything into memory at once. There simply isn't room for holding every part of a large game in the very limited memory of the device.

- Free up as much memory as possible when your application generates a warning that memory is running low; otherwise, your application risks summary termination.

Dealing with Touch Input

Touch input on the iOS is one of its trademark features: The device wowed everyone when it came out because it's accessible, intuitive, and downright easy to interact with. A large part of that is due to its clever reactions to touches onscreen, and the iOS makes it incredibly easy to respond to the user touching the screen.

Touch input has a history of being treated as another way of dealing with mouse input. This was largely true, back in the days when you could deal only with one touch at a time. But these are the days of multitouch, and it's time to deal with input in a sensible manner.

The long and storied life of a UITouch

Pick up your iPhone or iPad, turn it on, and tap the screen. Congratulations: You just made the CPU do an incredible amount of work!

Touches on the iOS are broken up into several stages: began, moved, stationary, ended, and canceled. Almost all touches that you work with go through the majority of them:

- **Began:** A touch begins when a finger hits the screen.

- **Moved:** The touch moves when the finger moves over the screen.

- **Stationary:** The touch is still on the screen, but has not moved any further.

- **Ended:** The touch ends when the finger lifts from the screen.

✔ **Canceled:** A touch is canceled when something interrupts the usual flow of touch information. This could be a phone call coming in (which always interrupts your application), a dialog appearing onscreen (such as when you receive a text message), or the view controller that the touch interacts with being replaced with a different view controller.

So, how is your code supposed to deal with all this complexity? When your view implements the right methods, those methods get called whenever a set of touches changes state. By tracking the different states that touches can be in, your view can figure out what the user's trying to do.

The stages of a touch

Initially, a touch belongs to the application's window. Only one window is ever onscreen at a time because only one application is onscreen at a time.

When a window detects that a touch has occurred, it takes the position of the touch in the window and works out which view the touch corresponds to through a recursive hit test. A *recursive hit test* takes the touch's position and figures out which of the window's subviews that position corresponds to; then, it instructs that subview to do its own check to see whether any of *its* subviews correspond to that position.

The end result of this is that the touch information is finally sent to the lowest-level view in the view hierarchy that can handle touch events.

When a touch lands on a view, it doesn't change views. If you tap a button and then drag your finger away from the button, that button still receives information about the touch until the finger lifts from the screen.

Touches begin

When a touch starts, the view that it's associated with receives the `touchesBegan:withEvent:` message. Here's a sample implementation of how you might handle a touch beginning inside a view:

```
- (void) touchesBegan:(NSSet*)touches withEvent:(UIEvent*)
        event {
  // do something with the touches that just landed on the
      view

}
```

"Hang on," you say, "Why is `touchesBegan:withEvent:` sent an NSSet? And what's this UIEvent thing?" This is a quirk of the touch handling system. All the methods that deal with the different phases of a touch don't receive individual touches. This is because iOS has multitouch technology all throughout its workings — it assumes that there *could* be many touches working at once in a view and sets up things so that it's easy for an app developer to work with them.

To that end, when you deal with new touch information, your method is sent an NSSet object that contains all the touches that changed states.

An *NSSet* is basically an array that promises to not include any duplicates. Sets are useful when you want to have a collection of objects and you don't care about the order that they're stored in. Thus, when `touchesBegan:withEvent:` is called, the method is passed the set of all touches that just landed onscreen.

There's also the matter of that UIEvent object. The *UIEvent object* can be thought of as the actual event that triggered the touches being created and passed to the view, and it includes information, such as when the event started or the event type.

Touches move

When a touch is dragged across the screen, the view that the touch belongs to is sent the `touchesMoved:withEvent:` message:

```
- (void) touchesMoved:(NSSet*)touches withEvent:(UIEvent*)
            event {
   // do something with the touches that moved on the view
}
```

This message is very similar to touchesBegan — in fact, it's practically identical. The only difference is that the collection of touches that the method receives is the set of touches that have moved — it won't contain touches that are within the view, but have not moved.

This collection of touches is *not* the total set of touches that's on the view; it's only the touches that moved.

With this method, you can update your application to deal with finger movement. In the section, "Processing Touches," later in this chapter, we show you how to enable the user to drag views around onscreen.

Touches end

This method receives the set of touches that have just been lifted from the screen:

```
- (void) touchesEnded:(NSSet*)touches withEvent:(UIEvent*)
         event {
  // do something with the touches that ended
}
```

Touches are canceled

A touch can be canceled if the view controller is dismissed or the application stops being the active application onscreen. The `touchesCancelled:withEvent:` method receives a set of touches that changed states, along with the event that caused it:

```
- (void) touchesCancelled:(NSSet*)touches
         withEvent:(UIEvent*)event {
  // do something with the touches that were cancelled
}
```

`touchesCancelled:withEvent:` is spelled with two L's.

Dealing with the Canceled phase is important, because when a touch is canceled, it indicates to your application that it shouldn't follow through with the action it was performing as a result of those touches.

Responding to Gestures

After your application has been notified about touch events, it looks at the touches and figures out what the user wants to do with them. Simple gestures can be interpreted easily — a touch starts and then ends, and the application performs an event when the touch ends. More complicated gestures depend on looking at the touch itself. So, how can you get a touch out of the NSSet object that you're given?

If you don't care about the number of touches that you're dealing with, you can send the NSSet the `anyObject` message, which makes the set return just that — any object it feels like.

This makes sense mostly when you don't mind which touch you're dealing with, as long as it's a touch.

The NSSet of touches that's sent to all touch handling methods is a collection of UITouch objects. Each one of these objects represents a finger onscreen, and you can get information about them by sending messages to them.

One of the most useful messages that the UITouch class responds to is the `locationInView:` message. This method takes a UIView as a parameter and returns a CGPoint that describes where, relative to that view, the touch is. This lets you figure out where a touch is and how it's moved.

Processing Touches

In the *Traffic* game, you want to make a car react to touch input. Start by letting the user drag around a car. Add the new method in Listing 7-1 to Vehicle.m.

Listing 7-1: Vehicle.m

```
- (void)touchesBegan:(NSSet *)touches withEvent:(UIEvent
         *)event {
  UITouch* touch = [touches anyObject];
  self.center = [touch locationInView:[self superview]];
}
```

This code runs when the user touches the car onscreen. The code works by taking an object from the set of touches provided to it and working out its position in the vehicle's superview (which is the game board.) After the code has that position, it sets the center position of the vehicle to the location of the touch.

The real trick to this code is in how it gets access to the UITouch object that represents the user's finger onscreen. All methods that track touches are given an NSSet object, which contains UITouch objects. The UITouch objects sent to `touchesBegan:withEvent:` are touches that are brand new. The UITouch objects that are sent to `touchesMoved:withEvent:` are touches that have gone through the Began phase and have since moved.

Because you're interested only in a single touch on each individual Vehicle class, you can ask the NSSet object for any object, which causes the NSSet to return one object of its own choosing.

Next, make the car follow the user's fingertip as she drags it around the screen. This means that you need to respond to moving touches. The code for touches moving around the screen is almost identical. Add the method in Listing 7-2 to Vehicle.m.

Listing 7-2:   Vehicle.m

```
- (void)touchesMoved:(NSSet *)touches withEvent:(UIEvent
          *)event {
  UITouch* touch = [touches anyObject];
  self.center = [touch locationInView:[self superview]];
}
```

The code is pretty much the same! All you're doing is taking the location of a touch and setting the location of the vehicle to the touch's position. To test this behavior, build and run the application. Your vehicle now responds to your touch! Drag the vehicle around the screen. This is the basis for how the player interacts with the game — by dragging around cars.

Chapter 8

Creating the Game Architecture

*T*o build a good game, you have to create a plan for it. You may be tempted to build an application piece by piece, but having a solid plan to build upon generally improves the quality of your final build.

Think of building a game as figure painting: You end up with a better result if you start with sketches. In this chapter, we put together the game's architecture and discuss a few ways of putting together the game. We also take a look at the different screens that the user looks at as he moves through the application.

Putting on Your Architect's Hat

Planning for a game requires laying out all the screens and breaking up each by feature. For this sample game *Traffic*, we walk through the game itself and how the components of the game work together.

Lots of this walk-through involves looking at the different view controllers used in the application because view controllers manage the individual sections of your application, making them good for organizing the different screens in the app.

View controllers, screens, and features

Because only one view controller is ever visible at a time, view controllers are a good way to think about the different screens. Each view controller is responsible for displaying information to the user, getting feedback from the user, and acting as the go-between for the user and the game's internals. We cover view controllers in more detail in Chapter 4, so head there if you want a quick refresher!

There are several things you need to keep in mind when designing the architecture of your game:

- ✔ **Most games have heaps of features, and it's important to break them up between screens.** Otherwise, users likely get overloaded with options and information. You have to keep things organized and keep a balance between simplicity and functionality.

- ✔ **Work out how the behind-the-scenes objects work, and how they drive the game forward.** At a game's core, it has a collection of *game objects,* which are the things onscreen that are a part of the game. In this game, these are the cars and lanes (as opposed to the buttons, switches, and other devices, which are controls that manage the game without strictly being a part of the game itself).

- ✔ **You need a single object managing every game object.** This keeps objects in order and controls game-wide events, such as the game ending.

Game loops

For an action-based game like *Traffic,* you need to keep things moving. The best way to achieve this is with a *game loop.* This updates the game on a regular basis and tells all objects in the game to update. The game loop is an infinite loop that runs continuously, updating the game world and then getting things ready for the screen to be drawn.

A typical game loop looks like this:

1. Move every object that needs moved.

   Check whether this caused any events, such as cars crashing or points going up.

2. When the game ends, stop looping.

3. Go to Step 1.

This isn't the only way to construct a game — this is simply the method that we chose when designing the game. A game loop is easy to think about, easy to code, and easy to describe. Additionally, a game loop is also appropriate for a game with lots of things moving and interacting with one another.

If you create a turn-based strategy game, you might want to design your game around an event-based model. *Event-based models* are application designs in which your application doesn't loop at all but rather waits for user input before doing anything. This simplifies your design quite a bit, and it also reduces the amount of work that the game needs to do, which reduces the amount of battery usage.

We don't cover event-based architectures in this book. An excellent resource for advanced techniques like this is *Game Programming Gems*, by Mark DeLoura (Charles River Media). But game loops are best for busy, interactive games.

Timers and frame rates

With a game loop, your application loops repeatedly, and every time it loops, it moves things around. We take a closer look at how things get moved.

A *frame* is the work that gets done every time the game loops around. We use this term quite a bit in this chapter.

Imagine that you have a car onscreen and you want it to move across the screen. Sounds simple, right? Every frame, you'd take the car's position, add (say) 3 pixels, and move the car to the new position you just calculated.

The problem is that method of calculating movement doesn't work too well — what you see is the object moving around the screen erratically, alternating between fast and slow. That's not much fun to watch, and if you ran the same game on faster hardware, the car would speed up!

What causes erratic behavior? Each frame isn't guaranteed to take the same amount of time to process and draw on the screen. This is often caused by the complexity of the graphics onscreen — if the operating system needs to draw lots of stuff, the frame takes longer, which means the game loop takes longer to go from one frame to the next.

If you want smooth movement, think in terms of movement over time instead of movement between individual frames.

Imagine that you want the car to move across the screen at a constant speed of 5 pixels per second. That is, no matter how many frames are drawn during that second, by the end of those frames, the car will have moved a total of 5 pixels.

This means that during every frame, you need to take the car's speed and work out how much time has elapsed since it was last moved. After you have this information, you can solve the equation. Simply multiply the speed by the time and you get the change in distance, which you can then use to update the car's position onscreen.

The benefit that comes from doing this is that this method for calculating the game's speed still works well even if the time needed to draw each frame changes. If you suddenly add a whole bunch of cars onscreen, the *frame rate* (the number of frames drawn per second) might drop, but that won't affect how fast each car appears to move.

How can you calculate the frame rate? One method is to keep a clock running and use it to figure out how long the last frame took. Follow these steps:

1. **When the game starts, store the current time in a variable.**

   A quick way of doing this is to use the timeIntervalSinceReferenceDate method in NSDate. The reference date is the first instant of January 1, 1970, GMT.

   ```
   // NSTimeInterval is in seconds
   NSTimeInterval currentTime = [NSDate
         timeIntervalSinceReferenceDate];
   ```

2. **During the main loop of the game, compare the (updated) current time to the stored time by subtracting the stored time from the current time.**

   This gives you *delta time* — the amount of time it took to render the last frame.

   ```
   NSTimeInterval deltaTime = [NSDate
         timeIntervalSinceReferenceDate] - currentTime;
   ```

3. **Store the current time into the time variable so that you can perform the same calculation next frame.**

   ```
   NSTimeInterval currentTime = [NSDate
         timeIntervalSinceReferenceDate];
   ```

When you develop the main game loop in Traffic, you'll be following a very similar technique, though the source of the time information will come from a slightly different source.

Game objects and your app

In a game, the user sees and interacts with several objects inside the game. The most obvious object is the car: The user sees it and drags it around, and the car also moves up the screen. Therefore, the cars need to respond to the user touching them. A few other objects in the game are a bit less visible. For example, the three lanes onscreen create cars and place them onscreen at the right time. The other important game object — the Traffic Controller — is invisible; it doesn't appear onscreen. Instead, the Traffic Controller runs the game loop and keeps track of car movement, collisions, and cars reaching the end of the road.

The game loop in the Traffic Controller repeats these actions for every frame:

- ✔ For every car that's onscreen, the game loop calculates its new position onscreen based on its speed and the frame rate and then moves the car to its new position.

- ✔ The game loop checks whether any cars are colliding. Cars collide if the images overlap onscreen. If cars collide, show the game over screen (which we discuss in the "The game over screen" section, later in this chapter) and stop the game.

- ✔ The game loop checks whether a car moves off the top of the screen. If this happens, the loop then verifies whether the car was in the correct lane when it left the screen. If the car was in the correct lane, the game loop adds to the amount of time the player has remaining. Finally, the game loop removes the car from the game.

- ✔ The game loop subtracts the amount of time needed to process the last frame from the amount of time the player has left. If the amount of time left is zero (or less than zero), the loop shows the game over screen and stops the game.

Designing the Screen Flow

A game is structured around different screens:

- ✔ Some screens let the user access other screens.
- ✔ Some screens let the user access settings.
- ✔ One special screen is the game itself.

Each screen's view controller is designed separately in Interface Builder and stored as separate files. This is a great way to conserve the limited iPhone resources because you keep all the different images and objects needed for each screen separate and load them only when they need to be shown.

The main menu

The *main menu* is the jumping-off point for all other features; it's the screen the user sees first. Therefore, the main menu needs to look good. If the user doesn't like the look of the game in the first few seconds, she'll hit that Home button faster than you can say "but this game took ages to make!"

Functionally, the main menu (see Figure 8-1) is nothing more than buttons that trigger other screens to appear. Each button, when tapped, causes the appropriate screen to load and show to the user; when the user's done with the screen, the main menu reappears.

Figure 8-1:
The outline
of the main
menu.

The game screen

The *game screen* (the *Traffic* game screen, as shown in Figure 8-2) is where all the action happens. Here's where the actual game play takes place, and it's where the user spends most of his time.

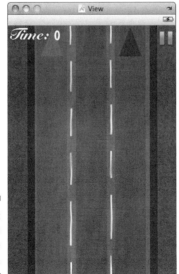

Figure 8-2:
The outline
of the game
screen.

In terms of overall construction, the game screen is pretty simple: It's a background image with lanes and cars put on top of it, as well as a few labels and buttons that give the player feedback and control over the game. In addition, the game screen manages the Traffic Controller because the game controller is closely tied to what's visible onscreen.

The stuff that's shown onscreen can get a little complex. In addition to cars being added to the screen and moved around, other content might appear on top of the game, causing the rest to fade out. This might happen when a player pauses the game or when the game ends.

Additionally, game stopping events cause other screens to be overlaid. These views are designed in Interface Builder and are programmatically added to the view hierarchy when they're needed.

The pause screen

The *pause screen,* as shown in Figure 8-3, is a view that sits on top of the game screen; it's semi-transparent and consists of nothing but a giant Pause image, along with an End button. Tapping on the Pause image resumes the game; tapping the End button ends the game and takes the player back to the main menu.

Figure 8-3:
The outline of the pause screen.

The pause screen appears when the user taps the Pause button (the one at the top-right of the game screen) when playing the game, which lets her take a break from the action. The pause screen also appears when the application stops being the foreground application (which happens when the user presses the Home button on the iPhone, sending the app to the background) and when the application gets an interruption (such as a phone call, text message, or a push notification).

When the user taps the background image, the pause screen disappears and game play resumes.

The game over screen

The game over screen, as shown in Figure 8-4, appears when the game ends, which can happen because of a few things. The game can end when cars crash; the game can also end during a multiplayer game (which you find out about in Chapter 15), when the other player crashes a car or disconnects from the game.

The game over screen is very similar in construction to the pause screen: It appears on top of the game screen and is semi-transparent to let the player see the game in the background. This helps the player see that she's still in the context of a game, rather than a menu or any of the other screens.

The game over screen starts with just a Game Over image, which takes the player back to the main menu after a short delay. In Chapter 16, you add some features that let the player post his high score to Facebook.

Figure 8-4:
The outline
of the game
over screen.

The high scores screen

When the player plays the game, she racks up a score. Scores aren't of much use when the game ends, unless the game keeps track of them to let the player see how well she does. The high scores screen lets the player see her top four scores.

The high scores screen, as shown in Figure 8-5, is built of a background image, four text labels used to show the screen, and a button that takes the player back to the main menu. We discuss the high scores screen in a lot more detail in Chapter 11.

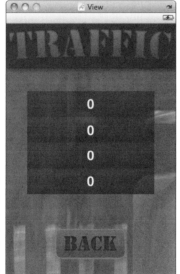

Figure 8-5:
The outline of the high scores screen.

The settings screen

No matter how good a designer you are, you're not likely to get everything just right for every single different person who plays the game. Some people might not like the sound effects or might not want music. The settings screen lets players customize their game.

The settings screen, as shown in Figure 8-6, shows the settings to the user, lets the user make changes to those settings, and makes sure those settings are stored for later use.

The settings screen is built of a background image, a button that takes the user back to the main menu, and controls that allow the user to see and change the settings.

Figure 8-6:
The out-
line of the
settings
screen.

Chapter 9

Creating the Game Controller

· ·

· ·

*I*n this chapter, we discuss the core object that runs and manages a game from start to finish: the *Traffic Controller.* The Traffic Controller is an example of a *controller object* — an object that makes sure the game runs properly.

The role of this object is to manage every other object in the game. The Traffic Controller deals with how much time the player has left, with moving all the objects around the screen, with pausing and un-pausing, and with multiplayer support. The Traffic Controller is a large object, purely because it has a lot to do; if this game were any more complex, it'd be worth breaking up the code into a few objects.

The Traffic Controller is created when the game screen displays onscreen. The controller sets up a timer to move things around the screen at a constant speed, causing objects to move around onscreen; it also detects events, such as cars crashing or reaching the end of the road. Finally, this controller also responds to the user pausing the game, which means that the timer needs to be stopped when the user tells the game to pause (and resume when the game is un-paused).

Because the Traffic Controller is the largest single part of the game's overall code, we go through it step by step in this chapter.

We're only talking about the iPhone in this chapter. We adapt everything for the iPad in Chapter 19.

Creating the Traffic Controller Files

You can't code the Traffic Controller without creating files for it first. What you have to do is to create an empty object, add it to the application, and build functionality into it. You do this throughout the rest of this chapter, as you follow the steps.

To create the new object that controls the game, follow these steps:

1. **In Xcode, create the files TrafficController.h and TrafficController.m by choosing File⇨New File and selecting the Objective-C Class template. Choose NSObject from the Subclass of drop-down list, and click the Next button.**

2. **When prompted, name the class TrafficController.**

When you've gone through these steps, you'll have a new, empty class in your project called TrafficController.

You need to add an instance of the TrafficController object to the game board so that it loads along with every other item on the board.

Next, we show you how to add this class to the game itself in Interface Builder. Technically, you could add this object manually with code, but later, we show you how to connect existing game board objects to the controller. Adding the object to the application with Interface Builder means that the nib file for the TrafficViewController, which we discuss in Chapter 5, creates and links the TrafficController for you, which saves you from writing code. (That's *always* a good thing.)

Follow these steps to add the class:

1. **Open TrafficViewController.xib in Interface Builder. Drag an NSObject from the Library window and drop it in the Document window.**

   The Document window looks like Figure 9-1.

2. **Select the new object, and choose Identity Inspector from the Tools menu.**

   The Identity Inspector opens.

Figure 9-1:
Adding the
new object.

3. Replace the text in the Class field with TrafficController.

This changes the type of the object to TrafficController, which means that a TrafficController object will be loaded when the view controller loads, rather than a plain NSObject (which is the default).

After you complete these steps, you've successfully added the TrafficController object to the view controller.

Now, an instance of TrafficController is created whenever the application loads the TrafficViewController nib file.

The TrafficController object is also removed when the TrafficViewController class is *de-allocated* (removed from memory).

Registering Cars

The cars are moved directly by the TrafficController class — the controller takes each car and moves it up the screen a little bit on every frame. To do this, the controller needs to know about every car. Therefore, when a car is added to the board, the controller adds that car to a list. Then, when the controller wants to move cars, it simply goes through its list of cars and updates them.

After creating this list, you need to store the list in the TrafficController. You can use an NSMutableArray for this. *NSMutableArray* is a class that allows you to store objects as a list; additionally, you can add and remove objects whenever you like, which makes it perfect for this situation.

Follow these steps to add the vehicles list to the TrafficController class.

1. **Add the list variable to TrafficController.h by modifying it to look like the following code:**

```
#import <Foundation/Foundation.h>

@class TrafficViewController;

@interface TrafficController : NSObject {
   NSMutableArray* vehicles;
}

@end
```

The bold in the preceding code is what you need to change.

2. **Set up the list when the TrafficController object loads with the following code (add it to TrafficController.m):**

```
- (void)awakeFromNib {
  vehicles = [[NSMutableArray arrayWithCapacity:10]
       retain];
}
```

Instead of doing the setup in an `init` method, do it in the awakeFrom-Nib method because the object is loaded from the interface file rather than created by your code. For more details on why, have a look at the sidebar "Waking from nibs," later in this chapter.

This code sets up the list of vehicles by creating a new NSMutableArray object (with an initial capacity of ten objects, though this increases as needed). This code also retains the new object to keep the object from being released without your knowledge.

3. **Add the method that allows cars to be registered, by adding the following code to TrafficController.m:**

```
- (void)registerVehicle:(Vehicle*)vehicle {
  [vehicles addObject:vehicle];
}
```

This code takes a Vehicle object, and adds it to the list of registered vehicles.

4. **Import the necessary header file at the start of TrafficController.m.**

Add the following lines of code to the top of TrafficController.m:

```
#import "Vehicle.h"
#import "TrafficViewController.h"
```

At this stage, make the Traffic Controller aware of the Traffic View Controller. This is necessary for a couple reasons:

✔ You need a way to add new cars to the game board, and the only way you can do that is to create new Vehicle instances and add them as sub-views of the Traffic View Controller's view.

✔ You also want to overlay views, such as the game over view or a pause screen. Again, the only way to do that is to add the view as a subview of the Traffic View Controller's view.

To connect the Traffic Controller to the Traffic View Controller, follow these steps:

1. **Add the new IBOutlet variable to Traffic Controller by modifying TrafficController.h so that it looks like the following code:**

```
#import <Foundation/Foundation.h>

@class TrafficViewController;

@interface TrafficController : NSObject {
  NSMutableArray* vehicles;
  TrafficViewController* viewController;
}

@property (nonatomic,retain) IBOutlet
        TrafficViewController* viewController;

@end
```

Waking from nibs

Objects that are created in Interface Builder are pre-prepared objects that are initialized, pre-pared, and then freeze-dried when you save the xib document. A *nib file* is a collection of pre-prepared objects, ready to be loaded into your application. They used to have the extension .nib; the extension is now .xib, but every-one still calls them nibs.

When your application loads a nib, every object that's included in the xib document is rehy-drated (if you'll excuse the tortured dried food metaphor) and brought back to work.

One thing that's important to note about this process is that these objects are sent the init method only once — when they're created in Interface Builder. That's because init is sent to

an object only right after it's created from scratch, and objects that are prepared in Interface Builder are objects that have been created already.

However, having an object know when it's woken up and put back to work is handy. The object doesn't receive the init message again because it already received it when it was made in Interface Builder. Instead, Cocoa Touch sends the object the awakeFromNib message when the object loads from the nib.

This method allows your object to do setup tasks when it starts working. In the Traffic Controller's case, it creates the array that's used for storing the vehicles it later manages — something that can't be designed in Interface Builder.

Next, connect the TrafficViewController object to the new `viewController` Outlet you just created. To do this, follow these steps:

1. **Open TrafficViewController.xib in Interface Builder.**

   Find this file in the list of source files in Xcode.

2. **Hold down the Control key and click Traffic Controller, and then drag the mouse to the File's Owner.**

   The list of potential outlets you can connect appears.

3. **Choose viewController, and then save the file by pressing ⌘+S.**

When the nib file loads and the Traffic Controller is brought back to life, it restores its connection to the view controller. Your code can then use the viewController variable to talk to the view controller.

Creating the Game Timer

In Chapter 8, we discuss the game loop and how it's central to how the game operates at the lower level. The basic concept of the *game loop* is that it moves the cars a small amount, checks whether anything interesting happened as a result of that movement, waits for the iPhone to update the screen, and then repeats the whole process.

To make the game loop work over and over, you need a method to make your application repeatedly do something; a great way to do this is with a CADisplayLink object. *CADisplayLink* keeps an eye on the drawing system used by iOS and sends messages to your code every time the screen updates. This makes CADisplayLink perfect for applications that need to repeatedly update content on the screen, such as *Traffic*.

To use CADisplayLink, you have to create it, give it a target object to send messages to, and then add it to the run loop. After that's done, the CADisplayLink calls a method on your target object every time the screen finishes its drawing. You set this behavior up later in this section.

To make moving objects work in the game loop, you need to work out how much time has passed since the display finished drawing the last frame. Fortunately, CADisplayLink makes this really easy! By asking the CADisplayLink object for its `timestamp` property, you can find out when the last frame finished drawing. If you compare that to the current time, you know how much time the frame took to draw — and that's the information you need to know to work out how far to move the cars!

CADisplayLink objects can also pause. A *paused* CADisplayLink doesn't send messages to its target object. If your entire game's movement is driven by these update messages, pausing the CADisplayLink also pauses the game.

The timer must run very quickly to ensure that the game plays smoothly. The human eye sees anything that changes appearance more than 24 times a second as continuously moving — that's how television and movies work. The display link runs at around 60 frames a second, which is easily smooth enough to fool the human eye into thinking that something is moving.

At first, the loop method doesn't do anything visible — all it does is run constantly. We show you how to add stuff to the loop function over time until it runs the entire game.

To create the display link, and the methods that it needs, follow these steps:

1. **To add the display link variable to the Traffic Controller class, modify TrafficController.h so that it looks like the following:**

```
#import <Foundation/Foundation.h>
#import <QuartzCore/QuartzCore.h>

@class TrafficViewController;

@interface TrafficController : NSObject {
  CADisplayLink* displayLink;

  NSMutableArray* vehicles;
  TrafficViewController* viewController;
}

@property (nonatomic,retain) IBOutlet
        TrafficViewController* viewController;


@end
```

2. **To create the startGame method, add the following code to TrafficController.m:**

```
- (void)startGame {
  displayLink = [CADisplayLink
        displayLinkWithTarget:self selector:@
        selector(update:)];
  [displayLink addToRunLoop:[NSRunLoop mainRunLoop]
        forMode:NSRunLoopCommonModes];

}
```

This method kicks off the game. Rather than awakeFromNib, you do this in a separate method to allow for maximum flexibility. You want to be able to control when the game starts, rather than automatically starting it when the view loads onscreen.

In this method, you create and prepare the CADisplayLink, and then add it to the run loop. The Traffic Controller then receives calls to the update: method many times a second.

3. **To create the `update:` method, add the following code to TrafficController.m:**

```
- (void) update:(CADisplayLink*)sender {
}
```

Right now, the code in the update method doesn't do anything. However, this code will quickly become one of the most important methods in the entire game as you add more functionality to it.

After you have the structure of the main loop in place, add the features that make the game what it is. You do this in the following sections!

Setting up the View Controller

The view controller needs to tell the game to start playing when the game appears onscreen. At the moment, the game will start playing when it receives the startGame message. Make sure that message gets sent!

To do this, you need to update the TrafficViewController so that it knows about the TrafficController, and sends the startGame message when the view appears on the screen.

To do this, follow these steps:

1. **Make the TrafficViewController class aware of the TrafficController class.**

   To do this, add the following code to TrafficViewController.h, replacing the existing code in it:

```
#import <UIKit/UIKit.h>

@class TrafficController;

@interface TrafficViewController : UIViewController {
       TrafficController* gameController;
}
```

```
@property (nonatomic, retain) IBOutlet
        TrafficController* gameController;

@end
```

This code adds an outlet variable called `gameController`, which will be used to work with the TrafficController that you added to the interface file in the first section.

2. **Make the game start up when the view appears.**

   To do this, remove the old viewWillAppear: method from the class, and add the following method to TrafficViewController.m:

   ```
   @synthesize gameController;

   - (void) viewWillAppear:(BOOL)animated {
           [gameController startGame];
   }
   ```

   The `viewWillAppear:` method is run when the view appears on the screen. In this code, it tells the TrafficController object to start the game.

3. **Connect the TrafficViewController to the TrafficController.**

   To do this, open TrafficViewController.xib in Interface Builder. Hold down the Control key, and drag from the File's Owner to the Traffic Controller object, and select gameController from the list that pops up.

   Save the file by pressing ⌘+S.

Keeping Track of the Clock

Because *Traffic* is a *timed* game — the game ends when time runs out — you need to know how much time is left before the game ends. By default, the game starts with 30 seconds of time, which ticks away as the game plays. More time is added to the clock when a car leaves the road and is on the right lane.

We show you how to store the amount of time remaining in an instance variable and to reduce the amount of time left in every frame by the amount of time that's elapsed. You also need to store the timestamp of the most recent frame, which you use when calculating the frame rate of the game.

To add this feature, follow these steps:

1. **To add the timeRemaining variable to the Traffic Controller class, modify TrafficController.h so that it looks like the following code.**

```
#import <Foundation/Foundation.h>
#import <QuartzCore/QuartzCore.h>

@class TrafficViewController;

@interface TrafficController : NSObject {
  CADisplayLink* displayLink;

  NSMutableArray* vehicles;
  double timeRemaining;
  double lastTimestamp;


  TrafficViewController* viewController;
}

@property (nonatomic,retain) IBOutlet
        TrafficViewController* viewController;


@end
```

2. **To subtract the amount of time elapsed every frame, update the code in the update method so that it looks like this:**

```
-(void)update:(CADisplayLink*)sender {
  if (lastTimestamp <= 0) lastTimestamp = sender.
      timestamp;
  CGFloat deltaTime = sender.timestamp -
      lastTimestamp;

  timeRemaining -= deltaTime;

  lastTimestamp = sender.timestamp;
}
```

In this code, you calculate the time elapsed since the last frame, and then subtract the amount of time taken from the amount of time left in the game. If the lastTimestamp variable is zero or less, then the game has just started, so the lastTimestamp variable is set to the current timestamp.

3. **Give the player 20 seconds of time when the game starts.**

Update the awakeFromNib: method by adding the following line of code to the end:

```
timeRemaining = 20;
```

Right now, the game will count down the clock until the amount of time remaining reaches zero, but then it will keep going, and the amount of time remaining goes into negative numbers. We show you how to fix this bug in the section "Making the Game End" later in this chapter, when you add the game over screens. For now, we show you how to make the lanes add new cars to the game!

Creating Cars from Lanes

To have the game provide a steady stream of cars, you need to have the game create new cars at the position of the lanes. To be as flexible as possible, the Traffic Controller doesn't store the starting positions of the cars in the code — in fact, if you did that, you'd end up with errors when the size of the screen changes (like it does when you move to the iPad in Chapter 19). Instead, the controller uses the lane positions onscreen as starting points and allows for any number of lanes.

Here's how lanes work in the game: Every traffic lane onscreen is a view — a special subclass of UIView, in fact — that has extra code added to it that enables it to participate in the game.

When the game starts, every lane gets in touch with the Traffic Controller and registers. This allows the Traffic Controller to keep track of all the lanes in the game, which is handy later when you add the code that checks whether a car is in the right lane.

To make this registration system work, you need to create a new NSMutable-Array instance variable in TrafficController, which acts as the list of registered lanes. Use an NSMutableArray instead of an NSArray because NSArray's contents can be set only when the array is created, which doesn't work for this purpose — the list of lanes needs to be set up after all the objects load, which happens after the Traffic Controller object finishes setting itself up.

Registering lanes

Follow these steps to add the variable that stores all the lanes onscreen, to add a method that allows lanes to register themselves after they load from the nib, to create the class for the lane objects, and to get them to register themselves when they load:

1. **Add the lane array to the Traffic Controller by modifying TrafficController.h to look like the following:**

```
#import <Foundation/Foundation.h>
#import <QuartzCore/QuartzCore.h>

@class TrafficViewController;

@interface TrafficController : NSObject {
  CADisplayLink* displayLink;

  NSMutableArray* vehicles;
  NSMutableArray* lanes;

  double timeRemaining;
  double lastTimestamp;
  TrafficViewController* viewController;
}

@property (nonatomic,retain) IBOutlet
      TrafficViewController* viewController;


@end
```

2. **Allocate and initialize this list when the Traffic Controller loads from the nib by modifying the awakeFromNib method in TrafficController.m so that it looks like the following:**

```
- (void)awakeFromNib {
  vehicles = [[NSMutableArray arrayWithCapacity:10]
      retain];
  lanes = [[NSMutableArray arrayWithCapacity:3]
      retain];
}
```

3. **Add the `registerLane:` method to the Traffic Controller by adding the following code to TrafficController.m:**

```
- (void)registerLane:(Lane*)lane {
  [lanes addObject:lane];
}
```

This method adds a new lane to the list of lanes that the Traffic Controller knows about.

4. **Create the Lane class by choosing File⇨New File, and in the New File dialog that opens, create a new NSObject subclass called Lane.**

5. **Add the following code to Lane.h:**

```
#import <UIKit/UIKit.h>
```

```
@class TrafficController;

@interface Lane : UIView {
        TrafficController* controller;
}

@property (nonatomic, retain) IBOutlet
        TrafficController* controller;


@end
```

6. **Add three views for the lanes in TrafficViewController.xib:**

   a. *Drag in three UIView objects from the Library window onto the view controller.*

   b. *Resize these objects so that they're long and narrow — like each of the lanes in the background image of the view.*

   c. *Change the background colors of these views to green, red, and blue and then set them up so that the lane on the left is green, the middle lane is red, and right lane is blue.*

   You might also want to make the background colors semi-transparent. To do this, change the opacity of the color by sliding the opacity bar at the bottom of the color picker; it's up to you!

7. **Change the views to be lane objects, rather than UIViews:**

   a. *Select all views and open the Identity Inspector by pressing ⌘+4 or choosing Window⇨Identity Inspector.*

   b. *Change the class of the views from UIView to Lane.*

   To change the class of the views, select them, open the Identity Inspector by pressing ⌘+4, and change the Class from UIView to Lane.

8. **Connect the controller outlet of each of the Lanes to the Traffic Controller:**

   a. *Hold down the Control key, click Lane, and drag to the Traffic Controller.*

   b. *Choose* `controller` *in the list that appears.*

   The lanes need to register themselves with the Traffic Controller as well as tell the controller that a new car should be created.

Once you complete these steps, the lanes are ready to start creating cars, and TrafficViewController.xib should look like Figure 9-2.

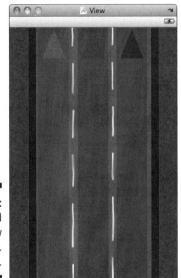

Figure 9-2:
The finished
TrafficView
Controller.
xib.

Updating the Vehicle class

We need to update the vehicle class so that it's possible to create vehicles given a file name. Right now, vehicles will only use the RedCar.png image — we need to change this, which we'll do by changing the initWithFrame: method to initWithName: (which takes the name of an image.)

Additionally, we need to add a speed variable to the Vehicle class, which controls how quickly vehicles move up the screen.

Finally, we need to include a slowed variable, which controls whether or not the car is traveling at half-speed (something that we'll make happen when the user is dragging the car around the screen.)

1. **Update the Vehicle.h file to include the new variables and new method name**

   Replace the contents of this file with the following code (new code is in bold):

   ```
   #import <UIKit/UIKit.h>

   @class TrafficController;
   @class Lane;

   @interface Vehicle : UIView {
     UIImage* image;
     TrafficController* controller;
     CGFloat speed;
     BOOL slowed;
   ```

```
}

- (id)initWithName:(NSString*)name;

@property (assign) CGFloat speed;
@property (nonatomic, retain) TrafficController*
        controller;
@property (readonly) BOOL slowed;

@end
```

2. **Update the initWithFrame: method in Vehicle.m (now initWithName:)
    to use the following code:**

```
- (id)initWithName:(NSString*)name {
  UIImage* loadedImage = [UIImage imageNamed:name];
  CGRect rect = CGRectMake(0, 0, loadedImage.size.
        width, loadedImage.size.height);
  self = [super initWithFrame:rect];
  image = [loadedImage retain];
  speed = 125;
  self.opaque = NO;
  self.backgroundColor = [UIColor clearColor];
  return self;
}
```

3. **Synthesize the new variables.**

    Add the following line of code to Vehicle.m, after the @implementation
    line:

```
@synthesize speed, slowed;
```

Once you're done, the Vehicle class is ready to be used by the Traffic
Controller.

Creating new cars

Lanes also create new cars. To achieve this, add a timer inside the Lane
class, which, when it triggers, tells the Traffic Controller to create a new car
at the Lane's position.

To tell the Traffic Controller to do this, the code you add will use the connection to the Traffic Controller that you created in the preceding section.

To make the lanes create cars, follow these steps:

1. **Add the car start timer to the Lane class and add the declarations of
    the methods that are used to start and stop the lane from creating cars
    by updating the code in Lane.h so that it looks like the following:**

```
#import <UIKit/UIKit.h>

@class TrafficController;

@interface Lane : UIView {
  NSTimer* carStartTimer;
  TrafficController* controller;
}

@property (nonatomic, retain) IBOutlet
      TrafficController* controller;

-(void)start;
-(void)stop;

@end
```

2. **Add the code for the Lane class by adding the following code to Lane.m:**

```
#import "Lane.h"
#import "TrafficController.h"

@implementation Lane

@synthesize controller;

- (void) awakeFromNib {
  [controller registerLane:self];
  srandom(time(NULL));
  [self start];

}

- (void) start {
  long newStartTime = random() % 200;
  carStartTimer = [NSTimer scheduledTimerWithTimeI
      nterval:newStartTime / 1000.0 target:self
      selector:@selector(startTimerFired:)
      userInfo:nil repeats:YES];
  [carStartTimer retain];
}

- (void)startTimerFired:(NSTimer*)timer {
  // pick a random number of milliseconds to fire
      again at

  long newStartTime = random() % 1500 + 500;

  [timer setFireDate:[NSDate dateWithTimeIntervalSince
      Now:newStartTime / 1000.0]];
```

```
  [controller startCarFromLane:self];

  NSLog(@"Starting new car");
}

-(void)stop {
  [carStartTimer invalidate];
  [carStartTimer release];
  carStartTimer = nil;
}

@end
```

With this code, you create four methods for this class:

- The first runs when the object loads from the nib, and is used to register the lane with the Traffic Controller and to signal itself to create cars.

- The second method creates, prepares, and schedules the car-creating timer; it picks a random start time and tells the timer to call the third method when the timer goes off.

- The third method is the most important one: It tells the Traffic Controller to create and add a new car. This method also reschedules the timer to go off after a random amount of time.

- The fourth and final method stops the lane by disabling the timer, which makes the lane stop telling the Traffic Controller to make cars.

3. Import Lane.h at the start of TrafficController.m.

The TrafficController class needs to know about Lane objects, so add the following line of code to the start of TrafficController.m:

```
#import "Lane.h"
```

After the lane object is set up to instruct the Traffic Controller to create a car, get the Traffic Controller to do something about it. The Traffic Controller needs to maintain a list of all the cars that are currently on the road. This is necessary because, during the game loop, the Traffic Controller takes every car and moves it up the screen by a small amount on every frame. To do this, the Traffic Controller needs a way to refer to all those cars.

The Traffic Controller refers to cars in the same way that it refers to lanes — as a mutable array. This array has objects added to it when a car enters the game and removed from it when a car leaves the game.

Add the following code to TrafficController.m. This code picks a random number for the car, which it uses to determine the color of the car. The code then creates the car and adds it to the list of currently active cars in the game; it also positions the car at the bottom of the screen:

```objc
- (void) startCarFromLane:(Lane*)starter {

  NSString* carType;

  int type = random() % 3;

  switch (type) {
    case 0:
      carType = @"GreenCar";
      break;
    case 1:
      carType = @"RedCar";
      break;
    case 2:
      carType = @"BlueCar";
      break;
  }

  Vehicle* v = [[Vehicle alloc] initWithName:carType];

  [viewController.view addSubview:v];
  [self registerVehicle:v];

  v.controller = self;

  CGPoint position;
  position.x = starter.center.x;
  position.y = 480;
  v.center = position;

  [v release];
}
```

The Traffic Controller now knows about every single car in the game, and it's time for it to do something with that knowledge. That's right; time for those cars to move!

Moving Cars Around

To move cars around, start by expanding the update: method. When this method runs, every car moves up the screen a certain distance. This distance is calculated based on the speed of the car and the time elapsed since it was last moved.

Assume that the screen is updated 30 times a second. So, if you have a car that's moving at, say, 100 pixels a second, all you need to do is multiply the speed by the time. One hundred pixels a second multiplied by 1/30 second equals 3.33 pixels. This means that the car needs to be moved up the screen 3.33 pixels during the frame.

To make things a little easier to modify later, your code will do this calculation every frame, rather than calculating once and hard-coding the result. This way, it's possible to change the speed of cars.

Updating car positions

Adding the capability to move cars is straightforward. Go over every car that the Traffic Controller knows about and update its position:

1. **Add the car movement code to the `update:` method so that it looks like the following:**

```
-(void)update:(CADisplayLink*)sender {
  if (lastTimestamp <= 0) lastTimestamp = sender.
        timestamp;
  CGFloat deltaTime = sender.timestamp -
        lastTimestamp;

  timeRemaining -= deltaTime;

  for (Vehicle* v in vehicles) {
    // move it!

    CGPoint position = v.center;
    CGFloat speed = v.speed;
    position.y -= speed * deltaTime;

    v.center = position;

  }

  lastTimestamp = sender.timestamp;
}
```

2. **Run the game.**

   Every time a lane creates a car, the car moves up the screen.

At the moment, cars can still be dragged around the screen, even when they move up the road. What you want is to let the user drag the cars from lane to lane and constrain that movement so that cars aren't dragged off the road, or dragged down or up. In the next section, we show you how to do that.

Moving between lanes

To enable movement between lanes (but not off the road), you need to tie together the list of lanes and cars. When the user drags the car, the game checks which lane the user's finger is on top of. Then a variable inside the car indicates which lane the car is trying to move to. After that's set up, modify the update: function to make cars move sideways from lane to lane at a fixed speed.

To easily check which lane is underneath the user's finger, add a method to Traffic Controller that takes a point onscreen and works out which lane object, if any, occupies the space where the point is.

We also show you how to add a variable to the Vehicle class that lets it keep track of which lane object it's currently on or moving toward. Follow these steps:

1. **Add the laneAtPoint: method to the Traffic Controller by adding the following code to TrafficController.m:**

```
-(Lane*)laneAtPoint:(CGPoint)point {
  for (Lane* lane in lanes) {
    if (CGRectContainsPoint([lane frame], point))
      return lane;
  }
  return nil;
}
```

This code checks all the registered lanes and figures out whether the point given to the method happens to be inside any of them. If the point given to the method happens to be inside a lane, then that lane is returned; if the point is not inside a lane, it returns nil.

2. **Add the goalLane variable to the Vehicle class by modifying the code in Vehicle.h so that it looks like the following:**

```
#import <UIKit/UIKit.h>

@class TrafficController;
@class Lane;

@interface Vehicle : UIView {
  UIImage* image;
  TrafficController* controller;

  CGFloat speed;
  Lane* goalLane;

}

- (id)initWithName:(NSString*)name;

@property (assign) CGFloat speed;
```

```
@property (nonatomic, retain) TrafficController*
        controller;
@property (nonatomic, retain) Lane* goalLane;

@end
```

The goalLane variable is used by the Vehicle class to keep track of the lane that it's trying to move toward.

3. **Synthesize the property that was just added, in Vehicle.m.**

   Add the following line of code to Vehicle.m, just under the `@implementation` line.

   ```
   @synthesize goalLine;
   ```

4. **Remove the old touch handling code by deleting the methods `touchesBegan:withEvent:` and `touchesMoved:withEvent:` in Vehicle.m.**

   You replace them with updated touch handling code in a moment.

5. **Add the new touch handling code that checks for the location of the user's finger and the lanes onscreen by adding the following code to Vehicle.m:**

   ```
   - (void)touchesMoved:(NSSet *)touches
           withEvent:(UIEvent *)event {
     UITouch* aTouch = [touches anyObject];

     // does this touch intersect with a lane? ask the
           controller
     Lane* lane =  [controller laneAtPoint:[aTouch
           locationInView:self.superview]];

     if (lane) {
       self.goalLane = lane;
     }
   }
   ```

   This code takes the location of the touch onscreen and asks the Traffic Controller about what lane is under the user's finger. The vehicle then sets its goalLane variable to the lane that the user points at, which is used to move the car from side to side.

6. **Add the following code to the update: method in TrafficController.m to make the cars move toward their target lanes:**

   ```
   -(void)update:(CADisplayLink*)sender {
     if (lastTimestamp <= 0) lastTimestamp = sender.
           timestamp;
     CGFloat deltaTime = sender.timestamp -
           lastTimestamp;

     timeRemaining -= deltaTime;
   ```

```
for (Vehicle* v in vehicles) {
// move it!

CGPoint position = v.center;

CGFloat speed = v.speed;

position.y -= speed * deltaTime;

CGFloat lateralSpeed = 200;

if (v.goalLane != nil) {
  CGPoint goalLanePosition = v.goalLane.center;

  CGFloat deltaX = fabs(goalLanePosition.x -
    position.x);
  if (deltaX < 3)
    position.x = goalLanePosition.x;

  if (position.x > goalLanePosition.x)
    position.x -= lateralSpeed * deltaTime;
  else if (position.x < goalLanePosition.x)
    position.x += lateralSpeed * deltaTime;
}

v.center = position;

}

lastTimestamp = sender.timestamp;
}
```

This code works if the car is to the left or right of its goal lane, and it applies a slight amount of sideways movement to the car if it needs to move. This code also works if the car is close enough to the lane, in which case, it snaps the vehicle to the center of the lane — this keeps all the cars in an orderly line.

The cars can now be dragged from lane to lane, but when they reach the top of the road, they keep going. If you play the game for a while at this point, you notice that it gets slower and slower because the game never removes cars from the road — it just adds more and more to the game. The fact that you can't see them anymore doesn't mean that they don't have to be processed in the game's update loop. In the next section, we show you how to fix this.

Removing Cars from the Game Board

When a car moves off-screen, the application needs to remove it so that the car won't be drawn and won't be updated. This is also the perfect point to add the capability to detect whether the car was in the correct lane when it left the screen. When a car is removed from the game, the game needs to check whether it's on the correct lane; if the car is in the correct lane, the game gives the player more time. (More on this in a later section in this chapter, "Making the Game End," when you add the countdown timer!)

You first need to add an extra step to the `update:` method that checks whether a car has gone off-screen. Simply check whether the car's frame intersects with the screen's frame. If the car doesn't intersect with the screen's frame at all, it's completely off-screen, and therefore, invisible and eligible to be removed.

After moving the car up the screen, we show you how to check whether the car's off-screen. If the car is off-screen, call the `vehicleReachedEndOf-Road:` method that handles this event. This method initially doesn't do very much, but later it gives more time to the player.

When this method is called, it removes the car from the game view by instructing it to remove itself from its superview. After that, there's no reason for the object to stay in memory or to be included in the game's update loop — it'd simply add to the amount of processing that the game needs to do. The obvious thing for the `vehicleReachedEndOfRoad:` method to do would be to remove the car from the `vehicles` array — after all, it's a mutable array, right?

Actually, that would cause a crash because you aren't allowed to modify an array that you currently loop over! Remember that in the `update:` method, the game examines every car in the `vehicles` array by using a for-in loop. If you modify the array during this loop, Cocoa Touch gets confused and crashes.

The solution is to keep *two* arrays — one for the vehicles and one for the vehicles you're going to delete. When a vehicle is being deleted, it's added to the list of vehicles that needs to be removed. Then, when the `update:` method is done working with the list of vehicles, it removes the vehicles that were added to the second list.

Essentially, you're deferring the deletion of the object!

To make cars remove themselves from the game, follow these steps:

1. **Add the `vehiclesToDestroy` variable and its property to TrafficController.h:**

   ```
   #import <Foundation/Foundation.h>
   #import <QuartzCore/QuartzCore.h>
   #import "Vehicle.h"
   #import "Lane.h"

   @class TrafficViewController;
   ```

```
@interface TrafficController : NSObject {
  CADisplayLink* displayLink;

  double lastTimestamp;

  double timeRemaining;
  NSMutableArray* vehicles;
  NSMutableArray* vehiclesToDestroy;
  NSMutableArray* lanes;

  TrafficViewController* viewController;
}

@property (nonatomic,retain) IBOutlet
        TrafficViewController* viewController;
@property (assign) BOOL paused;

- (void)startGame;
- (void)stopGame;
- (void)registerVehicle:(Vehicle*)vehicle;
- (void)registerLane:(Lane*)lane;
- (void) startCarFromLane:(Lane*)starter;
- (Lane*)laneAtPoint:(CGPoint)point;

@end
```

2. **Allocate and initialize the vehiclesToDestroy variable by modifying the `awakeFromNib` method in TrafficController.m so that it looks like the following:**

```
- (void)awakeFromNib {
  vehicles = [[NSMutableArray arrayWithCapacity:10]
        retain];
  lanes = [[NSMutableArray arrayWithCapacity:3]
        retain];
  vehiclesToDestroy = [[NSMutableArray
        arrayWithCapacity:10] retain];
}
```

The new variable needs to be created when the game starts.

3. **Add the code that checks whether the car has gone off-screen by modifying the `update:` method so that it looks like this:**

```
-(void)update:(CADisplayLink*)sender {
  if (lastTimestamp <= 0) lastTimestamp = sender.
        timestamp;
  CGFloat deltaTime = sender.timestamp -
        lastTimestamp;

  timeRemaining -= deltaTime;

  for (Vehicle* v in vehicles) {
    // move it!
```

```
     CGPoint position = v.center;

     CGFloat speed = v.speed;

     if (v.slowed) {
       speed *= 0.5;
     }

     position.y -= speed * deltaTime;

     CGFloat lateralSpeed = 200;

     if (v.goalLane != nil) {
       CGPoint goalLanePosition = v.goalLane.center;

       CGFloat deltaX = fabs(goalLanePosition.x -
         position.x);
       if (deltaX < 3)
         position.x = goalLanePosition.x;

       if (position.x > goalLanePosition.x)
         position.x -= lateralSpeed * deltaTime;
       else if (position.x < goalLanePosition.x)
         position.x += lateralSpeed * deltaTime;
     }

     v.center = position;

     if (position.y < -50) {
       [self vehicleReachedEndOfRoad:v];
     }

   }

   lastTimestamp = sender.timestamp;
}
```

This code checks every car to see whether its position's y-coordinate on the screen has gone above –50 pixels, which is far off-screen and invisible to the user.

4. **Add the code that adds the vehicle to the vehiclesToDestroy list by adding the method in the following code to TrafficController.m:**

```
- (void)vehicleReachedEndOfRoad:(Vehicle*)v {
  [v removeFromSuperview];
  [vehiclesToDestroy addObject:v];
}
```

This code removes the car from the screen and adds it to the list of cars that need to be removed from the game entirely.

5. **Add the code that removes the car from the game if it's on the vehiclesToDestroy list by modifying the update: method so that it looks like the following:**

```objc
-(void)update:(CADisplayLink*)sender {
 if (lastTimestamp <= 0) lastTimestamp = sender.
        timestamp;
  CGFloat deltaTime = sender.timestamp -
        lastTimestamp;

  timeRemaining -= deltaTime;

  for (Vehicle* v in vehicles) {
    // move it!

    CGPoint position = v.center;

    CGFloat speed = v.speed;


    if (v.slowed) {
      speed *= 0.5;
    }


    position.y -= speed * deltaTime;

    CGFloat lateralSpeed = 200;

    if (v.goalLane != nil) {
      CGPoint goalLanePosition = v.goalLane.center;

      CGFloat deltaX = fabs(goalLanePosition.x -
        position.x);
      if (deltaX < 3)
        position.x = goalLanePosition.x;

      if (position.x > goalLanePosition.x)
        position.x -= lateralSpeed * deltaTime;
      else if (position.x < goalLanePosition.x)
        position.x += lateralSpeed * deltaTime;
    }

    v.center = position;

    if (position.y < -50) {
      [self vehicleReachedEndOfRoad:v];
    }


  }

  for (Vehicle* v in vehiclesToDestroy) {
    [vehicles removeObject:v];
  }

  lastTimestamp = sender.timestamp;
}
```

After you add this code, your game can theoretically run forever without running out of memory: The vehicles are created by the lanes and removed from the game when they leave the screen.

Earning More Time

If a car's off-screen and it was in the correct lane, you need to reward the player for a job well done. Do this by giving the player more time. To detect whether a car has gone off-screen in the right lane, you first have to get the cars to keep track of which lane they're heading toward. There are three lanes on the screen, so there must be three types of cars, each one heading to a different part of the road.

For convenience, keep with the red, green, blue color scheme. When a lane creates a car, the car has a number assigned to it that identifies which lane it's trying to get to. Each of the lanes onscreen is given the same number. For example, the left lane is lane 0, the middle lane is lane 1, and the right lane is lane 2.

These numbers also select the color used for the car. Because the left lane is red, a car that tries to get to the left lane is given the red car image (and so on for the other two lanes). These numbers are *tags,* and they're quite straightforward to add to the Car class — you just have to add another integer property.

They're also very easy to add to views, which is why we suggest you use numbers in the first place. Every single view has a built-in tag property, which is an integer! This feature exists in Cocoa Touch to let you quickly search for a view, given that you know its tag.

In Traffic, use the tags feature to associate cars with lanes. Here are the steps:

1. **Add the goalTag variable and property to the Vehicle class.**

    The goalTag variable is an NSInteger, and it should be an `assign` property. Add code to Vehicle.h that declares an instance variable and property, and then add the code to Vehicle.m that synthesizes the variable.

2. **Add the BlueCar.png and GreenCar.png to the project.**

    You'll find these images in the resource collection you downloaded in Chapter 1.

3. **Add the code to choose the image for the vehicle when it's created and to set the goal lane, by updating the `startCarFromLane:` method so that it looks like the following:**

```
- (void) startCarFromLane:(Lane*)starter {

  NSString* carType;

  int type = random() % 3;

  switch (type) {
    case 0:
      carType = @"GreenCar";
      break;
    case 1:
      carType = @"RedCar";
      break;
    case 2:
      carType = @"BlueCar";
      break;
  }

  Vehicle* v = [[Vehicle alloc] initWithName:carType];

  [viewController.view addSubview:v];
  [self registerVehicle:v];
  v.goalTag = type;

  v.controller = self;

  CGPoint position;
  position.x = starter.center.x;
  position.y = 480;
  v.center = position;

  [v release];
}
```

After the cars know which lane to head to, the next step is to add the code that checks whether the car was in the correct lane when it left the screen.

4. **Add the code that updates the timeRemaining variable when a car drives off in the right lane by updating the `vehicleReachedEndOfRoad:` method in TrafficController.m so that it looks like the following:**

```
- (void)vehicleReachedEndOfRoad:(Vehicle*)v {
  [v removeFromSuperview];
  [vehiclesToDestroy addObject:v];

  if (v.goalTag == v.goalLane.tag) {
    timeRemaining += 2.0;
  } else {
    // car did not reach goal; no reward
  }
}
```

The core of the game is done. You have one thing left to add before the game is properly playable: making the game end!

Detecting Collisions

In *Traffic,* games usually end when two cars collide; therefore, you need to add some code to check whether the cars collide. For this purpose, a collision occurs when two cars overlap onscreen. How do you know whether they overlap? By using the magic of CGRectIntersectsRect! This method takes two CGRects, and returns TRUE if they intersect each other.

If two cars' frames intersect, they've collided. If they've collided, the game is over! To check for a collision, add the code that checks to the `update:` method, during the stage when it updates every car onscreen. After the car has been moved and checked to see whether it's gone off the edge of the screen, it's then checked against every *other* car to see whether it's collided with it. If the cars have collided, boom! Game over! When a collision happens, a new `vehicle:collidedWithVehicle:` method is called. This method ends the game.

To add the collision detection, follow these steps:

1. **Add the code that checks for collisions to the `update:` method:**

```
-(void)update:(CADisplayLink*)sender {
  if (lastTimestamp <= 0) lastTimestamp = sender.
      timestamp;
  CGFloat deltaTime = sender.timestamp -
      lastTimestamp;

  timeRemaining -= deltaTime;

  for (Vehicle* v in vehicles) {
    // move it!

    CGPoint position = v.center;

    CGFloat speed = v.speed;


    if (v.slowed) {
      speed *= 0.5;
    }


    position.y -= speed * deltaTime;

    CGFloat lateralSpeed = 200;
```

```
  if (v.goalLane != nil) {
    CGPoint goalLanePosition = v.goalLane.center;

    CGFloat deltaX = fabs(goalLanePosition.x -
      position.x);
    if (deltaX < 3)
      position.x = goalLanePosition.x;

    if (position.x > goalLanePosition.x)
      position.x -= lateralSpeed * deltaTime;
    else if (position.x < goalLanePosition.x)
      position.x += lateralSpeed * deltaTime;
  }

  v.center = position;

  if (position.y < -50) {
    [self vehicleReachedEndOfRoad:v];
  }

  // is the car colliding with any others?
  for (Vehicle* otherVehicle in vehicles) {

    // If this other vehicle is the current vehicle,
    //   then ignore it (since you can't collide with
    //   yourself!)
    if (otherVehicle == v) continue;

    // inset by 7 pixels to provide a degree of
    //   tolerance
    CGRect myRect = CGRectInset(v.frame, 7,7);
    CGRect otherRect = CGRectInset(otherVehicle.
      frame, 7, 7);
    if (CGRectIntersectsRect(myRect, otherRect)) {
      [self vehicle:v collidedWithVehicle:
      otherVehicle];
      return; // the game ends after this, don't
      bother continuing the game loop
    }
  }
}

for (Vehicle* v in vehiclesToDestroy) {
  [v removeFromSuperview];
  [vehicles removeObject:v];
}

lastTimestamp = sender.timestamp;
}
```

2. **Add the method `vehicle:collidedWithVehicle:` to TrafficController.m:**

```
- (void) vehicle:(Vehicle*) aVehicle
        collidedWithVehicle: (Vehicle*) otherVehicle {
   // game over, man

   if (!displayLink.paused)
     [self togglePause];

   [viewController displayGameOver];
}
```

This code pauses the game and instructs the view controller to display the game over screen you prepare in the section "Making the Game End," later in this chapter.

Updating the Counter

The time-remaining indicator lets the user know that time is running out, and the only way to know this is for the amount of time remaining to show up on the screen.

This means that you need to display a counter at the top of the screen. You also need to detect when the time has gone below zero, and end the game.

Start by adding the counter. Follow these steps:

1. **Open TrafficViewController.xib in Interface Builder.**

2. **Drag in a UIImageView from the Library window, and set it up to show the Time: image.**

   To do this, select the new image view you just added, and open the Attributes Inspector by pressing ⌘+1. Change the Image field at the top of the Inspector to Time-Text.png, which you find inside the resources bundle you download in Chapter 1.

   After you do that, resize the image view to fit the image by pressing ⌘+=, and then move the image view to the top-left of the view.

3. **Drag in a UILabel from the Library window, and place it just to the right of the Time: image.**

   This label will be used to show the time. It needs to use the Marker Felt font and be yellow. Modify the font and color values in the Attributes Inspector.

After the clock is in place, you need a way for the TrafficViewController object to be able to update it. This means you need an outlet for the clock, and a method for the TrafficController to call to update the clock.

To do this, follow these steps:

1. **Add following code to TrafficViewController.h, replacing its existing contents:**

```
#import <UIKit/UIKit.h>

@class TrafficController;

@interface TrafficViewController : UIViewController {
        TrafficController* gameController;
        UIView* pauseOverlay;
        UIView* gameOverOverlay;
        UILabel* timeRemainingLabel;
}

@property (nonatomic, retain) IBOutlet
        TrafficController* gameController;
@property (nonatomic, retain) IBOutlet UIView*
        pauseOverlay;
@property (nonatomic, retain) IBOutlet UILabel*
        timeRemainingLabel;
@property (nonatomic, retain) IBOutlet UIView*
        gameOverOverlay;
- (void) displayGameOver;
- (IBAction) pauseGame:(id)sender;
- (IBAction) endGame:(id)sender;
- (void) setTimeRemaining:(CGFloat)time;

@end
```

This code adds the outlets that you need for the clock, and also adds outlets for the Traffic Controller, pause screen and game over screen, and actions for controlling the game flow. You make use of these additional outlets and actions in the next two sections; in the meantime, you work with just the `timeRemainingLabel` variable and the `setTimeRemaining:` method.

2. **Add the following code to TrafficViewController.m, replacing its existing contents:**

```
#import "TrafficViewController.h"
#import "TrafficController.h"

@implementation TrafficViewController

@synthesize gameController;
@synthesize pauseOverlay;
@synthesize gameOverOverlay;
```

```
@synthesize timeRemainingLabel;

- (void) viewWillAppear:(BOOL)animated {
        [gameController startGame];
}

- (void)setTimeRemaining:(CGFloat)time {
        timeRemainingLabel.text = [NSString
        stringWithFormat:@"%.1f", time];
}

@end
```

The new method you add, setTimeRemaining:, sets the value of the text field to the time value that was sent to the TrafficViewController.

3. Connect the TrafficViewController class to the clock label.

To do this, open TrafficViewController.xib in Interface Builder. Hold down the Control key, and drag from the File's Owner to the label you added at the top-right. Choose timeRemainingLabel from the list that appears.

After you complete these steps, the view controller knows how to update the time remaining label. There's one last thing to do: The label needs to be updated on every frame, showing the amount of time left.

To add this feature, follow these steps:

1. Add the following lines of code to the end of the update: method in TrafficController.m:

```
[viewController setTimeRemaining:timeRemaining];

if (timeRemaining < 0) {
  // game over!
  if (!displayLink.paused)
    [self togglePause];
  [viewController displayGameOver];
}
```

This code tells the view controller to update the time remaining clock, showing the amount of time left to the user. It then checks to see if the player is out of time; if so, it pauses the game and tells the view controller to display the game over screen (which you prepare in the "Making the Game End" section later in this chapter).

2. Play the game.

When you play the game, you'll see the time ticking down.

Next step: Add the capability to pause!

Pausing the Game

It's highly likely that the player will, at some point, need to pause the game in order to take a break. To do that, a few things need to occur. First, the game needs to freeze all movement by stopping the update loop, and stopping all lanes from creating new cars. Second, the game needs to show a screen that indicates that the game is paused.

Pausing the game isn't enough, though, because the user also needs to be able to *un*pause the game. Unpausing undoes everything pausing does — it gets rid of the paused screen, it re-activates all lanes, and it resumes the game's update loop.

Creating the Paused View

When the player pauses the game, the game needs to show a screen that indicates this action. This screen will be superimposed on top of the game, showing the frozen cars.

To create the pause view, you create a separate view in Interface Builder, but you don't add it to the view controller's view. Instead, it will sit, waiting to be displayed; when it needs to appear, your code will manually add it. When the pause screen needs to disappear, your code will also manually remove it.

Here's how to create the Paused view:

1. **Add the "End-Button.png", "GameOver.png", "Paused.png" and "Pause-Button.png" images to the project.**

   You'll find them in the resource collection from Chapter 1.

2. **Create a new empty view in TrafficViewController.xib.**

   To do this, open TrafficViewController.xib in Interface Builder. Open the Library by pressing ⌘-Shift-L, and drag a View from the Library to the Document window.

   Rememeber, don't drag it into the main canvas! The view window shouldn't appear on the screen until it's needed.

   Once you've dragged in the view, double click it to open it in a new window. You now have two canvases: one for the paused view, and one for the game view.

3. **Make the view semi-transparent.**

   Select the new view, and open the Attributes Inspector by pressing ⌘-1. Un-check the "Opaque" checkbox in the Inspector, and change the "Background" drop-down list to "Clear Color".

4. Add the "Paused" image button to the paused view.

This giant button will actually look like a giant image view, but it will be used for un-pausing the game when the user taps it.

To do this, drag in a UIButton from the Library and place it in the paused view. Using the resizing handles, resize it so that it fills the entire view.

5. Set up the "Paused" button.

To do this, open the Attributes Inspector by pressing ⌘-1, and change the "Type" drop-down to "Custom". This changes the button to one that doesn't show rounded corners, which is exactly what you want.

Once you've changed the button's type, change the button's background image by entering "Paused.png" in the Inspector's "Image" field.

6. Add the "End Game" button.

There's one last button to add to the game view: the Pause button itself, which actually pauses the game and makes the screen you just created appear.

Figure 9-3:
The finished pause view.

To add this button, follow these steps:

1. Open the main game view in TrafficViewController.xib.

2. Drag in a new UIButton. Position it at the top-right of the view.

3. Change the button's type to Custom, and its image to Pause-Button.png.

Pausing

After the pause view is set up, you need to make the game actually pause itself. To do this, you add code to the TrafficViewController that handles the pause button being clicked.

To add this code, follow these steps:

1. **Add the `togglePause` method to the TrafficController class.**

   To do this, add the following code to TrafficController.m:

   ```
   - (void)togglePause {
     displayLink.paused = !displayLink.paused;
     if (displayLink.paused) {
       // make all vehicles not respond to user
           interaction
       for (Vehicle* v in vehicles) {
         v.userInteractionEnabled = NO;
       }
       // make all lanes stop sending cars
       for (Lane* l in lanes) {
       [l stop];
       }
     } else {
       // make all vehicles respond to user interaction
       for (Vehicle* v in vehicles) {
         v.userInteractionEnabled = YES;
       }
       // make all lanes start sending cars
       for (Lane* l in lanes) {
         [l start];
       }
     }
   }
   ```

   This code toggles the paused state of the display link: If it's unpaused, it pauses the link, and if it's paused, it unpauses. This causes the display link to start or stop sending `update:` messages. Once the display link has been set up, the code disables (or enables, depending on the new pause state) all of the cars and lanes, preventing them from participating in the game.

2. **Add the `isPaused` method to the TrafficController class.**

   To do this, add the following code to TrafficController.m:

   ```
   - (BOOL) isPaused {
     return displayLink.paused;
   }
   ```

   This code simply returns the current pause state of the display link.

3. **Add the `pauseGame:` method to the TrafficViewController class.**

   To do this, add the following code to TrafficViewController.m:

```
-(IBAction) pauseGame:(id)sender {
  [gameController togglePause];
  if ([gameController isPaused]) {
    [self.view addSubview:pauseOverlay];
  } else {
    [pauseOverlay removeFromSuperview];
  }
}
```

   This code tells the game controller to toggle its pause state, and then checks to see if the game is now paused or not. If the game is now paused, the pause screen that you created earlier is displayed. If the game is *not* paused, the pause overlay is removed from the display.

4. **Connect the Traffic Controller to the pause screen and the Pause button.**

   Now that your code has these methods and outlets, you need to attach them to elements in your interface.

   Open TrafficViewController.xib in Interface Builder. Hold down the Control key, and drag from the File's Owner to the pause view in the Document window. Select pauseOverlay from the list that appears.

   Once that's done, hold down the Control key and drag from the Pause button to the File's Owner, and select pauseGame from the list that appears.

   Finally, repeat the same procedure for the little Pause button at the top-right of the game screen.

After you complete these steps, you can run the game and pause it.

There's one step left: showing the game over screen.

Making the Game End

Making the game play is all well and good, but all good things must come to an end, and that includes games!

Creating the game over view

The game over view needs to look basically identical to the pause view, but with a difference: The game over view can't be dismissed by the user, but will instead simply stay on the screen for a second or two before the application returns to the main menu.

This means that the game over view can be a lot less complicated. To add this view, follow these steps:

1. **Create a new empty view in TrafficViewController.xib.**

   As with the pause view, drag a view from the Library into the Document window. Double-click on this new view to open it.

2. **Make the view semi-transparent.**

   Select the new view, and open the Attributes Inspector by pressing ⌘+1. Uncheck the Opaque check box in the Inspector, and change the Background drop-down list to Clear Color.

3. **Drag a UIImageView from the Library into the new view.**

   After you drag it in, resize it so that it fills the entire view.

4. **Change the image of the view to the game over image.**

   Do this by selecting the image view, opening the Attributes Inspector, and changing the Image field to GameOver.png.

After you complete these steps, the game over view is ready to be displayed.

Handling the Game Over event

One of the methods that the rest of the game refers to is `displayGameOver`. In this section, you add this method, which displays the game over screen, and makes the game return to the Main Menu after 1.5 seconds.

To end the game, the application needs to tell the navigation controller to get rid of the current view controller, which will return the user to the main menu.

However, you can't just return to the main menu as soon as the game ends, because that would surprise the player. Instead, you need to add a slight delay. A simple way to add this delay is to put the code that returns to the main menu in a separate method, and then tell iOS to run this method in 1.5 seconds' time.

To add this behavior, follow these steps:

1. **Add the `displayGameOver` method to the TrafficViewController class.**

   To do this, add the following method to TrafficViewController.m:

```
-(void)displayGameOver {
  [self.view addSubview:gameOverOverlay];
  // Wait 1.5 seconds and go to the main screen
  [self performSelector:@selector(endGame:)
        withObject:nil afterDelay:1.5];
}
```

This code displays the game over screen, and then sets up the end-Game: method to be called in 1.5 seconds.

2. **Add the `endGame:` method to the TrafficViewController class.**

   To do this, add the following method to TrafficViewController.m:

```
- (IBAction) endGame:(id)sender {
  [self.navigationController
      popViewControllerAnimated:NO];
}
```

   This code makes the TrafficViewController vanish from the screen, returning the player to the main menu.

   There's one last thing to do: The pause screen includes a button that takes the player back to the main menu. At least, it *should,* but right now, it doesn't. Fortunately, adding this feature is easy.

3. **Connect the End Game button to the `endGame:` method.**

   To do this, open the pause screen inside TrafficViewController.xib. Hold down the Control key, and drag from the End Game button to the File's Owner. Select endGame: from the list that appears.

Whew! You've set up a lot, but after you do all of this, the core game play is finally ready. Congratulations!

Chapter 10

Using the Debugger

Developing games can be a pretty hectic process, and sometimes when you work late at night, the coding mistakes flow more freely than the useful code, especially when you spill coffee on your keyboard, causing it to do nothing but repeat semicolons constantly. (Not that that's ever happened to us, of course.)

You're probably wondering why top-shelf programmers like us would ever make coding mistakes, much less need to fix them. (You were wondering that, right?) Sadly, we do need to use the Debugger fairly regularly because, in the immortal words of a famous former U.S. Vice President, "Stuff happens."

This chapter covers how to detect errors in your code with the powerful debugging tools that Apple provides. We tell you about the most common errors, and how the debugging tools can help you find and fix each and every one. We discuss how, and why, errors can occur in your code (and what you need to do to prevent and fix them).

Figuring Out What Debugger Can Help You Do

Thankfully, the Debugger built into Xcode is both powerful and, in glorious Apple tradition, pretty easy to use. The Debugger that Xcode features is based on a GDB tool, which was created by a variety of fiercely intelligent men with beards in the distant past (and then modified by Apple to support Objective-C and such).

What sort of "stuff" can the Debugger help you fix? When developing games, that "stuff" comes in three categories:

✔ **Syntax errors:** Compilers — the Objective-C compiler in Xcode is a case in point — expect you to use a certain set of instructions in your code. Those instructions make up the language the compiler understands. When you type **If** instead of **if**, or the subtler **[view release}** instead of **[view release]**, the compiler suddenly has no idea what you're talking about and generates a syntax error.

Syntax errors are the most obvious errors, simply because your program doesn't compile (or can't run) until all these are fixed. Generally, syntax errors spring from typographical errors. (And yes, the errors can be pretty penny-ante stuff — an *I* for an *i*, for goodness' sake — but it doesn't take much to stump a compiler.)

In Figure 10-1, you can see an example of a syntax error. This one was kindly pointed out to us by Xcode's friendly little Debugger feature (more on him later). We accidentally included an extra colon when calling the `setTitle:` method.

An error resulted because the compiler couldn't quite figure out what we were doing. The description of the error appears next to the part of code that the compiler couldn't understand.

You can generally ignore the subsequent errors after the first syntax error because they may be the result of that first error. In this case, because of the first error, that line and the next ones were treated as a single instruction.

✔ **Runtime errors:** Runtime errors cause your program to stop executing — it *crashes,* in other words, as in "crashes and burns to much wailing and gnashing of teeth." Something might have come up in the data that you hadn't expected (a division by zero error, for example), or maybe the result of a method dealt a nasty surprise to your logic, or perhaps you sent a message to an object that doesn't have that message implemented. Sometimes you even get some build warnings for these errors; often the application simply stops working or *hangs* (stops and does nothing). Or the app shuts down, and you get the (not particularly helpful) message in Figure 10-2.

Figure 10-1:
A syntax error. Oops.

```
- (void)viewDidUnload {

    [self setTitle::@"My view controller"];
                     ⊘ Expected expression before ':' token
}
```

Figure 10-2:
An
unexpected
quit.

Debugging terminated.

✔ **Logic errors:** Your literal-minded game does exactly what you tell it to, but sometimes you unintentionally tell it the wrong thing and then it coughs up a logic error. In Figure 10-3, everything looks fine — not an error sign in sight — except when you try to pause the game and you discover that the game keeps running. This is the exact opposite of what you want.

Look closely at this chunk of code:

```
- (void)togglePause {
    paused = paused;
    ...
```

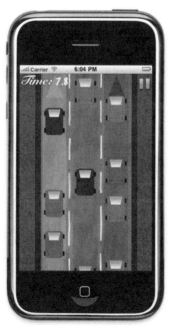

Figure 10-3:
Oh, great
— it works
backwards.

See the assigned value of paused to paused? The code should have been assigned the negated value of paused. Here's how the code should look:

```
paused = !paused;
```

Not being able to guess what we *really* wanted, it did what we *told* it to. The program worked, but not the way we intended it to.

Syntax errors, runtime errors, and logic errors can all be pains in the behind, but you don't need to think of them as insurmountable roadblocks. You're still on your way to an entertaining iOS game. In this chapter, we show you how to use the Debugger to remove at least some of these obstacles. The Debugger works best for runtime errors, but as we point out later, it can also help you track down logic errors.

Using the Debugger

In Figure 10-4, we deliberately created a situation that causes a runtime error. We divide by zero — a mathematical no-no that any respectable fifth grader would berate us for. This enables us to show you how to approach runtime errors in general.

Figure 10-4:
Results of division by zero.

```
int i;
i = 1/0;                    ⚠ Division by zero
```

Here's the drill: After introducing a boneheaded error while writing code in Xcode, we chose Build⇨Build and Run. The application started and then immediately shut down, but the compiler was kind enough to tell us what we did wrong.

You can see in the top of Figure 10-4 that we got a warning message `Division by zero`. Pay attention to those warnings: Sometimes the subsequent message can help you more precisely understand what the compiler is complaining about.

Before you scoff and say that we should've caught such a basic error — okay, you're right to scoff — we want to point out three things:

✔ In the middle of development, we may have been pelted with compiler warnings that we didn't really need to take care of because they had no impact on the execution of the program. As a result, we might not have noticed one more compiler warning that actually *did* have an impact — a big one.

✔ If the game was a bit more complicated (and they often are), we could conceivably end up dividing by zero without realizing it. (Remember, stuff happens.)

✔ If you happen to save this code and then build it again, you don't see the compiler warning in the status bar because there were no changes to that file — so it wouldn't be recompiled. (This is definitely something to remember.) This is one reason to set the Xcode Building preference Build Results Window: Open During Builds to Always — it continually reminds you about those warnings by making sure the Build Results Window: Open During Builds automatically opens every time you build.

How can the Debugger help determine the source of a runtime error like this one? The next section gives you the details.

Debugging your project

To use the Debugger, start by building the application in another way. You tell Xcode to compile the project and then launch the application alongside the Debugger. The Debugger watches your application and pauses execution if your code hits a breakpoint, or if there's an app-stopping error. Follow these steps:

1. **Add the following code to the end of the application:didFinishLaunchi ngWithOptions: method in TrafficAppDelegate.m:**

   ```
   int i = 0;
   i = 1/0;
   ```

2. **With the project open in Xcode, click the Breakpoints button in the Project window toolbar.**

   The Build and Run button changes to Build and Debug (as shown in Figure 10-5). This time, after you build and run the program, you see a few different things.

   You get a message in the status bar of the Project window in Figure 10-5:

   ```
   Program received signal:  "EXC_ARITHMETIC".
   ```

   The Debugger strip is visible in the Project window, just above the Editor view, as shown in Figure 10-5. There are also a number of buttons for your clicking pleasure, which we get to shortly.

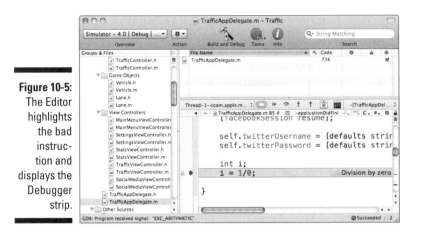

Figure 10-5:
The Editor
highlights
the bad
instruc-
tion and
displays the
Debugger
strip.

The Debugger strip is a collection of controls that lets you manage what the debugger is doing while you inspect your application. You can see it on the right hand side in Figure 10-5 between the code editing area and the file list.

3. **In Xcode's Editor view in Figure 10-5, notice the red arrow that shows you the instruction that caused the program to crash.**

   That's the Debugger pointing out the problem. Even more informa-tion is available though. As shown in Figure 10-5, the mouse pointer is positioned above the i on the offending line. You can see the Debugger datatip displaying the value of i.

4. **Position the mouse pointer above 'self', as shown in Figure 10-6, and then move it over the disclosure triangle.**

   A Debugger datatip that shows the appDelegate's instance variables displays. The datatip is a small yellow window that appears on top of the window, which gives you a brief overview of the variable you're looking at.

Figure 10-6:
A Debugger
datatip.

▶	TrafficAppDelegate *	**self**	0x752ce40

5. **Select the up and down arrows next to** [TrafficViewController viewDidLoad] **in the Debugger strip to see the stack (as shown in Figure 10-7).**

The *stack* is a trace of the objects and methods that got you to where you are now.

For example, main called UIApplicationMain — which sent the [UIApplication_run] message and so on, which eventually ended up in [TrafficAppDelegate application:didFinishLaunching with Options], and then finally to [TrafficViewController viewDidLoad]. That's where this little problem reared its ugly head.

Okay, the stack isn't really all that useful in this particular context of dealing with our boneheaded attempt to divide by 0, but it *can* be very useful in other contexts. In a more complex application, the stack can help you understand the path that you took to get where you are. Seeing how one object sent a message to another object — which sent a message to a third object — can be really helpful, especially if you didn't expect the program flow to work that way.

Looking at the stack can also be useful if you're trying to understand how the framework does its job and in what order messages are sent. As we discuss later in this chapter in the "Using Breakpoints" section, using a *breakpoint* can stop the execution of my program at any point and trace the messages sent up to that point. So don't despair; you have options. Even more information is available, though — it comes to you in the Debugger window.

 6. **Click Show Debugger in the Debugger strip in the Project window, or choose Run➪Debugger from Xcode's main menu.**

The 'Show Debugger' button is the picture of the spray-can in front of a window. This is one of the rare cases where you'll see Apple make a visual pun — after all, bug spray kills bugs, doesn't it?

Alternatively, press Shift+⌘+Y.

The Debugger window appears.

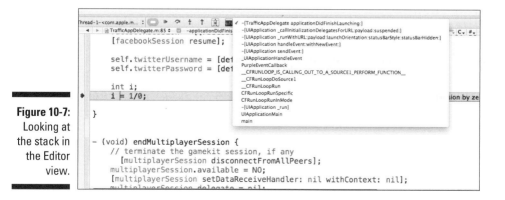

Figure 10-7:
Looking at
the stack in
the Editor
view.

Using the Debugger window

Even though the Debugger officially runs in the background, you have to open the Debugger window explicitly the first time you choose Run➪Debugger.

Figure 10-8 shows the Debugger window; it has everything that's in the Editor window, but you can see your stack and the variables in scope at a glance. The Debugger window also has some extra functionality we show you in the upcoming section "Using Breakpoints."

In the upper-left pane, you can see the same stack from the Editor window.

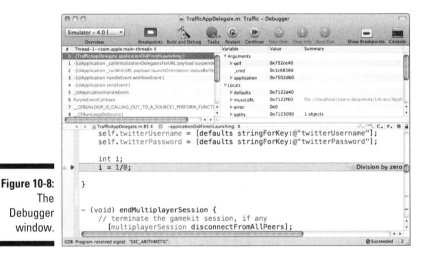

Figure 10-8: The Debugger window.

Your window may not look exactly like ours. That's because Xcode gives you lots of ways to customize the look of the Debugger window. You could, for example, choose Run➪Debugger Display from the main menu and tweak the way you want your Debugger window to look. We chose Source Only from that menu — so that only the source code appears in the bottom pane. You could, of course, have checked the Source and Disassembly option in the same menu if you had a hankering for checking both the source code *and* the assembly language (if you really care about assembly language); in that case, the bottom pane divides down the center into two panes, with the source code on the left and the assembly code on the right.

We wouldn't actually expect you to use the Source and Disassembly option at this point. But sometimes, as you explore interfaces, things don't look the way they used to. This usually occurs because a different display option has been chosen — either by accident or on purpose.

Examine the top-right pane in the Debugger window. You see a display of the program object's variables. Click the disclosure triangles next to `self` and the application, and you can see the application delegate's instance variables that you saw in the datatip in the Editor window.

This is useful for a couple of reasons:

- ✔ **Checking variables:** If the view doesn't display the correct data, look in the Variable column to see what the value of the variable actually is. If the value is correct here, you can conclude that either it gets changed by mistake later or you display something other than what you intended to display.

- ✔ **Checking messages sent:** Some logic errors you may encounter are the result of what some people call a *feature* and others call a *design flaw* in Objective-C. For some reason, which isn't particularly important here, Objective-C, unlike some other languages, allows you to send a message to a `nil` object *without* generating a runtime error. If you do that, expect to see some sort of logic error because a message to a `nil` object simply does nothing (we call this a feature, for the record).

  When things don't happen how you expect, you might have a real logic error in your code. But consider one other possibility: Maybe an object reference hasn't been set, and you're sending the message into the ether.

  How can you use the Variable column to help with that? Simple. If you look at an object reference instance variable and its value is 0x0, any messages to that object are simply ignored. So when you get a logic error, the first thing to check is whether any of the object references you use have 0x0 as their values, informing you that the reference was never initialized.

As you can see, the Debugger can be really useful when your program doesn't do what you expect. For the blatant errors, the Debugger can show you exactly what's going on when the error occurred. The Debugger provides a trail of how you got to where you are, highlights the problem instruction, and shows your application's variables and their values at that point. Had the cause of the error in this case been more subtle, looking at the value of the variable would've given a good hint about what was going on.

What's just as valuable is how the Debugger can help with logic errors. Sending a message to `nil` isn't uncommon, especially when you make changes to the user interface and forget to set up an outlet, for example. In such situations, the capability to look at the object references can help. What can really help you with that is the capability to set breakpoints, which we discuss in the following section.

Using Breakpoints

Xcode's Debugger feature is a great tool to track down runtime errors, as we discuss earlier in this chapter. We want to highlight another useful feature of the Debugger — its capability of setting breakpoints. If you're stymied by a logic error, setting breakpoints is a great way to break that jam.

A *breakpoint* is an instruction to the Debugger to stop execution at that instruction and wait for further instructions. By setting breakpoints at various methods in the program, you can step through its execution, at the instruction level, to see exactly what it does. You can also examine the variables the program sets and uses, which allow you to determine whether the problem is there.

In Figure 10-9, a breakpoint is set simply by clicking in the far-left column of the Editor window. When you set a breakpoint, a blue marker appears in the left column that indicates the line where the breakpoint is located. (We also deleted the statement that caused the division by zero error.) When the program is built and run again (as shown in the Debugger Editor window in Figure 10-10), the program stops executing at the set breakpoint. (You would also see that same thing in the Editor window.)

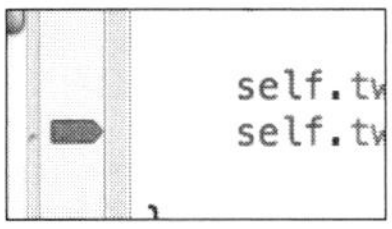

Figure 10-9:
Setting a
breakpoint.

We also clicked the triangle next to `self`, which shows the view controller's variables. If we had clicked viewController under appDelegate, you'd see the same thing, or you could've stayed in the Editor window and used the datatip.

Under the appDelegate variables is the VARIABLE and its value, which is `nil`. If you'd wanted to do something with VARIABLE at this point, that click would've shown that you tried to do something with a variable that hadn't been initialized with the value needed. In other words, this wouldn't have been a good time in the program flow to display the VARIABLE variable.

Say you wanted to see precisely when that variable was set. You could execute the program instruction by instruction, simply by clicking the Step Into button on the Debugger toolbar. You would have executed METHOD; (after a brief stop at @synthesize VARIABLE) and then gone on to the next line of code, as shown in Figure 10-11. You'd keep clicking that Step Into button at every instruction until you got to where you wanted to be (which, by the way, can be a long and winding road).

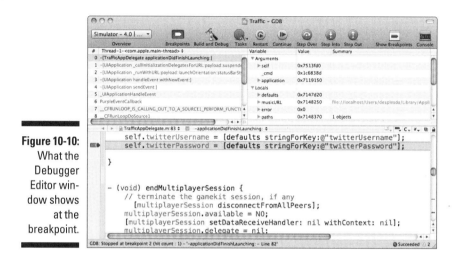

Figure 10-10:
What the Debugger Editor window shows at the breakpoint.

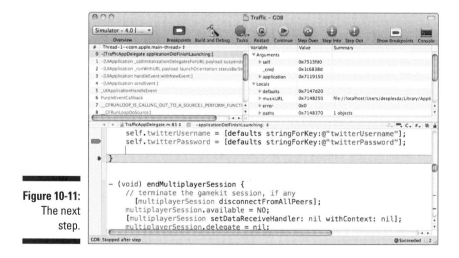

Figure 10-11:
The next step.

The Debugger window gives you a number of other options to make your way through your program in addition to the Step Into button. For example, you could use one of the following buttons:

- ✔ **Step Over** gives you the opportunity to skip over an instruction.

- ✔ **Step Out** takes you out of the current method.

- ✔ **Step Into** takes you into the method that the current line of code is about to call.

- ✔ **Continue** tells the program to keep on with its execution.

- ✔ **Restart** restarts the program. (You hoped maybe if you tried running the program again it would work?)

To get rid of the breakpoint, simply drag it off to the side. You can also right-click the breakpoint and choose Remove Breakpoint from the pop-up menu that appears.

Using the Static Analyzer

Xcode has a Build and Analyze feature (also known as the Static Analyzer) that analyzes your code. The results show up like warnings and errors, with explanations of where and what the issue is. You can also see the flow of control of the potential problem. We say *potential* because the Static Analyzer can give you false positives.

In Figure 10-12, we deliberately created a memory leak. A *memory leak* is when you create an object and then never release its memory back to the system — the memory taken up by that object can't be used by your program, which reduces the amount of memory left to your application. This is a bad thing! In this case, we allocated a new TrafficViewController and then did nothing with it:

```
TrafficViewController* anObject =
                    [TrafficViewController alloc];
```

We then chose Build⇨Build and Analyze. In Figure 10-13, you can see the results in the Project window. A notice appears with a little blue icon that says

```
Potential leak of an object allocated on line 86 and
            stored into 'anObject'
```

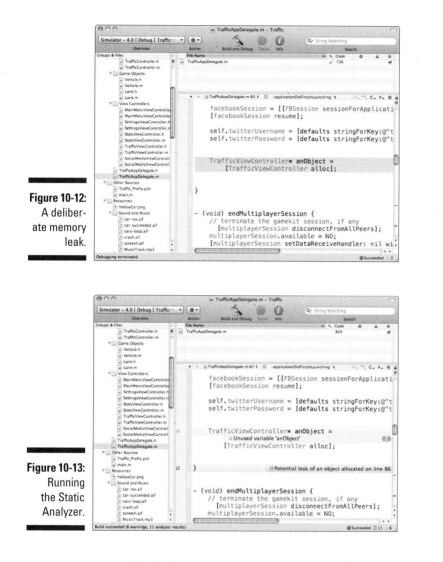

Figure 10-12: A deliberate memory leak.

Figure 10-13: Running the Static Analyzer.

If we click the little blue icon, we get a trace of what happened to cause the problem; you can see this in Figure 10-14.

There's an (Instruments) app for that

Although the Static Analyzer can help you detect memory leaks, the real champ at doing that is Xcode's Instruments application, which also lets you know how your application uses iPhone resources, such as the CPU, memory, network, and so on. The Instruments application is included as part of the Apple iPhone SDK.

The Instruments application allows you to observe the performance of your application while running it on the iPhone, and to a lesser extent, while running it on the Simulator. Here, *instrument* means a specialized feature of the Instruments application that zeroes in on a particular aspect of your game's performance

(such as memory usage, system load, disk usage, graphics, and the like) and measures it. What's really neat, however, is that you can look at these different aspects simultaneously along a timeline — and then store data from multiple runs so you get a picture of how your game's performance changes when you tune it.

The Instruments application is a powerful piece of software. It has so many features that an in-depth discussion is beyond the scope of this book. We discuss it briefly again when we cover OpenGL ES in Chapter 23, but for the most part, we leave it for you to explore on your own.

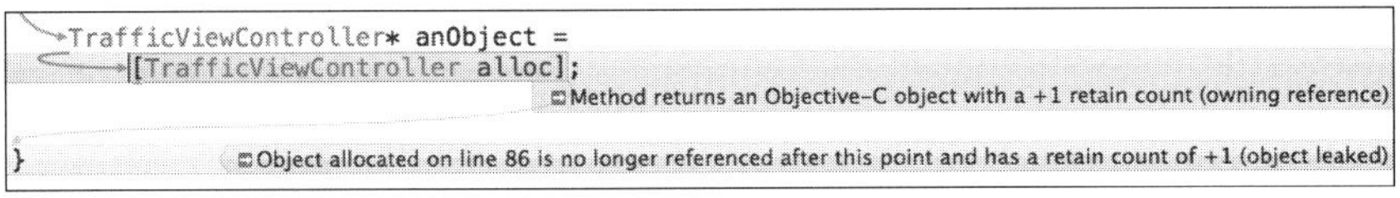

Figure 10-14:
The expanded Static Analyzer warning.

First we get the warning:

```
Method returns and Objective-C object with a +1 retain
count (owning reference)
```

Then in the next line, the icon says

```
Object allocated on line 86 is no longer referenced after
          this point and
has a retain count of +1 (object leaked)
```

Notice that the results refer to line numbers. That's why we explain how to turn on line numbers in Xcode in Chapter 3.

As we mention earlier, memory management is a big deal on the iPhone. Before you attempt to get your game into the App Store, or even run it on anyone's iPhone, make sure it delivers the promised features and game play, and also avoids the unintentional misuse of iPhone resources. Keep in mind that the iPhone, as cool as it may very well be, is nevertheless somewhat resource-constrained when it comes to memory usage and battery life. Such restraints can have a direct effect on what you can (and can't) do in your application.

Finally, before you continue on with the rest of the project, don't forget to remove the crashing bug you introduced earlier in the chapter!

Just because the iPad looks like a bigger iPhone doesn't mean it has any additional resources. The iPad actually has exactly the same amount of memory as the iPhone 3GS — the iPhone 4 actually has more memory than the iPad!

Chapter 11

Keeping Score in Your Game

In This Chapter

▶ Saving, storing, and working with scores

▶ Working with chroot jails

▶ Keeping score with TrafficController

▶ Displaying high scores

A determined player dropping coins into an arcade machine in an endless quest for the perfect high score is one of the classic images in video games. Although the iPhone and the iPad don't have built-in coin-collection slots (not yet, anyway), there's good reason to include a high-scores system in a game.

One of the best ways to reward a player for playing your game is to give her a solid number that represents how well she did while playing your game. If you give people something they can point to that demonstrates how skilled they are, they're more likely to come back to try and beat that.

Scores suit this purpose very well. Keep track of the player's score over the game (or over many games), and you've given her a reason to come back and try to beat the score.

Score-Keeping in Traffic

When you consider what elements of the game to make into a scoring system, look at the individual things that the player is rewarded for in-game. In other words, think about the small triumphs that the player earns while playing and then turn those into a numeric value. These small triumphs are dubbed the *smallest unit of victory,* or you may hear them referred to as *victory atoms* — it sounds like something out of a 1960s sci-fi movie.

Achievements and other "scores"

A numeric score has been the traditional way of tracking how well the player does. However, a numeric score isn't the only way that the player can be given an indicator of how well he's doing. In the past ten years, in-game achievements have been an increasingly popular form of rewarding players. *Achievements* are a complex topic and come in many forms, but the core idea behind them is that the game awards a trophy for achieving a goal within the game. Usually, these goals aren't directly related to the content of the game itself; that is, earning an achievement doesn't reward the player in-game. Rather, the goals are often about demonstrations of a skill that don't necessarily translate into something the game would reward the player for.

Some of the best examples of achievements in games can be seen in Valve Software's *Team Fortress 2*. These achievements are a challenge, but they don't earn the player anything — they're simply fun to have and encourage game play. Some of the best achievements in *Team Fortress 2* include the Rasputin (awarded to those who "in a single life, get shot, burned, bludgeoned, and receive explosive damage") and the Communist Mani-Fisto (for those who "kill an enemy with a critical punch"). The descriptions are funny, the achievements are a challenge to get, and the whole thing is worth bragging about to your friends.

Achievements are often tied in to a publicly viewable profile, which allows users to show off to their friends. This makes achievements a good replacement for high scores in games where points aren't as applicable.

So, what are the individual victories in the *Traffic* game? If you were making a shooter game and the player's goal was to destroy spaceships, the smallest unit of victory would be each spaceship destroyed. However, *Traffic* is a game about getting cars into the right slots and earning more time to play the game. Therefore, the smallest unit of victory in *Traffic* is when a car goes down the right lane.

One simple way of handling scoring would be to give points every time the player succeeds in diverting a car to the correct lane. You could give points when a car goes into the correct lane and show a running tally.

That may be an appealing idea, but here's a better one. You already show a numeric figure during game play — the amount of time the player has remaining! You don't need to show more than one number onscreen if you can avoid it; plus, you'd have to show the numbers close together, which could confuse the player. The solution is to take that existing number — the time remaining — and turn it into a score.

You can judge a player's level of achievement based on how long he lasts in the game. The game gets harder and harder as time goes on, and it gets more and more difficult to keep from crashing. This means that you have a score — how long the player lasts.

Using this value for your score means that you don't have to display any other information onscreen, which is a huge bonus for a fast-paced game — the less the player gets distracted with, the better.

Storing not just the *best* score but *several* best scores is often the most effective thing to do. Although beating the best score is a challenge, beating your second-best score is easier to do, and is almost as rewarding. Game design is all about finding ways to reward your players, so you want to give your players as many ways to be rewarded as possible.

With this in mind, we take a look at how you're going to save your high scores.

Saving Scores

After you decide what your score is going to be, figure out how you can actually store the score to be accessed. **Remember:** High scores need to stay around until the player manages to beat them, so it's important to store these scores where they're going to persist. You don't want the scores to be lost when the user quits the game.

The two ways to store information on an iOS device are in *NSUserDefaults* (the preferences system) or by writing a file to the file system. NSUserDefaults is easier to use from a coding point of view, but it's better suited for storing individual values and getting them back later. This works well if you store only one score value, but you're scoring the top scores, plural. Rule out using NSUserDefaults for the scoring system in this case, and use the file system.

Storing files in chroot jails

"So, what are you in for?"

You may not realize it, but all iOS applications are in jail. Specifically, every application exists in a *chroot jail,* or a section of the file system. (See the nearby sidebar "Chroot jails" for more information on these mythical constructs.) Chroot jail means that an application can see only the folders and files that the iOS allows it to. This keeps applications from interfering with one another and from accessing information that they shouldn't.

Apps have full access to their jail and can read and write to their heart's content. The *jail* is where applications can store documents, files, and settings. Every application's jail is backed up by iTunes when the user syncs her iPhone, iPod touch, or iPad. Therefore, if you ever lose your device, you can restore your backup to a new device without losing any data.

Where your application exists in iOS contains several important directories, and they all have different uses. These are also the locations where you can potentially store the information about high scores:

✔ **Documents:** This is the directory in which Apple recommends you store files and data that should be backed up regularly. If you wrote a system for saving and loading the game's state, you'd store the save-game files here. This folder is backed up by iTunes.

Documents is the best place to put the information because the contents are backed up by iTunes and the files won't be purged by the system.

✔ **Library/Preferences:** This is the directory that stores the preferences you save through NSUserDefaults.

Don't directly touch the files that are stored here. Instead, use NSUserDefaults to access the data that is kept in the Library/Preferences folder. This folder is also backed up by iTunes.

✔ **Library/Caches:** This is the directory that stores support files that you want to last after the application quits but don't necessarily have to be backed up.

This is often useful for images downloaded from the Internet — you *could* download them again when you want the user to see them, but it's a lot faster just to store them in this folder. This folder is *not* backed up by iTunes when you sync the device, so don't put any files in here that your application can't easily replace.

✔ **tmp:** This directory is your application's scratchpad for temporary files that you use during your application's operation.

You should always delete files from this folder that you aren't using, to avoid wasting space on the user's device; additionally, the system might delete files from this folder when your application isn't running. This means that your application can't guarantee that files that are put in this folder will be around the next time it goes to open them. This folder is also *not* backed up by iTunes when you sync the device.

Chroot jails

Why is the section of the file system that applications live in called a chroot jail? You have to go back to the old UNIX file system, which the iOS adopted, to find out. UNIX organizes its files in one big system; all directories and files are in the / folder — the *root* of the file system.

UNIX was designed for multiple users accessing the system at the same time, and a system needed to be developed that would keep users from getting in the way of others. The *chroot* system works by *ch*anging the *root* of an application — meaning that the application can't get any files that it shouldn't.

For example, say you have a program that needs only to deal with files in a certain folder — /Applications/MyApp/ImportantStuff/ — and nowhere else. You *could* set up a system that uses UNIX permissions that allow the program to access only its designated folder, but a simpler and more elegant solution would be to simply put it in a chroot jail, rooted at /Applications/MyApp/ImportantStuff. For the program, its designated folder is now / — it

can't get any files above that level because to the program, they don't exist.

Repeat this process for every application that you want to run on your device without letting them get in each other's way, and you have the same system as iOS. This system has a bunch of security benefits — for instance, it's practically impossible to write a virus for iOS because the only files that the virus application has access to are its own files. This also means that you can't write a malicious application that reads the user's e-mail and uploads it to the Internet because the user's e-mail is stored outside the chroot jail.

This process can also get annoying: It makes communication among applications tricky because you can't share files among them. Is chroot jail a good solution? Well, it's certainly the safest solution, and as you've seen from the iPhone's popularity, it doesn't appear to get in the way of the platform's success. You be the judge!

File formats

After you decide where to put the information, consider what format the information will be in. What you save to disk is just a collection of numbers. These numbers are then stored in descending order (so that the biggest number — in this case, the longest time — appears first in the list).

To store this in memory, use an NSArray object that contains NSNumber objects. *NSNumber* is a class that allows you to store a number in an object, rather than as a plain, old `int`. Storing the data as an object means you can use the data in other classes that expect to deal with objects, such as arrays, dictionaries, and other useful tools. Each NSNumber object would store the time that the player lasts, and the NSArray would store each number in sorted order. Sounds perfect!

But what about saving to disk? Well, NSArray (along with many other useful classes) can write itself to disk! As long as the NSArray contains objects of only certain classes — these classes, specifically NSString, NSNumber, NSData, NSDictionary, and NSArray — it can be written out to a file in a single method call and read back in just as easily.

This method is `writeToFile:atomically:`, and it takes as its parameters:

- An **NSString object** that contains the path that you want the file written to

- A **Boolean value** that indicates whether you want the file to be guaranteed to be written entirely or not at all

The `writeToFile:atomically:` method returns YES if the file was written successfully and NO if the file failed to be written (or if the NSArray contains anything that can't be written quickly to disk with this technique).

The strategy for working with the high scores is now clear. Here's how the process will work:

1. When the application starts, it reads the high scores file into an NSArray, which it keeps in memory.

2. When the user finishes a game, his score is added to the array, which is then resorted so that the top score appears at the start of the array and the lowest score appears at the bottom.

3. When the application terminates, the high scores list (stored as an array) is written to disk.

Storing the Scores

While the game runs, store the high score list as an NSArray containing NSNumber object, which is managed by the app delegate (the object that serves as the manager of the entire application). In this example, use NSMutableArray for your array class because you're going to add more scores to it at run-time.

NSMutableArray is a subclass of NSArray. Normally, NSArray objects can't be modified after they're created: You can only look at the contents of the array and you can't add, remove, or replace any objects. This allows the internal implementation of the array to work a little faster, because it knows that the order of objects will never change. NSMutableArray, on the other hand, *does* allow adding, removing, and replacing objects at the cost of a little bit of efficiency. However, because you're changing the scores list while the game is played, you need to use the mutable version. In any case, this won't cause any performance issues, because you rarely have to use the array.

Creating the scores list

Creating the scores list is pretty simple; add the property to the app delegate. Listing 11-1 shows what TrafficAppDelegate.h looks like after you're done.

Listing 11-1:   TrafficAppDelegate.h

```
#import <AVFoundation/AVFoundation.h>

@interface TrafficAppDelegate : NSObject
           <UIApplicationDelegate> {
   UIWindow *window;
   UINavigationController *navigationController;

   NSMutableArray* scoresList;
}

@property (nonatomic, retain) IBOutlet UIWindow *window;
@property (nonatomic, retain) IBOutlet
           UINavigationController *navigationController;

@property (nonatomic, retain) NSMutableArray* scoresList;

@end
```

Add an NSMutableArray property dubbed scoresList to TrafficAppDelegate (see the bold code in Listing 11-1).

Don't forget to synthesize the scoresList property in the implementation of TrafficAppDelegate as well by adding the appropriate @synthesize directive at the top of TrafficAppDelegate.m.

Loading the scores list

Loading the scores list happens in a couple stages. First, you need to work out the path for where you keep the file. Second, you need to actually load the file from the file system and use the contents.

You also need to watch out for the situation where you can't read in the file. This happens if the file is corrupt or doesn't exist — and the file won't exist the first time the application is launched. If the file can't be read for any reason, the code you'll write shortly will create an empty array.

Add the bolded code in Listing 11-2 to the `applicationDidFinishLaunching:` method in TrafficAppDelegate. This code asks the system for the string representing the path for the Document directory, and then builds a path to the scores file by appending "`scores.plist`" to the end of the string. The code then attempts to read in the scores from the file at that path; if it can't, it makes an empty mutable array. In both cases, the code retains the array that it ends up with.

Listing 11-2:   TrafficAppDelegate.m

```
- (void)applicationDidFinishLaunching:(UIApplication *)
          application {

  [window addSubview:[navigationController view]];
  [window makeKeyAndVisible];

  NSArray *paths = NSSearchPathForDirectoriesInDomains
          (NSDocumentDirectory, NSUserDomainMask, YES);
  NSString *documentsDirectory = [paths objectAtIndex:0];

  NSString* scoresListPath = [documentsDirectory
          stringByAppendingPathComponent:
          @"scores.plist"];

  scoresList = [[NSMutableArray arrayWithContentsOfFile:
          scoresListPath] retain];

  if (scoresList == nil) {
    scoresList = [[NSMutableArray array] retain];
  }
}
```

Working with Scores

The user's score is tracked through the game, but nothing particularly interesting happens to it until the game ends. When the game ends, the user's score needs to be submitted to the high scores list. This means that the object in charge of the game — the TrafficController — lets the app delegate know that a new score exists. You also need to set up the TrafficController class to keep track of the total accumulated time that the game has been played for.

Adding scores to the list

You're storing scores as NSNumber objects inside an NSMutableArray. To use the NSMutableArray class, simply tell it to insert new objects, and it keeps them around for you.

However, your high scores list has another requirement — you need to show the top scores at the top of the list. This means that you need to store the scores in a sorted order so that the best scores are at the start of the list, followed by the second-best score, and so on. The advantage of storing the scores like this is that you can simply get the first four items in the array and display them: this technique is fast to code and even faster to run.

To sort an array of NSNumber objects, the array needs to compare them all against each other to figure out the order. Luckily, all NSNumber objects respond to the `compare:` message; to sort the array, you just tell the array to sort itself by sending the `compare:` message to all objects.

When writing the high scores to disk, you need to do something very similar to what you did when you loaded the scores: Figure out where you need to store the file and then tell the array to write itself to that location.

Here you need to add a single method, `addHighScore:`, that takes a score, adds it to the scores list, re-sorts the list, and then saves the list to disk. Follow these steps to do so:

1. **Add the method declaration for `addHighScore:` to TrafficAppDelegate.h.**

   To do so, add the following code to the interface for TrafficAppDelegate. This code tells the rest of the application that the TrafficAppDelegate has a method for adding a new high score:

   ```
   -(void)addHighScore:(float)score;
   ```

2. **Add the method definition for `addHighScore:` to TrafficAppDelegate.m.**

   To do so, add the method in Listing 11-3 to TrafficAppDelegate.m. This new method takes the new high score, puts it in a new NSNumber object, and inserts it into the array. The method then tells the array to re-sort itself, to keep the highest scores toward the front of the array.

Listing 11-3: TrafficAppDelegate.m

```
- (void)addHighScore:(float)score {
    [scoresList addObject:[NSNumber
            numberWithFloat:score]];

    [scoresList sortUsingSelector:@selector(compare:)];
    NSString* scoresListPath = [documentsDirectory string
            ByAppendingPathComponent:@"scores.plist"];
        scoresList = [[NSMutableArray arrayWithContents
            OfFile:scoresListPath] retain];
    [scoresList writeToFile:scoresListPath
            atomically:YES];
}
```

After you make your score-keeping system capable of adding new high scores, keeping them in order, and saving them to disk (by writing them to the file), make the rest of the code add new high scores to this system.

To do this, make the TrafficController keep track of the user's score during the game and then make the TrafficController send a high score to the TrafficAppDelegate when the game ends.

Keeping score in TrafficController

If you've followed along so far, TrafficController only keeps the amount of time the player has left, which constantly decreases and increases over time. However, you need to store the amount of time the player has been playing. For this, you need to add a second variable that never goes down. Follow these steps to do just that:

1. **Add the CGFloat variable, dubbed timeTotal, to TrafficController.**

   Because this variable never needs to be accessed from outside the class, TrafficController instead tells TrafficAppDelegate about new scores at the end of every game; the variable doesn't need to be a property. Add the variable to the class's interface (the new line is bolded in the code below).

   See the following code to see how TrafficController.h looks after this change is made:

   ```
   #import <Foundation/Foundation.h>
   #import "Vehicle.h"
   #import "Lane.h"

   @class TrafficViewController;
   ```

```
@interface TrafficController : NSObject {
        NSTimer* gameTimer;
        NSTimer* countdownTimer;

        CGFloat timeTotal;
        CGFloat timeRemaining;
        NSMutableArray* vehicles;
        NSMutableArray* vehiclesToDestroy;
        NSMutableArray* lanes;

        TrafficViewController* viewController;

        BOOL paused;

}

@property (nonatomic,retain) IBOutlet
       TrafficViewController* viewController;
@property (assign) BOOL paused;

- (void)startGame;
- (void)stopGame;
- (void)registerVehicle:(Vehicle*)vehicle;
- (void)registerLane:(Lane*)lane;
- (void) startCarFromLane:(Lane*)starter;
- (void)vehicleReachedEndOfRoad:(Vehicle*)v;
- (void)togglePause;
- (Lane*)laneAtPoint:(CGPoint)point;
- (void)vehicleBeganMovement;
- (void) vehicle:(Vehicle*) aVehicle
        collidedWithVehicle: (Vehicle*) otherVehicle;

@end
```

2. **Add the following code to the method `decrementTime:` in TrafficController.m to update the total time while the game is played.**

When time is taken away from the player, you also add onto their total time spent playing the game by the same amount:

```
- (void)decrementTime:(NSTimer*)timer {
  timeRemaining -= 0.1;
  timeTotal += 0.1;

  [viewController setTimeRemaining:timeRemaining];

  if (timeRemaining < 0) {
    // game over!
    if (!paused)
      [self togglePause];
```

```
        [viewController displayGameOver];
    }
}
```

3. Add code to TrafficController that adds a new high score when the game ends, no matter what the reason is.

Whenever the game ends, stopGame is called. To make this method add a new score, add the following code to the end of the stopGame method in TrafficController.m. This code gets a reference to the app delegate and then tells it to add the current score to the scores list:

```
- (void)stopGame {
  [gameTimer invalidate];

  for (Lane* l in lanes) {
    [l stop];
  }

  [lanes removeAllObjects];
  [vehicles removeAllObjects];

  // update the high scores
  TrafficAppDelegate* delegate = [[UIApplication
      sharedApplication] delegate];
  [delegate addHighScore:timeTotal];
}
```

Hang in there; you're almost done! Your code now loads high scores, adds scores when the game ends, and stores the high scores file on the disk when the app quits. You have one last thing to do: Show the scores to the user!

Displaying the High Scores List

Time to build the high scores list in Interface Builder and then connect the list to its data when ready. The high scores will display on a separate screen. This is mostly because they take up a large amount of space to be viewed easily, and you want to give them focus when the user looks at them.

Therefore, you need to create a new UIViewController subclass to manage the screen.

Creating the scores screen

Follow these steps to build the screen and then add the button on the main menu that displays the screen:

1. **Create a new UIViewController subclass and call it StatsViewController.**

   Do this by pressing ⌘+N, and selecting UIViewController Subclass from the grid that appears. Click Next, and name the file StatsViewController.m when prompted.

2. **Open StatsViewController.xib in Interface Builder and then set up the view controller.**

   To set up the view controller:

   a. Drag in the menu's background image from the Library, as well as a Back button.

   b. Set the type of the button to Custom and its image to Back.png.

   You can find this image in the resources you download in Chapter 1.

3. **Drag in four UIImageView controls from the Library, with the image set to ScoreBackground.png.**

   These form the background for each of the four top scores you set.

4. **Drag in four UILabel controls from the Library, and put them in the center of each of the row images.**

5. **Make the labels light yellow and center the text.**

Once you're done with these steps, the high score screen is ready for viewing. You can see the result in Figure 11-1. The next step is to make the controls you just added show the scores to the player.

Making scores visible to the player

After the screen is set up, make the score displays that you added in the preceding section actually show the scores to the player! To do this, add instance variables for each of the labels to StatsViewController so that it knows where to put the scores. These variables also need to be IBOutlets so that Interface Builder knows that they can be connected to the objects you just created in your interface.

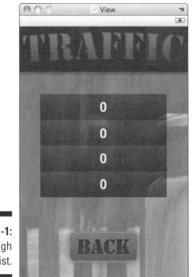

Figure 11-1:
The high
scores list.

Follow these steps to make StatsViewController get the top four scores from the app delegate and display them:

1. **Add four IBOutlets for UILabels in the interface for StatsViewController to StatsViewController.h and call them score1, score2, and so on.**

   For a refresher on creating and working with IBOutlets, take a look at Chapter 5, where you build the majority of the game's interface.

   To return to the game, the high scores screen needs a way to go back to the main screen. To do this, you need to add a method that is called when the Back button is pressed.

2. **Add a new IBAction method dubbed goBack:.**

   When you're done, StatsViewController.h looks like this:

   ```
   #import <UIKit/UIKit.h>

   @interface StatsViewController : UIViewController {
     UILabel* score1;
     UILabel* score2;
     UILabel* score3;
     UILabel* score4;
   }
   ```

```
@property (nonatomic, retain) IBOutlet UILabel*
        score1;
@property (nonatomic, retain) IBOutlet UILabel*
        score2;
@property (nonatomic, retain) IBOutlet UILabel*
        score3;
@property (nonatomic, retain) IBOutlet UILabel*
        score4;

- (IBAction) goBack:(id)sender;

@end
```

3. **In Interface Builder, connect the first label to score1, the second label to score2, and so forth.**

   To make the labels and the button do something, they need to be connected to the StatsViewController.

   Connect them in the right order, or your scores appear out of order. That would confuse the player, and a confused player is a player who's not coming back to play your game.

4. **Connect the Back button to the goBack: action.**

5. **Add code to StatsViewController that loads the scores and displays them.**

   Replace the code in StatsViewController.m with the following code. This code includes two methods: goBack: and viewWillAppear:.

   The goBack: method is run when the user taps the Back button. This method instructs the navigation controller that manages the high scores screen to go back to the previous screen, without doing any animation.

   The second method that's added is viewWillAppear:. This code is run when the view is about to appear onscreen: the code retrieves the already sorted list of scores from the app delegate and displays the first four in the UILabels that you just set up.

   Before displaying onscreen, the scores are formatted so that they appear with one decimal point, just like they do in-game:

```
#import "StatsViewController.h"
#import "TrafficAppDelegate.h"

@implementation StatsViewController

@synthesize score1, score2, score3, score4;

- (IBAction) goBack:(id)sender {
```

```
    [self.navigationController
        popViewControllerAnimated:NO];
}

- (void)viewWillAppear:(BOOL)animated {
    TrafficAppDelegate* delegate;
    delegate = (TrafficAppDelegate*)[[UIApplication
        sharedApplication] delegate];

    NSArray* scores = [delegate scoresList];

    score1.text = [NSString stringWithFormat:@"%.1f",
        [[scores objectAtIndex:0] floatValue]];
    score2.text = [NSString stringWithFormat:@"%.1f",
        [[scores objectAtIndex:1] floatValue]];
    score3.text = [NSString stringWithFormat:@"%.1f",
        [[scores objectAtIndex:2] floatValue]];
    score4.text = [NSString stringWithFormat:@"%.1f",
        [[scores objectAtIndex:3] floatValue]];
}

@end
```

You're done! Your game now has a fully-functioning high scores system. Play the game, set a high score, and go look at it displayed in the list. Then, try to beat your score.

Chapter 12

Storing User Preferences

*1*n this chapter, you discover how to present and work with settings in your application, how to store those settings so that your device remembers them, and how to make the controls of your application interact with the settings.

Face it: Users love having control over their software. The ability to tweak a setting, however minor, gives them the ability to make the software work for them, rather than forcing them to work along the preset guidelines of their computer. Additionally, you'll remember that one of the key principles of a fun game is that a good game gives players control. This applies to the non-game parts of the applications you build, too!

The iOS provides you with a simple and easy-to-use system, dubbed *NSUserDefaults,* for working with application settings. We explore this system in great detail throughout this chapter.

Designing Settings

Before you can add user settings to your application, it's very important to take a moment and think about exactly what settings you want to expose to the user.

As with all Apple products, the iPhone and iPad's philosophy of application design is about making the right assumptions about what the user wants. Ideally, there should be very few areas of your application where you can't make a definite assumption that works for at least four fifths of your users. For these areas where you *can't* make an assumption, provide a means to let the user decide what he wants.

The idea is that too many settings are an indication of poor application design. The concept applies to games as well; in fact, it's probably even more applicable than it is for other applications! (Would you want to play a game if you had to set up all the rules? Of course not — that's the job of the game designer, not the user!)

Figuring out what settings to add

Here are the two kinds of settings:

- ✔ Settings that allow the user to provide important information necessary to run the application (such as usernames and passwords)
- ✔ Settings in which the user has a few predefined options to choose from

In the context of games, there are only a few areas where you don't know what the user wants or where you actually need the user to provide information. These are

- ✔ **Sound:** The user might want music, or he might not. Additionally, the user might (or might not) want sound effects. Users need the ability to control these factors.
- ✔ **Logging in to social networks:** For instance, how to add the ability to post updates to Facebook to the application. For this to work, you need information from the user about how to access her social network. We cover these settings in Chapter 16.

Because this game doesn't have much in the way of customizable elements in the way that the game is played, you don't need to include other settings. However, a more complex game might expose other options such as difficulty, car color, and the background image used in the game.

Giving the user control (s)

After you identify the settings that you need to expose user control, you need to consider how you're going to let the user actually change them.

The iOS has a number of useful controls, all designed for different purposes. The *switch* control, as shown in Figure 12-1, is designed for a Yes/No setting. You've probably seen this control all over your iPhone.

Figure 12-1:
The switch
control.

Switches are simple to use. All you need to do is add the switches to your interface in Interface Builder and then connect them to the object that needs to know about what state the object is in (see "Building Custom Settings Interfaces," later in this chapter, where we discuss how to add and set up these controls). When the switch changes from Yes to No (or vice versa), your object receives a message, giving it the opportunity to record the changed setting.

The application records settings with a mechanism called NSUserDefaults; read on to find out more.

Getting Familiar with NSUserDefaults

NSUserDefaults is a simple system for storing user preferences. At the highest level, you can do three useful preference information tasks with it:

- ✔ Store data from your app in the preferences database.
- ✔ Read data out of the preferences database and into your app.
- ✔ Provide default values for when the user hasn't yet set any preferences.

NSUserDefaults also lets you store *default objects.* These can be any of the following:

- ✔ Integers, floating point numbers, and Boolean values
- ✔ Strings, URLs, dates, and data objects
- ✔ NSArrays and NSDictionaries, as long as they contain only default objects

This limitation on the kinds of data you can store in the preferences database means that it's light, simple, and easy to use. Each setting that you store in the preferences database is mapped to a string. This means that you can ask the database for the Should Play Background Music setting, for example; you don't need to invent complex codes to refer to your settings.

The strings used to name each setting are *keys*. The data attached to these keys are *values*.

One thing to keep in mind is that NSUserDefaults is one of the oldest pieces of code that exists in iOS. It dates back to the old days of NeXT Computer, the company that Steve Jobs founded when he left Apple in 1985 (he later returned to Apple). Consequently, the application programming interface (API) for NSUserDefaults has a few eccentricities:

- ✓ **The word default is used everywhere.** When talking about NSUserDefaults, *default* means a setting, but it can also mean the setting value used when the user hasn't changed the setting. Additionally, the object that represents the defaults database is called the *defaults object*.

- ✓ **NSUserDefaults is a special class; there's only one instance of it at any one time.** You get access to this instance by asking NSUserDefaults for the standardUserDefaults like so:

```
NSUserDefaults* defaults = [NSUserDefaults standardUserDefaults];
```

For the defaults database to contain some default values, you actually need to provide these values to the database before you load settings from it.

Treat NSUserDefaults like this:

1. **Call [NSUserDefaults standardUserDefaults] to get the standard user defaults object (which is the object that represents the preferences database).**

2. **Tell the defaults object about what all the default settings are.**

   The *default* settings are the settings that the application has when you first launch it. You provide the default settings by giving the defaults object an NSDictionary that contains the initial settings information.

3. **When the user changes a setting, tell the defaults object about it.**

   You do this by sending a new value to the defaults object.

   The defaults object records this new value and keeps it around, even after your application exits.

4. **When you need to know what the value is for any given setting, ask the defaults object.**

   You do this by sending the defaults object a request for the current value of the setting you're interested in.

- If you're asking for a setting that the user has changed, the defaults object gives you the value it provided in Step 3.

- If the user *hasn't* changed that setting, the defaults object gives you the value that you provided in Step 2.

Pretty straightforward, huh?

Providing default values

After getting a reference to the NSUserDefaults object, here's how you provide the default settings. The default settings need to be contained in an NSDictionary object, in which you store the keys and values of the default settings. The dictionary looks like this when you're finished constructing it:

```
NSDictionary defaultsDictionary = [NSDictionary
        dictionaryWithObjectsAndKeys: @"first default
        value", @"name of first setting", @"second
        default value", "name of second setting", nil];
```

Here are a few things to look out for when you use this method to construct a dictionary:

- **Provide the keys and values in a back-to-front order.** For each key-value combination in the dictionary, provide the value first and *then* the key.

- **Values need to be Objective-C objects.** If you need to provide something, such as a number, wrap it in an NSNumber object. We talk about how to do this after this bullet list.

- **The list of values and keys needs to end with a `nil` value.** The reason you end the list with `nil` is because this last value indicates that the list has ended — it's a somewhat odd little quirk of Objective-C.

Values, such as BOOLs (Objective-C's word for Boolean true-or-false values), integers, and floats, need to be stored in objects. The object designed for this purpose is NSNumber, and it's a cinch to use. To store a BOOL value in an NSNumber, all you need to do is this:

```
NSNumber myNumber = [NSNumber numberWithBool:YES];
```

"Should Play Music" and "Should Play Sound Effects" are the settings that the application needs to deal with at this point. That means that the default values dictionary for the *Traffic* game needs to look like this:

```
[defaults registerDefaults:[NSDictionary
        dictionaryWithObjectsAndKeys: [NSNumber
        numberWithBool:TRUE], @"shouldPlayMusic",
        [NSNumber numberWithBool:TRUE],
        @"shouldPlaySFX", nil]];
```

This code is how you do the first two steps of using the preferences database —
you got access to the setting database and provided some initial values.

Once you've given the preferences database this dictionary, your app has
some default settings for the "shouldPlayMusic" and "shouldPlaySFX" values.
Time to use them.

Reading settings

To get access to the settings stored in the defaults database, all you need to
do is ask for them:

✔ To get a BOOL value out of the database (don't add this code to your
  project — these are just examples):

```
BOOL myBool = [defaults boolForKey:@"bool setting name"];
```

✔ To get out an int or float is very similar:

```
int myInt = [defaults integerForKey:@"int setting name"];
float myFloat = [defaults floatForKey:@"float setting name"];
```

✔ To get out an Objective-C object is just the same:

```
NSString* myString = [defaults objectForKey:"object setting name"];
```

The objectForKey: method can be used for getting any valid
Objective-C object from the defaults database, not just NSStrings.

Simple!

Writing settings

Putting settings into the database is easy and can be done at any point in the
application. Values you put in the database stay around forever, until they're
changed later. Here's how you put a BOOL value in the preferences database.

```
[defaults setBool:YES forKey:@"bool setting name"];
```

That's all you need to do to! The next time you ask for the setting, you get the updated value. To store a value for a different setting, just change the key string that you give the method in the second parameter.

Building Custom Settings Interfaces

To present settings to the user and let her manipulate them, you need to have some sort of onscreen control for each setting that the user can work with.

Using controls

So far in *Traffic*, the only things you've worked with have been images, buttons, labels, or custom views that you have complete control over (that is, the view objects that represent the cars). But that's not all that exists in the Cocoa Touch universe!

The list of controls in the Interface Builder library includes things like sliders, text fields, segmented controls, and all manner of interesting and fun things that your user can play with!

The way that controls notify other objects about important events (such as button taps and switches changing state) is through a variation on the delegate pattern (which we discussed in Chapter 4), called the Target-Action pattern. In this pattern, the control sends an object a message when an event occurs, and it's up to you to control what the object is and what message is sent.

Exploring the Target-Action pattern

The *Target-Action* pattern is when an object sends an Objective-C message to another object (the *target*) when the user performs an action, such as tapping or modifying the control.

If you set up the buttons for the main menu in Chapter 5, you were connecting the Touch Up Inside event to an action. This is known as a *sent action* — the control sends the action to a receiving object.

The id, not the ego

The id type is a special type in Objective-C. Simply put, id refers to an object of any type. All Objective-C objects are ids. The difference between id and the class NSObject (which is the superclass of every object in this project) is that NSObject defines a bunch of methods and properties, whereas an id is simply an object.

With an id, you can send it messages but you have no idea what messages it responds to.

id could respond to no messages at all! This makes id a useful type for expressing the idea of having an object where you don't expect to know what class it is.

The id type is used as a placeholder for when you want to deal with objects of any kind rather than objects of a specific class.

Lots of different actions exist:

- ✔ Buttons have actions, such as Touch Up Inside — the user touched the control and lifted his finger while still inside the control (in other words, he tapped the control).
- ✔ Sliders have actions, such as Value Changed — the user dragged her finger over it, changing the value represented by the control.

These actions are sent as simple Objective-C messages.

You've used these kinds of actions in this book, whenever you connected a button to a method. The IBAction methods you've implemented are methods that are called in response to an action.

Running a method in response to a button-press is all well and good, but what about when you need to know about the state of the control that sent a Value Changed action? That's when the (id) sender parameter comes in.

Every IBAction method takes a single parameter dubbed sender, which is an id type.

The sender parameter is the object that sent the message in response to the user event. You can use this parameter to get information about the object that sends messages. Imagine you have an object with the following method:

```
- (IBAction) somethingHappened:(id)sender;
```

Imagine that you have a UISwitch, which lets you choose between a Yes and No value, and you've hooked up the Value Changed event to the somethingHappened: method. Now, when you tap the switch, the somethingHappened: method runs — and sends the UISwitch object as the sender.

To treat the parameter as a UISwitch and send UISwitch-related messages to it, you first need to cast the sender parameter to the UISwitch type. This is pretty simple, and you see it done in the second line of the following method. After that's done, you can get at the switch's value and then do something useful with it. Hooray!

```
-(IBAction) doSomething:(id)sender {
  // cast the sender to UISwitch
  UISwitch* switch = (UISwitch*) sender;

  // get the new value of the switch
  BOOL switchState = switch.on;

  // go and do something useful with switchState!
}
```

Building Settings in Traffic

With all the preceding code and setup that you've done in mind, time to build the settings interface used in the *Traffic* game. To do this, you need to set up the view controller that contains the controls used for manipulating the settings. Then, write the code that responds to changes in those controls.

Adding the variables

To avoid getting a reference to the NSUserDefaults instance in every class, create instance variables in the TrafficAppDelegate class to store the settings. Load the value from NSUserDefaults into these variables when the application starts and store their value back into NSUserDefaults when the application exits.

Follow these steps to make TrafficAppDelegate.h ready to use settings. You can see the finished product in Listing 12-1.

To make the modifications necessary to store the settings:

1. **Add the instance variables for storing the settings.**

2. Make properties for both of the variables you added.

Every @property you declare in a .h file needs to have a corresponding @synthesize (see Chapter 6 on what you need to do to work with properties).

When you're done, TrafficAppDelegate.h looks like Listing 12-1. The bold code marks the new additions.

Listing 12-1:   TrafficAppDelegate.h

```
@interface TrafficAppDelegate : NSObject
           <UIApplicationDelegate> {
  UIWindow *window;
  UINavigationController *navigationController;

  BOOL shouldPlayMusic;
  BOOL shouldPlaySFX;

  NSMutableArray* scoresList;
}

@property (nonatomic, retain) IBOutlet UIWindow *window;
@property (nonatomic, retain) IBOutlet
           UINavigationController *navigationController;
@property (assign) BOOL shouldPlayMusic;
@property (assign) BOOL shouldPlaySFX;

@property (nonatomic, retain) NSMutableArray* scoresList;

-(void)addHighScore:(float)score;

@end
```

Loading the default settings

When the application delegate has somewhere to keep the settings, add the code that loads the settings. Add code to the applicationDidFinishLaunching:withOptions: method, which is sent to the application delegate right after the application finishes launching. (We know! Cocoa Touch is full of surprises.)

In this method, you follow the setup routine that we outline in the "Getting Familiar with NSUserDefaults" section earlier in this chapter: Get a reference to the NSUserDefaults object, provide it with the default settings, and finally read the user's settings.

To load the settings, add the bolded code in Listing 12-2 to the `application DidFinishLaunching:withOptions` method in TrafficAppDelegate.m.

Listing 12-2:   TrafficAppDelegate.m

```
- (void)application:(UIApplication*) application didFinish
         LaunchingWithOptions:(NSDictionary*)options
         {
[window addSubview:[navigationController view]];
[window makeKeyAndVisible];

NSUserDefaults* defaults = [NSUserDefaults
         standardUserDefaults];

[defaults registerDefaults:[NSDictionary
         dictionaryWithObjectsAndKeys: [NSNumber
         numberWithBool:TRUE], @"shouldPlayMusic",
         [NSNumber numberWithBool:TRUE],
         @"shouldPlaySFX", nil]];

self.shouldPlayMusic = [defaults
         boolForKey:@"shouldPlayMusic"];
self.shouldPlaySFX = [defaults
         boolForKey:@"shouldPlaySFX"];

// Load the high scores list
NSArray *paths = NSSearchPathForDirectoriesInDomains
         (NSDocumentDirectory, NSUserDomainMask, YES);
NSString *documentsDirectory = [paths objectAtIndex:0];

NSString* scoresListPath = [documentsDirectory
         stringByAppendingPathComponent:
         @"scores.plist"];

scoresList = [[NSMutableArray arrayWithContentsOfFile:
         scoresListPath] retain];

if (scoresList == nil) {
  scoresList = [[NSMutableArray array] retain];
}

}
```

Saving the settings on exit

After you've added the code in the previous section, the application loads the settings and keeps them around for later use, but you have a problem —

the values of the shouldPlayMusic and shouldPlaySFX variables aren't stored back into the NSUserDefaults.

The way to correct that is by saving the changes when the application is about to exit. Every application, right after the user presses the Home button to leave the application, is given a small amount of time to run in the background before the app is suspended and doesn't run any more code (until the user opens it again.) This is your application's chance to save data and preferences. When the application knows it's going into the background, it sends its delegate the `applicationDidEnterBackground:` message.

When your application delegate receives the `applicationWillTerminate:` message, it doesn't have very much time to clean up before the iOS forcibly quits your application. iOS devices need to feel quick and responsive, and if an app takes a long time to quit, the user gets frustrated with the device as a whole.

This means that you have less than a second to finish, so don't do anything time-intensive, such as talking to the Internet or saving large files. Fortunately, storing preferences is done in a flash and takes next to no time at all.

Add the new method in Listing 12-3 to TrafficAppDelegate.m. When you're done, your application loads settings and saves them back when the application quits!

Listing 12-3: TrafficAppDelegate.m

```
- (void)applicationDidEnterBackground:(UIApplication *)
            application {
  NSUserDefaults* defaults = [NSUserDefaults
            standardUserDefaults];

  [defaults setBool:shouldPlayMusic
            forKey:@"shouldPlayMusic"];
  [defaults setBool:shouldPlaySFX
            forKey:@"shouldPlaySFX"];
}
```

Constructing the view controller

If you've followed along so far, now is the time to create the user interface that allows the user to see the state of the application's settings — and to make changes to them.

You need to create a new screen to hold the controls, which means adding a new view controller. Start by creating the files needed for the view controller and then make the main menu take the user to the new screen. To do so, follow these steps:

1. **Create the view controller files:**

   a. *Choose File⇨New File and then select the UIViewController subclass in the New File dialog box that appears (see Figure 12-2).*

   b. *Make sure that the With XIB for User Interface check box is selected and that both the UITableViewController Subclass and Size View for iPad check boxes are not selected.*

   c. *When prompted to give the file a name, call it* SettingsViewController.

   You add controls to the SettingsViewController shortly; for now, leave it empty.

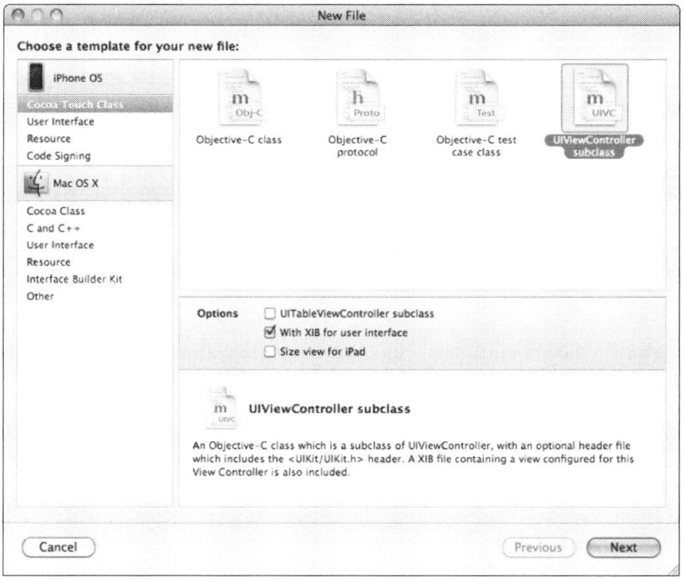

Figure 12-2:
Creating the files.

2. **Add the new method in the following code to MainMenuViewController.m.**

```
-(IBAction) showSettings:(id)sender {
  SettingsViewController* settings =
       [[SettingsViewController alloc]
       initWithNibName:
       @"SettingsViewController" bundle:nil];
  [self.navigationController
       pushViewController:settings animated:NO];
}
```

This method creates a new SettingsViewController and pushes it onto the navigation controller's stack, making it visible to the user.

3. **Import the SettingsViewController.h file at the top of MainMenuView Controller.m.**

To do this, modify MainMenuViewController.m so that it looks like this:

```
#import "MainMenuViewController.h"
#import "TrafficAppDelegate.h"
#import "TrafficViewController.h"
#import "StatsViewController.h"
#import "SettingsViewController.h"

@implementation MainMenuViewController
```

Perfect! Once you've added this code, you'll be able to run the application, tap on the Settings button, and see the settings screen.

After the methods are in place, follow these steps to add a button that triggers this code and displays the new view controller:

1. **Open the MainMenuViewController.xib file in Interface Builder, by double-clicking on the file.**

2. **Connect the Settings button to the `showSettings:` method:**

   a. *Control-drag from the button onto the MainMenuViewController.*

   b. *Select the* `showSettings:` *method from the list that appears.*

   You just connected the button to the method. When the user taps the button, the `showSettings:` method is called.

3. **Save all open files and run the application.**

Building the Settings Interface

If you've followed along so far, add the necessary elements to the SettingsViewController that makes it do what you want it to.

We walk you through the steps in detail, but here's an overview of what you need to do: Add the background image so that the screen fits in visually with the rest of the application, and then add a way to go back to the Main Menu and hook a button to it.

Next, add the actual settings-related elements. Add two UISwitches to the screen and attach them to IBOutlets so that the controller knows which switch is which. (Try saying that ten times quickly.)

When the view controller is about to appear onscreen, ask the application delegate about the state of the two settings. You then tell the two switches to be either on or off, as needed. Finally, add two IBAction methods to the SettingsViewController — one for each switch. Hook up these methods and use them to update the settings stored in the application delegate. Time to get started!

Building the interface

To show a settings screen to the user, start by building up the interface and adding all of the UI elements:

1. **Add the background image:**

   a. *Open SettingsViewController.xib in Interface Builder.*

   b. *Drag out a UIImageView from the Library and into the view controller's view, set it to Background.png (the same image you used in MainMenuViewController), move it, and resize it so that it fills the screen.*

2. **To add the Back button, drag out a UIButton from the Library and place it at the bottom of the screen.**

   Following the same method as the buttons on the Main Menu, use the image Back.png, which is included in the resources you downloaded in Chapter 1.

3. **To add two labels, drag out a pair of UIImageViews from the Library and then set them up to use the Music-Text.png and Sounds-Text.png files.**

   You find these files in the game's resource collection, which you can download by following the instructions in Chapter 1.

4. **To add two switches, drag out a pair of UISwitch controls from the Library and then move them so that they're next to a label.**

   The Settings interface looks like Figure 12-3.

Coding the SettingsViewController Class

When developing the view controller that drives the settings screen, add the code that drives these controls. Start by creating the header file for the SettingsViewController object. You need three methods: one to go back to the main menu, and one each for the two switches.

You also need to create IBOutlet variables for both switches so that you can set them up with the necessary values when the view appears. Take the code in Listing 12-4 and replace the contents of SettingsViewController.h with it.

Figure 12-3:
The Settings interface.

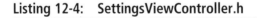

Listing 12-4:   SettingsViewController.h

```
#import <UIKit/UIKit.h>

@interface SettingsViewController : UIViewController {
  UISwitch* musicSwitch;
  UISwitch* sfxSwitch;
}

- (IBAction) changedMusicSetting:(id)sender;
- (IBAction) changedSFXSetting:(id)sender;

@property (nonatomic, retain) IBOutlet UISwitch*
          musicSwitch;
```

```
@property (nonatomic, retain) IBOutlet UISwitch*
        sfxSwitch;

- (IBAction) goBack:(id)sender;

@end
```

Now add the code that drives the interface. Replace the code in SettingsViewController.m with the code in Listing 12-5.

Listing 12-5:   SettingsViewController.m

```
#import "SettingsViewController.h"
#import "TrafficAppDelegate.h"

@implementation SettingsViewController

@synthesize musicSwitch;
@synthesize sfxSwitch;

- (void) viewWillAppear:(BOOL)animated {
  TrafficAppDelegate* delegate;
  delegate = (TrafficAppDelegate*)[[UIApplication
          sharedApplication] delegate];

  musicSwitch.on = delegate.shouldPlayMusic;
  sfxSwitch.on = delegate.shouldPlaySFX;
}

- (IBAction) goBack:(UISwitch*)sender {
  [self.navigationController
          popViewControllerAnimated:NO];
}

- (IBAction) changedMusicSetting:(UISwitch*)sender {
  TrafficAppDelegate* delegate;
  delegate = (TrafficAppDelegate*)[[UIApplication
          sharedApplication] delegate];

  delegate.shouldPlayMusic = sender.on;
}

- (IBAction) changedSFXSetting:(id)sender {
  TrafficAppDelegate* delegate;
  delegate = (TrafficAppDelegate*)[[UIApplication
          sharedApplication] delegate];

  delegate.shouldPlaySFX = sender.on;
}

@end
```

Each of these methods is run in response to an event:

- ✔ **viewWillAppear::** This method is called when the view is just about to appear onscreen, and it's the controller's chance to do any last minute changes to the view. SettingsViewController uses this opportunity to ask the application delegate about the settings and sets the switches' states accordingly.

- ✔ **goBack::** The `goBack:` method is called when the Back button is pressed. This method removes the current view controller from the navigation controller (the one that manages all view controllers in the application), which sends the user back to the main menu.

- ✔ **changedMusicSetting: and changedSFXSetting::** These are very similar methods. All they do is get a reference to the app delegate and then set the settings based on the appropriate switch's state.

Connecting all of the code

To make the settings screen do useful work when the user interacts with it, you need to connect the code to the interface:

1. **To connect the Music switch to the SettingsViewController, Control-drag from the Music switch to the Settings View Controller and then choose the `changedMusicSetting:` method in the menu that pops up.**

2. **To connect the sound switch to the Settings View Controller, Control-drag from the Sound Effects switch to the `changedSFXSetting:` method.**

3. **To connect the Back button to the `goBack:` method, Control-drag from the button onto the SettingsViewController and select the `goBack:` method from the list that appears on the screen.**

4. **Connect the Settings View Controller to the switches.**

   You need to connect the `musicSwitch` and `sfxSwitch` variables to the switches (otherwise, the code in `viewWillAppear:` doesn't work). The reason you need to make two sets of connections for the switches is because one set of connections is for the actions that the switches send, and the second set of connections is to make the class able to talk to the switches and set their values.

   • Control-drag from the Settings View Controller to the Music switch. Choose `musicSwitch` from the Outlets menu that appears.

- Do the same for the Sound Effects switch: Control-drag from the Settings View Controller to the Sound Effects switch, and choose `sfxSwitch` from the Outlets menu that appears.

5. **Run the application, change the settings, quit, and then run the application again.**

   The controls remember their configuration. Hooray!

Chapter 13

Death, Taxes, and iOS Provisioning

*B*enjamin Franklin once said, "In this world nothing can be said to be certain, except death and taxes." We've discovered one other certainty in this earthly vale of tears: Everybody has the same hoops to jump through to get a game 1) onto an iOS device and then 2) into the App Store — and nobody much likes them, but there they are.

So you're working on your game, running it in the Simulator, as happy as a virtual clam, and all of a sudden you think you're ready to get it into the App Store. The first hurdle is getting the app to run on the phone.

Before we take you through that process, an important heads up:

As you've been going through this book, we would expect that you've tried a shortcut here and there. We've been known to do that ourselves. Some of them probably worked, and others didn't. And if they did work, all the more power to you.

But when it comes to both provisioning and getting your app into the store, you have two rules to follow:

▶ Rule 1: There are no shortcuts. You have to do everything *exactly* the way Apple says.

▶ Rule 2: See Rule 1.

For most developers, getting their games to run on the iPhone and iPad during development can be one of the most frustrating things about developing software for the iPhone. The sticking point has to do with a rather technical concept called *code signing*, a rather complicated process designed to ensure the integrity of the code and positively identify the code's originator. Apple requires all iPhone applications to be digitally signed with a signing certificate — one issued by Apple to a registered iPhone developer — before the application can be run on a development system and before they're submitted to Apple for distribution. As we mention earlier, this signature authenticates the identity of the developer of the application and ensures that there have been no changes to the application after it was signed. As to why this is a big deal, here's the short and sweet (and, to our ears, convincing) answer: Code signing is your way of guaranteeing that no bad guys have done anything to your code that can harm the innocent user.

Now, as we said, nobody really likes the process, but it's doable. In this chapter, we're going to start by giving you an overview of how it all works by jumping right to that point where you're getting your application ready to be uploaded to the App Store and then distributed to end users. We realize we're starting at the end of the process, which for all practical purposes begins with getting your application to run on a device during development. We're doing the overview in this order because the hoops you have to jump through to get an application to run on a single iPhone during development are a direct consequence of code signing, and of how Apple manages it through the App Store and on the device. Everything in this chapter applies equally to iPhones, iPads and iPod Touch devices.

After the overview, which will give you some context for the whole process, We'll revert back to the natural order of things and start with getting your application to run on your iPhone during development.

How the Process Works

It's very important to keep clear that there are *two* different processes that you'll have to go through: one for development and one for distribution. Both of these processes produce different, but similarly named certificates and profiles, and you need to pay attention to keep them straight. We start with the *distribution* process — how you get your game to run on *other people's iPhones.* Then we go back and talk about the *development* process — how to get your game running on *your iPhone* during development.

The Distribution process

Before you can build a version of your game that will actually run on your users' iPhones, Apple insists that you have the following:

✔ **A Distribution Certificate:** An electronic document that associates a *digital identity* (which it creates) with other information that identifies you, including a name, e-mail address, or business that you have provided. The Distribution Certificate is placed on your *keychain* — that place on your Mac that securely stores passwords, keys, certificates, and notes for users.

✔ **A Distribution Provisioning Profile:** These profiles are code elements that Xcode builds into your application, creating a kind of "code fingerprint" that acts as a unique *digital signature*.

After you've built your game for distribution, you then send it to Apple for approval and distribution. Apple verifies the signature to be sure that the code came from a registered developer (you) and hasn't been corrupted. Apple then adds its own digital signature to your signed application. The iOS will only run applications that have that digital signature. Doing it this way ensures iPhone owners that the applications they download from iTunes have been written by registered developers and haven't been altered since they were created.

To install your distribution-ready application on a device, you can also create an *Ad Hoc Provisioning Profile,* which allows you to actually have your application used on up to 100 devices.

Although the system for getting apps on other people's iPhones works pretty well, leaving aside the fact that Apple essentially has veto rights on every application that comes its way, there are some significant consequences for developers. In this system, there really is no mechanism for testing your application on the device it's going to run on:

✔ You can't run your game on an actual device until it's been code-signed by Apple, *but* Apple is hardly going to code-sign something that may not be working correctly.

✔ Even if Apple did sign an game that hadn't yet run on an iPhone, that would mean an additional hassle: Every time you recompiled, you'd have to upload the app to the App Store again — *and* have it code-signed again because you had changed it, *and* then download it to your device.

Bit of a Catch-22 here.

The Development process

To deal with this problem, Apple has developed a process in which you can create a *Development Certificate* (as opposed to a Distribution Certificate that we explain in the preceding section) and a *Development Provisioning Profile* (as opposed to a Distribution Provisioning Profile that we also explain in the preceding section). It's easy to get these confused — the key words are Distribution and Development. With these items in hand, you can run your game on a *specific* device.

Remember, this process is required only because of the code-signing requirements of the distribution process.

The Development Provisioning Profile is a collection of your App ID, Apple device UDID (a Unique Device Identifier for each iPhone), and iPhone Development Certificate (belonging to a specific developer). This Profile must be installed on each device on which you want to run your application code. (You find out how that is done later in this chapter.) Devices specified within the Development Provisioning Profile can be used for testing only by developers whose iPhone Development Certificates are included in the Provisioning Profile. A single device can also contain multiple provisioning profiles.

It's important to realize that a development provisioning profile (as opposed to a distribution one) *is tied to a device and a developer.*

Even with your provisioning profile(s) in place, when you compile your program, Xcode will build and sign (create the required signature for) your application *only* if it finds one of those Development Certificates in your keychain. Then, when you install a signed application on your provisioned device, the iOS verifies the signature to make sure that (a) the application was signed and (b) the application has not been altered since it was signed. If the signature is not valid or if you didn't sign the code, the iOS won't let the application run.

This means that each Development Provisioning Profile is also tied to a particular Development Certificate.

And to make sure the message has really gotten across:

> A Development Provisioning Profile is tied to a *specific device* and a *specific Development Certificate.*

> Your application, during development, must be tied to a specific *Development Provisioning Profile* (which is easily changeable).

The process you're about to go through is akin to filling out taxes: You have to follow the rules, or there can be some dire consequences. But if you do follow the rules, everything works out, and you don't have to worry about it again. (Until it's time to develop the next great game, of course.)

While this is definitely not our favorite part of iPhone software development, We've made peace with it, and so should you. Now we'll go back to the natural order of things and start by explaining the process of getting your device ready for development. We're happy to give you an overview of the process, but it will be up to you to go through it step by step on your own. Although Apple documents the steps very well, do keep in mind that you really have to carry them out in exactly the way Apple tells you. There are no shortcuts! But if you do it the way it prescribes, you'll be up and running on a real device very quickly.

With your game up and running, it's time for the next step: getting your creation ready for distribution. (We find that process to be somewhat easier.) Finally, you'll definitely want to find out how to get your game into the App Store. We aim to please, so we spell out those steps as well. After that, all you have to do is sit back and wait for fame and fortune to come your way.

This is the way things looked when we were writing this book. What you see when you go through this process yourself may be slightly different from what you see here. Don't panic. It's because Apple changes things from time to time.

Provisioning Your Device for Development

Until just recently, getting your application to run on the iPhone during development was a really painful process. In fact, we had written a 30-page chapter on it, detailing step after painful step. Then, lo and behold, right when we had put the finishing touches on our *magnum opus,* Apple changed the process and actually made it much easier. In fact, the process is now so easy that there's no real need for us to linger over the details. (Okay, we have some mixed feelings about that — but they're mostly *relief.*)

Here's the drill:

1. **Go to the iPhone Dev Center Web site at**

   ```
   http://developer.apple.com/iphone
   ```

   The Program Portal button appears in the iPhone Developer Program section on the right side of the Web page, as shown in Figure 13-1. (Well, the button appears if you're a Registered Developer. You took care of that, right? If not, read Chapter 3 for more on how to register.)

2. **Click the iPhone Developer Program section's iPhone Provisioning Portal button.**

   The Provisioning Portal screen appears, as shown in Figure 13-2.

Figure 13-1:
The gate-way to the Program Portal.

iPhone Developer Program

iPhone Provisioning Portal ❯

iTunes Connect ❯

Apple Developer Forums ❯

Developer Support Center ❯

3. **If you're a Team Admin or Team Agent, or are enrolled in the Developer Program as an individual, use the Development Provisioning Assistant to create and install a provisioning profile and iPhone development certificate.**

We explain this process in the next section.

You need these certificates to build and install applications on the iPhone. But you knew that.

You've already identified yourself to Apple as one of two types of developers:

✔ If you're enrolled in the Developer Program as an **individual**, you're considered a Team Agent with all the rights and responsibilities.

✔ If you're part of a **company**, you've set up a team already. If not, click the Visit the Member Center Now link in the center of the screen to get more info about setting up a team and who needs to do what when.

This screen changes on a regular basis, so don't be surprised if it looks different when you visit it.

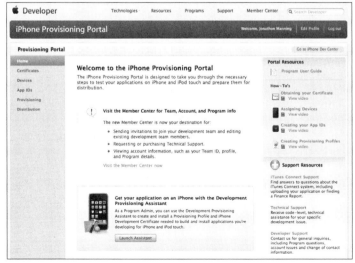

Figure 13-2:
Behold the iPhone Developer Program Portal.

Getting your Development Provisioning Profile and iPhone Development Certificate

The first thing you need to do is generate a Development Certificate. The How-To's video, "Obtaining Your Certificate," in the right column of the Provisioning Portal does a stellar job of explaining how to do that.

The first choice is to click the Launch Assistant button and simply go through the process.

As we mention earlier in the chapter, to run an application you're developing for iOS, you must have a Provisioning Profile installed on the device on which you're running your app, as well as a Development Certificate on your Mac. The whole point of the Development Provisioning Assistant is to guide you through the steps to create and install your Development Provisioning Profile and iPhone Development Certificate.

Development and Distribution stay off each other's turf. The Development Provisioning Assistant creates a *Development* Provisioning Profile, not *Distribution* Provisioning Profile. You have to use the Provisioning section of the Program Portal to create a Distribution Provisioning Profile required for distribution to customers on the App Store. We get to that later in the chapter.

Here's what the Development Provisioning Assistant has you do:

1. **Choose an App ID.**

   An App ID is a unique identifier that is one part of your Development Provisioning Profile.

   Using the Assistant creates an App ID that *cannot* be used with the Apple Push Notification service, nor can it be used with In App Purchase or the Game Center. If you've previously created an App ID that can be used with the Apple Push Notification service or for In App Purchase, you *can't* use the Assistant to create a Development Provisioning Profile. This is not a big deal; you just have to follow the steps the Assistant follows on your own.

2. **Choose an Apple Device.**

   Development provisioning is also about the device, so you have to specify which particular device you're going to use. You do that by providing the Assistant with the device's Unique Device Identifier (UDID), which the Assistant shows you how to locate using Xcode.

3. **Provide your Development Certificate.**

   Because all applications must be signed by a valid certificate before they can run an Apple device, you should have created one at this point. If not, the How-To's video, Obtaining Your Certificate, in the right column of the Developer Portal does a stellar job of explaining how to do that.

4. **Name your Provisioning Profile.**

   A Provisioning Profile pulls together your App ID (Step 1), Apple device UDID (Step 2), and iPhone Development Certificate (Step 3). The assistant steps you though downloading the profile and handing it over to Xcode, which installs it on your device.

You also have a second choice. After you've created your Development Certificate, just go back to programming. Yep, Xcode (well, Xcode version 3.2.3 and newer, to be precise) will actually auto-provision your device for you. It will

1. Create an App ID for you — AppStore ID

2. Create a provisioning profile for your Team Provisioning Profile

3. Automatically download the profile to your device

All you need to do is plug in your device.

To start this process, here's what you do:

1. **Choose Window⇨Organizer from Xcode's main menu to open the Organizer window. Then plug in your device.**

   You can see the result of this action in Figure 13-3.

2. **Click the Use For Development button.**

   Xcode will ask you for your iPhone Provisioning Portal logon (the same Apple ID you use to log in to the iPhone Dev Center). You can see Xcode's polite prompting in Figure 13-4.

3. **Supply the need username and password and then click Log In.**

   You end up in (or back in) your Project window.

4. **In the Project window, choose iPhone Device as the active SDK in the drop-down menu in the upper-left corner, as shown in Figure 13-5.**

   You can then build your application and have it installed on the provisioned device. You can see that in Figure 13-5, we also have Distribution as one of my active configuration options. Not to worry; you'll be there soon.

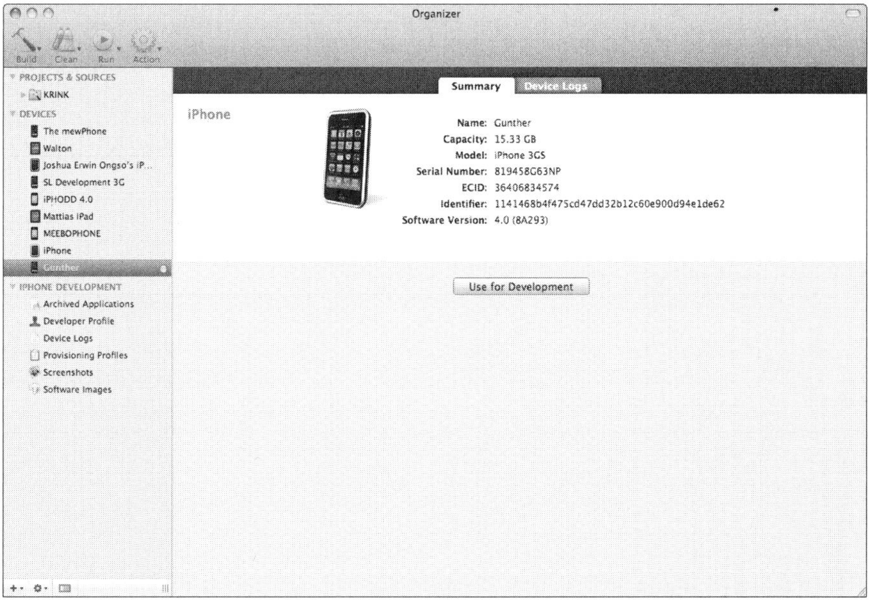

Figure 13-3:
Use this
device for
develop-
ment

Figure 13-4:
Log in,
please.

When you build and run your app, Figure 13-6 shows the (somewhat alarm-
ing) message you get. To get beyond this roadblock, just click Install and Run
and you are there.

Just as with the Development Provisioning Assistant, the App ID that will
be created *cannot* be used with the Apple Push Notification service, In App
Purchase, or Game Center. If you've previously created an App ID already
that can be used with the Apple Push Notification service or for In App
Purchase, you *can't* use the Assistant to create a Development Provisioning
Profile. This is not a big deal; you just have to follow the steps the Assistant
follows on your own.

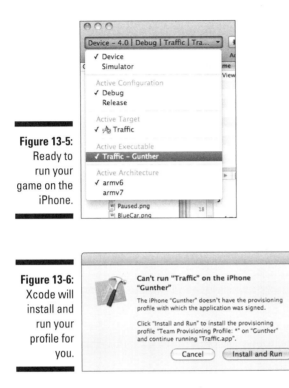

Figure 13-5:
Ready to run your game on the iPhone.

Figure 13-6:
Xcode will install and run your profile for you.

Provisioning Your Application for the App Store

Although there's no dedicated assistant to help you provision your application for the App Store, that process is actually a little easier — which may be there isn't an assistant for it. Start at the provisioning portal (refer to Figure 13-2), but this time select Distribution from the menu on the left side of the page. Something similar to the screen in Figure 13-5 appears — it offers you an overview of the process and links that take you where you need to go when you click them.

You actually jump through some of the very same hoops you did when you provisioned your device for development — except this time you're going after a distribution certificate.

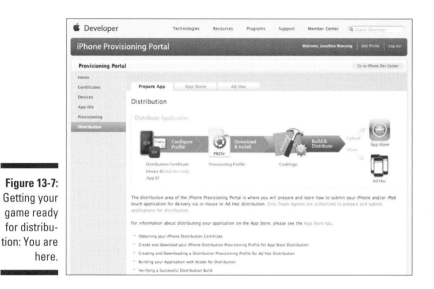

Figure 13-7:
Getting your
game ready
for distribu-
tion: You are
here.

Follow these steps to get your provisioning profile for the App Store:

1. Obtaining your iPhone Distribution Certificate.

   To distribute your iOS game, a Team Agent has to create an iPhone Distribution Certificate. This works much like the Development Certificate, except only the Team Agent (or whoever is enrolled as an Individual developer) can get one. Clicking the Obtaining Your iPhone Distribution Certificate link (shown in Figure 13-7) leads you through the process.

2. Create your iPhone Distribution Provisioning Profile for App Store Distribution.

   To build your game successfully with Xcode for distribution via the App Store, first you have to create and download an App Store Distribution Provisioning Profile — which is (lest we forget) *different* from the Development Provisioning Profiles we talk about in the previous section.

   Clicking the Create and Download Your iPhone Distribution Provisioning Profile link (again, shown in Figure 13-7) leads you through the process.

   Apple will accept an application only when it's built with an App Store Distribution Provisioning Profile.

   If you had Xcode create your development profile for you, you can use the App ID it created here.

3. When you're done creating the Distribution Provisioning Profile, download it and drag it into Xcode on the Dock.

   That loads your Distribution Profile into Xcode, and you're ready to build an app you can distribute for use on actual iPhones.

4. (Optional) You can also create and download a Distribution Provisioning Profile for Ad Hoc Distribution.

   Going the Ad Hoc Distribution route enables you to distribute your game to up to 100 users without going through the App Store. Clicking the Creating and Downloading a Distribution Provisioning Profile for Ad Hoc Distribution link (refer yet again to Figure 13-7) leads you through the process. (Ad Hoc Distribution is beyond the scope of this book, but the iPhone Developer Program Portal has more info about this option.)

5. Build your application with Xcode for distribution.

   After you download the distribution profile, you can build your application for distribution — rather than just building it for testing purposes, which is what you've been doing so far. It's a well-documented process that you start by clicking the Building Your Application with Xcode for Distribution link (shown in Figure 13-7).

6. Verify that the build worked.

   Click the Verifying a Successful Distribution Build link (refer to Figure 13-7) to get the verification process started. In this case, we find there are some things missing in the heretofore well-explained step-by-step documentation, so we'll help you along.

   If you check the handy documentation that's part of the Verifying a Successful Distribution Build link, it tells you to open the Build Log detail view and confirm the presence of the `embedded.mobile provision` file. In Chapter 3, we show you how to keep the Build Results window open, but if you haven't been doing that, choose Build➪Build Results.

   Depending on the way the way the Build Results window is configured, you may see a window showing only the end result of your build, as in Figure 13-8, which shows that, yes, your build was in fact successful. To get the actual log of the process, you have to change Errors & Warnings Only in the drop-down menu in the scope bar to All Messages as we have in Figure 13-9.

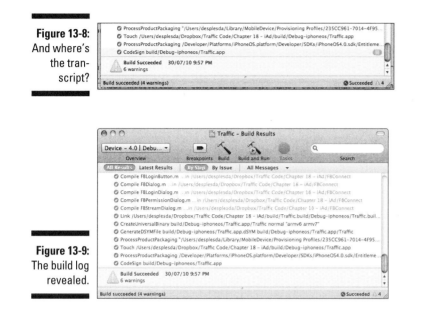

Figure 13-8: And where's the transcript?

Figure 13-9: The build log revealed.

7. At this point, you'd be wise to do a couple of prudent checks:

- Verify that your application was signed by your iPhone Certificate. To do that, select the last line in the build log — the one that starts with CodeSign. Then click the icon at the end of the line, as we have in Figure 13-10.

  In Figure 13-11, you can see that it was signed by my iPhone Certificate. (Okay, you may need a magnifying glass, but trust us it's there, and make sure yours is, too.)

- Verify that the embedded.mobileprovision is there and is located in the Distribution build directory and is not located in a Debug or Release build directory.

  To do that, search for embedded.mobileprovision in the Search field in the upper-right corner of the Build Results window, as we did in Figure 13-12. You see two matches. We chose the second one, and again clicked the icon at the end of the line to see more. We can see that it's there, and the directory it's building to is Distribution-iphoneos.

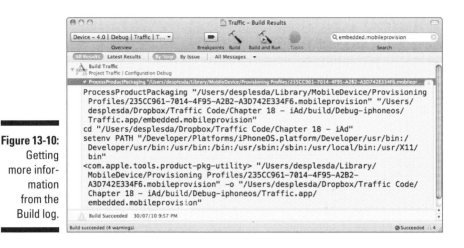

Figure 13-10:
Getting more information from the Build log.

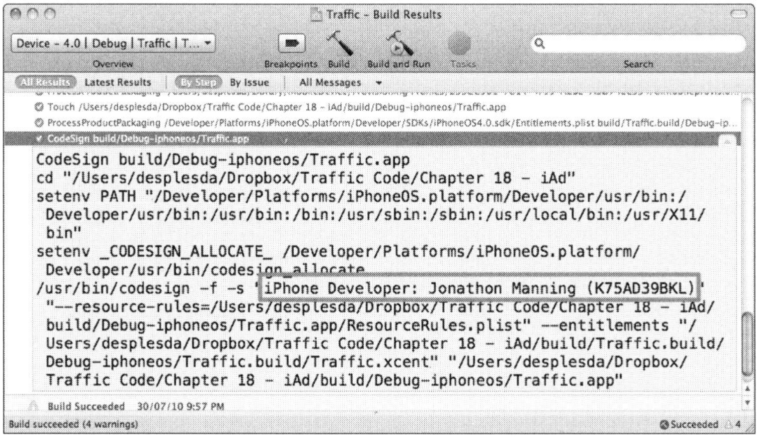

Figure 13-11:
The app has been signed by our iPhone Certificate.

When you've done this elaborate (but necessary) song and dance, you're ready to rock 'n roll. You can go to iTunes Connect — your entry way to the App Store. This is where the *real* fun starts.

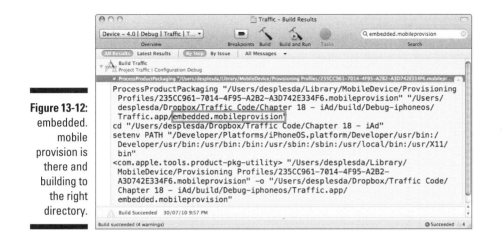

Figure 13-12: embedded. mobile provision is there and building to the right directory.

Getting Your Content in the App Store via iTunes Connect

Welcome to the world of forms, policies, and procedures. All these are well documented by Apple, so we won't bore you (and more importantly us) by rewriting the Apple instructions.

There's also another reason for you to dive into the Apple instructions yourself. Remember Rule 1 — there are no shortcuts, so you need to follow the process exactly as Apple has documented it.

The exact details of the process, and all the rules, can be found in the Developer Guide. The link to download it is found at the bottom of the main iTunes Connect page in Figure 13-13. Follow it religiously (okay, enough already).

Although the rules may seem arbitrary, we're going to cut the folks at Apple some slack here — given the number of apps they have to approve, there'd be absolute chaos if they didn't have a strict procedure in place.

But what we *can* do for you is give you an overview of the process so that what you have to do makes sense in the overall context. We also share with you some of the things We've learned in submitting my eight (and maybe even more by the time you read this) apps to the store.

Your portal into the world of fame, fortune, and forms is iTunes Connect. iTunes Connect is a group of Web-based tools that enables developers to submit and manage their applications for sale via the App Store. It's actually the very same set of tools that the other content providers — the music and video types — use to get their content into iTunes. In iTunes Connect, you can check on your contracts, manage users, and submit your game with all its supporting documentation — the *metadata,* as Apple calls it — to the App Store. This is also where you get financial reports and daily/weekly sales trend data (yea!).

You get here by clicking on the iTunes Connect link in the iPhone Developer Program section of the iPhone Dev Center page. (Refer to Figure 13-1.) Before you can do anything, you're asked to review and accept the iTunes Distribution Terms & Conditions. After taking care of that chore, you land on the iTunes Connect page shown in Figure 13-13.

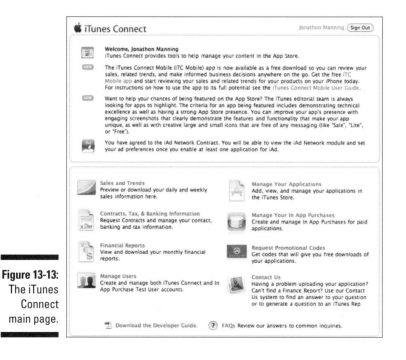

Figure 13-13:
The iTunes
Connect
main page.

When you want to add an game to the App Store or manage what you already have there, the iTunes Connect main page is your control panel for getting that done.

You'll probably find yourself returning time and again to three specific sections of the iTunes Connect page — the Manage Users section the Contract, Tax & Banking Information section; and the Manage Your Applications section — so we take the time to explain those bits in greater detail in the next few pages.

Manage Users

Users in this context means you and your fellow team members, not any future potential users of your app. Click the Manage Users link to find out what tools are available for managing how you and your team communicate about what's what with your app. When creating and editing an iTunes Connect user account, you can define user roles and *notifications* — the type of e-mails your fellow team members will receive regarding the main iTunes Connect account. When setting up accounts, keep in mind that you have four distinct user roles to choose from: Admin, Legal, Finance, and Technical.

Contract, Tax & Banking Information

After you've set up your various user accounts, proceed to the Contracts, Tax & Banking module. In this module, you need to complete the paid application agreements and provide financial information relating to payment and tax withholdings from the sale of your apps.

If you plan on selling your game, you need to have your paid commercial agreement in place and signed before your game can be posted to the App Store.

If your game is free, you've already entered into the freeware distribution agreement by being accepted into the iOS Developer Program; however, there is still a contract setup that free application contracts will need to go through before your game will go live in the App Store.

We're not going to charge for the Traffic game, but just like with anything else at Apple, contract approval can take a while, so you should probably fill out the contract information just to get it out of the way. If you're going to charge for your games, then make sure you research pricing first — we're not going to go into the theory behind it here, it would take a book of its own! It's worth studying some popular games to get idea of how they're priced — start with the ones we recommend in Chapter 28.

If you're going to charge for your game, you have to provide even more information. Most of it is pretty straightforward, except for some of the banking information, which you do need to have available. To change some of the information after you've entered it, you have to e-mail iTunes technical support. It behooves you to get it right the first time.

Here's what we're talking about:

- **Bank name**
- **Bank address**
- **Account number**
- **Branch/Branch ID**
- **ABA/Routing Transit Number or SWIFT Code:** What this number is will depend upon where your bank is located. For United States banks, this number is the first nine digits of that long number at the bottom of your checks that also contains the account number. If you aren't sure what the routing number is, contact your bank. For non-U.S. banks, you may have to enter the SWIFT Code instead. You have to get that from your bank. The process also provides look-up function to help you out.

Take it from us: It's far easier if you have all bits and pieces together *before you start the actual upload process,* rather than having to scramble at 3 a.m. to find some obscure piece of information Apple wants. (The Bank SWIFT Code was the one that got us.)

Uploading your information

After you've set the wheels in motion, you can then go back to the iTunes Connect main page and upload your data. At this point, you can start the application-upload process by clicking the Manage Your Applications link on the iTunes Connect main page. Make sure you've dealt with out the requisite Contracts, Tax & Banking Information.

The first time you enter the Manage Your Applications page in iTunes Connect, you see a blank page. After you've uploaded your first binary, you can see your application(s) listed here.

To begin adding an application, click the Add New Application button. Follow the instructions.

But before you actually start the process, you have to have some things ready. We cover this in the next section.

What you need to get your game into the App Store

To start with, there's a link on the iPhone Dev Center page, under News and Information labeled: Tips on Submitting Your App to the App Store.

This page has information on Keywords, Assigning a Rating for Your App, and some other tips. Read it!

Apple is very strict about some things, and we speak from firsthand experience.

The first time we submitted an app to the App store, we received a polite, but firm e-mail rejecting it because our icon used an iPhone. When we resubmitted our app, it was rejected a second time because we used an iPhone image as the image in one of the menus. At the time of our first submissions, we really didn't think this whole image stuff was a big deal — hey, this was early on in the process — but what a difference a few rejections can make. Take it from us: Apple wants you to follow its guidelines. Period.

We fixed both of those issues, and you can now find our games in the App Store.

So how do you get your game into the App Store? Actually, the Uploading Your Application to the App Store part is pretty easy. The hard part is collecting all the little bits of information you'll need to enter into all the text fields in the upload page.

Here's an overview of the kind of information you'll need (for more information, download the Developer Guide using the link at the bottom of the iTunes Connect page— see Figure 13-13):

✔ **Metadata:** The ever-present data about data. Here's what Apple wants from you:

- *Application Name:* The name must conform to guidelines for using Apple trademarks and copyrights.

  Apple takes this very seriously, as evidenced by Apple sending a cease-and-desist order to Neal's ISP when he tried (innocently) to use iPhoneDev411 as his domain name. (A word to the wise: Don't mess with Apple.)

- *Application Description:* When you go through the process of uploading your data, the field you have to paste this into says you're limited to 4,000 characters. Apple suggests no more than 580 characters so customers can view your entire iTunes Connect

Application Description without clicking the More button in the App Store.

This is what users will see when they click your app in the App Store, so it's important that this description be well written and that it point out all your app's key features. Check out the descriptions of some of the games we recommend in Chapter 28 for some inspiration.

Don't include HTML tags; they will be stripped out when the data is uploaded. Only line breaks are respected.

- *Device:* Basically, we're talking iPhone and/or iPod touch and/or iPad.

- *Primary Category:* There will be a drop-down menu from which to choose the primary category for your app. There are about 20 choices, ranging from Business to Games to Social Networking to Travel to Utility.

Your first category should probably be Games.

- *Secondary Category:* (Optional) Same categories as the primary category.

- *Rating Information:* Later, you'll be asked to provide additional information describing the content. You'll see things like Cartoon or Fantasy Violence, Simulated Gambling, Mature/Suggestive Themes, and so on. For each type of content, you'll need to describe the level of frequency for that content — None, Infrequent/Mild, Frequent/Intense. This allows you to set your rating for your application for the purpose of parental controls on the iPhone App Store.

Apple has strict rules stating that an app must not contain any obscene, pornographic, or offensive content. Oh and by the way, it's entirely up to Apple what is to be considered offensive or inappropriate.

- *Copyright:* We use a line like this one:

© Copyright Neal Goldstein, Jon Manning & Paris Buttfield-Addison 2010. All rights reserved.

You can get the copyright symbol, in Word at least, by choosing Insert⇨Symbol and then selecting the copyright symbol. If you have any questions about copyright registration, talk to your lawyer or check out `www.copyright.gov`.

- *Version Number:* People usually start with 1.0. Then, as you get more and more suggestions and "constructive criticism," you can move on to 1.1, and someday even version 2.0.

- *SKU Number:* A Stock Keeping Unit (SKU), any alphanumeric sequence of letters and numbers that is used to uniquely identify your application in the system.

   Be warned — this SKU number is not editable after you submit it.

- *Keywords:* Keywords that describe your game. These are matched to App Store searches. Spend some time on this one. Keywords can be changed only when you submit a new binary, or if the application status is Rejected, or Developer Rejected. Keywords must be related to your application content and cannot contain offensive or trademarked terms. You may not use other app names or company names as keywords. Keywords can be single words or phrases, and the text field is limited to 100 characters. Your App Name and Company are already searchable, so you don't need to include them in your list.

- *Support URL for the Company:* You need a support URL, which basically means you need a Web site, which isn't that hard.

   If you don't have a Web site yet and don't know how to build one, just go to your friendly ISP, find a domain name, get a package designed for folks who don't know HTML, and build yourself a Web site. Later on, you can get a hold of David Crowder's *Building a Web Site For Dummies,* 3rd Edition, which can help you build a "more professional" site. There will be a link to your support URL on the application product page at the App store, and this is the link users will click on if they need technical support from you or have a question about your app.

- *Support E-Mail Address:* (For use by Apple only) Likely, this address will be the one you used when you registered for the developer program.

- *Demo Account – Full Access:* Test accounts that *the App Store reviewers can use to test your application.* Include usernames, passwords, access codes, demo data, and so on.

   If you provide one, make sure the demo account works correctly. You'd hate to have your app rejected because you didn't pay attention to setting up a demo account correctly.

- *End User License Agreement (EULA):* (Optional) If you don't know what this is, don't worry. It's the legal document that spells out to the end users what they're agreeing to do in order to use your app.

   Fortunately, the iTunes Store has a standard EULA. By this time, we think it probably knows what it's doing — but you should read it anyway before you use it.

- *Availability Date:* When your application will be available for purchase.

- *Application Price:* Free is easier, but if you want to get paid, you have to select a price tier. The last time we tried it, you couldn't see the pricing matrix unless you had first selected one. To help you along, Tier 1 is US$0.99 and so on.

- *Localization:* Additional languages (besides English) for your meta-data. You can have your text and images in Italian in all Italian-speaking stores, for example.

- *App Store Availability:* The territories in which you would like to make your application available. (The default is all countries iTunes supports.)

✔ **Artwork:** A picture is worth a thousand words, so the App Store gives you the opportunity to dazzle your app's potential game players with some nice imagery:

- *iPhone/iPod touch Home Screen Icon:* Your built game must have a 57-x-57-pixel icon included for it, following the procedure we show you back in Chapter 5. This icon is what will be displayed on the iPod touch or iPhone home screen. You can find an icon for Traffic in the resources you downloaded in Chapter 1.

- *Large Application Icon:* This icon will be used to display your game on the App Storefront. It needs to meet the following requirements:

  512 x 512 pixels (flattened, square image)

  72 dpi (dots per inch)

  JPEG or TIFF format

- *Primary Screenshot:* This shot will be used on your *application product page* in the App Store.

  Apple doesn't want you to include the iPhone status bar in your screenshot. The shot itself needs to meet these requirements:

  320 x 460 portrait (without status bar) minimum

  480x 300 landscape (without status bar) minimum

  320x 480 portrait (full screen)

  Up to four additional optional screenshots can be on the application product page. These may be resized to fit the space provided. Follow the same requirements listed in this bullet.

- *Additional Artwork:* (Optional) If you're really lucky — we mean *really* lucky (or that good) — you may be featured on the App Store. Apple will want "high-quality layered artwork with a title treatment for your application," which will then be used in small posters to feature your application on the App Store.

The wait begins.

Avoiding the App Store Rejection Slip

During his opening Worldwide Developer Conference (WWDC) keynote address in June of 2010, Apple CEO Steve Jobs mentioned that there are now over 225,000 applications available. He also said that 15,000 applications are submitted per week, and that 95 percent of all apps submitted are approved within one week.

That's a pretty high approval rate. But just to be sure, it wouldn't hurt to know what was up with the 5% that _did_ get rejected. It turns out the majority of those rejected were rejected for one of the following reasons:

✔ The app doesn't function as advertised by the developer.

✔ The app uses private API's.

✔ The app crashes.

Sounds reasonable, but in addition to the Big Three, there are a few other reasons why apps are rejected. Keep the following in mind so that Apple smiles benignly down on your app:

✔ **Use the same icon for the app (the bundle icon) and the App Store page icon.** Make sure the bundle icon for your app is the same image as the 513-pixel version for your App Store page.

✔ **Icons must be different for _lite_ and _pro_ versions (such as free and paid versions).** Use a different icon image for app and page for a lite version than the one you use for the pro version.

✔ **Don't use any part of an Apple image and certainly none of the company's trademark images or names.** Your app can't include any photos or illustrations of the iPhone, including icons that resemble the iPhone, or any other Apple products, including the Apple logo itself. (You can read about my experience with this in the section "Knowing what info to have in hand to get your app into the App Store," earlier in this chapter.)

Your app can't include the word _iPhone_ in its title.

If there is any doubt in your mind, it pays to read Apple's posted Guidelines for Using Apple's Trademarks and Copyrights, which you can find at

```
www.apple.com/legal/trademark/guidelinesfor3rdparties.
    html
```

✔ **If you use any of Apple's user interface graphics, you must use them in the way they were intended.** For example, the blue + button should be used only to add an item to a list.

✔ **Don't infringe on other trademarks.** Your app's title, description, and content must not potentially infringe upon other non-Apple trademarks or product likenesses.

✔ **Keywords can get you in trouble.** Keyword terms must be related to your app's content. It should be obvious, but some developers do it: You can't use offensive terms. And it's a big no-no to refer to other apps, competitive or not.

✔ **Don't include pricing information in your app's description and release notes.** Your app's marketing text — the application description and release notes — should not include pricing information, mostly because it would cause confusion in other countries due to pricing differences.

✔ **Don't mention Steve Jobs.** Apple will reject any app that mentions Steve Jobs in any context.

✔ **Don't try to fool the ratings.** Apps are rated accordingly for the highest (meaning most adult) level of content that the user is able to access. If you hide it, they will find it.

Now What?

Wait some more. As of June 30, 2010, 85 percent of new apps, and 95 percent of app updates were approved with one week (and this was a busy time since developers were submitting apps updated to iOS).

Chapter 14

Giving Your Game Music and Sound

Sound is a huge part of conveying the mood of your game. As you might expect, it's also important for letting the player know what has happened. You don't feel like you're playing an action game unless you hear a satisfying BANG to accompany the sight of your enemies flying into the air with arms flailing and — well, you get the idea. Sound effects have a strong impact on people, and they help draw the player into the world of your game.

Sound on the iPhone and iPad is slightly tricky because of the different kinds of audio that exist, and because all iOS devices inherit a legacy from the iPod. Because you're working on iPod hardware, you're working with systems designed by people who believe that sound is *really* important, and it needs to be played at maximum quality with next to no lag.

In this chapter, we show you how to add a number of sound-related things to the game. We cover how to add background music, which sets the mood of the game; ambient background audio, which solidifies the tone of the game; and sound effects, which serve to reinforce the visual events happening onscreen.

Speakers are built into most devices. You'll find them on every model of iPhone and iPad, but you won't find them on every iPod touch. Every iOS device has a headphone jack, though, so the user can hear sound if they're wearing headphones. (An iPod touch would not be a very good iPod if you could not hear music on it.)

Recognizing the Purpose of Sound in a Game

In games, audio is important. That may seems like a simple and obvious piece of advice, but you need to know *why* your game has to make noises. If your game makes sounds, those sounds have two completely different and simultaneous effects on the user:

✔ It lets the player know that something has happened.

✔ It sets the mood and tone for the game.

The player is being told, through the way your game sounds, how he should feels when playing the game.

What music does

Music is generally responsible for setting the underlying tone of the game, and for setting the pace of play. For example:

✔ A low-pitched, slow song makes the player feel nervous and play cautiously

✔ A happy, fast song gets the player's blood pumping and encourages vigorous play.

A great example of a game that uses music to its fullest potential is *Half-Life 2*, by Valve Corporation. This game, set ten years after aliens invade Earth, uses low, growling music when things are meant to be quiet and tense and uses fast-paced, beat-heavy music during action-oriented scenes like gunfights.

People react powerfully to music. Play a series of minor chords at someone, and you'll make her feel slightly tense. Play a series of major chords, and she'll start feeling slightly chipper.

The effects are generally very subtle, and you can't expect to set the mood for your game through music alone. That said, music helps set up the base of the mood that you're trying to establish, and you can cement it through the proper use of art, sound effects, and game play.

What sound effects do

Games are all about players reacting to events. To react to events, people need to know that they happened. The two most common ways to notify the user that something's happened is to either

✔ Show him through visual means (a fancy way of saying by showing stuff onscreen)

✔ Make a noise

More and more hardware is coming out that provides more options to notify the player of events — the iPhone, for example, has a built-in vibrating buzzer — but sound and visuals are still the most flexible way to communicate specific things to the user.

A sound effect cements what the eye sees. If you watch a silent video clip of someone walking, it doesn't have the same effect as watching the same video with sound. Sound effects help your brain confirm that what you see is actually happening.

Sound effects are also useful for letting the player know about things that she can't see. This includes someone sneaking up behind you or an alarm that something bad is happening somewhere else.

Finally, in addition to letting the player know about events, sound effects help set the mood and tone. Good sound effects fit in with the music and with the visual theme of the game, and they help reinforce the setting that you're trying to convey to the player.

Understanding Playback on iOS

iPhones and iPads were once just iPods. This means that if there's one thing that iOS does well, it's making noises. From a coding perspective, you need to be aware of two main kinds of audio when working with sound: uncompressed and compressed audio.

Uncompressed audio

Uncompressed audio is sound that is, well, not compressed. This means that no mathematical trickery is performed to give the sound a smaller file size: It's simply stored and played back, with very little processing needed.

Uncompressed audio takes up more space, but it doesn't use up very much CPU power. This means that lots of different sounds can be played at once, and playback can start instantly. This makes uncompressed sound perfect for audio that needs to react quickly to the player; for example, sounds that form a part of the user interface or sound effects that are triggered by in-game events.

Uncompressed audio can quickly take up a lot of space if it's reasonable quality and more than a few seconds in duration. That's where compressed audio comes in.

Compressed audio

Compressed audio is audio that's been manipulated so that it takes up much less space while still sounding the same (or close to the same, depending on how much compression is used) as uncompressed audio. Compressed audio needs a lot more CPU power to play back. Compressed audio also takes a little bit of time to start playing — not a lot, but the delay can be noticeable, especially on slower devices, such as the iPhone.

Compressed audio is suitable for long-running sound that doesn't have to respond quickly to the user. This makes compressed audio perfect for music and other background sounds, which are meant to set the scene for the user and add depth to the experience.

Compressed audio is played back through dedicated hardware on iOS devices; therefore, the battery drain that you'd normally have to suffer is greatly reduced. However, the dedicated compressed audio hardware can play only one stream of audio at a time. So if you want to play more than one compressed sound at the same time, you're going to force the CPU to play it, which drastically reduces your user's battery life. Avoid this situation as much as you can: You don't want your application to be the one that the user avoids because she doesn't want her battery to be eaten up.

Media playback on iOS

iOS has two main toolkits to play audio:

- ✔ **Audio ToolBox** is a lower-level set of functions that give you total control over how your audio plays. You can load, generate, play, and generally do everything you could possibly want to do with your audio, and it all happens very quickly.

  The downside is that Audio ToolBox a little complicated: You often have to do a lot of set up in the code.

> ✔ **AVAudioPlayer** is a very simple and clean Objective-C class that allows you to load and play audio of any kind. AVAudioPlayer is powerful and gives you very simple control over your audio.
>
> The downside is that an AVAudioPlayer object is required for each of the sounds you intend to play. If you have lots of little sounds, this can get complicated.

You can deal with audio in iOS in several other ways, but these two are the most promising for the sample game in this book. Others include *OpenAL,* designed for 3D positional audio, and *Audio Units,* which allow you to modify audio by passing it through a series of miniature programs before sending it to the speaker.

This book focuses on AVAudioPlayer and Audio ToolBox, but you can find more information on Audio Units in the Apple iPhone Reference Library online at `http://developer.apple.com/iphone/library/documentation /Audio/Conceptual/AudioUnitLoadingGuide_iPhoneOS/ Introduction/Introduction.html`. You can get more information on OpenAL at `http://benbritten.com/2008/11/06/openal-sound-on-the-iphone`.

Playing Background Music

Start with the background music for the game because it's straightforward to set up and gives a great setting for the game.

You can find the background music track in the assets that you downloaded back in Chapter 1.

AVAudioPlayer

For this example, make the TrafficAppDelegate object responsible for running the background music. Put the control of background music in the application delegate because not many objects stay around for the entire run of the game. The game play-related objects exist only while the user plays the game and not while she uses the menus.

We're using AVAudioPlayer for the background music, because AVAudioPlayer is great for playing back compressed audio files. For the shorter sound effects, we'll be using Audio ToolBox later on in the section "Audio ToolBox and system sounds."

Here's the overall flow of music playback:

1. When the application starts, your code creates an AVAudioPlayer object, and tells it to load the music file.

2. The application checks the user settings and decides whether the user has specified that he wants sound.

    • If the user wants music, the audio player plays back the file, and keeps playing it until the application quits or the user turns off the music.

    • If the user doesn't want music, the audio player just sticks around.

3. If the user changes his preferences in the Settings menu, the background music starts (or stops) at once.

Now that you have an overview of the process, time to get started with the code that makes some noise.

Loading the content

To play back content with an AVAudioPlayer, give the player an NSURL that points to the file that you want to play. An *NSURL* is an object that points at a location, which can be on the Internet or on your iPhone's or iPad's flash drive.

You need to write the code that adds an AVAudioPlayer to TrafficAppDelegate and then loads the music file. But before you can do that, you have to do a little bit of set up.

Setting up the project

To start working with AVAudioPlayer, you'll need to set up your project so that you have access to the necessary files.

1. **Add the MusicTrack.mp3 file to the project's Resources folder (you'll find this folder in the sidebar in Xcode).**

    If you don't have this file, look at Chapter 1, where you can get all the info you need on getting the resources for the project.

2. **Right-click the Frameworks folder in your project and add the AVAudioFoundation.framework to the project.**

    This framework contains AVAudioPlayer, which you need to set up your background music.

3. Import the framework and add the AVAudioPlayer variable:

 a. *Import <AVAudioFoundation/AVAudioFoundation.h> in TrafficAppDelegate.h.*

 b. *Add an AVAudioPlayer variable to TrafficAppDelegate.h and call it musicPlayer.*

When you're done, TrafficAppDelegate.h looks like Listing 14-1. The code in bold is the code that's been added.

Listing 14-1:   TrafficAppDelegate.h

```
#import <AVFoundation/AVFoundation.h>

@interface TrafficAppDelegate : NSObject
          <UIApplicationDelegate> {
  UIWindow *window;
  UINavigationController *navigationController;

  BOOL shouldPlayMusic;
  BOOL shouldPlaySFX;

  AVAudioPlayer* musicPlayer;

  NSMutableArray* scoresList;
}

@property (nonatomic, retain) IBOutlet UIWindow *window;
@property (nonatomic, retain) IBOutlet
          UINavigationController *navigationController;
@property (assign) BOOL shouldPlayMusic;
@property (assign) BOOL shouldPlaySFX;

@property (nonatomic, retain) NSMutableArray* scoresList;

-(void)addHighScore:(float)score;
@end
```

After you add the necessary pieces, make your application load and play the file!

Playing the content

The music plays only when the user's preferences are set up to allow it. Fortunately, if you've followed along so far, you've already done the majority of the work needed to set up sound playback. All you need to do is tell the audio system to start playing back sound! Follow these steps:

1. Modify `applicationDidFinishLaunching:withOptions:` in TrafficAppDelegate to look like the following code and make sure that you place the code before the point where you read in the settings.

```
- (BOOL)application:(UIApplication *)application did
        FinishLaunchingWithOptions:(NSDictionary*)
        options {
[window addSubview:[navigationController view]];
[window makeKeyAndVisible];

NSUserDefaults* defaults = [NSUserDefaults
        standardUserDefaults];

NSURL* musicURL = [NSURL fileURLWithPath:[[NSBundle
        mainBundle] pathForResource:@"MusicTrack"
        ofType:@"mp3"]];
NSError* error;

musicPlayer = [AVAudioPlayer alloc];
[musicPlayer initWithContentsOfURL:musicURL
        error:&error];
musicPlayer.numberOfLoops = -1; // loop forever
[musicPlayer retain];
// ... but don't start playing yet

[defaults registerDefaults:[NSDictionary
        dictionaryWithObjectsAndKeys:
[NSNumber numberWithBool:TRUE], @"shouldPlayMusic",
        [NSNumber numberWithBool:TRUE],
        @"shouldPlaySFX",nil]];

self.shouldPlayMusic = [defaults
        boolForKey:@"shouldPlayMusic"];
self.shouldPlaySFX = [defaults
        boolForKey:@"shouldPlaySFX"];

// Load the high scores list
NSArray *paths = NSSearchPathForDirectoriesInDomains
        (NSDocumentDirectory, NSUserDomainMask, YES);
NSString *documentsDirectory = [paths
        objectAtIndex:0];

NSString* scoresListPath = [documentsDirectory
        stringByAppendingPathComponent:@"scores.
        plist"];

scoresList = [[NSMutableArray arrayWithContentsOf
        File:scoresListPath] retain];

if (scoresList == nil) {
  scoresList = [[NSMutableArray array] retain];
}

}
```

This code locates the URL of the file MusicTrack.mp3 and then creates an AVAudioPlayer that loads the file pointed to by that URL. This code sets the player to repeat forever but doesn't tell it to start playing yet. You get to that in a second, but now for something a little tricky.

So far whenever you've worked with properties, you've *synthesized* them, or told the Objective-C compiler to create the setter and getter methods for you (which used to be a real pain to do by hand for each property, believe me).

But sometimes you want a little bit more out of your properties. Remember how you stored shouldPlayMusic as a BOOL property? Wouldn't it be nice to have the music play the moment you set that property to TRUE, rather than explicitly telling the app delegate to play music?

You do just that in the following step, by implementing your own version of `setShouldPlayMusic:`. The instant the user changes the settings, the music starts or stops. Nice and simple!

 2. **To control music playback to TrafficAppDelegate, add the following method to TrafficAppDelegate.m.**

```
-(void)setShouldPlayMusic:(BOOL)play {
  shouldPlayMusic = play;

  if (play) {
    if (![musicPlayer isPlaying]) [musicPlayer play];
  } else {
    if ([musicPlayer isPlaying]) [musicPlayer stop];
  }
}
```

This code is called whenever the shouldPlayMusic property's value changes. setShouldPlayMusic: changes the instance variable that stores the information and then starts or stops the music player based on the property: If the user says that music should start playing, then the music player starts making sound come out of the speaker.

 3. **Run the game to test it.**

If you have the music turned on, you hear it. Otherwise, go to the Settings menu and turn it on.

If you turn off the music, it stops!

Playing Sound Effects

Sound effects are the noises that play in response to something happening in the game. Before you add sound effects, figure out what noises you actually need in the game. For the *Traffic* game, you need these sounds:

- ✔ Cars changing lanes
- ✔ Cars crashing
- ✔ Cars reaching the end of the right lane
- ✔ Starting a new game

You also should include the traffic background noises to really set the mood, but that's something that doesn't require precise timing to match up with what's happening onscreen. We get to that later in this chapter in the "Playing background audio" section.

We discuss using AVAudioPlayer earlier in this chapter in the "Playing Background Music" section, and it's a great class for playing audio files when you need only one instance of that file playing music, background audio, and so forth. But what about sounds that could play a few times at once? One example is when a car changes lanes — another car could (and probably will) change lanes before the sound effect triggered by the last lane change finishes playing, thus requiring its own sound effect.

To tell the system to play a new sound on top of other sounds, without potentially getting in the way of these other sounds, take a stroll through the mystical world of system sounds.

Audio ToolBox and system sounds

System sounds, despite the name, don't belong to the system. *System sounds* are a simple way of binding an uncompressed audio file to an ID number and then telling the iOS to play the sound associated with that number. System sounds are an incredibly fast and flexible way to deal with short sounds, and it's absolutely perfect for playing back sound effects.

To access these magical tools, make use of the *C framework,* widely regarded as the *mother tongue* by all developers older than 35. Don't get us started on those Fortran heathens. (This framework isn't written in Objective-C.)

If you write Objective-C, you already know C.

Here are three key things to know about playing sounds with the system sounds application programming interface (API):

- ✔ Sounds are referred to with SystemSoundIDs (which are just integers).
- ✔ You create SystemSoundIDs with the AudioServicesCreate SystemSoundID function.
- ✔ You play SystemSoundIDs with the AudioServicesPlaySystemSoundID function.

You need only to follow a few rules:

- ✔ System sounds can be only 30 seconds or shorter.

- ✔ System sounds must be uncompressed audio. You can't use MP3s.

- ✔ The system sound API doesn't allow for timing or positioning — it's only for simple sound playback.

If you've followed along so far, you're ready to add sound to the project and have cars make noises when they change lanes or crash into each other. Follow these steps:

1. **To add the Audio ToolBox framework to your project, right-click the Frameworks folder and add the AudioToolbox.framework framework to your ever-growing collection.**

2. **Add the crash.aif and screech.aif files to the project's Resource folder.**

   You find these resources in the files you downloaded in Chapter 1!

3. **Import `<AudioToolbox.h>` in TrafficController.h.**

   Because the TrafficController knows about all movements, you make it responsible to play sounds.

4. **To add the sound IDs for the car crash and tire screech noises:**

   a. Add the instance variables — a pair of SystemSoundID variables, screechSoundID and crashSoundID — to TrafficController.

   These variables store references to the sounds, which we show you how to load shortly.

   b. Add the declaration for the vehicleBeganMovement method, which takes no parameters and returns void.

   This method is used by vehicles to tell the TrafficController that the vehicle started changing lanes. The TrafficController responds by playing a noise.

   When you're done, TrafficController.h looks like this:

   ```
   #import <Foundation/Foundation.h>
   #import <QuartzCore/QuartzCore.h>
   #import <AudioToolbox/AudioToolbox.h>

   @class TrafficViewController;

   @interface TrafficController : NSObject {
     CADisplayLink* displayLink;

     NSMutableArray* vehicles;
   ```

```
    NSMutableArray* lanes;
    NSMutableArray* vehiclesToDestroy;

    double timeTotal;
    double timeRemaining;
    double lastTimestamp;
    TrafficViewController* viewController;

    SystemSoundID screechSoundID;
    SystemSoundID crashSoundID;
}

@property (nonatomic,retain) IBOutlet
        TrafficViewController* viewController;

- (void) vehicleBeganMovement;

@end
```

5. **To load the sound files, update the awakeFromNib method in TrafficController so that it looks like the following code:**

```
- (void)awakeFromNib {
  vehicles = [[NSMutableArray arrayWithCapacity:10]
        retain];
  lanes = [[NSMutableArray arrayWithCapacity:3]
        retain];
  vehiclesToDestroy = [[NSMutableArray
        arrayWithCapacity:10] retain];

  NSURL* screechURL = [NSURL fileURLWithPath:[[NSBundle
        mainBundle] pathForResource:@"screech"
        ofType:@"aif"]];
  NSURL* crashURL = [NSURL fileURLWithPath:[[NSBundle
        mainBundle] pathForResource:@"crash"
        ofType:@"aif"]];
  AudioServicesCreateSystemSoundID((CFURLRef)
        screechURL, &screechSoundID);
  AudioServicesCreateSystemSoundID((CFURLRef)crashURL,
        &crashSoundID);

  timeRemaining = 20;
}
```

This new code creates NSURLs that point to the files you want to load and then creates SystemSoundIDs from them.

6. **Play a sound when a vehicle reports that it's begun moving.**

To do so, create a method that the Vehicle class calls when the vehicle begins to move. Add the method in the following code to TrafficController.m:

```
- (void)vehicleBeganMovement {
   TrafficAppDelegate* delegate = [[UIApplication
        sharedApplication] delegate];
   if (delegate.shouldPlaySFX)
     AudioServicesPlaySystemSound(screechSoundID);
}
```

This code checks with the app delegate to see whether the application can play sound effects and then plays the sound if it's allowed.

When you're done, add the method declaration for vehicleBegan Movement to TrafficController.h. You want other classes to know that the method exists.

7. **Make the vehicles report when they've begun moving.**

   Add the following method to Vehicle.m:

   ```
   - (void)touchesBegan:(NSSet *)touches
         withEvent:(UIEvent *)event {

     [controller vehicleBeganMovement];
   }
   ```

   This code lets the Traffic Controller know that movement has begun, triggering the sound playback.

8. **Add the following code to `vehicle:collidedWithVehicle:` to play a sound when a car crashes.**

   You already have a method that runs when a car crashes — it's `vehicle:collidedWithVehicle:` in TrafficController. This is the perfect place to put the sound that plays the crash sound effect.

   ```
   - (void) vehicle:(Vehicle*) aVehicle
         collidedWithVehicle: (Vehicle*) otherVehicle {
   // game over, man

     TrafficAppDelegate* delegate = [[UIApplication
         sharedApplication] delegate];
     [delegate addHighScore:timeTotal];

     if (delegate.shouldPlaySFX)
       AudioServicesPlaySystemSound(crashSoundID);

     if (!displayLink.paused)
       [self togglePause];

     [viewController displayGameOver];
   }
   ```

9. **Launch the game, test your new sounds, and check that your settings do what they're supposed to by turning the sounds on and off and confirming that sounds play (or don't play) as they're supposed to.**

Playing background audio

The background audio doesn't rely on any interactions with the user — it's just there. The background audio plays when the game starts and stops when it ends, all the while looping. Sounds like a perfect use for AVAudioPlayer!

This audio player goes in the view controller because you want to tie the audio starting and stopping to the view controller appearing and disappearing, respectively, and putting the code in the view controller is the easiest way to achieve that. Here's how:

1. **Add the file cars-loop.aif to the project's resources.**

   The file is part of the resources bundle you downloaded in Chapter 1. If you don't have the file, go straight to Chapter 1 to discover how to download the files for the project.

2. **Import the AVFoundation header, add an AVAudioPlayer to Traffic ViewController.h, and call the AVAudioPlayer background AudioPlayer.**

   When you're done, TrafficViewController.h looks like this:

```
#import <UIKit/UIKit.h>
#import <AVFoundation/AVFoundation.h>

@class TrafficController;

@interface TrafficViewController : UIViewController {
  TrafficController* gameController;
  UIView* pauseOverlay;
  UIView* gameOverOverlay;
  UILabel* timeRemainingLabel

  AVAudioPlayer* backgroundAudioPlayer;
}

@property (nonatomic, retain) IBOutlet
        TrafficController* gameController;
@property (nonatomic, retain) IBOutlet UIView*
        pauseOverlay;
@property (nonatomic, retain) IBOutlet UILabel*
        timeRemainingLabel;
@property (nonatomic, retain) IBOutlet UIView*
        gameOverOverlay;
```

```
- (void) displayGameOver;
- (IBAction) pauseGame:(id)sender;
- (IBAction) endGame:(id)sender;
- (void) setTimeRemaining:(CGFloat)time;

@end
```

3. **Load and prepare the audio player when the view loads by adding the method in the following code to TrafficViewController.m:**

```
- (void) viewDidLoad {
  NSURL* backgroundURL = [NSURL
       fileURLWithPath:[[NSBundle mainBundle]
       pathForResource:@"cars-loop" ofType:@"aif"]];

  backgroundAudioPlayer = [[AVAudioPlayer alloc] init
       WithContentsOfURL:backgroundURL
         error:nil];

  backgroundAudioPlayer.numberOfLoops = -1;
  [backgroundAudioPlayer retain];
}
```

This code runs when the view is loaded from the nib file. The code creates a URL that points to the background sound resource, creates an audio player with that URL, and tells it to loop. The code doesn't start playback yet, though.

4. **Play the background audio when the view appears by adding the following code to TrafficViewController.m:**

```
- (void) viewWillAppear:(BOOL)animated {
  [gameController startGame];

  TrafficAppDelegate* delegate = [[UIApplication
       sharedApplication] delegate];
  if (delegate.shouldPlaySFX)
    [backgroundAudioPlayer play];

}
```

This code runs when the view actually appears onscreen: The code gets a reference to the app delegate and sees whether sound effects are turned on. If they are, the background audio player begins playback.

5. **Import the TrafficAppDelegate.h file in TrafficViewController.m.**

To do this, add the following line of code to the start of TrafficViewController.m:

```
#import "TrafficAppDelegate.h"
```

Your application now has both music and sound effects. To add more sound effects, follow the same pattern:

- ✔ **To loop sound effects or sound effects that use compressed audio,** use an AVAudioPlayer.
- ✔ **For one-off sound effects,** use system sounds.

We include ten sound effects in the bundle of resources from Chapter 1. Challenge yourself to add them to the game where you think they'll be most useful!

Part III
The Social Aspects

The 5th Wave   By Rich Tennant

"Until we work the kinks out, David will be providing the audio portion of our game demonstration."

In this part . . .

This part takes the example game, *Traffic,* and kicks it up a notch by adding social features, such as wireless multiplayer and Facebook connectivity.

We also show you how to connect your game to the outside world through external display support, which gives your game a party atmosphere! Here's a breakdown of each chapter:

- ✔ Chapter 15 covers the integration of Apple's Game Kit framework, allowing your games to talk to each other wirelessly for multiplayer action.

- ✔ Chapter 16 brings in the power of Facebook, letting you know the basics of having your game and users interact with Facebook and their friends from within your game.

- ✔ Chapter 17 gets you social in a physical sense — discussing how to increase the party atmosphere by allowing your game to display things on an external display, such as a TV!

- ✔ Chapter 18 gives you an alternative way to bring in some cash, through Apple's iAd.

Chapter 15

Building Multiplayer Games with Game Kit

*T*he history of video games has always included multiplayer games. Even games like *Pong,* one of the great ancestors of today's video games, were designed to let two people play together. If you visit an arcade, you'll find rows of games that let you play against or with your friends.

When you bring multiplayer game play into the mix of your game, everything changes. The game now also depends on your interactions with a very, very complex mechanism that's far more intricate than any game you could possibly design: That mechanism, of course, is a human being.

When you develop games for the iOS OS, you have access to a number of tools that makes the design and creation of multiplayer games significantly easier than it used to be. This is made possible by *Game Kit,* a framework that Apple introduced in iOS OS 3.0 (then called *iPhone OS).* Game Kit makes finding other devices that want to play your game a snap and sending and receiving data to and from them a cinch. We won't bore you with a rant about how kids have it so easy these days, but this is the easiest it's ever been to get started with multiplayer games.

Most iPhones and the iPad have Bluetooth and Wi-Fi technology built into them, which further facilitates multiplayer game play. *Bluetooth,* if you're one of the five remaining people who don't have one of those funky earpieces, is a short-range wireless networking technology designed for networking devices. Bluetooth is pretty fast and has very low latency, which makes it perfect for games. When you develop your games, be aware of the hardware features you use.

Game Kit and the Simulator

To test any multiplayer code you write, you need to have more than one iPhone OS device. The iPhone Simulator unfortunately doesn't know how to talk via Bluetooth, so your only way to test it is to load your code on two iPhones, iPod touches, or iPads.

If you have only one test device, it might be worth borrowing another from a friend. In the long-term, you could contact the people at Apple and pester them to support Game Kit over Bluetooth in the Simulator. Maybe if enough people ask, Apple will respond.

Game Kit is available on all iOS hardware — iPod touches, iPhones and iPads alike.

The first generation of the iPod touch doesn't have Bluetooth. The original iPhone won't work either. Sorry, you'll have to upgrade!

Understanding the Basics of Game Kit

To understand how Game Kit works, you have to understand a couple underlying concepts that the framework is built around. The two main things that you work with when building a Game Kit application are sessions and peers:

- **Sessions:** Think about multiplayer games as rigidly organized, formal meetings. When you think about a meeting, it isn't just the people who attend it, it's also the place and time where it's held, the meeting topic, who's taking notes, who's responsible for bringing the donuts.

  A *session* is the object that keeps track of the meeting. The session knows when devices connect and when they disconnect, and provides management functions for dealing with all data transmission.

- **Peers:** If a session is the meeting itself, *peers* are the people in the meeting. Peers are the Objective-C objects that represent other devices that talk to each other in the session.

  Peers send and receive data to other peers. That's all they do, but like writing a book, it's a job that's a lot harder than it sounds. Peers need to know who they're talking to, who's in charge of what information, and what their responsibilities are to the other peers participating in the session.

Game Kit comes with a very useful, pre-prepared object — the *peer picker controller* — that makes it simple to find peers for your game. This tool can look for people over Bluetooth and Wi-Fi. Using the peer picker controller is only a little more complicated than telling it to appear and waiting for it to tell you which peer the user selected. (We'll start working with the peer picker controller in the section "Starting the session.")

Designing a Multiplayer Version of a Single-Player Game

Turning a single-player game into a multiplayer one depends on the type of game that you build. The two major kinds of multiplayer games are competitive and cooperative. The best option for your game depends on the type of game you're writing. For an action game, it's more likely that you'll want to make a competitive multiplayer game; a puzzle game might easily be a cooperative multiplayer game. But there are no absolute rules about what sorts of game play work for what kinds of games!

We take a quick look at these two kinds of game play to see what best fits the sample game, *Traffic,* you've created throughout this book.

Competitive multiplayer

Competitive multiplayer games are the most well-known form of multiplayer. Competitive multiplayer games pit one player directly against another player (or multiple players against everyone); there can be only one winner. The majority of multiplayer games are competitive: Just take a look at any of the Quake games, which are probably the most famous multiplayer games, by id Software. Other strong examples of competitive multiplayer include

- ✔ Real-time strategy games, such as the *Command & Conquer* series, by Electronic Arts
- ✔ Side-scrolling beat-'em-ups, such as the *Dead or Alive* series, by Tecmo

If the game that you build has a lot of independent actors that the player faces off against, such as monsters or other bad guys, it's a fairly straightforward step to add human players as another entity to square off against.

Cooperative multiplayer

Cooperative multiplayer games place two players on the same side and challenge them to work together toward a common goal. Cooperative multiplayer game play is a little more rare than competitive, which may be because fighting against another person can be fun. But cooperative game play can be incredibly rewarding. An increasing number of modern shooter games are turning to cooperative game play to make the single-player portion of the game more interesting. This approach was made especially famous by the *Gears of War* series, developed by Epic Games.

 Competitive game play can be easily turned into cooperative game play by taking two opposing players, putting them on the same side, and adding a computer-controlled challenge for them to deal with. Although this challenge can be pretty simple to think up, it does require a lot of effort to implement. This challenge can come from

- ✔ A clever computer-controlled opponent, which requires the developer to design and develop a clever artificial intelligence (which is a huge topic that can, and does, fill hundreds of books).

- ✔ Outside factors that both players must team up against to deal with (such as time running out or a constant stream of powerful, but mindless monsters).

  A great example of the cooperative approach is the *Serious Sam* series, developed by Croteam. The cooperative multiplayer component of this game essentially drops all the players into the single-player game, but increases the number of mindless enemies charging at them, which gives everyone a challenge that they all share.

Cooperative games are all about giving players the ability to help each other, while still placing them in danger (well, simulated video game danger, anyway). If you play alongside another person, you can get help and offer help: This bond really solidifies the fun that your game can offer.

Picking the paradigm

Given these two (admittedly broad) kinds of game play, which one works best for the *Traffic* game? The core of *Traffic* is the race against the clock. The passage of time isn't really something that you can outsmart: The player's only tools are her nimbleness and her ability to make quick decisions. This means that there's no easy role for an opposing player to step into. Sure, you could give the opposing player the ability to throw obstacles at the other, but that doesn't really seem like enough for them to do.

Game Kit, Game Center, and Social Gaming

Originally, Game Kit was introduced as just a framework for locating, managing, and communicating with peers on a network. With iOS 4, Apple introduced a companion framework for Game Kit, called *Game Center*. Game Center is a collection of extra classes, features, and methods that integrate with Game Kit and allow you to add social gaming features to your game.

Game Center allows your game to store information about how the user is doing on Apple's servers, and tie in to the user's Apple account. In Chapter 11, we discussed the concept of Achievements and how they can be used to track and reward player progress through your game. Game Center allows you to keep track of these achievements using Apple APIs, which saves you time to develop and implement them.

Additionally, Game Center allows you to match up your user with their friends for online gameplay.

You can learn all about using the extra Game Center features by reading the documentation for Game Kit, available online at `http://developer.apple.com/iphone/library/documentation/GameKit/Reference/GameKit_Collection/index.html`.

Additionally, the content from Apple's World-Wide Developer Conference in 2010 is available for free to all registered iOS developers, and you can download the presentations via iTunes, by visiting `http://developer.apple.com/videos/wwdc/2010/`.

While advanced features, such as achievements, are beyond the scope of this book, if you're interested in learning more we particularly recommend the Game Kit and Game Center presentations, where you'll see the Apple engineers who actually wrote the framework explain how to use it.

In that case, drop competitive game play and see what you can do in the area of cooperative game play. To keep the game design from getting too complex, both players need to face the same challenge: in this case, the clock. How, then, can you let them help each other?

One simple method to let players assist each other is to have two players share the game board. At first glance, that method makes sense; there's lots to take care of, and you'd be better at beating the clock if both players help move the cars. However, the game board is really small, and it's difficult to avoid crashes caused by two players moving their cars into each other by accident. You need to find a way that lets players play in their spaces but still provide a means for them to help each other.

A player beats the clock by moving his cars into the right lanes. That means that a good player might have some extra time. One way that a player can help his partner is to send her some extra time. That way, a player who's in a bad situation can get some help from a player who does slightly better. Additionally, this way, both players don't interfere with one another.

The final thing you have to think about is the game-over condition. In single-player mode, crashing cars or running out of time ends the game. But if two players are on separate boards, what happens when one player crashes and the other one doesn't? (That's something that's guaranteed to happen — how often do you suspect you'll see simultaneous crashes?) One way to deal with this problem is to make car crashes or timeouts end the game for both players. For simplicity's sake, this is the method we use in this chapter, but there are more creative ways of dealing with it.

Communicating between players

In multiplayer games, the players often need to communicate with each other. In the preceding section, you decided that the multiplayer component of *Traffic* involves players playing separate games, but one player can send time to the other. Additionally, when the game ends for one player, it ends for both.

This means that peers must be able to say four things to each other during the session. These messages aren't English sentences intended for the players to read: They're usually simple numeric codes, which are easier to send across the network, intended for the peers. Nonetheless, the meaning remains the same. Here are the "messages" that can be sent (in the code, you'd actually send numeric codes that represent each type of message, rather than strings of text):

✔ **Hey, we should start a game!:** This is the first message that can be sent. This message means that both peers can talk to each other, and they can begin playing the game and interacting with the user.

✔ **Here, I just sent *X* seconds of time to you!:** This message means that the user sent some of her time to the other player; the receiving party increases his remaining time and trusts that the sending party decreases her time accordingly.

Yes, you can easily make a version that cheats in this model. Designing a game that detects or stops cheating can get quite complex; for a good primer on how to get started, search for Apple's "Secure Coding Guide" you'll find it in the Xcode documentation. It's a lengthy read, but it's worthwhile if you want to stop people from cheating!

✔ **Oh no, my game just ended!:** One of the players ends his game (due to running out of time or a car crash in the game), meaning that the other player needs to end her game as well.

✔ **Goodbye! I'm leaving!:** What happens when a peer disconnects from the session. This can happen in a number of ways; networks can be flaky, and wireless networks are doubly so.

The Bluetooth connection between the two devices isn't something your application has control over, and your game needs to deal with it appropriately when — not *if*, but *when* — it inevitably happens.

In this sample game, the most sensible course of action is to treat it as another Game Over message because there isn't much point in recovering.

Network connections can be broken by one of the peers quitting the app. Your application needs to handle a broken network connection by responding appropriately to the user, rather than appearing broken without any explanation. Good ways of dealing with failing connections include displaying text onscreen that lets the player know about it. For Apple's advice on good ways to show error information to users, look up "Alerts, Action Sheets and Modal Views" in the *iPhone Human Interface Guidelines (HIG)*, which Apple provides with Xcode. You can find the HIG online at

```
http://developer.apple.com/iphone/library/documentation/userexperience/
            conceptual/mobilehig/Introduction/Introduction.html
```

Updating the interface

Now that you know *what* messages are sent by the application, you need to think about *when* those messages are sent. What does the user do to trigger the network activity? Here we take a look at what needs to happen, network-wise, when the user plays the game:

✔ **Starting the game:** The game starts as soon as the session reports that another peer has connected.

To set up a multiplayer game, set up the session through the use of the Game Kit-provided peer picker controller, which provides its own user interface. To start this process and to differentiate between single-player and multiplayer games, add another button to the main menu that launches a new multiplayer game. You'll do this in the section "Adding the Button."

✔ **Ending the game:** The game ends when the other peer disconnects, when the other peer sends a Game Over message, when the player crashes his car, or when he runs out of time.

This doesn't require any new user interface at the moment; a Game Over is a Game Over.

✔ **Transferring time to another player:** This is the only in-game event that the user can deliberately choose to trigger. You can allow the user to trigger it by tapping a new button that you'll later add to the screen, in the section "Sending Extra Time."

Setting Up the Session

Start using Game Kit by setting up a session between two iPhone OS devices. You're first going to add the button that starts a new game and then add the code that's triggered when the button is pressed.

You're going to add overall session management code to the app delegate (see Chapter 4 for a refresher on what the app delegate is) and code that starts the session in the Main Menu View Controller. After the session management code is run, the app delegate is the delegate of the session and is informed when peers disconnect. Additionally, the Main Menu View Controller is the delegate of the peer picker controller and is informed when peers connect to the session.

Adding the framework to the project

To work with Game Kit, add it to your project. Add the framework, import the right headers into the TrafficAppDelegate.h file, and add a variable that holds a reference to the Game Kit session. Listing 15-1 has this code; new additions are in bold. To add the framework to the project, modify TrafficAppDelegate.h.

Listing 15-1: TrafficAppDelegate.h

```
#import <AVFoundation/AVFoundation.h>
#import <GameKit/GameKit.h>

@interface TrafficAppDelegate : NSObject
            <UIApplicationDelegate, GKSessionDelegate> {
  UIWindow *window;
  UINavigationController *navigationController;

  BOOL shouldPlayMusic;
  BOOL shouldPlaySFX;

  AVAudioPlayer* musicPlayer;

  NSString* scoresListPath;
  NSMutableArray* scoresList;

  GKSession* multiplayerSession;
}
```

```
@property (nonatomic, retain) IBOutlet UIWindow *window;
@property (nonatomic, retain) IBOutlet
        UINavigationController *navigationController;
@property (assign) BOOL shouldPlayMusic;
@property (assign) BOOL shouldPlaySFX;
@property (nonatomic, retain) NSMutableArray* scoresList;
@property (nonatomic, retain) GKSession*
        multiplayerSession;

-(void)addHighScore:(float)score;

@end
```

Follow these steps to add Game Kit to your project:

1. **Add the framework by Control-clicking (or right-clicking) the Frameworks folder in your project and choose Existing Frameworks in the Add menu.**

2. **Choose GameKit.framework in the list that appears and click the Add button.**

3. **At the top of the TrafficAppDelegate.h and MainMenuViewController.h files, add the line that imports the header file `<GameKit/GameKit.h>`.**

4. **Make the class conform to GKSessionDelegate by adding GKSessionDelegate to the list of protocols in the class declaration.**

   The list of protocols appears in angle brackets: < and >.

   This protocol contains methods, such as peers connecting or disconnecting, needed for dealing with the session.

5. **Create a property to hold the session by creating a new GKSession instance variable, dubbed multiplayerSession, in TrafficAppDelegate.**

6. **Make the multiplayerSession variable a non-atomic, retained property.**

   To do this, add the line in Listing 15-1 that begins with "@property." This sets up the variable so that other classes can access it.

   The Game Kit session is the responsibility of the app delegate, so this class needs to store it as a variable.

Once you're done with these steps, Game Kit is added to your project, and your class is now ready to start working with Game Kit. The next step is to make use of the Game Kit features!

Adding the button

You'll need to add the button that the user presses to start the game. While you add the button, you also need to add an Interface Builder outlet for it so that you can control it later.

The button needs to participate in the popping buttons animation that you set up in Chapter 6, so you need to be able to make it animate. The following code doesn't set up the button to animate, but you can quickly adapt the steps you went through in Chapter 6 to make it work.

Listing 15-2 contains the code that makes these changes.

Listing 15-2: MainMenuViewController.h

```
#import <UIKit/UIKit.h>
#import <QuartzCore/QuartzCore.h>
#import <GameKit/GameKit.h>

@interface MainMenuViewController : UIViewController
        <GKPeerPickerControllerDelegate> {
            UIButton* newGameButton;
            UIButton* multiplayerButton;
            UIButton* statsButton;
            UIButton* settingsButton;

            CAKeyframeAnimation* popAnimation;

}

@property (nonatomic, retain) IBOutlet UIButton*
        newGameButton;
@property (nonatomic, retain) IBOutlet UIButton*
        multiplayerButton;
@property (nonatomic, retain) IBOutlet UIButton*
        statsButton;
@property (nonatomic, retain) IBOutlet UIButton*
        settingsButton;

-(IBAction) newGame:(id)sender;
-(IBAction) showStats:(id)sender;
-(IBAction) showSettings:(id)sender;
-(IBAction) newMultiplayerGame:(id)sender;

@end
```

Follow these steps to add the Network button to the main screen. When the user taps on this button, the peer picker controller will appear, letting the user host or join a multiplayer game and to set up the MainMenuViewController class to act as an object that can deal with information that the peer picker controller provides:

1. **To add the button control, open MainMenuViewController.xib in Interface Builder, drag in a new UIButton from the Library, and place it between the New Game and Stats buttons, which should already be on the screen.**

2. **Add the button image by adding the file Network.png to the project's resources.**

   You can find the Network.png file in the project resources you download in Chapter 1.

3. **Customize the button by setting the type of the button to Custom and then change the image of the button to Network.png.**

   Select the button, and open the Attributes Inspector window. In that window, you'll be able to change the button type and image settings.

4. **Resize and reposition the button, if necessary, to make it fit with the others on the menu, as shown in Figure 15-1.**

   For a quick refresher course in resizing and repositioning controls, flip to Chapter 5.

Figure 15-1:
The new
Network
button in the
main menu.

5. **Add the outlet and action for the button in the header by opening MainMenuViewController.h and adding a UIOutlet for the UIButton you added in Step 1.**

   Look for the bold line in Listing 15-2 that begins with "@property" — this is the code you want to add for this step!

6. **Call the outlet 'multiplayerButton' and then add the newMultiplayer-Game: action for the button to trigger.**

   Look at the last bolded line in Listing 15-2 for the code you need to add for this step.

7. **In the class declaration for MainMenuViewController, add the GKPeerPickerControllerDelegate to the list of protocols the class conforms to.**

8. **In Interface Builder, connect the button you just added to the newMultiplayerGame action in the Main Menu View Controller.**

   For a refresher on connecting buttons to actions, head to Chapter 5!

9. **Connect the multiplayerButton outlet in the Main Menu View Controller to the button.**

   You'll also find handy hints on how to connect buttons to outlets in Chapter 5.

Once you're done with these steps, your code should look like Listing 15-2.

Starting the session

After you have the formalities out of the way, set up the session. When the player presses the Network button, you want the game to allocate, initialize, present a GKPeerPickerController, and set the MainMenuViewController to be its delegate. You also want to make sure that the game responds only to nearby connections — in other words, connections made over Bluetooth.

After you perform this setup procedure, the peer picker controller appears onscreen and asks the user whether he wants to host a game or look for one. After he makes a selection, the peer picker controller either waits for an incoming connection or displays a list of available peers to connect to.

Regardless of whether the user chooses to host or look for a game, the end result is that the peer picker controller informs its delegate — that's you — that a peer has connected. The peer picker controller also creates the session that both peers are connected to, and passes along a reference to that session to the delegate as well. Once your application has the prepared session, you then decide whether to begin the game and talk to the connected peer.

Follow these steps to add the peer picker controller to the main menu:

1. **Implement the `newMultiplayerGame:` method by adding the method in the following code to MainMenuViewController.m.**

This code creates a peer picker controller, sets up the current object as its delegate, tells the peer picker controller that you're interested in nearby peers, and then displays the controller on the screen:

```
-(IBAction) newMultiplayerGame:(id)sender {
  GKPeerPickerController* picker =
        [[GKPeerPickerController alloc] init];
  picker.delegate = self;
  picker.connectionTypesMask =
        GKPeerPickerConnectionTypeNearby;
  [picker show];
}
```

2. **Implement the `peerPickerController:didConnectPeer: toSession:` method.**

   This method is part of the GKPeerPickerControllerDelegate protocol, and is called when the picker successfully negotiates a connection with another peer and sets up a session.

   This code dismisses the picker, stores the session in the app delegate, sets up the app delegate as the *session's* delegate, and then begins a new game.

   Add the method in the following code to MainMenuViewController:

```
- (void) peerPickerController:(GKPeerPickerControl
        ler *)picker didConnectPeer:(NSString *)peerID
        toSession:(GKSession *)session {
  [picker dismiss];
  [picker autorelease];

  TrafficAppDelegate* delegate;
  delegate = (TrafficAppDelegate*)[[UIApplication
        sharedApplication] delegate];
  delegate.multiplayerSession = session;
  session.delegate = delegate;

  TrafficViewController* traffic =
        [[TrafficViewController alloc] initWithNibName
        :@"TrafficViewController" bundle:nil];

  [self.navigationController pushViewController:traffic
        animated:NO];
}
```

3. **Test the application.**

   For this step, you need two iPhone OS devices, and you need to build and install the application on both devices. We show you how in the next section.

Testing your game on multiple devices

Building and running an application on two iPhones, iPod touches, or iPads is a little tricky. Apple assumes that you work with only one device at a time, which means that building and running an app for one device is really easy. Building and running an app on two devices *at the same time* is kind of a pain, on the other hand. Follow these steps for your official *For Dummies* guide on how to build and test an application on two devices at once:

1. **Plug both devices into your computer and then give both devices recognizable names:**

   a. *Open iTunes.*

      In the sidebar of the application, you see the list of all connected devices.

   b. *Double-click the name of each device and give them both distinct names.*

      For the record, Jon's devices are Walton, Gunther, Helios, and Yuri; Paris's iPhone is Padd; and the names of Neal's devices are currently classified information.

2. **Open Xcode, and click the Overview drop-down list at the top left of the main window.**

   Take a look at the Active Executable section of the menu that appears: You see an entry for both of the connected devices. This is how you control which device you build and install on to.

3. **Select the first device you want to install the application on and then build and run the project by clicking the Build and Run button in the toolbar.**

   Xcode installs the project on the current device and runs the app.

4. **Close the application after it launches.**

5. **Click the Overview drop-down list and in the Active Executable section, select the second device and then build and run it.**

   Xcode installs the app on the second device and then runs it.

6. **Tap the application icon on your first device.**

   The application launches, while Xcode remains in a debugging connection with the copy of the app that's running on the second device.

7. **To test the game, install the app on both devices and then tap the Network Game button on both of them.**

   Both devices search for each other. And after a few seconds, they both show a list of nearby iPhone OS devices running the *Traffic* game.

8. On one of the devices, tap the name of the other device.

The other device displays a dialog box asking whether you want to accept or decline the invitation to play a game. If you tap Decline, things go back to showing nearby peers. If you tap Accept, both devices instantly start a new game.

Enabling In-Game Communication

When your games can find each other on multiple devices, add more inter-device interaction in the game. The class that you're going to put in charge of sending game play events is TrafficController. TrafficController already controls the single-player game, and it knows about what happens during game play, so give it the responsibility of informing other players of these events as well.

Before we get into the details of sending messages between devices, you need to take a look at how Game Kit deals with data that it *receives.* In addition to its delegates, Game Kit sessions also have *data receive handlers,* or objects that are sent the message `receiveData:fromPeer:inSession:context:` when the session gets a chunk of data from any of its connected peers.

To handle receiving data, you need to set up one object to implement this method and appropriately respond to the data that gets sent. You can send data to the connected peers at any point in the program, but you only receive data that's sent to you in this method.

Data that you receive from other peers is considered *untrusted* — it could be a normal, rule-abiding message, or it might be an attempt to cheat the rules or to compromise your security. In this book, we ignore this threat because we don't want to overly complicate the program with validation code. Just keep in mind that if you plan on making a complicated, rule-based game and distributing it, build your code so that it minimizes the risk of cheating. For more information on how to design your code to minimize these risks, we recommend the *Secure Coding Guide,* by Apple. You can find it online at

```
http://developer.apple.com/mac/library/documentation/
          Security/Conceptual/SecureCodingGuide
```

The guide is a little dry (in the same way that oceans are a little bit damp) but well worth the reading if you want to know the best ways to keep your applications from being hacked.

The last thing to take note of is that the data that gets sent between peers is just that — *raw data.* This means that the data is just unstructured bytes, without any kind of organization. The Game Kit deals exclusively in *NSData objects,* which are Objective-C objects that store chunks of raw information. Your program puts these objects together when sending data and takes them apart when receiving them. Fortunately, Cocoa Touch has some brilliant built-in classes that make this a snap. With that in mind, start putting together the messages that your game sends.

Archiving objects

To send messages over the network, convert those messages into NSData objects. To create these objects, use a technique built into Cocoa — archiving. *Archiving* is Cocoa's term for taking data that's in your program and turning it into an NSData object, which can then be saved to disk or sent over the network. To convert an NSData object back into its original form, you *un-archive* it.

Here's how archiving works in Cocoa: When an object is told to archive itself, it's given an NSArchiver object to work with. The object then communicates with the archiver and tells it all about itself. The object explicitly stores every piece of information that it thinks is worth keeping; if the archiver simply yanked the object out of memory and stored that, un-archiving the object would get really complicated.

In Chapter 12, you store user preferences by telling the NSUserDefaults object to store values for specific keys. Archiving works exactly the same way. An object tells an archiver to store objects, numbers, and other values along with strings that act as references to those values. Later, when you need to un-archive that information, you simply pass the archiver those same keys to get back the information.

After the archiver has all the information you want it to have, tell it to finish and then get back the data as an NSData object. After you have that NSData object, you can tell the Game Kit session to send it to the other player. Next, you need to create a method that constructs a Game Over message.

Constructing the message's NSData object

The first message that you implement for the game is the message that tells all connected peers that the game is over. This method is called from a few different points in the program: Remember that the game can end via a couple ways. To avoid writing the code that prepares and sends the message more than once, put the message-sending code into a method and then call that method whenever the game ends:

1. **Add the sendGameOver method by adding the following code to TrafficController.m:**

```
- (void) sendGameOver {
  NSMutableData *data = [[NSMutableData alloc] init];
  NSKeyedArchiver *archiver = [[NSKeyedArchiver alloc]
      initForWritingWithMutableData:data];
  [archiver encodeString:@"GameOver"
      forKey:@"message"];
  [archiver finishEncoding];
  [archiver release];

  TrafficAppDelegate* delegate = [[UIApplication
      sharedApplication] delegate];

  [delegate.multiplayerSession sendDataToAllPeers:data
      withDataMode:GKSendDataReliable error:nil];

  [data release];
}
```

This code creates an NSMutableData object to store the bytes that you send later and then creates an NSKeyedArchiver that does the actual encoding. The code then builds up the message, tidies up everything, and then gets a reference to the Game Kit session that the app delegate is responsible for keeping track of. The method then tells the session to send the NSMutableData to all connected peers and to make sure that the data is guaranteed to arrive. Finally, the code releases the data because there's no reason to keep it around any longer.

After the applications can send the game-over packet, they need to be able to receive the packets that are sent to them.

Before you write the code that lets the application understand the packets, set up things so that the right objects receive the information in the first place.

2. **Set up the TrafficController as the data receive handler.**

Add the following code to the end of the awakeFromNib method in TrafficController.m. This code gets a reference to the app delegate and sees whether the multiplayer session is valid. If the session is valid, the code sets up the session to send all incoming data to this object:

```
- (void)awakeFromNib {
  vehicles = [[NSMutableArray arrayWithCapacity:10]
      retain];
  lanes = [[NSMutableArray arrayWithCapacity:3]
      retain];
  vehiclesToDestroy = [[NSMutableArray
      arrayWithCapacity:10] retain];
```

```
NSURL* screechURL = [NSURL fileURLWithPath:[[NSBundle
    mainBundle] pathForResource:@"screech"
    ofType:@"aif"]];
NSURL* crashURL = [NSURL fileURLWithPath:[[NSBundle
    mainBundle] pathForResource:@"crash"
    ofType:@"aif"]];

AudioServicesCreateSystemSoundID((CFURLRef)
    screechURL, &screechSoundID);
AudioServicesCreateSystemSoundID((CFURLRef)crashURL,
    &crashSoundID);


TrafficAppDelegate* delegate = [[UIApplication
    sharedApplication] delegate];

if (delegate.multiplayerSession != nil) {
  // tell the multiplayer session to send received
      data to this object
  [delegate.multiplayerSession
      setDataReceiveHandler:self withContext:nil];
}
}
```

3. **To write the code that receives and deals with a Game Over message, add the method in the following code to TrafficController.m:**

```
- (void) receiveData:(NSData *)data fromPeer:(NSString
      *)peer inSession: (GKSession *)session
      context:(void *)context
{
  NSKeyedUnarchiver *unarchiver = [[NSKeyedUnarchiver
      alloc] initForReadingWithData:data];

  NSString* message = [unarchiver
      decodeObjectForKey:@"message"];
  if ([message isEqualToString:@"GameOver"]) {
    // the other player ran out of time!
    if (!paused)
      [self togglePause];
    [viewController displayGameOver];
  }
}
```

This code is called when the Game Kit session receives a chunk of data from another peer; the code prepares a keyed un-archiver to read that data and pulls out the object encoded with the message key. If that object is a string equal to GameOver, it triggers a game over screen.

4. **Test the game by launching the apps (don't forget to install updated copies on both devices!) and starting a new shared game.**

See the section "Testing your game on multiple devices," earlier in this chapter, if you need a refresher. Crash one car into another and watch them both show a game over screen at the same time.

Handling interruptions

In the interest of keeping things tidy, you need to make the application detect when it can't keep the connection going, which means it needs to end the game. This can happen when the devices are out of range or when one of the applications on either device quits (or crashes!).

Fortunately, the Game Kit session is quick to tell its delegate that the session's no longer happening by sending it the `session:peer:didChangeState:` message. All you have to do is account for when the session stops working, which you handle by triggering a game over screen:

1. **Add a method to TrafficController that shows a game over screen when told by adding the method in the following code to TrafficController.m.**

   ```
   - (void) peerDisconnected {
     // the other peer quit the game, so we should
          display a game over
     if (!paused)
       [self togglePause];
     [viewController displayGameOver];
   }
   ```

   You need a method that runs when the connection drops. All this method does is stop the game and show the game over screen.

2. **Add the code that detects when the connection drops to TrafficAppDelegate by adding the method in the following code to TrafficAppDelegate.m:**

   ```
   - (void)session:(GKSession *)session peer:(NSString *)
          peerID didChangeState:(GKPeerConnectionState)
          state
   {
     if (state == GKPeerStateDisconnected) {
       TrafficViewController* game =
          [navigationController topViewController];
       if ([game isKindOfClass:[TrafficViewController
          class]]) {
         [game.gameController peerDisconnected];
       }
     }
   }
   ```

This code runs whenever a peer changes its state in the session, whether she connects, leaves, attempts to connect, and so forth. You're interested only in when she disconnects because that's your clue that the connection is going south.

This code checks what state the peer is in. If the peer is disconnected, the code then needs to check what the currently presented view controller is. This is because the disconnection could conceivably happen when any view controller is displayed. You only want to present a game over screen when the game itself is being played. The game is being played when the current view controller is a TrafficViewController class; therefore, when the peer disconnects and the current view controller is a TrafficViewController, its `peerDisconnected` method is called.

3. **Test the application by running the game on both devices and starting a game.**

4. **Quit the app on one of the devices.**

   The other game ends as well.

For bonus points, consider adding user interface components, such as Alert dialogs, to let the player know there was a problem. To get started with Alert dialogs, take a look at the UIAlertView class. A quick guide to UIAlertView can be found online at `www.idev101.com/code/User_Interface/UIAlertView.html`.

Sending Extra Time

The final part of your multiplayer component is the ability for a player to send half of his time to the other player, in the event that he has extra time and wants to help a player in trouble. You need to add three parts to make this work:

- ✔ Add a button to trigger the sending of time.
- ✔ Construct the data packet that's sent.
- ✔ Adapt your data receive handler function to be able to deal with this new kind of message packet.

Writing the code that sends the have some extra time packet:

1. **Add the method that builds and sends the packet by adding the method in the following code to TrafficController.m:**

```
- (IBAction) sendGameTime:(id)sender {
  float timeToGive = timeRemaining / 2.0;
  timeRemaining -= timeToGive;
```

```
NSMutableData *data = [[NSMutableData alloc] init];
NSKeyedArchiver *archiver = [[NSKeyedArchiver alloc]
        initForWritingWithMutableData:data];
[archiver encodeInt:@"SendTime" forKey:@"message"];
[archiver encodeFloat:timeToGive forKey:@"time"];
[archiver finishEncoding];
[archiver release];

TrafficAppDelegate* delegate = [[UIApplication
        sharedApplication] delegate];
[delegate.multiplayerSession sendDataToAllPeers:data
        withDataMode:GKSendDataReliable error:nil];

[data release];
}
```

This code is very similar to the game-over packet sender. The difference is that the message string that gets sent is different (to differentiate between time and game-over packets), and the code also encodes a number that represents the amount of time this peer sends to the other.

This code also removes half of the player's remaining time. (Try to resist the temptation to make a cheating version that doesn't subtract time.)

2. **Add the method to the class interface by adding the following method declaration to TrafficController.h:**

   ```
   - (IBAction) sendGameTime:(id)sender;
   ```

   Because this method will be called by tapping a button, you need to declare to the outside world that you have the method and it's an IBAction. As we discussed in Chapter 6, an *IBAction* is simply a method that has IBAction set as its return value type and accepts one parameter, which is an `id` variable. This indicates to Interface Builder that the method is designed to run in response to the user performing an action, such as pressing a button.

3. **Adapt the data receive handler by adding the following code to the `receiveData:fromPeer:inSession:context` method (in TrafficController.m):**

   ```
   - (void) receiveData:(NSData *)data fromPeer:(NSString
           *)peer inSession: (GKSession *)session
           context:(void *)context
   {
     NSKeyedUnarchiver *unarchiver = [[NSKeyedUnarchiver
           alloc] initForReadingWithData:data];

     NSString* message = [unarchiver
           decodeObjectForKey:@"message"];
   ```

```
if ([message isEqualToString:@"GameOver"]) {
  // the other player ran out of time!
  if (!paused)
    [self togglePause];
  [viewController displayGameOver];
} else if ([message isEqualToString:@"SendTime"]) {
  // we just received some time from the other
    player
  float bonusTime = [unarchiver
    decodeFloatForKey:@"time"];
  timeRemaining += bonusTime;
}
}
```

The bolded code checks whether the message is `SendTime`, in which case, it decodes the amount of time that the other player sent and adds it to the stockpile. This code adds to the existing code in `receive-Data:` and allows the application to receive and understand the `SendTime` message.

4. **Add a Send Time button by opening TrafficViewController.xib in Interface Builder, dragging a button into the main game view, and setting its label to Give Time.**

5. **Set up the button to trigger the `sendGameTime:` action in TrafficController.**

   Do this by Control-dragging from the button onto the TrafficController and selecting `sendGameTime:` from the window that pops up. The results appear in Figure 15-2.

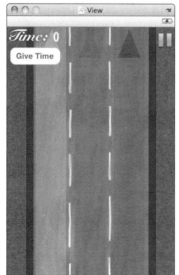

Figure 15-2:
The Give Time button in the TrafficView Controller.

You have one last bit of tidying up to do. In single-player games, the Send Time button is pointless because you don't have anybody to send the time to, so disable the button in single-player mode. Follow these steps to do so:

1. **Add an outlet for the Send Time button in the TrafficViewController interface declaration:**

   ```
   IBOutlet UIButton* sendTimeButton;
   ```

2. **Connect the Send Time button in Interface Builder to the newly created outlet.**

   Use the same process as with every other button you've connected take a look in Chapter 6 for the details, if you need a refresher!

3. **Add code to TrafficViewController to disable the button in single-player mode.**

   Add the following code to the end of the viewWillAppear: method in TrafficViewController.m:

   ```
   - (void) viewWillAppear:(BOOL)animated {
       TrafficAppDelegate* delegate = [[UIApplication
            sharedApplication] delegate];

       [gameController startGame];
       if (delegate.shouldPlaySFX)
       [backgroundAudioPlayer play];

       if (delegate.multiplayerSession == nil) {
         sendTimeButton.hidden = YES;
       }
   }
   ```

   This checks the state of the multiplayer session. If the multiplayer session isn't there, it's a single-player game. The Send Time button is then hidden for single-player games.

You're done. Go play with your friends!

Chapter 16

Game, Meet Facebook

Developing a community around the games you create is as important as developing the games themselves, and letting your game talk to the wider world beyond the single device that it runs on is critical to its success. After the game play and the hard infrastructure work are done, you still need to give your game a portal to the outside world.

Chapter 15 is all about Game Kit and how you can use it to give your game the capability to socialize with a nearby device so that your players can play with their friends. Talking to a nearby device is great, but don't forget that a whole world is out there! This chapter tackles adding Facebook support to your game; we discuss why Facebook is essential and how to add it.

If you've dutifully followed along in this book chapter by chapter, you probably haven't used any frameworks that weren't created and provided by Apple in the iOS Software Development Kit (SDK) yet. That all changes now.

Facebook support is provided by Facebook, not Apple. When you add Facebook support to your game, don't forget that you now deal with two entities: Apple, which wants the iPhone and iPad to be a simple and pleasant user experience, and Facebook, which wants to safeguard its user's privacy. Finding the happy balance between these two views isn't difficult, but it is something to keep in mind when you work on your game.

What you see when you acquire and add the Facebook SDK to your project may be slightly different from what you see here. Don't panic: The download site changes from time to time. The general process remains the same.

Looking at Facebook

Facebook is a social networking Web site that allows users to create pro-files and maintain a list of their friends. Friends can send each other private messages and post publicly viewable messages to their personal profiles. Facebook shot to popularity in 2006, and at the time of this printing is the most heavily used social network in the world, with more than 350 million users worldwide.

Facebook allows developers to host all manner of applications inside the platform. Lots of things are possible on the Facebook platform: You can update a user's status, share virtual items among people, display content to users, and do many other things.

Facebook's been in the news quite a lot over the past few years, primarily because of its surging popularity. From an application developer's perspec-tive, however, it's worthwhile to take a closer look at the individual actions that people can perform on Facebook. After you know what people can do with Facebook, you can figure out how to make your application work with Facebook.

Facebook has three main parts:

- ✔ **Stored information:** When a person signs up to Facebook, the first thing that she's asked for is a set of personal information — where she lives, what college she goes to (or went to), what her favorite TV show is, and so forth. This information is then posted on her profile for others to see. Who those others are depends entirely on the user: She can restrict her profile to her closest friends or make it public.

- ✔ **Friend connections:** Facebook is all about making connections with friends, family, co-workers, and other acquaintances. Every Facebook account has a set of connections to other accounts. These connected accounts are *Friends* (regardless of how well you may actually know these people), and accounts that are friends with each other have access to each other's information.

- ✔ **News feeds:** Every account on Facebook has a stream of small status update messages, which are posted by the user and read by his friends. These messages can be anything — what the user's up to, communica-tion between people, and so forth.

What's particularly exciting for an iPhone developer is that Facebook pro-vides code that lets you work with user information and friend connections as well as post to his news feed.

Exploring the Uses of Facebook

Before we look at the possibilities Facebook enables for your game in a deeper way, take a look at what the Facebook SDK lets you do:

- ✔ It seamlessly connects users' Facebook accounts and information with your iPhone app.
- ✔ It enables users to connect and share experiences with friends who also use your iPhone app.
- ✔ It allows users to share information and actions in your iPhone app with their friends on Facebook.

Social gaming toolkits

Facebook isn't the only tool available for adding social elements to your game. Several excellent frameworks and toolkits are available to developers that allow you to let people connect with their friends inside the game. These are two such frameworks:

- ✔ **Game Center** is a social network for games and is built right into iOS. Game Center, developed by Apple and available in iOS 4.1 and later, allows you to store high scores in a publicly accessible leader board, to let your friends find each other over long distances (as well as simplify the actual network connection process), and to track in-game achievements on Apple's servers.

  Game Center is also an app, available on iOS 4.1 and later, that lets users keep track of how they do in all the games they play. Game Center is also how players find each other for multiplayer games, how players can see the high scores that the game has posted to it, and how they see the achievements they earn.

Game Center is so huge that there simply isn't any other room to discuss it in this book. However, a great place to read about how to add Game Center to your games is the *Game Center Overview,* which is Apple's hub for Game Center information. You can access this site by visiting its home page: `http://developer.apple.com/iphone/gamecenter`.

- ✔ **OpenFeint** is a third-party framework that you add to your application. OpenFeint was developed before Game Center and is supported by a wide range of games. OpenFeint supports all the features of Game Center but is embedded directly in your game, much like Facebook is. One of the features that OpenFeint has that Game Center doesn't is chat — with OpenFeint, your players can talk to each other inside your game.

  You can find out more information about OpenFeint by visiting its Web site: `www.openfeint.com`.

These features sound pretty cool so far, don't they? But why should you bother? If a user cares enough about her high score within your game to talk about it on Facebook, won't she just post it there? Probably not. The more easily users can talk about your game (or the scores they get or actions that they take in your game), the more likely they are to do so. On its most basic level, the Facebook SDK for iPhone enables that.

For this sample game, let your users do something that's important to every single person: brag. Let your user post the amount of time he managed to play the game. Facebook takes care of displaying his times to his friends, which will (hopefully) make your user's friends more interested in checking out your game!

Working with Facebook

Facebook was a completely closed system until May 2007, when it launched the *Facebook Platform.* The platform allows developers to write programs — dubbed *Facebook applications* — that interact with Facebook. Users can browse for applications and add them to their profiles; when they do this, the application gets access to their information.

From a developer's perspective, a Facebook application is your way to present your functionality to Facebook. Applications can be as little as a name and a description — all Facebook needs is a way of dealing with your app.

To allow your application to talk to Facebook, you need to create an application on the Facebook Platform itself. This process ranges from extremely simple to extremely complex, depending on the type of application you want to build.

The process of preparing Facebook to work with your application involves registering, naming, and setting up an application inside the Facebook environment. The majority of this process is designed for those who build games or applications that live inside Facebook, such as FarmVille. Because you're building an iPhone game that only tangentially interacts with Facebook to post times, you just need to set up the bare minimum for a Facebook application.

Here's how you get started in setting up a Facebook application:

1. **Go to Facebook's Developer site at `www.facebook.com/developers/ apps.php`.**

   If you're not logged into Facebook, this page prompts you to log in or create an account.

2. **Click the Allow button to allow access to the Facebook Developer application on your profile, as shown in Figure 16-1.**

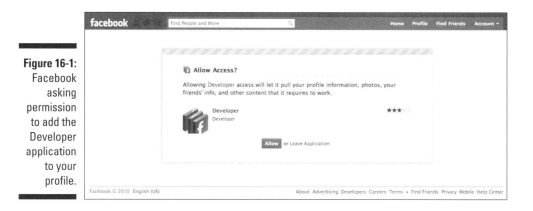

Figure 16-1:
Facebook
asking
permission
to add the
Developer
application
to your
profile.

If you prefer to create a Facebook account to use solely for development instead of using your regular Facebook account, you can. You might find this useful if you want to keep your personal information separate from your work — especially if you work in a team, where you wouldn't want to give other people your Facebook log-in details.

You enter the Facebook Developer application. After you're inside the Facebook Developer application, you see a screen similar to Figure 16-2. Existing applications that you've created display in the left column, and the details for the currently selected application display in the center.

Figure 16-2:
The
Facebook
Developer
application.

3. Create the new application by clicking the Set Up New Application button in the top-right corner of the Facebook Developer application.

The Create Application screen appears, as shown in Figure 16-3.

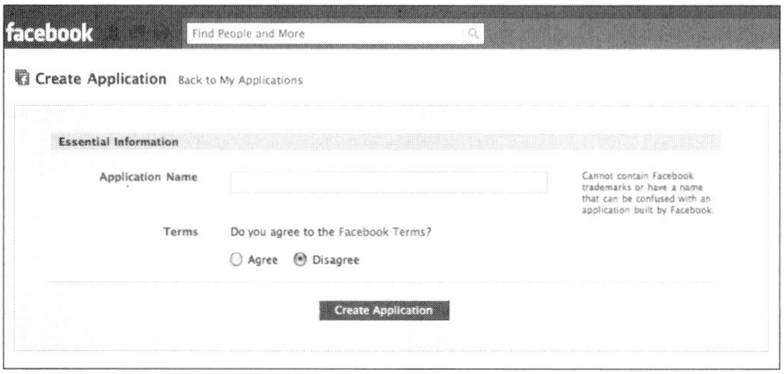

Figure 16-3:
The Create
Application
screen.

4. Enter your application's name, agree to the Facebook terms, and then click the Create Application button.

In this case, the application name is *Traffic* (the name can be different from your iPhone SDK project's name).

The Edit Application screen appears, with tabs for each set of Facebook application configuration options shown on the left of the screen.

5. In the Basic tab, copy your alphanumeric sequences — the application ID, API key, and secret — to an easily accessible text file on your computer.

This is everything you need to make your game connect to Facebook. With the alphanumeric sequences you copied, you can authorize your game to talk to Facebook and work with user profiles. In the following section, we show you how to acquire the Facebook Connect SDK for iPhone and actually make that connection.

Obtaining the Facebook SDK

Thankfully, acquiring the Facebook SDK for iOS isn't quite the Herculean task that becoming a registered iPhone developer is; it's a single step and after that, you're quickly ready to implement Facebook support.

Before you start with the code, take a look at how you're going to talk to Facebook. Facebook makes sure that you have access to its precious user information, so you need to jump through several hoops before you can do something potentially invasive, such as post on a user's feed. The following section "Facebook sessions and permissions" shows how Facebook works in your app.

Facebook sessions and permissions

At the center of all Facebook activity is the session. *Sessions* are your connection to Facebook — without a session, your application can't do anything. Sessions begin when a user signs in to Facebook and ends when the user signs out.

Sessions stick around between application launches. If your user signs in to Facebook and quits the application, when he signs back into Facebook, his session picks up where he left off. This, as you can imagine, saves him a huge amount of time and makes him more likely to use the Facebook integration you've built into your app.

However, your users can't just provide their usernames and passwords to start the session. If you want access to anything to do with their accounts — including posting on their news feeds — you need to ask your users for their explicit permission to do so. Without this permission, Facebook won't let you do anything to a user's profile.

Finally, all this session-starting and permission-getting needs to happen over the network. For every request you make, wait for the reply to come in — it isn't instantaneous.

To take a user from being not signed in to having her full permission to post on her feed, your application needs to follow these steps. (You add the code that does just this in the rest of this chapter; however, you don't need to do all this now. These are just the steps that the application must take to connect to Facebook.) Here are the steps your app follows:

1. **Display a log-in box that prompts the user to enter her username and password.**

   If the user declines to sign in, the process stops — if the user hasn't signed in, you can't post to her feed. If she provides her log-in credentials, however, you can continue.

2. **Send the request to start the Facebook session.**

   Facebook comes back and says that you have a session.

3. **Ask Facebook whether you have permission to post to the user's feed.**

   The code you add in the section "Checking for Permission," later in this chapter, does this by sending a message to Facebook that checks whether the user has already granted permission.

4. **When Facebook comes back, see whether the answer is yes or no.**

   Facebook returns information that informs you whether the user has granted permission to post to her feed.

   If the answer is yes, you're done — the application can post messages. However, if the application currently *doesn't* have permission, you need to perform two more steps.

5. **Display a dialog asking for permission to post to the user's feed.**

   This dialog is actually constructed for you by Facebook and sends the request to Facebook's servers when the user chooses to give or decline permission. After the user dismisses the dialog, Facebook contacts your application and informs you of the outcome.

   When Facebook says that you have permission, you're done. If the user has granted your application permission to post to her feed, you're set — you can post away.

   The other potential outcome of this process is that your user declines your application's request for permission, in which case, you need to stop because the user's made her point clear. No posting for you!

At the end of this process, your application knows whether it has the capability to post to a registered Facebook user's feed.

All the hoops that the application has to jump through are in the name of user security. Facebook allows users to have precise control over what happens with their profile, and with good reason, because there's a huge amount of sensitive information on that site. Now that you know what the conversation is like when talking to Facebook, time to get together some code.

Adding the Facebook iOS SDK to your project

To make your application work with Facebook, you need to include Facebook's SDK, which allows your code to talk to Facebook via Objective-C.

Follow these steps to add the Facebook SDK to your project:

1. **Point your browser to `http://github.com/facebook/facebook-iphone-sdk/zipball/master`.**

   Your browser downloads the latest version of the Facebook iOS SDK.

2. **Add the Facebook iOS SDK to the *Traffic* project.**

   Doing so lets you work with the classes needed to talk to Facebook. To add the Facebook Connect framework to your *Traffic* project:

   a. *Open the src folder in the unzipped Facebook iOS SDK download.*

   b. *Open the facebook-ios-sdk Xcode project file.*

      Xcode launches.

   c. *Drag the FBConnect group from the facebook-ios-sdk project into your game's Xcode project.*

Setting up the application delegate

To prepare the application delegate for Facebook in the game, you need to do two things:

✔ Include the Facebook headers and make the class into one that can work with Facebook sessions.

✔ Create a property that indicates whether the application has permission from Facebook to post to the user's page.

By doing the following steps, you make TrafficAppDelegate.h look like Listing 16-1.

Listing 16-1:   TrafficAppDelegate.h

```
#import <AVFoundation/AVFoundation.h>
#import "FBConnect.h"
#import <GameKit/GameKit.h>

@interface TrafficAppDelegate : NSObject
          <UIApplicationDelegate, FBSessionDelegate,
          GKSessionDelegate> {
  UIWindow *window;
  UINavigationController *navigationController;

  BOOL shouldPlayMusic;
  BOOL shouldPlaySFX;

  AVAudioPlayer* musicPlayer;

  NSMutableArray* scoresList;

  FBSession* facebookSession;
  BOOL hasFacebookPermission;

  GKSession* multiplayerSession;
}

@property (nonatomic, retain) IBOutlet UIWindow *window;
@property (nonatomic, retain) IBOutlet
          UINavigationController *navigationController;
@property (assign) BOOL shouldPlayMusic;
@property (assign) BOOL shouldPlaySFX;
@property (readonly) BOOL hasFacebookPermission;
@property (nonatomic, retain) NSMutableArray* scoresList;
@property (nonatomic, retain) GKSession*
          multiplayerSession;

-(void)addHighScore:(float)score;

@end
```

To prepare TrafficAppDelegate to work with Facebook, follow these steps:

1. **Import the FBConnect.h header file at the start of TrafficAppDelegate.h.**

   This lets the compiler know about the Facebook SDK code by including the FBConnect headers in your code in each file you intend to use them.

   This is needed to let your code know about the Facebook Connect classes that you'll work with.

2. **Make the class into something that can work as a Facebook session delegate by conforming to the FBSessionDelegate protocol.**

   To conform to the FBSessionDelegate protocol, add FBSessionDelegate to the list of names listed between the angle brackets (refer to the second bold line in Listing 16-1).

3. **Add a BOOL variable — hasFacebookPermission — to the interface (refer to the fourth bold line in Listing 16-1).**

4. **Add the property declaration for hasFacebookPermission.**

   This is done in the last bold line in Listing 16-1.

   You also need to synthesize it in TrafficAppDelegate.m, which you do in the next section.

Connecting to Facebook

After you prepare the application delegate for Facebook Connect, provide Facebook with the information that identifies your application: the API key and the application's secret.

You need to get your own key and secret. If you don't have them, the section "Working with Facebook," earlier in this chapter, shows the steps.

Listing 16-2 contains the code you need to add to the start of TrafficApp Delegate.m. Replace *your API key here* with the API key you got from the Facebook Developer site, and replace *your secret here* with the secret key you received.

Listing 16-2:   TrafficAppDelegate.m

```
#import "TrafficAppDelegate.h"
#import "MainMenuViewController.h"
#import "TrafficViewController.h"

static NSString* kApiKey = @"your API key here";
static NSString* kApiSecret = @"your secret here";
```

After you add your keys in TrafficAppDelegate.m, write the code that sends them off to Facebook.

Create, or resume, the Facebook session by changing the `applicationDid`
`FinishLaunching:withOptions:` method to look like the following (new
code is in bold):

```
- (BOOL)application:(UIApplication *)application didFinish
        LaunchingWithOptions:(NSDictionary*)options {
  [window addSubview:[navigationController view]];
  [window makeKeyAndVisible];

  NSUserDefaults* defaults = [NSUserDefaults
        standardUserDefaults];

  NSURL* musicURL = [NSURL fileURLWithPath:[[NSBundle
        mainBundle] pathForResource:@"MusicTrack"
        ofType:@"mp3"]];
  NSError* error;

  musicPlayer = [AVAudioPlayer alloc];
  [musicPlayer initWithContentsOfURL:musicURL
        error:&error];
  musicPlayer.numberOfLoops = -1; // loop forever
  [musicPlayer retain];
  // ... but don't start playing yet

  [defaults registerDefaults:[NSDictionary dictionaryWith
        ObjectsAndKeys:[NSNumber numberWithBool:TRUE],
        @"shouldPlayMusic", [NSNumber
        numberWithBool:TRUE], @"shouldPlaySFX",nil]];

  self.shouldPlayMusic = [defaults
        boolForKey:@"shouldPlayMusic"];
  self.shouldPlaySFX = [defaults
        boolForKey:@"shouldPlaySFX"];

  // Load the high scores list
  NSArray *paths = NSSearchPathForDirectoriesInDomains(NSD
        ocumentDirectory, NSUserDomainMask, YES);
  NSString *documentsDirectory = [paths objectAtIndex:0];

  NSString* scoresListPath = [documentsDirectory stringByA
        ppendingPathComponent:@"scores.plist"];

  scoresList = [[NSMutableArray arrayWithContentsOfFile:sc
        oresListPath] retain];

  if (scoresList == nil) {
    scoresList = [[NSMutableArray array] retain];
  }
```

```
facebookSession = [[FBSession
        sessionForApplication:kApiKey secret:kApiSecret
        delegate:self] retain];
[facebookSession resume];


  return YES;
}
```

This code makes the connection to Facebook and tries to resume the previous session (if one existed). If there is no session, the application will present a login box, to let the user sign in.

Checking for Permission

After the setup required to interact with Facebook, you can get to the more interesting stuff! Primarily, you need to add methods to your application delegate so that it can respond to Facebook events in the way Facebook Connect expects. This is made possible because your application delegate is set as the delegate of the session and your application delegate conforms to the FBSessionDelegate protocol.

Actually, the application doesn't yet fully conform to FBSessionDelegate. FBSessionDelegate classes need to implement the method `session:didLogin:`, which is called when the user successfully signs into Facebook.

We show you how to use this method to see whether your application has permission to post to the user's page. If the user hasn't granted permission, now is a perfect time to ask for it.

Facebook allows you to do almost anything with a user's profile, but the user needs to grant specific permission first. You can ask the user for this permission inside the app — you do that shortly — but before you do that, save the user's time and check whether the user already granted permission.

To perform this check, construct a Facebook query that represents the question "Does this application have access to the current user's stream?" After you send the query, wait for a response. If the response is yes, that's great! Otherwise, ask the user for the permission. Follow these steps:

1. **Create the request by adding the method in this code to TrafficAppDelegate.m:**

```
-(void)session:(FBSession *)session didLogin:(FBUID)uid {
         NSDictionary* params = [NSDictionary
    dictionaryWithObject:@"publish_stream"
    forKey:@"ext_perm"];
             [[FBRequest requestWithDelegate:self]
    call:@"facebook.users.hasAppPermission"
    params:params];
}
```

This method runs when the user successfully logs in and creates a request that asks whether the application has permission to publish to the logged-in user's stream. The method then sends that request for permission to Facebook.

2. **Deal with the request's response by adding the method in the following code to TrafficAppDelegate.m:**

```
- (void)request:(FBRequest*)request didLoad:(id)result
     {
  if ([request.method isEqualToString:@"facebook.
       users.hasAppPermission"]) {
    NSString* success = result;
    hasFacebookPermission = [success
        isEqualToString:@"1"];
    if (!hasFacebookPermission) {
      FBPermissionDialog* dialog =
         [[[FBPermissionDialog alloc] init]
         autorelease];
      dialog.delegate = nil;
      dialog.permission = @"status_update";
      [dialog show];
    }
  }
}
```

This code runs when any requests come back from Facebook. First, the code checks whether the request was the specific one that you're interested in the result of — specifically, whether the result is success or failure. The code gets the result of the request and checks whether it's a *1,* which indicates success. If the result is 1, the application notes that it has permission to post to the user's stream. If the result isn't 1, the code creates and presents a dialog that asks the user for that permission.

3. **Deal with the user signing out of Facebook by implementing the `sessionDidLogout:` method.**

When the user logs out of Facebook, you don't have permission to post to anyone's page. Take a look at this code for the method you need to add to TrafficAppDelegate.m:

```
-(void)sessionDidLogout:(FBSession *)session {
  hasFacebookPermission = NO;
}
```

This method runs when the user signs out of Facebook. The method is simple: All it has to do is note that you don't have permission to post to the user's stream (which makes sense, given that you can't actually talk to Facebook without that user being signed in).

Logging into Facebook

If you've followed along so far, your application can now resume a logged-in session, determine whether it has the permissions it needs, and ask for those permissions if it doesn't have them. What's missing?

You need to let the user actually log into Facebook. Thankfully, this is actually the simplest part of the process. Facebook Connect provides a convenient class — FBLoginButton — that already knows about the painstaking work you just did to set up the connection to Facebook. All you need to do is add this class to your interface, and then the user can log right into her account. Here's how:

1. **Open the SettingsViewController.xib file in Interface Builder and then add a plain UIView to the view.**

   Drag the UIView toward the bottom of the view and make it roughly in the shape of a short, wide button. UIView appears plain white in Interface Builder, but when you run the application, it appears as a proper button.

2. **Change the new view into a Facebook log-in button by selecting the view and pressing ⌘+4 to open the Identity Inspector window.**

   Alternatively, choose Identity Inspector from the Tools menu to open the Identity Inspector window.

3. **Change the class of the view from UIView to FBLoginButton and save the document.**

   To do this, enter **FBLoginButton** in the Class field. When the application launches, the view transforms from a plain, old white rectangle into a Facebook log-in button!

4. **Run the application, go to the settings screen, and log into Facebook.**

   That's it! The FBLoginButton knows about the FBSession that the app delegate has been working with, and the delegate receives the `session:didLogin:` message. You don't need to do anything more to let people sign on!

Posting to Facebook

After your player signs into Facebook, get the application to do something interesting with it — namely, give players the capability to brag.

Offer your user the chance to brag about his score at the Game Over screen. You'll have a Post to Facebook button, but it's usable only if the application knows it has permission to post to the player's page: If the user's logged out or hasn't granted permission, the button can't be used.

Creating the interface

To create the interface, create the buttons themselves. You need to modify TrafficViewController.h to let it know about the buttons. Listing 16-3 shows you the code.

Listing 16-3:   TrafficViewController.h

```
#import <UIKit/UIKit.h>
#import <AVFoundation/AVFoundation.h>
#import "FBConnect.h"

@class TrafficController;

@interface TrafficViewController : UIViewController
          <FBRequestDelegate> {
  TrafficController* gameController;
  UIView* pauseOverlay;
  UIView* gameOverOverlay;
  UILabel* timeRemainingLabel;
  IBOutlet UIButton* sendTimeButton;
  IBOutlet UIButton* postToFacebookButton;
  IBOutlet UIActivityIndicatorView* activity;

  AVAudioPlayer* backgroundAudioPlayer;
}

@property (nonatomic, retain) IBOutlet TrafficController*
          gameController;
@property (nonatomic, retain) IBOutlet UIView*
          pauseOverlay;
@property (nonatomic, retain) IBOutlet UILabel*
          timeRemainingLabel;
@property (nonatomic, retain) IBOutlet UIView*
          gameOverOverlay;

- (void) displayGameOver;
- (IBAction) postToFacebook:(id)sender;
- (IBAction) pauseGame:(id)sender;
- (IBAction) endGame:(id)sender;
- (void) setTimeRemaining:(CGFloat)time;
@end
```

Listing 16-3 contains several changes to TrafficViewController.h, which you make use of when working through the rest of this section. To create a Post to Facebook button, follow these steps:

1. **In Interface Builder, drag a UIButton from the library into the Game Over view and place it toward the bottom of the view.**

2. **In TrafficViewController.h, create a UIButton outlet and name it `postToFacebookButton`.**

3. **Create an action for the button to trigger when the user taps it and call this action `postToFacebook:`.**

4. **Connect the Traffic View Controller's postToFacebookButton outlet to the button, and then connect the Touch Up Inside event of the button to the `postToFacebook:` method.**

That's all you need to do as far as connecting the buttons go. Time to do the fun stuff — actually posting to Facebook.

Posting an update

Posting an update is simple. Remember the previous section "Checking for Permission," where you constructed a Facebook query to check whether the application has permission to post to the user's page? Well, posting an update happens in much the same way. Follow these steps:

1. **Make the view controller conform to the FBRequestDelegate protocol.**

   Refer to Listing 16-3 and add the FBRequestDelegate protocol to the list of protocols that the TrafficViewController class refers to.

2. **Implement the `postToFacebook:` method by adding the following code to TrafficViewController.m:**

```
- (IBAction) postToFacebook:(id)sender {
    NSString* statusText = [NSString
        stringWithFormat:@"I just beat the peak
        hour and lasted %.1f seconds in Traffic!",
        gameController.timeTotal];
    NSDictionary *params = [NSDictionary dictionaryWith
        ObjectsAndKeys:statusText, @"status", @"true",
        @"status_includes_verb", nil];
    [[FBRequest requestWithDelegate:self]
        call:@"facebook.users.setStatus"
        params:params];
}
```

3. **Implement the `request:didLoad:` method by adding the following code to TrafficViewController.m:**

```
- (void) request: (FBRequest*) request didLoad: (id) result
        {
   if ([request.method isEqualToString:@"facebook.
       users.setStatus"]) {
     NSString* success = result;
     if ([success isEqualToString:@"1"]) {
       // Go back to the main menu
       [self endGame:self];
     } else {
       // there was an error!
     }
   }
 }
```

This code is called when the Facebook request returns. This is your opportunity to deal with any potential errors.

4. **Make the view controller able to access the `timeTotal` variable when it posts to Facebook.**

Add the following line of code to TrafficController.h, before the @end line.

```
@property (readonly) double timeTotal;
```

Then, add the following line of code to TrafficController.m, after the @ implementation line.

```
@synthesize timeTotal;
```

Testing Everything

The final step is to test your game's interaction with Facebook. To do so, follow these steps:

1. **Launch your game.**

2. **On the settings screen in *Traffic*, tap the Connect with Facebook button to connect to Facebook within your application.**

Notice that the white box that you added in Interface Builder has turned into a good-looking button (as shown in Figure 16-4); that's the Facebook Connect library taking over the drawing of the view!

Figure 16-4:
The Facebook log-in button, drawn by Facebook Connect.

3. **Provide your Facebook log-in details.**

   After you log in, the application detects that you haven't granted the game permission to post to your feed, and it presents a dialog asking you to let it do this (as shown in Figure 16-5).

4. **Go back to the main menu, tap the New Game button, and play and finish a game (either by running out of time or crashing a car).**

   The Game Over screen appears, and you see the Post to Facebook button you added.

5. **Tap the Post to Facebook button.**

   Nothing happens for a few seconds, and then you return to the main menu.

6. **Check your Facebook profile.**

   You just posted your latest time to Facebook. Woo!

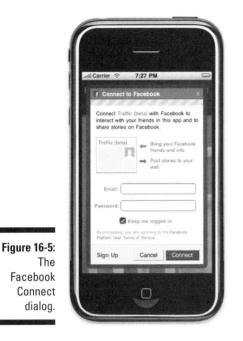

Figure 16-5:
The
Facebook
Connect
dialog.

Improving the User Experience

Congratulations! You've done the bare minimum needed to get your user's scores onto Facebook. Now make the user experience really shine.

Disabling the buttons

The first thing you do is disable the Facebook button if the user hasn't given the application permission to post to his feed. To do this, use the outlet for the button that you add earlier in this chapter in the "Creating the interface" section, to tell it to become dimmed and disabled. Follow these steps:

1. **Add this code to the viewWillAppear method in TrafficViewController to disable the button:**

```
- (void) viewWillAppear:(BOOL)animated {
    [gameController startGame];
    TrafficAppDelegate* delegate = [[UIApplication
            sharedApplication] delegate];
    if (delegate.shouldPlaySFX)
        [backgroundAudioPlayer play];
    if (delegate.multiplayerSession == nil) {
        sendTimeButton.hidden = YES;
    }
```

```
postToFacebookButton.enabled = delegate.
    hasFacebookPermission;
if (!postToFacebookButton.enabled)
  postToFacebookButton.alpha = 0.5;
}
```

This code asks the application delegate to see whether you have permission to post to the user's news feed. If you don't, the button is disabled and set as 50 percent transparent, which makes the button look untappable to the user.

2. **Test your code by running the application and logging out of Facebook before playing the game.**

   When the game ends, look at the Post to Facebook button: It's dimmed, and you can't use it.

Showing activity

The next step is to make the application do something animated and interesting while the user waits for the application to finish posting. To do this, add an *activity indicator,* which are those famous spinning circles that Apple made popular in the early 2000s. They're perfect for letting the user know that something's happening.

To add the activity indicator, create an outlet for referring to the control and then go back to Interface Builder and set it up. Follow these steps:

1. **Add an outlet for the control.**

   Refer to Listing 16-3 — notice how you're adding a UIActivityIndicator to the class.

2. **In Interface Builder, find the UIActivityIndicator control in the Library window (scroll through the list to find it), drag it into the Game Over view, and place it anywhere you like.**

   In the Library window, the activity indicator looks like Figure 16-6.

3. **Make the indicator be invisible when it's not needed:**

   a. *Select the newly added indicator.*

   b. *In the Attributes Inspector, select the Hide When Stopped check box.*

      The view appears only when it's spinning.

   c. *Choose Large White from the Style drop-down list to make the activity indicator look nicer against the dark background.*

   You can see the settings that you need to provide for the activity indicator in Figure 16-7.

Figure 16-6:
The activity
indicator
control in
the Library
window.

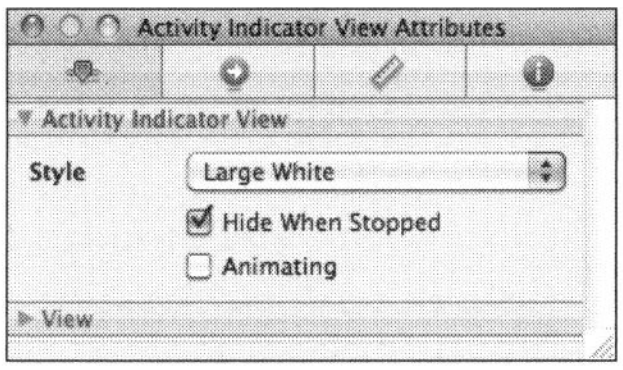

Figure 16-7:
The settings
you need for
the activity
indicator.

4. **Connect the Traffic View Controller's activity outlet to the activity indicator you just added.**

   To do this, hold down the Control key, and tap and drag from the file's owner to the activity indicator. Choose Activity from the list that appears.

After you follow these steps, the application can refer to the activity indicator. The next step is to actually make the indicator appear when it needs to. Here are the steps:

1. **Make the activity indicator appear when the user posts to Facebook by adding this code to the postToFacebook: method in TrafficViewController:**

```
- (IBAction) postToFacebook:(id)sender {
    NSString* statusText = [NSString
        stringWithFormat:@"I just beat the peak
        hour and lasted %.1f seconds in Traffic!",
        gameController.timeTotal];
    NSDictionary *params = [NSDictionary dictionaryWith
        ObjectsAndKeys:statusText, @"status", @"true",
        @"status_includes_verb", nil];
    [[FBRequest requestWithDelegate:self]
        call:@"facebook.users.setStatus"
        params:params];
    [activity startAnimating];
}
```

2. **Run the application and post your score to Facebook.**

   The activity indicator appears and starts spinning!

After going through these steps, you've put together a fully working Facebook application, along with a nice UI for it. Congratulations!

Chapter 17

External Displays

In This Chapter

▶ Discovering what external displays are

▶ Figuring out the differences among screens, windows, and views

▶ Updating *Traffic* to display extra content

A new feature in iOS 4 (and 3.2 on the iPad) is the ability to connect another display to your device and send pictures to it. Apple originally intended this to let users attach their big screen TVs to their iPods, iPhones, and iPads so they could watch movies with their home theatre system; however, in iOS 4, Apple also opened the application programming interface (API) to let developers (that's you!) work with the extra displays.

In this chapter, you find out about the different capabilities of external displays, how to connect one to your application, and how to make things appear on your other display.

To properly test on your hardware, you need a couple extra pieces of equipment. This chapter focuses on using the Apple iPad Dock Connector to VGA Adapter, because that's the connector most widely used with the iPad. You need to get one of those, or a similar connector, to test the features you'll be building in this chapter on real devices. Of course, having a display you can connect the iPad to also helps.

You can get an iPad Dock Connector to VGA Adapter at any Apple store or retailer.

You can attach external displays to an iPhone or iPod touch, if it's running iOS 4.0 or above. All of the code that you'll be writing in this chapter applies to projects running on the iPhone and iPhone 4. For this chapter, though, we'll be using the iPad. Feel free to make the iPhone version of the game run on your big-screen TV; the exact same techniques apply!

Doubling the Fun with an External Display

Attaching another display to your device means that you suddenly have a whole other extra area to display information to your user, as shown in Figure 17-1. Depending on the display you've connected, this display could be bigger than the iPad's built-in screen.

Figure 17-1:
Attaching an external display to an iPad.

An extra screen to show information to the user means you can do a wide range of interesting things. For example, you could

- Display statistics based on what the player does in the game
- Use the iPad as a game controller and show the game on the external display
- For a strategy game, show the game map on the large screen

Here are a couple differences to consider when designing a game that will be shown on an external display:

- **A tethered device is no longer mobile.** iOS devices are known for being able to be used anywhere, and letting the user pick them up and carry them away. As soon as you plug in a cable, though, everything changes. Because the device is now connected to a screen via the cable, the user can't pick up her iPad and walk away, or twist and tilt the device without being careful not to snag the cable on something.

✔ **Tethered iPads are held differently.** If you're making a racing game, where you hold the sides of the device and tilt the device, your user is used to gripping the device around the edges of the screen. However, if a screen is plugged in, the edges of the device are now no longer flat and smooth — there's a giant connector and cable poking out of one of the sides. Keep in mind how your users will hold the device when running your game, both connected and disconnected.

✔ **External displays aren't touchable.** The iPad's screen allows the user to interact with the application, but you can't put buttons, sliders, or controls of any kind on an external display. If you place these controls on the external display, the user can see them, but can't work with them at all. External displays are terrible for interactive content, but they are fantastic for non-interactive content — that is, telling the user about things.

Looking at Screens, Windows, and Views

Important differences are among windows, views, and screens, which we explain in the rest of this section. If you read Chapter 4, you already know about *views,* which are the regions of the screen where drawing happens. Views are used to actually put pictures onscreen, and if you've followed along so far, you've used them a lot to display everything to the user. Views are represented by the UIView class.

Every view that can be seen by the user is put inside a *window,* which is similar to a view but takes up the entire screen. Before the advent of multiple displays in iOS applications, pretty much every application had only one window. The window is the container for every single view that's shown to the user, and this includes every single view controller as well. Windows are represented by the UIWindow class.

A *screen* is the name that Cocoa Touch gives to the physical piece of hardware that displays the application to the user. The screen is the actual LCD built into the iPhone, iPad, and iPod touch. Windows are displayed on screens; if the window isn't on a screen, the user can't see it or its contents. Screens are represented by the UIScreen class.

Every single iOS device used to have the same resolution display (320 pixels wide x 480 pixels high), but that's not true anymore. For more information, see the sidebar "Pixels and points."

Because screens can be a bunch of different sizes, check what resolution they run at. To check the size of a screen, get a reference to the appropriate UIScreen object and ask for its `size` property. (We show you how to do that later in this chapter, in the "Sending the output" section.) Notice that we just said "the *appropriate* UIScreen object." Before iOS 3.2, only one screen was ever available to your app, which was the screen built in to the hardware — the so-called *main screen.*

Pixels and points

The Retina display, built into the iPhone 4, has a screen resolution of 640 pixels wide and 960 pixels high. However, every iPhone application made before the iPhone 4 assumes the screen is 320 pixels wide.

To get around this problem, Apple made a subtle change to how the display system works. On iPhone 4 devices, the screen still reports that it's 320 wide — but it's 320 *points* wide, rather than pixels. On iPhone 4, each screen point is 2 pixels wide and high. On lower-resolution devices (that is, the iPod touch, iPhone 3G and 3GS, and the iPad), each screen point is 1 pixel wide and 1 pixel high.

For more information on using high-resolution displays, Chapter 19 shows games that run on both the iPad and iPhone.

The upshot of this is that your application still works fine on the Retina display because the coordinate system remains the same. For more information on how these coordinate system shenanigans work, check out Apple's documentation; search the Apple Reference Library for *View Programming Guide for iPhone OS*. (This search will also bring up the *Table View Programming Guide* and the *Scroll View Programming Guide*. Both are good, but the document you're after is just the *View Programming Guide*.)

With the iPad (and with every device running iOS 4), however, many screens can be connected at once. (At the time of writing, you can only connect one other display to your device, but this could change in the future!)

Detecting extra displays

To get access to the list of screens attached to the device, ask the UIScreen class for the `screens` property. This property is an NSArray of UIScreen objects, each of which represents a connected display. This array always contains at least one object — the device's built-in display.

You can find out about screens in other ways. Every time the user connects a screen to your device, iOS posts the UIScreenDidConnectNotification. To handle this notification, tell Cocoa Touch that you want to know whenever the notification is posted. To make this happen, write some code like this:

```
// In the start-up part of your code...
NSNotificationCenter* defaultCenter =
          [NSNotificationCenter defaultCenter];
[defaultCenter addObserver:self
                selector:@selector(screenAttached:)
                     name:UIScreenDidConnectNotification
                   object:nil];

// Elsewhere in your code...
- (void) screenAttached:(NSNotification*)notification {
  // A screen was attached! Do something about it!
}
```

You can write similar code for handling the UIScreenDidDisconnectNotification, which sends when the user unplugs a screen, and UIScreenDidChangeNotification, which sends when a screen changes (for example, when the user changes the resolution of the display). All you have to do is change the name of the notification that you're adding an observer for.

UIScreenDidConnectNotification is sent only when the user plugs in an external display *after* your application launches. To find out about the screens that are *already* plugged in when the application launches, use the UIScreen's `screens` method to get the full list.

Differentiating among screens

Different screens run at different resolutions. If you plug in a high-definition television, you could run at a resolution of 1280 x 720; if you plug in an old, bulky CRT monitor, you could run at a resolution as low as 640 x 480. Therefore, you have a few challenges when designing your user interface. You aren't guaranteed to have the same size or shape screen, because different screens likely have different aspect ratios (for example, a wide screen TV is a different shape than an older style TV).

Keep an eye out for potential user interface issues when designing content for external displays and never assume that the user has the same kinds of external displays that you have.

Running different screen modes

In addition to different sizes, a lot of screens can also run in different *modes*. For example, a computer monitor could run at 800 x 600, 1024 x 768, or 1280 x 800. Cocoa Touch can figure out what modes a UIScreen object supports. You can also tell a UIScreen object to use a mode, by setting the `currentMode` property.

Because of performance, you need to be aware of the different possible screen resolutions. If you've ever played a modern game on an old computer, you already know that one of the tricks to get a decent frame rate is to reduce the game's resolution — you sacrifice visual quality for speed.

The frame rate is the rate at which your game is drawing itself to the screen. A high frame rate means a smoother-looking game. You should aim for a frame rate of 30 frames per second — anything less than this will look choppy, and could annoy the user.

Performance is even more important when talking about low-powered devices, such as the iPhone and iPad. *Remember:* These devices are powerful for their size, but they are still small devices! To get a decent frame rate, you might have to have the display render at a lower resolution. To do this, get the list of screen modes that your UIScreen supports.

Screen modes are represented by the UIScreenMode object and can be accessed by asking the UIScreen object for its `availableModes` property. You can also find out what mode the screen uses at the moment by asking for its `currentMode` property. Finally, you can set the screen resolution by setting the `currentMode` property to a mode that you think is most appropriate (keeping in mind, of course, that you only use a mode that the screen has reported it supports).

Using the extra display

After you know all about the differences among the various kinds of external displays, how can you go about actually using them?

The following steps are the basic process to put stuff on another display. We'll show you how to accomplish these in the section "Sending the Output."

1. Get the UIScreen that represents the screen you want to put the content on.

2. Create a UIWindow to contain the views that show the information you want to display.

   You can load this from a nib file, or you can make it yourself; it's often easiest to load the UIWindow from a nib file, which is what we show you in the section "Creating the window."

3. Set the `screen` property of the UIWindow to the UIScreen you want it to appear on.

4. Set the size of the UIWindow to match the size of the screen that it will appear on.

5. Tell the UIWindow to be visible.

After you make the window visible on the external screen, you can treat the views in the window just like any other — set their content, move them, and so forth. And they appear on your TV!

Adapting Your Game

To show you how this external display stuff works, we show you how to use a second display to indicate how long a user has played the current game. The first stage to adding external display support to *Traffic* is to create the extra window to be shown on the external display (see the next section for details!). This window contains a single UILabel, which contains the time.

Next, add the code to the TrafficViewController that detects the presence of an external display. If the user has a display connected when the view appears onscreen, the window resizes to match the size of the screen and displays onscreen. After that's done, update the label with the time. You'll find all of the code for this in the next section!

Creating the window

To get started, you'll need to first create the window that will end up being displayed on the screen. You'll also need to add some variables to the TrafficViewController class to make this happen. Read on to learn how to do it!

1. **Open TrafficViewController.xib in Interface Builder.**

   You'll find it in the Resources folder in your project.

2. **Create the new UIWindow for display on the external monitor:**

   a. *Drag in a new UIWindow object from the library into the list of objects in TrafficViewController.xib.*

   b. *Rename this UIWindow External Window.*

3. **Drag in a UILabel from the Library, and put it somewhere near the top of the window.**

4. **Add the outlet for the new window.**

   To put the new window on the external display, you need your code to be able to refer to it. Therefore, modify the interface for TrafficViewController so that it looks like the following code (additions are in bold):

```
#import <UIKit/UIKit.h>
#import <AVFoundation/AVFoundation.h>
#import "FBConnect.h"

@class TrafficController;

@interface TrafficViewController : UIViewController
        <FBRequestDelegate> {
  TrafficController* gameController;
  UIView* pauseOverlay;
  UIView* gameOverOverlay;
  UILabel* timeRemainingLabel;
  IBOutlet UIButton* sendTimeButton;
  IBOutlet UIButton* postToFacebookButton;
  IBOutlet UIActivityIndicatorView* activity;

  UIWindow* externalWindow;

  AVAudioPlayer* backgroundAudioPlayer;
}

@property (nonatomic, retain) IBOutlet UIWindow*
        externalWindow;
@property (nonatomic, retain) IBOutlet
        TrafficController* gameController;
@property (nonatomic, retain) IBOutlet UIView*
        pauseOverlay;
@property (nonatomic, retain) IBOutlet UILabel*
        timeRemainingLabel;
@property (nonatomic, retain) IBOutlet UIView*
        gameOverOverlay;

- (void) displayGameOver;
- (IBAction) postToFacebook:(id)sender;
- (IBAction) pauseGame:(id)sender;
- (IBAction) endGame:(id)sender;
- (void) setTimeRemaining:(CGFloat)time;

@end
```

5. Connect the window to the view controller.

Once you're done, the window is ready to be shown on screen.

Sending the output

After you have a window set up properly, make it appear on the external display. The first step is to check whether an external display is connected. If an external display isn't connected, you obviously shouldn't (and can't) do anything with it.

If an external display is connected, get the size of the display, resize the window to fit the display, and make the window appear onscreen:

1. **Detect the external display.**

   If the number of screens attached to the device is more than one, you know you have got an external display attached.

   To detect the display, modify the viewDidLoad method in TrafficViewController so that it looks like the following code:

   ```
   - (void) viewDidLoad {
     NSURL* backgroundURL = [NSURL
          fileURLWithPath:[[NSBundle mainBundle]
                            pathForResource:@"cars-
          loop" ofType:@"aif"]];
     backgroundAudioPlayer = [[AVAudioPlayer alloc] initW
          ithContentsOfURL:backgroundURL
                            error:nil];
     backgroundAudioPlayer.numberOfLoops = -1; // loop
          forever
     [backgroundAudioPlayer retain];


     if ([UIScreen screens] > 1) {
       // We have a connected display

       // The internal display is screen 0;
       // the external one is screen 1.
       UIScreen* externalScreen = [[UIScreen screens]
          objectAtIndex:1];
     }
   }
   ```

External displays and the Simulator

Because the Simulator is so useful, you've probably done a lot of development and testing inside it rather than spending heaps of time testing on real devices. At this stage, though, you might be wondering, "How can I plug in my HDTV into the iPhone Simulator?"

The answer, you might be astounded to hear, is that you can't. You shouldn't try to push your TV cable through the LCD to reach the virtual iPhone. Doing this will only break your computer. We have verified that this does not work. (It cost Jon the price of a new laptop, after his failed experiment.)

To simulate an external display, you can tell the iPhone Simulator that a TV Out device is connected. To do this, choose Hardware⇨TV Out. A list of different resolutions available appears. If you select one, the iPhone Simulator simulates a monitor being plugged into your device.

Note: Connecting a virtual TV Out monitor in the simulator doesn't send the UIScreenDidConnectNotification to your application; instead, it quits your application and returns to the home screen. You'll need to launch your application again after connecting the TV Out device.

2. **Resize the external window and attach the external window to the external display.**

   You'll need to get the current screen mode of the external display to work out the proper size for the window.

   To resize and attach the window, modify the code you just wrote so that it looks like the following:

```
if ([UIScreen screens] > 1) {
  // We have a connected display

  // The internal display is screen 0; the external
      one is screen 1.
  UIScreen* externalScreen = [[UIScreen screens]
      objectAtIndex:1];

  UIScreenMode* currentMode = externalScreen.
      currentMode;

  CGRect rect = CGRectZero;
  rect.size = currentMode.size;
  externalWindow.frame = rect;

  externalWindow.screen = externalScreen;
  [externalWindow makeKeyAndVisible];
}
```

This code figures out the size of the connected screen and creates a CGRect that's the same size as the connected screen. This code then sets the frame of the external window to that rectangle and makes the window appear on the external screen.

You have only one last thing left to do: Display useful content on the external display. Follow these steps:

1. **Add a new UILabel outlet and a new method to TrafficViewController by modifying the code in TrafficViewController.h so that it looks like the following code:**

```
#import <UIKit/UIKit.h>
#import <AVFoundation/AVFoundation.h>
#import "FBConnect.h"

@class TrafficController;

@interface TrafficViewController : UIViewController
        <FBRequestDelegate> {
  TrafficController* gameController;
  UIView* pauseOverlay;
  UIView* gameOverOverlay;
  UILabel* timeRemainingLabel;
  IBOutlet UIButton* sendTimeButton;
  IBOutlet UIButton* postToFacebookButton;
  IBOutlet UIActivityIndicatorView* activity;

  UIWindow* externalWindow;
  UILabel* timeElapsedLabel;

  AVAudioPlayer* backgroundAudioPlayer;
}

@property (nonatomic, retain) IBOutlet UILabel*
        timeElapsedLabel;
@property (nonatomic, retain) IBOutlet UIWindow*
        externalWindow;
@property (nonatomic, retain) IBOutlet
        TrafficController* gameController;
@property (nonatomic, retain) IBOutlet UIView*
        pauseOverlay;
@property (nonatomic, retain) IBOutlet UILabel*
        timeRemainingLabel;
@property (nonatomic, retain) IBOutlet UIView*
        gameOverOverlay;

- (void) displayGameOver;
```

```
- (IBAction) postToFacebook:(id)sender;
- (IBAction) pauseGame:(id)sender;
- (IBAction) endGame:(id)sender;
- (void) setTimeRemaining:(CGFloat)time;
- (void) setTimeElapsed:(CGFloat)time;

@end
```

This outlet is connected to the label that you added to the external window earlier and is used to show the amount of time the player has been playing the game. And the new method updates the text of the label.

2. **In TrafficViewController.xib, connect the label in the external window to the timeElapsedLabel outlet.**

   We go through how to connect objects to outlets earlier in this book — check out Chapter 6 for more examples.

3. **Resize the label so that it's a little bit longer than its default size.**

   The label needs to accommodate the entire size of the text it will display, without cutting off anything.

4. **Add the `setTimeElapsed:` method by adding the following code to TrafficViewController.m:**

```
- (void)setTimeElapsed:(CGFloat) time {
  timeElapsedLabel.text = [NSString
        stringWithFormat:@"Time elapsed: %.1f", time];
}
```

   This code updates the text inside the label, based on the time value it receives from the Traffic Controller.

5. **Make the Traffic Controller update the time (or label) by modifying the `update:` method in TrafficController.m so that it looks like the following:**

```
[vehicles removeObject:v];
}

[viewController setTimeRemaining:timeRemaining];
[viewController setTimeElapsed:timeTotal];

if (timeRemaining < 0) {
```

When you run the game on the iPad with an external display connected, you see the amount of time the player has spent in the game appear on the external display. Hooray!

Don't forget, you can display any content you like on the external display. One of the best examples of a game that does this very well is *Chopper 2*, which allows you to plug your iPad into a big-screen TV and play the game in high definition. Search for it on the App Store. (We'll remind you about it again in Chapter 28!)

Chapter 18

iAd

Up until now, all the technologies that we cover have existed with the primary goal of making great games and apps. In this chapter, we discuss how to build the original iPhone version of the *Traffic* game while integrating the *iAd framework* — a framework that exists with the singular purpose of making you, the developer, money.

A native drop-in solution for making money off advertisements inside your application is an important new feature of the iOS Software Development Kit (SDK) 4.0 and above, so be sure you fully understand both how to use it and the ramifications of taking an advertising-supported approach to your games.

In this chapter, we take the completed iOS version of the *Traffic* game, as it stood at the end of Chapter 17, and add iAd powered advertising to it. Along the way, we discuss the best practices for using ads, such as where you should and shouldn't use them, as well as how to test your implementation and some general tips and tricks. At the time of writing, iAd is only available for the iPhone and does not yet work on the iPad, but that's likely to change in the future.

Using iAd

iAd is one of the great new features of iOS and the iPhone 4.0 SDK. And, lucky for you, iAd is aimed squarely at increasing developer happiness. How? By increasing the size of your bank account!

iAd offers an alternative means to make money with your game. Instead of charging your customers for your game, Apple sells ads and delivers them directly to your game while you reap the profits. As shown in Figure 18-1, advertisements are received from Apple's iAd service and displayed in the designated places within your game.

AdKit is the framework provided by Apple that is responsible for downloading the ad content from their servers, and displaying the ad in your application. When the user taps on the ad in your application, they see the full ad, and you get money.

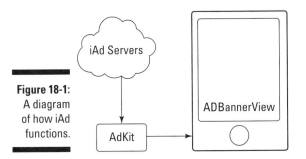

Figure 18-1:
A diagram
of how iAd
functions.

Joining the iAd Network

Sign up for the iAd network in a few steps:

1. **Point your browser to http://itunesconnect.apple.com.**

   A page similar to the one shown in Figure 18-2 appears. Apple does change this site occasionally, so when you get there, it may look a little different.

   See Chapter 13 for a refresher on the basics of iTunes Connect.

| | Store | Mac | iPod + iTunes | iPhone | Downloads | Support |

iTunes Connect

Apple ID

Password

Forgot Password...   Sign In

Figure 18-2:
The iTunes
Connect
login page.

2. **Enter your Apple ID and password, and then click the Sign In button.**

3. **Click the Contracts, Tax, & Banking Information link, as shown in Figure 18-3.**

   The Contracts, Tax, & Banking Information page appears.

Figure 18-3:
The
Contracts,
Tax, &
Banking
Information
link.

4. **Select the Request Contract check box for the iAd Network and then click the Submit button (see Figure 18-4).**

   The terms and conditions of the contract appear.

   If you want a refresher on the rest of iTunes Connect, see Chapter 13.

Figure 18-4:
Requesting
the iAd
contract.

5. **Read and agree to the terms and conditions.**

   Once you've agreed to the conditions, you're registered to deliver iAd advertisements in your app — you're ready to roll.

6. **Click through and fill in the details for the Contact Info, Bank Info, and Tax Info columns (see Figure 18-5).**

   Check out Chapter 13 if you want a refresher of this stuff. Also, we're developers, not lawyers, so you might want to talk to your by-the-hour buddy for some tips. Once you're done, click the "Done" button, which takes you back to the main iTunes Connect screen.

Figure 18-5:
The information that you'll need to give to Apple.

Your Contracts In Effect

Contract Number	Contract Region	Contract Type	Contract Download	Contact Info	Bank Info	Tax Info	Effective Date	Expiration Date	Contract in Effect
MS1431908	All (See Contract)	Paid Applications	✓	Edit	View/Edit	Edit	March 07, 2010	August 02, 2010	⊘
MS1931796	World	Free Applications	N/A	N/A	N/A	N/A	June 10, 2010	August 02, 2010	⊘

Done

You're officially registered for iAd. The next section shows you how to incorporate it into your games.

ADBannerView

The essence of iAd is the *ADBannerView,* which is another subclass of UIView. A section of your interface is dedicated to displaying an advertisement that the user can tap at any time. The view automatically retrieves new advertisements from Apple, and you're paid when a user interacts with an advertisement.

A view controller must manage any parts of your interface where you intend to include an ADBannerView because tapping an ad causes another view to display modally. Only view controllers can display a view modally.

A view that appears *modally* appears on top of an existing view and requires that users interact with it before they can return to the existing (parent) view. More often than not, these views take up the full screen (though there are exceptions, including dialogs).

The ADBannerView uses a delegate — *ADBannerViewDelegate* — to customize its behavior, such as when and how to show new advertisements, to pause your game during ad interactions, and to control the behavior of user interaction with the iAd. Complying with the ADBannerViewDelegate protocol is necessary, even if you don't care about hiding the iAd view if no ad is available or suspending any underlying elements of your app when the iAd is engaged.

An ADBannerView must always be one of two sizes:

- ✔ 320 x 50 for portrait view
- ✔ 480 x 32 for landscape view

Implementing iAd

Using the *Traffic* example throughout this book, put an iAd on the *Traffic* main menu screen; it would annoy users if you put an ad in the middle of the game, and the other screens are fairly transient locations. The main menu is the part of the interface users see the most, with the exception of playing the game itself.

Open MainMenuViewController.xib in Interface Builder and, one by one, select each of the four buttons you have and move them up a little. The first button — New Game — ends up a little closer to the top of the screen, and the following buttons (Network, Stats, and Settings) are significantly closer to each other. Take a look at Figure 18-6 to get the idea.

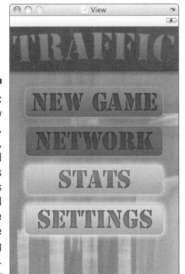

Figure 18-6:
The New Game, Network, Stats, and Settings buttons rearranged to make room for the positioning of iAd.

Add the iAd.framework framework to the project before continuing. For a refresher on how to add a framework to your project, head back to Chapter 14, where you added the audio frameworks to the application.

You need to add an ADBannerView to the menu. Just like in Chapter 5, use the Interface Builder Library window to browse the objects available — look for the iAd object. After you find the iAd object, drag it into the main menu and position it at the very bottom of the screen.

After you do this, you have something that resembles Figure 18-7.

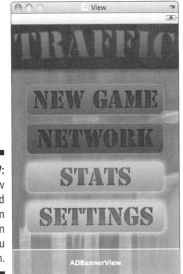

Figure 18-7: iAd view positioned cleanly on the main menu screen.

You need to set the delegate of the ADBannerView you just added to the file's owner proxy object (which we discussed in Chapter 3). Follow these steps to set up the outlet and delegate:

1. **Open MainMenuViewController.xib in Interface Builder. Select the ADBannerView in the view window.**

2. **In the Connections tab of the Inspector window (choose Tools⇨ Connections Inspector, if you can't find it onscreen) drag from the little circle next to the delegate outlet to the File's Owner object in the MainMenuViewController.xib window.**

   The File's Owner object flashes, and the delegate of your ADBannerView is set to the MainMenuViewController class you created.

3. **Set the alpha (or transparency) of the ADBannerView to 0 by switching to the Attributes Inspector (click the left-most tab at the top of the Inspector window) and dragging the Alpha slider to 0.**

In the next section, you'll write code that ensures the ADBannerView is set only to fully opaque if there's actually an ad to display, so making it default to completely invisible is a sensible move.

4. **Save the MainMenuViewController.xib file, leave Interface Builder, and return to Xcode.**

Conform to My Protocol, Baby

If you've followed along so far, you have an app that loads an iAd from Apple's server, and which would display the iAd if it wasn't invisible. (Go ahead and run the application — the only visual difference is that the main menu is moved to the new position!)

Cute, but not particularly useful for the purposes of rubbing yourself in hard-earned iAd dollars. The ad needs to be shown to the user, if you want to make money!

Add the following import to MainMenuViewController.h:

```
#import <iAd/iAd.h>
```

Also, add the ADBannerViewDelegate protocol to the interface line:

```
@interface MainMenuViewController : UIViewController
        <GKPeerPickerControllerDelegate,
        ADBannerViewDelegate>
```

As we point out at the beginning of this chapter, ideally if there's no iAd to display, the user should never see the iAd view (even if it's just an empty frame — well, especially if it's just an empty frame!) To that end, you need to allow the ADBannerView to elegantly fade into view if an ad is available. And if, for some reason, it's displayed and an ad becomes unavailable (such as if the device loses its connection to the computer Internet, heaven forbid!), it needs to elegantly fade the broken iAd out of view.

First, look at how you make the ADBannerView appear when an iAd is available. Add the following code to MainMenuViewController.m:

```
-(void)bannerViewDidLoadAd:(ADBannerView *)banner {
    [UIView beginAnimations:nil context:NULL];
    [UIView setAnimationDuration:1];
    [banner setAlpha:1];
    [UIView commitAnimations];
}
```

If you're reading this book from cover to cover, this is familiar to you because you did pretty much the same thing in Chapter 6. In Chapter 6, you made the buttons change their size onscreen, which made them look like they're popping into existence. For the banner view, you make the opacity change from 0 (fully transparent, which was what you set up in Interface Builder) to 1 (fully opaque).

If you build and run your game now, the main menu pops into view as usual, and the iAd banner gracefully fades up when it fetches an iAd (or in this case, a test iAd) from Apple's server. Take a look at Figure 18-8 for what this looks like.

Of course, if no iAd is available, you don't want anything to display. To that end, add the code to make the ADBannerView hide the banner if there's no iAd to display. Add the following code to MainMenuViewController.m:

```
-(void)bannerView:(ADBannerView *)banner
        didFailToReceiveAdWithError:(NSError *)error {
    [UIView beginAnimations:nil context:NULL];
    [UIView setAnimationDuration:1];
    [banner setAlpha:0];
    [UIView commitAnimations];
}
```

Pretty simple! All you do here is animate the *alpha* (that is, the transparency) of the ad view back to 0 (fully transparent) so that the ADBannerView disappears if there's no iAd to display.

You can test this by disconnecting your computer from the Internet and running the new code — you return to seeing a running version of Figure 18-8.

Figure 18-8:
Apple's test iAd displayed after fading into view.

Part IV
The iPad

"It's a docking system for the iPad that comes with 3 bedrooms, 2 baths, and a car port."

In this part . . .

In this part, we overhaul the game on a technical and philosophical level — for the iPad (and the iPhone 4). This part gets you ready to go with Apple's iAd system for selling advertising within your game so you can make a little coffee money on the side. We tell you how to best approach building, designing, and converting games for the iPad. We also use new things like gesture recognizers (to reduce the pain in detecting gestures, such as a pinch) and cool things like OpenGL ES (for adding fancy 3D effects).

Finally, this part tells you how to add a few nifty bonus features to your game to boost the chances of its success. Here's a breakdown of each chapter:

- ✔ Chapter 19 gives you the lowdown on the whole new world that the iPad represents, and what that means for your game design and development.

- ✔ Chapter 20 overhauls *Traffic* for the iPad, adding multiple lanes of cars.

- ✔ Chapter 21 adds a nifty speed control using Apple's powerful new gesture recognizer system.

- ✔ Chapter 22 takes *Traffic* into the third dimension, in the simplest way possible, using the mighty power of OpenGL ES.

- ✔ Chapter 23 builds on your newfound OpenGL ES knowledge and discusses how to add objects to the 3D space.

- ✔ Chapter 24 takes those objects and gives them some flair — by adding textures.

- ✔ Chapter 25 kicks the game up a level by adding some cool finishing touches to round off things.

Chapter 19

The World of the iPad

*I*n this chapter, we lead you on a journey into a whole new world: that of Apple's latest type of mobile device. That's right — it's not a romantic ballad by Sir Tim Rice, it's the iPad!

More than a few people purchased an iPad right off the bat, and if you were one of the enthusiastic few to have grabbed one on launch day, you know what a fascinating little gadget it is. (We shan't mention which of the authors was crazy enough to line up at 3 a.m. to get one.)

This chapter covers the design differences you need to keep in mind when writing applications and games for the iPad, as well as how to transition your application from one that runs on only the iPhone to one that runs on the iPad as well.

Introducing the iPad

Before we go any further we need two vital pieces of information:

- ✔ The iPad *is not* a big iPhone.
- ✔ The iPad *is* just a big iPhone.

Got it? No? Hmm, perhaps further explanation is in order. Here we explain what we meant:

- ✔ The iPad has a lot in common with the iPhone:
    - It runs the same OS.
    - It's built around the idea of the user directly manipulating information by using a touchscreen.

- It's designed to be connected to the Internet a lot of the time.

- It runs the majority of the same apps, albeit with a much bigger screen.

✔ At the same time, the iPad is quite different from the iPhone:

- It doesn't fit in the user's pocket, so it's less likely to be carried around by the user at all times.

- The larger screen also means that there's more room for graphical detail and more room for the user's hands to move around.

- Whereas the iPhone is usually held with one hand and manipulated with the other, the iPad is used differently — it can be used by one hand, but it's also often placed on a flat surface and worked on with both hands.

- Because the iPad is a lot larger, it's also heavier. This means that games that involve holding and rotating the device make the user's arms a lot more tired: A racing game that has the player turn the iPad around like a steering wheel gets tiring quickly!

Discovering the New Rules for iPad Apps

Apple has a set of recommendations for iPad applications, and they also apply to games. Here are some of the ways in which the iPad differs from the iPhone. Keep these in mind when you're developing your game.

Multiple orientations

Applications need to make an effort to support all orientations — both portrait and landscape need to be supported and upside-down versions of each.

The iPad is a device that adapts itself to how it's held. When you use an iPad, you often change how you hold it based on what's comfortable. Additionally, when you pick up an iPad and turn it on, the device needs to be ready for you to use instantly, rather than you rotating it until you can work with it.

This isn't a hard-and-fast rule: Not all applications make sense in both portrait and landscape modes. Many wide screen applications (such as many racing games, and Apple's Keynote presentation software) don't support displaying in portrait mode because those apps don't make that much sense when squeezed and resized to fit the portrait orientation.

Therefore, design your games with the *aim* of supporting all orientations. For space reasons, we don't cover adapting *Traffic* as a landscape application, but any games that you write need to start out with this idea in mind.

More room for hands

The larger screen on the iPad means that there's more room for hands to move around the screen. Because the physical screen space on the iPhone is small, the user moves her fingers only small distances when she plays games. On the iPad, though, there's plenty of room, and the user has to move her entire arm to reach from one corner of the screen to the other.

To avoid making your user have to reach too much, keep related controls close to each other. The farther away a control is from the user's hand, the less likely it is he'll want to use it, unless he really has to.

This issue is mitigated a little bit by the fact that the user is more likely to use both hands, but it's still a factor. Design your game so that the user can quickly get at the stuff he cares about!

Two people, one device

Remember this when you're designing iPad games: The iPad is a great device for sharing game play with other people.

With the large screen, two people have room to play the same game, which can be an incredible experience. In Chapter 20, we show you how to update *Traffic* to support multiple-person game play on the same screen. Also, think about how you could turn your own games into games you can share with friends.

The best kind of marketing is word of mouth, and the best kind of word of mouth is where your user shares the game experience with their friends. By letting players share the game together, you're more likely to get another sale!

Adapting Traffic for the iPad

To put *Traffic* on the iPad, you need to make a few changes. The first of these changes is to take the iPhone version of the project, and then convert it to a project that builds and runs on the iPad. Fortunately, this is a simple process that's built right into Xcode and is known as *transitioning*.

Transitioning the project

The iPhone version of the *Traffic* project is composed of one target. A *target* is Xcode's name for an application that it builds, and you can have multiple targets inside a single Xcode project. Use this to your advantage to keep the project's resources separate — you can still play the same iPhone version of the game while you upgrade the iPad version.

The single target — *Traffic* — compiles the code that you've written and turns it into an iPhone application. Transitioning the project means adding a new target that takes the code and turns it into an iPad application.

The iPad application can't use the exact same resource files as its iPhone counterpart. The iPad app can use a lot of them, but it can't use the same Interface Builder files, for example, because they just aren't the right size. Fortunately, transitioning the project to use the iPad creates a second Resources folder, which contains a duplicate set of the xib files. These xib files are used only in the iPad version of the application, while the originals are used in the iPhone version.

You can then modify these iPad-only copies and adapt the entire interface to be something completely different for the iPad version. (If you follow along, by the end of Chapter 24, the game will be hugely different! You add, among other things, a new background system and update the game play for the larger screen.)

Deciding how to transition

You have two ways to transition a project from the iPhone to the iPad:

- ✔ Create two different targets in your project: One target is aimed at the iPhone, and the other is aimed at the iPad.
- ✔ Create a *universal* application that works on both the iPhone and the iPad.

You might choose one route over another for various reasons. First, upgrading your application to a universal application means that the user can purchase your game once and run it on both the iPhone and the iPad without buying it a second time. Depending on your views, this might be a good thing or a bad thing!

Creating a universal application means that your application needs to do a little bit more work to tell the difference between running on an iPad and running on an iPhone. However, running on an iPhone and iPad for no extra cost can be a huge selling point.

Creating two versions of your application allows you to sell both versions of the application separately; it also means you need to manage both versions.

In this book, you create both applications. Chapters 1–18 focus on the creation of the iPhone version. From this chapter to the end of the book, all extra features we discuss are for the iPad version.

With all that in mind, bite the bullet, grit your teeth, and transition the project! Follow these steps:

1. **Select the *Traffic* target from the drop-down menu at the top-left of the Xcode project window, as shown in Figure 19-1.**

Figure 19-1:
Selecting
the *Traffic*
target.

2. **Choose Project⇨Upgrade Current Target to iPad to transition the target.**

   A dialog appears, asking you how you want to transition the application — either by upgrading the single target to be universal or adding a new iPad target.

3. **Select the "Two device-specific applications" option, and click the "OK" button to create two targets.**

   A new Resources-iPad folder and a new Traffic-iPad target are created in your project structure. The Resources-iPad folder contains copies of the nib files you've created if you worked through the earlier chapters — only they've all been scaled to match the iPad's resolution of 1024 x 768. Time to resize them all!

After following these steps, you'll now have two separate applications — one for the iPhone, and one for the iPad.

Resizing the views and menus

To make the game look its best on the iPad, you need to reposition the elements of the game's screens so that they're properly located on the bigger screen. Follow these steps to make the application look best on the iPad:

1. **Reposition and resize the buttons and the background image on the main menu.**

   To do this, follow these steps:

   a. Open MainMenuViewController.xib and then resize the background image to fill the screen by changing the content scale mode to Scale to Fill.

   To change the content scale mode, select the background image, and open the Attributes Inspector. The content scale mode selector is near the middle of the window.

   b. Move the buttons so that they're positioned as they are in Figure 19-2.

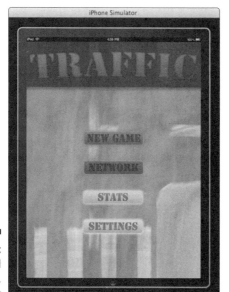

Figure 19-2:
The updated
main menu.

2. Reposition and resize the controls for the high scores screen.

This is exactly the same process as Step 1, but in this case, you're working on the StatsViewController.xib file. Reposition the views so that
they're in the center of the screen and resize the background image so
that it fills the screen.

3. Reposition and resize the controls for the settings screen.

Same as Steps 1 and 2 — only now, you're working in
SettingsViewController.xib.

Reposition the views so that they're in the center of the screen and
resize the background image so that it fills the screen.

4. Reposition and resize the views in the game screen.

Open up TrafficViewController.xib. Similarly to the previous steps,
resize the background image, make it Scale to Fill, and reposition and
resize the lanes so they stretch from the top of the screen to the bottom.

5. Center the game over and pause screens.

The game over and pause screens, when they're displayed on the
screen, are placed at the top-left hand corner of the screen. Without any
changes to the size of the views, they'll appear as a tiny region at the
top-left, and make the game look broken. Time to fix this!

The easiest way to correct this visual issue is to expand the game over
and pause screens to fit 1024 x 768 pixels, and then place the visible
components of these screens in the center.

Resize the game over view, and the pause screen, so that they're 1024 x 768, and then reposition the views and controls that are inside them.

To resize the views, select the window and open the Size Inspector by pressing ⌘-3. Set the Width and Height fields to 1024 and 768 respectively, and make sure that the X and Y fields are both set to 0.

Before you play with the iPad version, you'll need to understand how to work with the two targets that are now managed inside Xcode. In the next section, you'll find out how to accomplish this!

Managing multiple targets

To manage both targets that now exist in your project, start by looking at the Build Configuration drop-down list in the top-left of the main Xcode Project window. If you open this list, you see a list of build options, as shown in Figure 19-3.

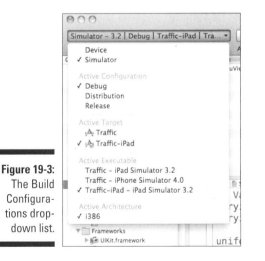

Figure 19-3:
The Build Configurations drop-down list.

About halfway down the list is the Active Target section. This controls which target Xcode builds when you click the Build & Run button. To select the iPad target, follow these steps:

The Active Target control is useful when you develop two different applications inside the same project and want to control which target you work on.

1. **Open the Build Configuration list and then choose the Traffic-iPad target.**

2. **Click the Build and Run button to build the iPad version of the game, which installs and runs it on the iPad Simulator.**

High-resolution Screens

The iPad's display is a lot bigger than the old iPhone's display — the original iPhone has a display resolution of 320 x 480, and the iPad runs at an impressive 1024 x 768. As a consequence of this larger space, icons are bigger on the iPad. (Your icon needs to be 72 x 72 pixels, and called Icon-iPad.png.)

To make the application use this image for the icon on the iPad, simply add the file to the project by dragging it from the Finder to the Resources folder in Xcode. When you next build and run the game, the application will have an updated icon.

However, the iPad isn't the only device that has a bigger screen, and now's the perfect time to talk about it.

The Retina display

For the purposes of the *Traffic* game, the iPhone 4 is identical to previous versions of the hardware in almost all regards, except for one: the screen.

The resolution of the iPhone 4's display (which Apple's marketing dubs the Retina display) is double that of previous models, which means that the game now fits in a 640 x 960 screen. If you run the game on an iPhone 4, though, you'll find that the game still fills the entire screen.

This is because iOS automatically doubles the size of all images, text, and views used in the application. From iOS's point of view, the bigger resolution doesn't mean that there's more room for content, but rather that it's able to present things in more detail.

Because iOS takes this philosophy for drawing content on the Retina display, it pretends that the screen is still running at a resolution of 320 x 480. However, there's a subtle difference when running on iOS 4: instead of thinking about the screen in terms of pixels, you think of them in terms of *points*.

The iPhone's screen is 320 points wide, no matter what hardware you're running on. However, on an iPhone 4, there are 2 pixels for every point.

From a practical standpoint, this means that your code doesn't have to change to run on higher-resolution screens.

However, it does mean that images will be blown up and look blurry. Fortunately, this is something you can fix!

Starting in iOS 4, every time your code loads an image, it checks to see whether it's running on a high-resolution display. If this is the case, it then checks to see if there's a double-resolution version of the image you're trying to load. If it finds one, it loads that double-resolution image rather than the original file, and your code continues on its way! The upshot is that you'll have crisp, great-looking images on the high-resolution screen, and your code will still work on lower-resolution screens.

So, how does iOS find these high-resolution images? Like the rest of Apple's code, it expects you to follow strict conventions. A high-resolution version of an image is marked as such by including @2x at the end of the filename. As an example, the file RedCar.png would have a high-resolution counterpart called RedCar@2x.png. As long as you follow these simple rules, you'll get great-looking images on a great-looking screen!

We've included high-res versions of all of the imagery used in *Traffic* in the resources collection you downloaded in Chapter 1. Add those images to your project, and run it on an iPhone 4 to see the difference!

If you don't have an iPhone 4, you can test out how it looks in the iPhone Simulator. Here's how you turn your iPhone Simulator into an iPhone 4 Simulator:

1. **Open the iPhone Simulator.**

2. **Open the Hardware Menu, and choose Device⇨iPhone 4. The simulator will turn into an iPhone 4 Simulator.**

   Note that the iPhone 4 Simulator is treated as a different "device" to the iPhone Simulator, and *Traffic* won't appear on the home screen. You'll have to re-install it. Here's how:

3. **Go back to Xcode, and click the Build and Run button. The game will be installed in the iPhone 4 Simulator.**

You can go back and forth between the different versions of the hardware at any time.

Adding a better default image

When you convert the game to an iPad application, a lot of settings remain the same. This includes the default screen, which is the image that appears when the application is loading.

For the iPad, you need a bigger, more detailed launch screen. Here's how to add one to the project:

1. **Add the Default-iPad.png image to the project.**

   You'll find this image in the resources collection from Chapter 1.

2. **Set up the application to use this image on the iPad, by changing the Info.plist file.**

   Locate and open the Info.plist file, which is one of the original files created by Xcode when you started the project.

   Select one of the rows in the list, and click the "+" button at the right hand side of the list.

   Change the key in the left-hand column of the list to "Launch image (iPad)", and change the value in the right-hand column to "Default-iPad.png".

3. **Build and Run the application, by clicking the Build and Run button at the top of the Xcode window.**

When you launch the application, the higher-resolution image will appear!

Chapter 20

Adding Multiple Lanes for the iPad

In This Chapter

▶ Adapting the game to a larger screen

▶ Adding more complexity to the game

*T*he iPad provides a much larger canvas for the game to exist on than the iPhone, but simply scaling up the game to work on it isn't going far enough.

In this chapter, you expand the game to work on two different roads at once, and add some more game play elements for the player to think about when playing.

Designing Game Play for a Larger Screen

The iPad's larger screen means that more than one person can use the device at once, with a multiplayer game. If you have a game that you can share with your friends, you're likely to have even more fun — plus, as a developer, you're more likely to see increased sales!

Designing multiplayer games on a single screen is an idea that's been around for a very, very long time — in fact, the first games ever made used this technique. And this technique is still used to this day when the game developer knows that only one screen is available to use.

You can design two-player game play onscreen at once in a couple ways:

✔ **Split screen:** This shows two viewpoints on the game onscreen at once (see Figure 20-1).

This is very useful for when you have a game in which players are likely to change their position or orientation when playing (such as in racing games with each player driving around a world). A great, old example of such a game is *Mario Kart 64*, by Nintendo.

✔ **Single viewpoint:** Two players share a viewpoint that works for both (see Figure 20-2).

This works well for simpler styles of games, such as puzzles and simple strategy games. A great example of a shared-screen multiplayer game is *Little Big Planet*, by Media Molecule, or any of the *Super Smash Bros* games by Nintendo.

We'll be turning this version of the game into one that uses shared-screen multiplayer.

For *Traffic,* you adapt the game to allow two people to play it, but it works just as well for one person, too. Whereas the iPhone version of the game contains three lanes of cars, the iPad version of the game has six. In the iPhone game, all the cars travel in the same direction; in the iPad version, half the cars travel in the opposite direction (see Figure 20-3).

You'll be making these changes for two reasons:

✔ **Novelty:** The iPad version of the game needs to contain a few twists, just to be different.

✔ **Clarity:** When two players play on the same screen, you run the risk of players getting confused over who should control what parts of the game. By clearly dividing the game into two halves, each player's area of responsibility is obvious.

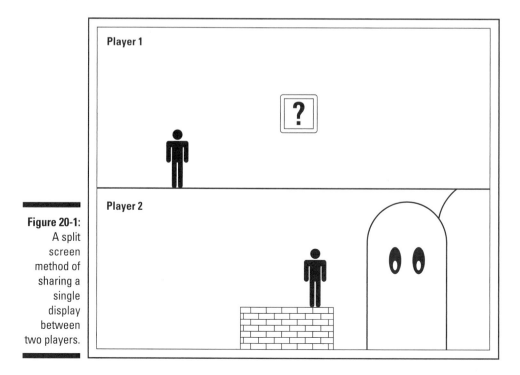

Figure 20-1:
A split screen method of sharing a single display between two players.

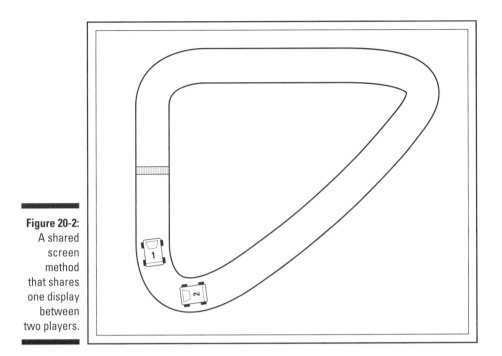

Figure 20-2:
A shared
screen
method
that shares
one display
between
two players.

Cars drive on the left in *Traffic.* Why? That's how Her Majesty would want it to be. Also, 60 percent of the authors of this book are Australian, which means that Neal got overruled.

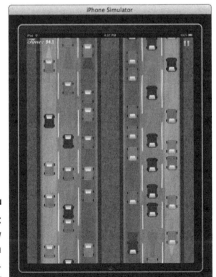

Figure 20-3:
The new
screen
layout.

Creating Additional Lanes and Multidirectional Cars

To adapt the game to use lanes going in opposite directions, you need to make a few changes to how Traffic Controller creates and manages the cars in the game. You also need to add extra lanes to the game screen. To minimize the amount of work needed to adapt the game to allow cars to move backward, build upon the code that exists already.

First, we show you how to duplicate the three lanes onscreen already (in the section "Adding extra lanes") and then move them to the other side of the screen so that you have six lanes. Because we don't want you to have to write a lot of code to support a reverse-direction version of the Lane class, we show you how to make use of the tags again.

Remember how the current three lanes you use are set up to use the tags 0, 1, and 2? If you need a refresher, you set this up in Chapter 9, when designing the overall game play. Well, for the iPad version, make the three new lanes use the tags 3, 4, and 5.

These new lanes all participate in the car creation system that you put together in Chapter 9 (that is, they use a timer to tell the Traffic Controller that a car needs to appear onscreen). However, here you modify the car creation code so that cars that are created by downward-facing lanes move down the screen.

Adding extra lanes

Expand *Traffic* for the iPad by making the new lanes:

1. **In Interface Builder, open TrafficViewController.xib. Select the background image view and change its image to Road-iPad.png to add the new background.**

   To change the image, open the Attributes Inspector by pressing ⌘-1 and change the Image field's contents to Background-iPad.png. You'll need to add the image to the project.

   You can find this image in the collection of resources you download in Chapter 1.

2. **In TrafficViewController.xib, select the three lanes, and then hold down the Option key and drag them to the right to duplicate the existing lanes.**

   A new copy of the lanes appears.

3. **Position these three lanes so that they go in the order of blue, then green, and then red by clicking and dragging the new lanes until they're in the right position.**

4. **Change the tags of the lanes.**

   To do this, select each of the lanes, and open the Attributes Inspector by pressing ⌘-1. At the bottom of the Inspector, you'll find a Tag field. Enter a number in this field to change the view's tag.

   The blue lane needs the tag 5; the green lane needs the tag 4; and the red lane needs tag 3.

The next step is to make the Traffic Controller aware of the differences between the left set of lanes and the right set. The lanes on the right side of the screen create cars that move down the screen. The lanes on the left side of the screen create cars that move up. You also set up each of the lane's tags so that the three lanes on the right have tags of 3 or greater. This means that you can very easily tell the difference between the two types of lanes.

Creating cars

For this game, cars that move downward have only a couple key differences from their upward-moving cousins:

- ✔ Every frame, their position is shifted down the screen, not up. (Surprise!)

- ✔ They appear at the top of the screen.

- ✔ They're drawn upside-down so that they don't look like they're driving backward.

- ✔ They're considered to have left the screen when they reach the *bottom* of the screen, rather than the top.

- ✔ Their goal lanes have tags of 3 or greater, *and* the cars are created by lanes with a tag of 3 or greater.

Basically, the extra code for the multiplayer version of *Traffic* turns the single player version on its head!

With this knowledge, you can build up your new cars. First, add the new code that detects when a downward-driving car needs to be created. A new vehicle needs to drive downward when the lane that created it has a tag of 3 or greater; additionally, the car needs to have a goal lane of 3 or greater. (Otherwise, the car's goal lane is in the other direction, and it could never reach it.)

The goal lane is currently selected by picking a random number between zero and two. You build on that by saying that if the lane that created the car is a downward-driving lane, the goal tag for the vehicle needs to increase by three. This makes the new vehicle aim toward getting to the bottom of the screen. To create cars that travel down the screen, follow these steps:

1. **Add the code that sets up cars created by the downward-driving lanes by modifying the method `startCarFromLane:` in TrafficController.m so that it looks like the following:**

   New code is in bold.

   ```
   - (void) startCarFromLane:(Lane*)starter {
     NSString* carType;

     int type = random() % 3;

     switch (type) {
     case 0:
       carType = @"GreenCar";
       break;
     case 1:
       carType = @"RedCar";
       break;
     case 2:
       carType = @"BlueCar";
       break;
     }

     Vehicle* v = [[Vehicle alloc] initWithName:carType];

     [viewController.view addSubview:v];
     [self registerVehicle:v];
     v.goalTag = type;

     v.controller = self;

     CGPoint position;
     position.x = starter.center.x;

     if (starter.tag >= 3) {
       // this car is on the right-hand side of the
           screen, and is moving down
       v.goalTag += 3;
     }

     v.center = position;
     [v release];
   }
   ```

The new code is in bold.

Additionally, you want to make the downward-driving car face the other way. This is actually pretty simple because all you need to do is to make iOS rotate the UIView that the car represents.

To do this, give the car view a *transform,* which is a value that tells the view how it should change how it's displayed.

We cover transforms in Chapter 6; you use Core Animation to animate the transform of the buttons on the main menu, making them perform that excellent popping animation. Transforms are really powerful and can be used to make a view move, skew, and rotate.

Rotating is what you want to do, so we show you how to make your cars rotate 180 degrees and face backward. You create a new transform with the CGAffineTransformMakeRotation function, which takes a rotation value (in radians) and returns a transform you can apply to a view. (To find out more about what a radian is, check out the sidebar, "Radians? Are they some sort of hippie group?" elsewhere in this chapter.)

2. **Make the cars face backward by modifying the code you just added so that it looks like this:**

```
if (starter.tag >= 3) {
  // this car is on the right-hand side of the
      screen, and is moving down
  v.goalTag += 3;
  v.transform = CGAffineTransformMakeRotation(M_PI);
}
```

By default, the cars appear at the bottom of the screen, but that won't do when the car needs to move toward there. The solution is to put downward-driving cars at the top of the screen and upward-driving cars at the bottom of the screen.

3. **To position the cars appropriately, modify the code you've been work-ing with so that it looks like this:**

```
if (starter.tag >= 3) {
  // this car is on the right-hand side of the
      screen, and is moving down
  v.goalTag += 3;
  v.transform = CGAffineTransformMakeRotation(M_PI);
  position.y = -50;
} else {
  position.y = viewController.view.bounds.size.
      height + 50;
}
```

Once you've added this code, the downwards-driving cars are created and positioned on screen, but won't move yet. In the next few steps, you'll fix this up!

Radians? Are they some sort of hippie group?

A *radian* is another way to describe a rotation. Whereas degrees are numbers between 0 and 360, a radian is a number between 0 and 2 times pi (about 6.283). *Pi,* as you might remember from high school math, is 3.141593 (or thereabouts); pi has certain special properties that are important when talking about circles or other circle-like things, such as rotations (as shown here).

So, when you create a rotation that turns an object around one half-circle, that rotation in radians is pi. See, Mr. Crenshaw from Geometry class was right after all: High school math is useful in the real world. Also, never eat in class.

360 degrees = 2π radians
90 degrees = π/2 radians

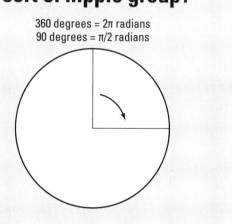

After you finish setting up the `startCarFromLane:` method, make the game loop move the cars appropriately. Like earlier in this chapter, use the vehicle's tag to figure out which direction it needs to move in: If the tag is 3 or greater, the car needs to move down the screen; if the tag is 2 or fewer, it needs to move up.

Also, check whether the car has moved off-screen. This has different meanings for the different kinds of cars:

✔ Upward-driving cars are off-screen after their y-coordinate goes below –50.

✔ Downward-driving cars are off-screen after their y-coordinate goes over the height of the screen.

Therefore, you need to make two changes: First, change how cars move — down the screen, not up; second, change how the controller detects when cars leave the board. To make these changes, follow these steps:

1. **To update the game loop to take the different directions of cars into account, modify the `update:` method so that it looks like the following:**

```
CGFloat speed = v.speed;


if (v.slowed) {
   speed *= 0.5;
}

if (v.goalTag < 3)
   position.y -= speed * deltaTime;
else if (v.goalTag >= 3)
   position.y += speed * deltaTime;

if (v.goalTag < 3 && position.y < -50) {
   [self vehicleReachedEndOfRoad:v];
} else if (v.goalTag >= 3 && position.y >= 1074) {
   [self vehicleReachedEndOfRoad:v];
}

CGFloat lateralSpeed = 200;
```

 2. **Run the game by clicking the Build and Run button at the top of the Xcode window.**

Cars appear, driving up and down both sides of the road.

Try not to drive your cars into oncoming traffic.

The new code is actually rather simple: For each car that appears on the road, the code checks whether the goal lane is 3 or greater, which indicates that the car drives down the screen. If this is the case, the code *increases* the car's y-coordinate, which moves the car farther down the screen.

The other piece of code checks whether the car moves too far off-screen; in the case of cars that drive down the screen, the code checks whether the car has gone too far down. And that's how you turn the game on its head!

Chapter 21

Using Gesture Recognizers

*G*esture recognizers were added to iOS when the iPad was launched, and they're an extremely flexible and useful feature. In this chapter, we tell you what gesture recognizers are, how to use them, and how to hook them up to the code running in your application.

Understanding Gestures

A *gesture* is one or two touches that move in certain ways. You use several gestures built into iOS every day; some of the more common examples include tapping, swiping, pinching, and dragging. In Chapter 7, you write code that does your own gesture recognition — the Vehicle objects can track the touches that the user drags over the screen, which controls how the cars move.

However, for more complex gestures, it doesn't make much sense to have the code that detects the gesture be so tightly coupled to the code that responds to the gesture, because detecting the gesture and responding to the gesture are two completely different things, and you don't want to write code that does both tasks at once — that leads to overly complicated code! This is especially true of gestures that are complex to detect, such as a pinch-and-rotate gesture.

To make things easier, you can use a *gesture recognizer*. Gesture recognizers are classes that you attach to views and which watch the touches that land on the view. If the touches match with the gesture that you're looking for, the gesture recognizer informs your code the user has performed the gesture, and that the code should react accordingly.

Gesture recognizers work on all iOS devices. In this chapter, we're focusing on the iPad, but the same code works just as well on the iPhone. Gesture recognizers are available on the iPad starting in iOS 3.2, and on the iPhone starting in iOS 4.0.

Detecting gestures

Several gesture recognizers are built into Cocoa Touch, and they're all based on the gestures that users have become used to when working with iOS. They are

- Tap
- Multiple tap
- Drag
- Pinch
- Rotate
- Long press (also known as press and hold)

When you create a gesture recognizer, attach it to a view and give the recognizer a target object to send a message to when the gesture recognizer does something interesting.

Some gesture recognizers are *one-time* — for example, a tap gesture recognizer has only one action (the tap itself). Some other gesture recognizers are *continuous,* such as the pinch gesture recognizer, which sends its action message over and over again while the user moves her fingers on the screen.

Exploring the states of a gesture recognizer

A gesture recognizer has a few states that it can be in, depending on the input from the user and the type of gesture that the recognizer is looking for. These states are *Possible, Began, Changed, Ended, Canceled,* and *Failed.* Some different types of gestures don't go through all the states; for example, a discrete gesture, such as a tap, doesn't need to watch continuously for changes because the user has either tapped the view or he hasn't.

A gesture recognizer always starts in the Possible state. In this state, the recognizer waits for more information before it can say that the user is performing a gesture. After the recognizer has received enough information and has decided that the user is performing the gesture it's looking for, it changes to the Began state. When the user continues to perform the gesture, the recognizer changes into the Changed State; finally, when the user completes the gesture, the recognizer changes to the Ended state.

A gesture recognizer can end in other possible states. For example, a gesture recognizer might detect what it thinks is a gesture that it's looking for, but then later realize that it's in fact not the right gesture. Say that a view has a tap recognizer attached, and the user places her finger on it. The recognizer instantly jumps into the Possible state and watches for what happens next. If the user drags her finger across the screen without lifting her finger, it's pretty clear that she's not tapping, but dragging. In this case, the gesture recognizer moves into the Failed state.

Finally, just like touches, gestures can be canceled. Cancelations are caused by events like phone calls coming in or when the view controller that the gesture recognizer belongs to is removed from the screen.

Separating gesture detection from action

The whole point of a gesture recognizer is to detach the recognition code from the action that the gesture provokes. This means that you write a lot less code, which means there are fewer opportunities for bugs to occur.

For *Traffic,* add a feature to the game that lets the player slow down the traffic on the road. Also add a speed limit sign to the middle of the screen that the player can pinch open and closed. When the user pinches the sign open, the speed limit gets larger and the cars on the road speed up. When the user pinches the speed limit sign closed, the cars slow down. (The speed limit on the sign doesn't change, because that just makes things more complicated to code.) This gives the player a measure of control over the pacing of the cars on the road and lets the player slow down things temporarily to perform some precise maneuvering. This also lets the player apply a speed boost to the cars.

You could've added this gesture recognition feature with your code, but that'd be boring and would distract from the game play goal that you want to achieve. Instead, let gesture recognizers do the heavy lifting for you!

Adding the Gesture Recognizer Code to Your Game

To add this functionality to *Traffic,* you first have to add the speed limit sign to the game screen and attach it to the view controller. Then, add the gesture recognizer and allow the user to pinch the view open and closed. Finally, attach this control to the Traffic Controller, which lets the player control the very fabric of time itself! (At least as far as your game is concerned, anyway.)

This is how the pinch gesture recognizer works: When the user pinches the view, the gesture recognizer lets the view controller know what the scale of the pinch is. This information is then sent to the Traffic Controller, which it uses to control the speed of the game. The gesture recognizer will also send the current scale of the pinch whenever the pinch changes size.

Remember how the Traffic Controller calculates the speed of all the cars on the road? The Traffic Controller takes the speed value stored in every car object and multiplies that by the frame rate to get a smooth movement. You're going to take that and add another factor into the calculation: the game speed.

The game's speed is 1.0 when running at normal speed, 0.5 when running at half speed, and 2.0 when running at double speed. You then control this variable by making the view controller update it when the speed limit is pinched. By multiplying the speed of all the cars by this number, all cars on the board speed up and slow down with barely a few extra lines of code.

When you code the gesture recognizer, it sends only the scale of the pinch gesture based on the size of the pinch when the gesture began. For example, if you pinch open a view until your fingers are twice as far apart as they were when the pinch began, the gesture recognizer reports that the pinch's scale is 2. However, if you lift your fingers and then pinch closed again, the scale is 0.5, not 1, because the scale is based on the size of the gesture when it began and not the size of the gesture when it was last used.

To work around this problem, the code in this chapter stores the most recently seen scale of the pinch gesture and takes this into account when calculating the pinch.

Adding the view

Follow these steps to add the speed limit sign to the game:

1. **Add the speed limit image view by opening TrafficViewController.xib and dragging in a new image view from the Library.**

2. **Set the view's image to SpeedLimit.png.**

   You can find this image in the resource collection you downloaded in Chapter 1.

3. **Resize the view to fit (by choosing Layout⇨Size to Fit) and move the view into the middle of the game screen, between the two strips of road.**

4. **Add the following code to TrafficViewController.h.**

   This code creates a new IBOutlet for the view in TrafficViewController, so that you can refer to it in your code, and then adds a new variable to keep track of the gesture's recorded scale. New code is in bold.

```
#import <UIKit/UIKit.h>
#import <AVFoundation/AVFoundation.h>
#import "FBConnect.h"

@class TrafficController;

@interface TrafficViewController : UIViewController
        <FBRequestDelegate> {
  TrafficController* gameController;
  UIView* pauseOverlay;
  UIView* gameOverOverlay;
  UILabel* timeRemainingLabel;
  IBOutlet UIButton* sendTimeButton;
  IBOutlet UIButton* postToFacebookButton;
  IBOutlet UIActivityIndicatorView* activity;

  UIWindow* externalWindow;
  UILabel* timeElapsedLabel;

  AVAudioPlayer* backgroundAudioPlayer;

  UIView* speedControlView;
  CGFloat speedScale;

}

@property (nonatomic, retain) IBOutlet UILabel*
        timeElapsedLabel;
@property (nonatomic, retain) IBOutlet UIWindow*
        externalWindow;
@property (nonatomic, retain) IBOutlet
        TrafficController* gameController;
@property (nonatomic, retain) IBOutlet UIView*
        pauseOverlay;
```

```
@property (nonatomic, retain) IBOutlet UILabel*
        timeRemainingLabel;
@property (nonatomic, retain) IBOutlet UIView*
        gameOverOverlay;
@property (nonatomic, retain) IBOutlet UIView*
        speedControlView;

- (void) displayGameOver;
- (IBAction) postToFacebook:(id)sender;
- (IBAction) pauseGame:(id)sender;
- (IBAction) endGame:(id)sender;
- (void) setTimeRemaining:(CGFloat)time;
- (void) setTimeElapsed:(CGFloat)time;

@end
```

5. **Synthesize the speedControlView variable in TrafficViewController.m.**

   Add the following line of code to TrafficViewController.m, after the @
   implementation line.

   ```
   @synthesize speedControlView;
   ```

6. **Connect the speedControlView outlet to the speed sign you just created.**

   To do this, select the speed sign, hold down the Control key, and click and drag from the speed sign to the File's Owner. A list of outlets will appear; click on speedControlView.

7. **Add the pinch gesture recognizer by modifying the viewDidLoad method in TrafficViewController.m so that it looks like this:**

   ```
   - (void) viewDidLoad {
     NSURL* backgroundURL = [NSURL
           fileURLWithPath:[[NSBundle mainBundle]
           pathForResource:@"cars-loop" ofType:@"aif"]];

     backgroundAudioPlayer = [[AVAudioPlayer alloc] initW
           ithContentsOfURL:backgroundURL  error:nil];

     backgroundAudioPlayer.numberOfLoops = -1;
     [backgroundAudioPlayer retain];

     UIPinchGestureRecognizer* pinchRecognizer
           = [[UIPinchGestureRecognizer alloc]
           initWithTarget:self action:@
           selector(handlePinch:)];
     [speedControlView addGestureRecognizer:pinchRecogni
           zer];
     [pinchRecognizer release];

     speedScale = 1.0;
   }
   ```

This code creates the pinch gesture recognizer, sets it up, and attaches it to the speed sign view. After it's been attached, it can be released.

The gesture recognizer is now set up to watch for pinching gestures applied to the speed sign.

Responding to the gesture

After your code is set up to recognize the gesture, add the following method which responds to information coming from the gesture recognizer. This changes the size of the speed sign, which gives the player some visual feedback on what he's doing, and also informs the Traffic Controller about the changes in the game's state (which will lead to the game's speed slowing down.)

This method also limits the pinch so that the user doesn't pinch the speed limit sign to be too big or too small. Add the method that handles events coming from the gesture recognizer. To do so, add the following code to TrafficViewController.m. This code takes the scale of the pinch gesture recognizer, and changes the transform of the speed sign to make it scale up or down based on the size of the pinch. If the pinch has ended, it records its size, which it uses in future calculations. Finally, the method informs the Traffic Controller about the changes in the game state:

```
- (void) handlePinch:(UIGestureRecognizer*)recognizer
       {
  CGFloat factor = [(UIPinchGestureRecognizer*)
       recognizer scale];
  factor *= speedScale;

  if (factor < 0.5) factor = 0.5;
  if (factor > 2.0) factor = 2.0;

  speedControlView.transform = CGAffineTransformMakeSc
       ale(factor, factor);

  if (recognizer.state ==
       UIGestureRecognizerStateEnded) {
    speedScale = factor;
  }

  gameController.gameSpeedFactor = factor;
}
```

This code takes the pointer to the gesture recognizer and casts it to a UIPinchGestureRecognizer class to get at the pinch-specific properties. The code then asks the recognizer for the gesture's scale and stores it in a variable.

However, the scale isn't remembered between gestures — every time you start a new pinching gesture, the scale starts at one, no matter how far apart your fingers are. Because you want to make your speed sign remember its size, the code multiplies the gesture's scale by the *last* scale of the view. After the code has done that calculation, the code makes sure that the scale doesn't go above 2 or below 0.5, which helps prevent some potential problems — if the scale gets too small, the user won't be able to pinch it open again, and if the scale gets too big, the view will be way too large (and the game will be moving way too fast). By limiting the range of the scale, this code nips these problems in the bud.

The code then makes the speed sign view actually appear bigger or smaller onscreen, depending on the calculated scale. To do this, the code makes a new transform based on the scale and applies it to the view. Finally, the gesture recognizer is asked whether the gesture has ended. This happens when the user lifts her fingers. This is your chance to store the current scale in the variable to be used next time.

The last thing that needs to happen is to inform the Traffic Controller about the changes. You do that by simply setting a property, which we show you how to do in the next section.

Slowing down time

The final part of adding this feature is to make the application actually slow down time. Well, sort of. You can't delay your fortieth birthday or make your kids stay cute longer, but you can add speed variability to *Traffic.* To handle this, add a new speed variable to the Traffic Controller that's controlled directly by the view controller. Then, make the in-game movement calculations take this speed variable into account. Follow these steps to do just that:

1. **Add a new gameSpeedFactor variable to TrafficController.h:**

   ```
   CGFloat gameSpeedFactor;
   ```

2. **Add the property:**

   ```
   @property (assign) CGFloat gameSpeedFactor;
   ```

3. **Synthesize this property in TrafficController.m.**

   Add the following line to TrafficController.m, after the `@implementation` line.

   ```
   @synthesize gameSpeedFactor;
   ```

4. **To make the movement calculations take speed into account, modify the `update:` method in TrafficController.m so that it looks like this:**

```
if (v.goalTag < 3)
  position.y -= speed * deltaTime * gameSpeedFactor;
else if (v.goalTag >= 3)
  position.y += speed * deltaTime * gameSpeedFactor;


  ...

  if (position.x > goalLanePosition.x)
    position.x -= lateralSpeed * deltaTime *
      gameSpeedFactor;
  else if (position.x < goalLanePosition.x)
    position.x += lateralSpeed * deltaTime *
      gameSpeedFactor;
}

v.center = position;
```

Up until now, the position of objects onscreen has been updated based on the speed of the car and the frame rate of the game. This updated code adds an extra factor into the calculation. When gameSpeedFactor is equal to 1, the car moves at full speed because the number of pixels it's moved up the screen is multiplied by 1.

When the gameSpeedFactor value is less than one, the number of pixels it's moved is reduced, making the car move slower. When the gameSpeedFactor is greater than one, the car moves more pixels per frame and consequently, moves faster.

5. **Make the game speed start at 1.0 by adding this code to the end of the awakFromNib method in TrafficController.m:**

```
gameSpeedFactor = 1.0;
```

By default, the variable starts at 0, which is no good — this means that the game would multiply all speeds by zero, making all cars stuck. This code fixes that problem.

And you're done! If you run the game and start playing, you can now control the speed of cars on the board by pinching the speed limit sign and making it bigger and smaller. Welcome to the wonderful world of gesture recognizers!

Chapter 22

Setting Up OpenGL

. . . .

In This Chapter

▶ Understanding OpenGL

▶ Setting up OpenGL contexts

▶ Drawing in 3D space

. . . .

*I*n this chapter, we take a dive into the wondrous world of drawing complex graphics using iOS and OpenGL. You find a lot of interesting and new content that is talked about in this chapter, but don't despair — the end result will eventually be fancy graphical effects, which are difficult to add in any other way!

By following the process shown in this chapter, you're going to put a background image behind the game that shows a road speeding past underneath the cars. This is pretty difficult to do using plain Cocoa Touch, but is quite straightforward in OpenGL, after you have things set up correctly.

"Behold, the Third Dimension!"

In science fiction, going into another dimension usually involves lots of electricity, cackling mad scientists, and lots of special effects. When drawing graphics using OpenGL, though, it's a lot quieter. You find less mad science and a little bit more math.

Fortunately, we're going to minimize the amount of extra knowledge that this book is going to drop on you by drawing a very simple scene. We discuss what this finished scene is in Chapter 23; in the meantime, it's worth knowing a little bit about what's going on behind the scenes.

By the end of this chapter, your game will look like Figure 22-1. Don't worry about the fact that it looks a lot simpler. In Chapter 23 and Chapter 24, you'll be making it a lot more complex again!

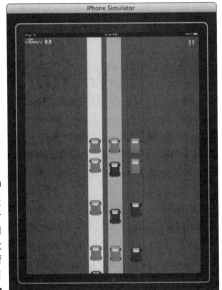

Working with 3D space

Previously, all of *Traffic* has been constrained to two dimensions: X and Y. As we've previously discussed, X means going sideways and Y means going up and down. These have been the two *axes* that we've been working in.

When dealing with three dimensions, though, we need to add another axis: the Z axis. The Z axis is at right angles to both the X and Y axes — X goes from left to right, Y goes up and down, and Z goes *into and out of* the screen. If you took an object and moved it along the Z axis, it would be moving toward you or away from you. It looks something like Figure 22-2.

When dealing with 2D graphics, you're mostly concerned with the location of pixels on a screen. When dealing with 3D space, you're dealing with the location of points in space, which are called *vertices*. Everything that you draw on the screen boils down to a collection of vertices (a vertex, plus a bunch of its colleagues).

However, at the end of the day, the user is still looking at a screen, which displays a 2D picture. This means that these 3D positions need to be converted into 2D so that they can be shown to the user.

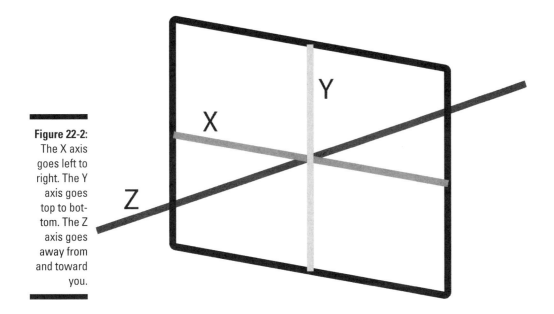

Figure 22-2:
The X axis
goes left to
right. The Y
axis goes
top to bot-
tom. The Z
axis goes
away from
and toward
you.

Fortunately, this tricky bit of math is already done for you by the graphics chip. The graphics chip is a separate processing unit that sits next to the CPU and runs independently. For the most part, the CPU and the graphics chip (also known as the GPU, or *graphics processing unit*) don't interact much, except when the CPU tells the GPU to draw something, or when the GPU tells the CPU that it's finished drawing a picture.

When you give a bunch of points to the graphics chip, it figures out how to draw them onto the screen, given a little bit of information from you, such as where the virtual "camera" is along with extra information like textures and lighting.

The way that you can tell a graphics chip to do this for you is by using a library called *OpenGL*.

A history lesson

In the bad old days (the early 1990s) you had a bunch of different ways of telling a graphics chip to draw something on the screen. This meant that if you wanted your game to run on more than one type of computer, you had to essentially write a whole different program for each type.

This led to games containing a list of the different graphics cards they supported, and gamers had to be very careful about matching games to their hardware.

Of course, this meant that hardware developers weren't able to develop their chips very far, because they had to be careful about not breaking compatibility with games. Eventually, a group of manufacturers declared that enough was enough, and that they'd all get together and build their cards in such a way that they could all be programmed using a shared interface.

This interface was known as the *Open Graphics Library* or *OpenGL*. OpenGL basically acts as a standard way of telling a graphics card about the stuff that needs to be drawn on-screen.

OpenGL was designed to be extremely flexible. It doesn't make any kinds of assumptions about the stuff that you're drawing; instead, it's only interested in stuff like lines and triangles, and it lets you build whatever complex system that you want to using that.

OpenGL is also designed to be very modular. The designers of OpenGL realized that despite the goal of making a standard graphics library that would work on every single graphics chip, 100 percent compatibility simply isn't possible. For example, suppose a graphics chip manufacturer like NVIDIA came up with a revolutionary way of drawing realistic lighting and wanted to get this new technology to market. OpenGL is run by a collection of companies (collectively known as the very sinister-sounding Khronos Group), and it takes time for new technologies to make their way throughout the entire industry.

To get around this problem, OpenGL allows chip manufacturers to create *extensions* to OpenGL. These are little add-ons to OpenGL that allow manufacturers to add new features in a standard way. This process means that the new and exciting technology gets to be used by the end user (that is, you), while at the same time, OpenGL doesn't get broken into a collection of competing standards.

Over time, extensions are folded into the main OpenGL specification, which makes OpenGL an increasingly more powerful library that remains compatible with the major graphics cards.

Tiny graphics powerhouses

This method of using extensions to break up features also means that it's possible to make specialized versions of OpenGL for different situations. One of these situations is when you have a very small, low-power device that doesn't have the same amount of resources that a high-powered desktop computer does. Such devices are instead designed to run a cut-down version of OpenGL, called *OpenGL for Embedded Systems,* or *OpenGL ES* for short.

Say, that whole "small, low-powered devices" thing sounds familiar!

The iPhone uses OpenGL ES to do all its drawing on the screen. The first iPhone used OpenGL ES 1.0 to do its drawing, and later versions of the hardware have slowly increased in functionality.

The current version of the hardware, the iPhone 4, runs OpenGL ES 2.0. This version of OpenGL ES is extremely fast, and it has several advanced features that only a few years ago were only found on top-of-the-line gaming computers. Because the iPad runs on very similar hardware to the iPhone 4, it also has similar abilities.

All this means that the iPhone and iPad are capable of doing some extremely interesting things with graphics.

How OpenGL Works

So, how do you actually use OpenGL to do drawing? To get started, it's worth taking a look at the things that OpenGL uses to compose a picture.

Contexts

An OpenGL context is like a little self-contained artist's studio. The context is where you set up your drawing, do all your rendering, and eventually show the picture to the user.

Primitives

A *primitive* is OpenGL's term for the base-level components that make up a 3D picture. Three different types of primitives exist:

- **Points:** A point is a single point in space. It's nothing more than a position described by 3D coordinates. When OpenGL draws a point, it draws a dot on the screen.

- **Lines:** A line is two connected points. You can make more complicated lines by chaining them together. When OpenGL draws a line, it simply figures out the location of the two points and traces a line between them.

- **Triangles:** A triangle is three connected points. Triangles are the most useful of the primitives, because when OpenGL draws them, it needs to work out what to draw inside the triangle. It's up to you to provide this information, and you can provide anything you like: any color, any picture, and any graphical element you like. By connecting a bunch of triangles, you can create any 3D image you like.

Seems pretty basic, no? Using these three different things, you can put together extremely complex scenes. Most of the time, you'll be working with triangles because they're the foundation for drawing surfaces. However, points and lines are also useful, such as when you want to draw simple or retro graphics on the screen.

How does this happen? When you combine lots of little triangles together, you can put together a very complex object. Figure 22-3 shows a picture of a 3D rock.

Figure 22-3:
A rock, drawn in 3D.

This rock is actually composed of 63 individual triangles, all connected together so that they form a rock shape. Each triangle then has a rock texture put on top of it, making it look more like a real lump of stone. You can see some of the triangles in Figure 22-4.

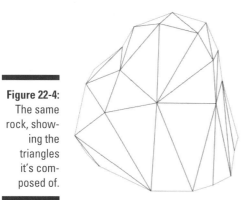

Figure 22-4:
The same rock, showing the triangles it's composed of.

Vertices

A vertex is the building block of all primitives:

- ✔ One vertex defines a *point.*
- ✔ Two vertices define a *line.*
- ✔ Three vertices define a *triangle.*

To do drawing in OpenGL, you give it a collection of vertices and tell OpenGL to draw them. That's it!

Of course, the trick to making great-looking graphics is to give OpenGL the right vertices that match up with the picture that you want to appear.

When you give OpenGL vertices, you also need to give it a little bit of information about them. This information includes the type of primitives you want OpenGL to make using them (points, lines, or triangles), which *shader program* you want to use to render them (more on this in a bit), along with many, many other details you can provide.

Each vertex can also receive extra information, which OpenGL uses when drawing them. These extra bits of information are known as *vertex attributes.* Some common attributes include color, texture coordinates, and position.

To give you an example of this being used, take a look at Figures 22-3 and 22-4 again. Look at how triangles are used to create the final picture. Every corner of each of the triangles is a vertex.

In Figure 22-5, we've highlighted a vertex. For this vertex to be drawn (and turned into triangles, which are turned into pixels), the vertex needs

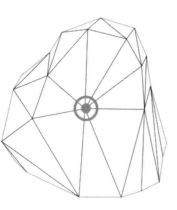

Figure 22-5:
A single
vertex on
the rock.

✔ A position attribute, which tells the graphics chip where to put it

✔ *Texture coordinates,* which tell the graphics chip how to draw the texture (more on this in Chapter 24)

These vertex attributes are useful during vertex processing, which is where OpenGL figures out how each vertex affects the final picture. Vertex attributes are also used during the process of *rasterization.*

Rasterizing

Thinking in abstract terms of points and triangles is all well and good, but the goal is to put pixels in front of the user. This means that every primitive needs to be converted to pixels, which is a process known as *rasterizing.*

Rasterizing is the process of figuring out where a primitive is on the screen, and coloring each pixel on the screen appropriately:

✔ If you're drawing a line, OpenGL needs to figure out which pixels on the screen are part of that line.

✔ If you're drawing a triangle, OpenGL needs to figure out which pixels are inside that triangle.

Each of these pixels that are filled in on the screen is known as a *fragment.*

After OpenGL has worked out which fragments need to be drawn, it then needs to work out what color each pixel needs to be filled in with. This depends on the vertex attributes attached to each vertex used to draw the primitive — for every fragment that needs to be drawn, OpenGL figures out what the values for the vertex attributes should be at that point, which is a process known as *interpolation.* OpenGL can then use these interpolated values to work out the color.

Buffers

After telling OpenGL to draw the fragments, the results end up in a *buffer.*

Buffers are regions of memory that are used to contain images. Buffers are important, because they're responsible for storing the picture that the user will see, after rendering is complete.

We look at buffers in more detail later in this chapter!

Shaders

We kind of glossed over vertex processing and fragment processing earlier. Given a bunch of vertices, how does OpenGL process them into pretty pictures during the rasterization process?

The answer is *it uses gypsy magic.*

Well, almost. It uses a very small program called a *shader.* You find two different kinds of shaders:

  ✔ *Vertex shaders* are methods that take a vertex and figure out how it should look.

  ✔ *Fragment shaders* are methods that work out the color for each pixel on the screen.

When you combine both a vertex shader and a fragment shader, you can render graphics. Here's what happens when you submit a vertex to OpenGL for drawing:

1. OpenGL takes the vertex and runs a piece of code that processes it, called a *vertex shader.*

   A vertex shader looks like this:

   ```
   void main() {
     // Put every vertex that this shader processes
     // at the position (0, 0, 0)
     // (Note: this shader doesn't do much useful work
     // since it puts all vertices at the same place)
     gl_Position = vec4(0.0, 0.0, 0.0, 0.0);
   }
   ```

2. OpenGL rasterizes the primitive and generates a bunch of fragments.

3. Each fragment to *another* piece of code is called a *fragment shader,* which works out which color the fragment should be.

   A fragment shader looks like this:

   ```
   void main() {
     // Make every fragment that this shader processes be
     // bright green, and completely opaque.
     gl_FragColor = vec4(0.0, 1.0, 0.0, 1.0);
   }
   ```

4. After all the fragments have been given colors, OpenGL writes the results into the render buffer.

The master plan for rendering

Rendering is a process that looks like this:

1. Set up the OpenGL context.

2. Give OpenGL the shader code you want it to use for rendering.

3. Send OpenGL a collection of vertices.

4. Display the resulting picture on the screen.

5. Repeat the process, 30 times a second.

We use this master plan in this chapter, Chapter 23, and Chapter 24, because each step is an important part in putting pixels on the screen.

The reason that this process is gypsy magic is because *you write both of these shaders.* You have complete control over how OpenGL draws the vertices you send to it, which means that you can create effects ranging from simple things like drawing a texture on a square to creating a reflective, refracting, shiny chunk of metal.

You can also draw different parts of your scene using different shaders. For example, you could write a plastic shader that mimics how light reflects off a ball and write a metal shader that mimics how light bounces off wood, and then draw two different objects in the same frame.

In this book, you'll be writing shaders that are a little less complex than that — your shaders will let you (eventually) display a texture on a rectangle. However, the capabilities of shaders are practically unlimited, and you can use them to create very fancy effects.

In OpenGL, shader programs are written in a language called *GLSL,* which stands for *OpenGL Shader Language.* GLSL was designed for the same reason as OpenGL — to let developers control the lower-level rendering systems in a standard way. (Previously, as you might imagine, every different graphics chip manufacturer had its own way, and you had to write shaders for every different manufacturer.)

Shaders and shader programs

To work with shader programs, you first need to write a vertex shader and a fragment shader. We show you how to do this in Chapter 23. After you have the shaders, you give the source code for each to OpenGL and tell it to compile them. After OpenGL has compiled the individual shaders, you tell it to link the shaders together, forming a shader program. Finally, you use your shader program to do the actual drawing.

Vertex shaders

A vertex shader is responsible for positioning a vertex in space. You might think that that's already been done, given that your application already submitted the vertex to OpenGL for drawing. And you're right! However, the vertex shader is responsible for letting you customize the position of the vertices, based on whatever parameters you want to provide. Vertex shaders are also useful for doing calculations like lighting and texture mapping, which we look at later in this chapter.

Fragment shaders

Fragment shaders are responsible for figuring out and providing a color to every fragment drawn by the renderer for a primitive. They take information that was calculated in the vertex shader and return a color.

Fragment shaders are *insanely powerful* and are limited only by your imagination and the capabilities of your hardware. We take a closer look at building shaders in Chapter 23.

Drawing stuff on the screen

Finally, after all the drawing is done, you need to tell iOS to show the buffer on the screen. This is as simple as just telling it to do so! After you've done this, the picture contained inside the frame buffer is put up on the screen for the user to look at.

The picture stays on screen for the next $\frac{1}{30}$ second or so, anyway. Then it's erased, and the whole process begins again.

OpenGL objects, names, and binding

Working with OpenGL means working with a collection of objects that exist on the graphics chip. These objects include shader programs, textures, render buffers, and other useful things.

However, OpenGL is a C-based library. This means that it was designed for a language that didn't include object orientation. (This is due to compatibility reasons: C is essentially the universal language of all computers, and a library that works in C can work everywhere — even in space!)

To allow developers to work with objects, the OpenGL designers hit upon a method of maintaining compatibility while still being extremely flexible.

Every OpenGL object is given a *name,* which is a number identifying it within your OpenGL context. This name is created when you *generate* an object on the graphics chip. When you want to start working with an object, you *bind* the object to a *target* inside the context, and then start doing work with it:

✔ A target is a category of objects. OpenGL only knows how to work on one object at a time, and it relies on you to tell it which one to focus on.

✔ When you bind an object to a target, you tell OpenGL which object to work on.

To give you an example of how this works, take a look at textures. You can have a huge number of textures in your game, but you can only be directly working with one texture at a time. To make a texture the currently selected texture, you bind it to the "texture" target. After you've done that, any work you do with textures is done with the currently bound object.

When you want to work with another object, you simply bind another object to the same target. When you're finished with an object and want to get rid of it, you *delete* it.

Here's how you work with a texture object, for example.

```
// Store the texture's name as an integer
GLuint myTextureName;

// Ask OpenGL to generate a name for the
// texture, and store it in myTextureName
glGenTextures(1, &myTextureName);

// Tell OpenGL to bind the name to the GL_TEXTURE_2D
// target, which makes OpenGL start using this texture
glBindTexture(GL_TEXTURE_2D, myTextureName);

// Do some work with the texture!

// Finally, delete the texture
glDeleteTextures(1, &myTextureName);
```

This pattern is used for every different type of object used inside OpenGL.

Using OpenGL in iOS

Now that you have a good look at the theory underneath OpenGL, it's time to take a look at how OpenGL works with the graphics technologies you've already been using.

OpenGL needs to play nicely with other graphics systems on iOS, and Apple has made that happen by tightly coupling Core Animation with OpenGL.

Core Animation layers

Every single UIView in an application is backed up by a *Core Animation layer.*
A *layer* is a region of memory used for storing an image. When the operating
system needs to show the contents of the screen, it takes every single visible layer and *composites* them — that is, it puts the layers together on the
screen so that layers sit on top of each other, shows layers underneath them
if they're transparent, and so on.

Here's a simpler explanation:

- ✔ *Layers* are the canvas where you do all your drawing.

- ✔ *Views* are responsible for showing those drawings to the user.

    A view can have many layers, but it always needs at least one.

If that description of a layer reminded you of a buffer in OpenGL, you're
exactly right! Because layers are essentially buffers, you can use them easily
with OpenGL. To do this, you simply tell OpenGL that the region of memory to
use for the frame buffer is the location of a Core Animation layer.

This means that OpenGL drawing can be contained inside a UIView. This is
really handy, because it means that you can still put together your interface
in Interface Builder, and add buttons, labels, and images. All the drawing happens inside a specialized subclass of UIView.

EAGLContext, a fountain of mysteries

In addition to having a place to store the drawn picture, OpenGL also needs
a context. This is also taken care of for you by iOS, through the use of the
EAGLContext class. EAGLContext is an Objective-C object that acts as the
container for an OpenGL context, allowing you to treat your OpenGL contexts
in an object-oriented way.

Usually, you'll only be dealing with one context at a time, but you still need
to set up an EAGLContext so that iOS knows how to handle OpenGL for your
application.

Displaying the frame buffer

To display the picture to the user, all that needs to happen is to tell the
EAGLContext to present the frame buffer. This makes iOS update the layer
with the drawn content, and the user gets to see the picture.

Setting Up OpenGL for Traffic

We now set up *Traffic* to use OpenGL. Because this is a fairly complex process, the end result of this chapter will only show a single-colored square on the screen. In the later chapters, we build upon this to turn the background into an exciting, fast-paced treat for the eyes.

Don't get too worried about making shaders at this point — it's not a lifelong job, and they're simple to put together. We build some simple ones in Chapter 23.

Several development environments can help you put together scenes using OpenGL available for purchase. We won't be covering them in this book, but a bit of quick searching on the Internet can reveal some useful things! We're particularly fond of the Unity game engine, which lets you build and develop a 3D scene using an all-in-one toolkit. You can find more information about Unity at www.unity3d.com.

Setting up the view

What you'll end up creating in this chapter, and others, is a rolling road underneath the traffic lanes. This will actually conflict with the ability for cars to drive down the road, so for the purposes of keeping the game less confusing for the player, you'll need to remove the downward-driving lanes. Don't worry — it's a simple change, and easily reversed.

To remove the downward-driving lanes, follow these steps:

1. **Open TrafficViewController.xib in Interface Builder. Select the three lanes at the right-hand side of the screen, which you added in Chapter 21. Delete them by pressing the delete key.**

2. **Move the remaining lanes to the center of the screen.**

   While you're here, you should also change the opacity of the lanes from semi-transparent to fully opaque, which will help them stand out against the background you'll be building in this chapter.

   To do this, select each of the lanes, and open the Attributes Inspector by pressing ⌘-1. Change the "Alpha" setting for each of the views to 1.0.

Creating the 3D view

To do 3D drawing in iOS, you need to have a region of the screen where the 3D content is displayed. All drawing on the screen is done via UIViews; therefore, we're going to make our own UIView subclass that does drawing through OpenGL.

To make this OpenGL UIView, you need to tell Cocoa Touch that you want to use a different Core Animation layer than the usual. You see, Core Animation is optimized around the application, putting an image on a layer and then displaying it for a long time; however, real-time graphics that are created by OpenGL need to be updated all the time, and using the standard Core Animation stuff isn't going to work.

Fortunately, a specialized Core Animation layer subclass is designed for use with OpenGL: CAEAGLLayer. (Try saying that seven times quickly.)

When a UIView is created, iOS sends it a message asking it what kind of CALayer subclass it should use as the *backing store* for the view — that is, the type of layer object used for storing the contents of the view. By default, the class returns CALayer, indicating that it wants a regular, plain old layer. To use CAEAGLLayer, your class needs to return something a little different.

First, we create the subclassed UIView, and then we start telling iOS about the OpenGL-related changes we want to make.

We call this OpenGL view class OpenGLTrafficView:

1. **Create the files for OpenGLTrafficView.**

   Choose File⇨New File. Create a new UIView subclass called OpenGLTrafficView.

2. **Make the class indicate that it wants to use CAEAGLLayer.**

   Add the following code to OpenGLTrafficView.m. This is a class method, which means that it's a method iOS can call without having to create an instance of the OpenGLTrafficView class.

   In Objective-C, some methods can be called on the class itself, even if no instances of the class are hanging around. In this case, iOS asks the class itself to provide information about itself:

   ```
   + (Class) layerClass {
     return [CAEAGLLayer class];
   }
   ```

3. **Delete the background image view inside TrafficViewController.xib.**

   Get rid of the background image. Where we're going, we don't need roads!

4. **Add an OpenGLTrafficView to the interface.**

   Drag out a UIView from the library, and change its class from UIView to OpenGLTrafficView in the Identity Inspector.

   Make this view fill the screen, and move it behind all the other views so that the buttons and labels appear on top.

5. **Add the OpenGL framework to the project.**

   Right-click the Frameworks folder in Xcode and choose Add⇨Existing Frameworks. Add the OpenGLES.framework framework.

6. **Import the OpenGL header files in OpenGLTrafficView.h.**

   While you're at it, include the Core Animation header and the Core Graphics header as well. We use them later.

   Add the following code to the start of OpenGLTrafficView.h:

   ```
   #import <UIKit/UIKit.h>
   #import <OpenGLES/ES2/gl.h>
   #import <OpenGLES/ES2/glext.h>
   #import <QuartzCore/QuartzCore.h>
   #import <CoreGraphics/CoreGraphics.h>
   ```

7. **Add the instance variables needed for the OpenGLTrafficView class.**

   The class needs to have references to a few pieces of information. These include the EAGLContext and the frame, depth, and color render buffers.

   Add the code in Listing 22-1 to OpenGLTrafficView.h.

Listing 22-1:   OpenGLTrafficView.h

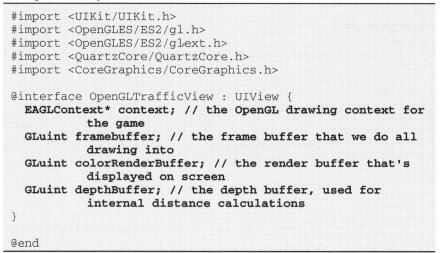

```
#import <UIKit/UIKit.h>
#import <OpenGLES/ES2/gl.h>
#import <OpenGLES/ES2/glext.h>
#import <QuartzCore/QuartzCore.h>
#import <CoreGraphics/CoreGraphics.h>

@interface OpenGLTrafficView : UIView {
  EAGLContext* context; // the OpenGL drawing context for
          the game
  GLuint framebuffer; // the frame buffer that we do all
          drawing into
  GLuint colorRenderBuffer; // the render buffer that's
          displayed on screen
  GLuint depthBuffer; // the depth buffer, used for
          internal distance calculations
}

@end
```

What are these "buffers" of which you speak?

Buffers are destinations for drawing. Whenever OpenGL draws some pixels, those pixels need to end up somewhere. Usually, that "somewhere" is the screen, but it doesn't have to be.

Think of a buffer as a canvas: Whenever you draw something onto it, it remembers what was drawn for later. You can also clear a buffer, which erases its contents.

Buffers are made up of a width, a height, and a storage type. This storage type determines what the buffer can be used for, and you find a few different storage types — black-and-white, grey-scale, and color are some of the more popular ones.

The way that OpenGL draws an entire screen is by drawing several batches of vertices into a buffer and then displaying that buffer onscreen. By waiting for the entire scene to finish drawing before letting the user see it, you avoid making your application flicker.

Frame buffers

This main buffer is known as the *frame buffer.* It's made up of a couple of other buffers, which are combined during the rendering operation to create proper 3D effects.

Usually, a frame buffer is the same size as the screen, and it uses a color storage type, which allows you to show full-color images to the user.

Render buffers

The frame buffer needs to draw information about the display from somewhere. This is almost always a *render buffer,* which is OpenGL's scratch pad for drawing primitives.

Depth buffers

The *depth buffer* contains information on how far away each pixel is from the camera. This buffer is used for figuring out whether an object is *occluding* (which is fancy graphics talk for *covering up*) another object.

When a primitive is drawn by OpenGL, it works out the fragments that should be drawn on the screen. Each fragment contains color information, but it also contains depth information. Simply put, every fragment knows how far away from the camera it is. When OpenGL is assembling the final picture, it knows that fragments closer to the camera should cover up fragments farther away from the camera.

The depth buffer is used for keeping track of this depth information, and it's a vital part of creating a believable 3D scene.

Creating the OpenGL context

After you have set up a UIView, it's time to get OpenGL ready to do its thing.

We start by creating a method in this class that prepares the OpenGL context and the various buffers needed by this application.

We also add the call to this method in the `awakeFromNib:` method. This method is run when the view is reconstructed from the Interface Builder file, and it's a useful point to do the necessary set up:

1. **Add the prepareOpenGL method to OpenGLTrafficView.**

    Add the code in Listing 22-2 to OpenGLTrafficView.m.

Listing 22-2:   OpenGLTrafficView.m

```
- (void) prepareOpenGL {
  context = [[EAGLContext alloc] initWithAPI:kEAGLRenderin
         gAPIOpenGLES2];
  [EAGLContext setCurrentContext:context];
}
```

2. **Call prepareOpenGL when the view starts up.**

    Add the code in Listing 22-3 to OpenGLTrafficView.m.

Listing 22-3:   OpenGLTrafficView.m

```
- (void) awakeFromNib {
  [self prepareOpenGL];
  [self render];
}
```

After this is done, the EAGLContext will be set up to do rendering using the OpenGL ES 2.0 API. Hooray!

Preparing the buffers

After creating the OpenGL context, the next step is to prepare the various pixel buffers we need for drawing things onto the screen.

Add the code in Listing 22-4 to OpenGLTrafficView.m. We have a lot to cover, so we're going to go through the code bit by bit so that you can see what's going on.

Listing 22-4:   OpenGLTrafficView.m

```
- (void) prepareOpenGL {
    context = [[EAGLContext alloc] initWithAPI:kEAGLRenderin
            gAPIOpenGLES2];
    [EAGLContext setCurrentContext:context];

    glGenFramebuffers(1, &framebuffer);

    glBindFramebuffer(GL_FRAMEBUFFER, framebuffer);

    glGenRenderbuffers(1, &colorRenderBuffer);

    glBindRenderbuffer(GL_RENDERBUFFER, colorRenderBuffer);

    [context renderbufferStorage:GL_RENDERBUFFER
            fromDrawable:(CAEAGLLayer*)self.layer];

    glFramebufferRenderbuffer(GL_FRAMEBUFFER, GL_
            COLOR_ATTACHMENT0, GL_RENDERBUFFER,
            colorRenderBuffer);

    GLint height, width;
    glGetRenderbufferParameteriv(GL_RENDERBUFFER, GL_
            RENDERBUFFER_WIDTH, &width);
    glGetRenderbufferParameteriv(GL_RENDERBUFFER, GL_
            RENDERBUFFER_HEIGHT, &height);

    glGenRenderbuffers(1, &depthBuffer);
    glBindRenderbuffer(GL_RENDERBUFFER, depthBuffer);

    glRenderbufferStorage(GL_RENDERBUFFER, GL_DEPTH_
            COMPONENT16, width, height);

    glFramebufferRenderbuffer(GL_FRAMEBUFFER, GL_DEPTH_
            ATTACHMENT, GL_RENDERBUFFER, depthBuffer);

    GLenum status = glCheckFramebufferStatus(GL_
            FRAMEBUFFER);
    if (status != GL_FRAMEBUFFER_COMPLETE) {
        // If the frame buffer is not complete, there's a
            problem, and we can't do
        // any rendering.
        NSLog(@"Failed to create a complete render buffer!");
    }

}
```

First, the code creates a new EAGLContext, which is the working environment in which OpenGL will do its drawing. An application can have multiple
contexts, but this application only needs one. (In fact, the majority of games
only need one.)

When the context is created, it's told to use OpenGL ES 2.0. You can make a context that uses the older OpenGL ES 1.1 system, but who wants to live in the past? (Several reasons exist for using OpenGL ES 1.1, which is why it's an option — these include compatibility and occasionally simpler code.)

```
context = [[EAGLContext alloc] initWithAPI:kEAGLRenderingA
        PIOpenGLES2];
[EAGLContext setCurrentContext:context];
```

After the context has been set up and iOS has been told to use it, it's time to create the objects that OpenGL needs to work with. First, you need to create a framebuffer, which is the buffer where the picture that the user will see is drawn into. To create it, you first ask OpenGL to generate a name for the object (which it stores in the frameBuffer variable) and then tell OpenGL to bind the object to GL_FRAMEBUFFER; this tells OpenGL to prepare the framebuffer, and also start using it:

```
glGenFramebuffers(1, &framebuffer);
glBindFramebuffer(GL_FRAMEBUFFER, framebuffer);
```

A framebuffer needs two *render* buffers to work:

✔ A color buffer is used to store the actual pixels to the user.

✔ The depth buffer is used for working out how to draw objects that are on top of each other.

These extra buffers are *attached* to the framebuffer to give the framebuffer the actual memory that it will use to store the picture. The color buffer is especially important, because iOS will use its contents to store pictures in the Core Animation layer that the user will see.

To connect the color buffer to the Core Animation layer, you need to tell iOS that the color buffer uses the Core Animation layer as its storage.

When the color buffer has been set up, it needs to be connected to the framebuffer:

```
glGenRenderbuffers(1, &colorRenderBuffer);
glBindRenderbuffer(GL_RENDERBUFFER, colorRenderBuffer);
[context renderbufferStorage:GL_RENDERBUFFER
        fromDrawable:(CAEAGLLayer*)self.layer];
glFramebufferRenderbuffer(GL_FRAMEBUFFER, GL_
        COLOR_ATTACHMENT0, GL_RENDERBUFFER,
        colorRenderBuffer);
```

After the render buffer has been created, the depth buffer then needs to be created. The depth buffer uses its own memory storage, and not a Core Animation layer, because it's not directly shown to the user, but rather is used by the rendering process in the background. To set up this memory storage, you need to tell OpenGL about the size of the rendering area, making sure that it's the same size as the color buffer (because the depth buffer needs to match, pixel for pixel, the color buffer.)

Depth buffers are render buffers that store information about how far away a pixel is from the camera and are useful when working out whether an object is occluding (covering up) another object.

To figure out the necessary size, we ask OpenGL to give us the width and the height of the color buffer, and use those values when telling OpenGL to set up the storage for the depth buffer.

The depth buffer also needs to know what *format* to store its information in. The format that's most often used is 16-bit; we don't have enough room to tell you why this is important, but Microsoft has a great article on depth buffering that explains the gory details: http://msdn.microsoft.com/en-us/library/bb976071.aspx. (Please note that this article actually discusses DirectX, which is Microsoft's system that does the same thing as OpenGL. However, the theory behind depth buffers applies just the same to both.)

```
GLint height, width;
glGetRenderbufferParameteriv(GL_RENDERBUFFER, GL_
        RENDERBUFFER_WIDTH, &width);
glGetRenderbufferParameteriv(GL_RENDERBUFFER, GL_
        RENDERBUFFER_HEIGHT, &height);

glGenRenderbuffers(1, &depthBuffer);
glBindRenderbuffer(GL_RENDERBUFFER, depthBuffer);

glRenderbufferStorage(GL_RENDERBUFFER, GL_DEPTH_
        COMPONENT16, width, height);

glFramebufferRenderbuffer(GL_FRAMEBUFFER, GL_DEPTH_
        ATTACHMENT, GL_RENDERBUFFER, depthBuffer);
```

After creating, preparing, and attaching the depth buffer, we can then ask OpenGL to check whether the framebuffer is ready for use. If it's ready, drawing can proceed! (If it's not, you have a problem, and you should check your code!):

```
GLenum status = glCheckFramebufferStatus(GL_FRAMEBUFFER);
   if (status != GL_FRAMEBUFFER_COMPLETE) {
     // If the frame buffer is not complete, there's a
            problem, and we can't do
     // any rendering.
     NSLog(@"Failed to create a complete render buffer!");
   }
```

Whew! That long chunk of code does a fair amount of stuff, all in the service of the Queen — uh, that is, in the service of setting up a render environment that can be used later.

After this is done, the first stage in the master plan is complete: The OpenGL context is now ready to draw an image.

Okay. Let's draw some pixels!

Rendering the 'scene'

This view shows a very simple scene.

It's so simple, it will be a marvelous example of your artistic purity and vision, while encapsulating a minimalist aesthetic that evokes passion and hot-tempered emotions in the audience.

We're going to make the entire view go dark red.

Add the code in Listing 22-5 to OpenGLTrafficView.m.

Listing 22-5: OpenGLTrafficView.m

```
- (void) render {
  glBindFramebuffer(GL_FRAMEBUFFER, framebuffer);

  glViewport(0, 0, self.bounds.size.width, self.bounds.
          size.height);

  glClearColor(0.5, 0.0, 0.0, 1.0);
  glClear(GL_COLOR_BUFFER_BIT);

  glBindRenderbuffer(GL_RENDERBUFFER, colorRenderBuffer);
  [context presentRenderbuffer:GL_RENDERBUFFER];
}
```

To do this, you need to step through a few things that OpenGL needs to do to fill the render buffer with red pixels.

First, you need to tell OpenGL to bind the framebuffer to the GL_FRAMEBUFFER target, which makes OpenGL aware that you're drawing into the framebuffer you set up:

```
glBindFramebuffer(GL_FRAMEBUFFER, framebuffer);
```

Next, you need to tell OpenGL about the size of the "viewport" that you're rendering into. The *viewport* is the area onscreen that shows the rendered content; to make the viewport fill the entire OpenGLTrafficView, you tell OpenGL that the viewport is the size of the view:

```
glViewport(0, 0, self.bounds.size.width, self.bounds.size.
        height);
```

Next, you perform the actual "drawing:" You tell OpenGL that you're clearing using a dark red color, and then you tell OpenGL to clear the color buffer. This fills the color buffer with dark red–colored pixels, and erases anything else that was already drawn:

```
glClearColor(0.5, 0.0, 0.0, 1.0);
glClear(GL_COLOR_BUFFER_BIT);
```

After clearing the buffer, you're done with drawing, and you need to show the results to the user. To make this happen, tell OpenGL to bind the render buffer to the GL_RENDERBUFFER target, which tells OpenGL that the current renderbuffer is the one you set up earlier (the one that's attached to the framebuffer.)

Then, tell iOS to show the results to the user by telling it to present the currently bound renderbuffer. After you make this call, the OpenGLTrafficView is filled with glorious pixels!

```
glBindRenderbuffer(GL_RENDERBUFFER, colorRenderBuffer);
[context presentRenderbuffer:GL_RENDERBUFFER];
```

Setting up the viewport in this manner means that drawing a vertex at the position of (–1,–1,0) puts it at the lower left of the screen, and drawing at (1,1,0) puts it at the upper right.

This effectively means that the virtual camera used for drawing the image is looking down the Z axis and is locked in place.

With this, you're now done with the initial setup of OpenGL. In later chapters, we turn this background into something fancy. Sit tight, 'cause things are going to get wild!

Chapter 23

Drawing with OpenGL

*N*ow that you have OpenGL properly set up, it's time to make it draw something useful on the screen. Over the next two chapters, you put together a background scene, drawn with OpenGL, that simulates a road speeding underneath the car's tires.

In this chapter, you discover how to write vertex and fragment shaders, and how to draw graphics using OpenGL. You also find out about some best practices when drawing OpenGL content.

At the end of this chapter, you'll be drawing a multicolored object underneath the game graphics. In the next chapter, you expand on this and turn it into a textured road.

We start by making the background multicolored, because it's a simple way to look at using both vertex and fragment shaders. We use this as a base to build on in the next chapter.

The Background Scene

In this chapter, we add some graphics that are being drawn by OpenGL but don't interfere with the graphics that we've already drawn. Instead, the existing game graphics sit on top of the OpenGL content, letting OpenGL enhance the overall mood of the game.

By the end of this chapter, you'll see something that looks like Figure 23-1.

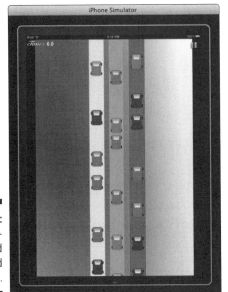

Figure 23-1:
The mul-
ticolored
background
rectangle.

The goal

Here's what the scene is going to look like by the end of the process: Underneath the cars, you'll see a road that is moving extremely quickly. This serves to increase the feeling of speed imparted by the game; up until now, the game's "camera" has been locked in place, and the cars have been the objects that are moving. By making the game look like the "camera" is also moving, you'll be making the game more exciting.

To get this going, you need to replace the existing background graphics with the OpenGL view and draw the contents into that.

The OpenGL content and the in-game content will exist on different layers and won't be able to interact with one another. This means that you can't draw OpenGL content on top of the cars — only underneath. For the purposes of setting up the background scene, however, this isn't a problem.

Setting up the background rendering

This background scene is going to need to animate, which means that it needs to be redrawn every frame. As you read in Chapter 9, the smartest way to do that is to use a CADisplayLink object, which sends a message to an object of your choosing every time the screen needs to be redrawn.

We're going to use this feature to make OpenGL redraw its contents every frame! First, we need to set up a display link object in OpenGLTrafficView. Then, we need to create the render method, which is responsible for drawing the entire scene. Follow these steps:

1. **Add the display link, and a variable to hold the shader program, to the OpenGLTrafficView class.**

   Modify the class definition in OpenGLTrafficView.h so that it looks like the following code.

   ```
   #import <UIKit/UIKit.h>
   #import <OpenGLES/ES2/gl.h>
   #import <QuartzCore/QuartzCore.h>
   #import <CoreGraphics/CoreGraphics.h>

   @class TrafficController;

   @interface OpenGLTrafficView : UIView {
     EAGLContext* context; // the OpenGL drawing context
           for the game
     GLuint framebuffer; // the frame buffer that we do
           all drawing into
     GLuint colorRenderBuffer; // the render buffer
           that's displayed on screen
     GLuint depthBuffer; // the depth buffer, used for
           internal distance calculations

     GLuint shaderProgram; // the shader program, used
           for positioning and shading the objects
     CADisplayLink* displayLink;

   }

   @end
   ```

2. **Set up the display link when the view is loaded.**

   You need to make the display link call the render method (which we create in a moment) every time the screen needs to be redrawn.

   To set up the display link, do the same thing that you did in Chapter 9 — set up the link so that it calls the render method and then add it to the run loop.

   When setting up the display link, you give it a target object, which it will send messages to, and a "selector" (a method name) to call. You then add it to the run loop, which makes it start sending messages to the target object.

   Finally (and this is optional), you tell it how often you want it to send these messages. By setting the frame interval to 2, you're telling the display link to send the render message every second frame.

Modify the `awakeFromNib` method in OpenGLTrafficView.m so that it looks like the following code:

```
- (void) awakeFromNib {
    [self prepareOpenGL];

    displayLink = [CADisplayLink
            displayLinkWithTarget:self selector:@
            selector(render:)];
    [displayLink addToRunLoop:[NSRunLoop mainRunLoop]
            forMode:NSRunLoopCommonModes];
    [displayLink setFrameInterval:2];
}
```

3. **Add the render method.**

Right now, this method is empty; shortly, we make it display OpenGL content every frame.

Replace the render: method in OpenGLTrafficView.m with the following code:

```
- (void) render:(CADisplayLink*)sender {
}
```

After you've added this code, you have finished a lot of the infrastructure. The next step is to actually draw something.

Writing Fragment and Vertex Shaders

In Chapter 22, you set up the OpenGL context and discovered vertex and fragment shaders. Just to refresh your memory, shaders are little functions that are run when OpenGL renders a frame. The code in a vertex shader is run for every vertex you send to OpenGL, and the code in a fragment shader is run for every pixel that ends up being drawn.

You need both a vertex shader and a fragment shader to draw a collection of vertices. Together, these shaders let their powers combine and form a *shader program*.

You're going to write one now!

Uniforms, varyings, and attributes — oh my!

Shader programs need to work with a bunch of different bits of information, and each bit of information falls under one of three different categories:

✔ **Uniforms:** A *uniform* is a piece of information that stays the same for the entire duration of a drawing operation. After you set a uniform to a value and tell OpenGL to draw something, it uses that value every time it runs the shader program. (You're free to change the uniform after the drawing is done and tell OpenGL to draw something different.)

✔ **Varying variables:** A *varying variable* is a piece of information that is calculated in the vertex shader and used by the fragment shader. Varying variables (also known as *varyings*) are so named because they *vary* from fragment to fragment.

Varyings are how you communicate between the different shaders in a shader program. If you declare a varying with the same name and type in both shader functions, they are treated as the same position in memory, which means that you can store a value in the vertex shader and read it out later in the fragment shader.

Varying variables are *interpolated* by OpenGL. When you give OpenGL a bunch of vertices, it needs to figure out what value to give to the fragment shader for every pixel that appears between the vertices. This is all taken care of for you, and the end result is that your fragment shader will have the right value of every varying variable depending on where in the primitive the fragment sits.

✔ **Vertex attributes:** A *vertex attribute* is like a uniform, but instead of being kept the same during a drawing operation, you're allowed to set a different value for every different vertex. This is important for doing things like setting the position and color for each of the different vertices you're drawing with. Vertex attributes can't be used in fragment shaders, so you need to pass the values from the vertex shader to the fragment shader using a varying.

The shader program that we write in this chapter is pretty simple. It takes two vertex attributes: color and position. The vertex shader takes the position attribute and uses it to place the vertex on the screen. It then passes the color attribute to the fragment shader (using a varying). The fragment shader takes the value of the color varying, and uses that to set the color of the fragment it's been told to draw.

The vertex shader

The vertex shader is written using GLSL, the C-like language that we briefly discussed in Chapter 22. GLSL shaders need to be kept in text files that are distributed with the application and loaded when the application starts up.

As we mentioned earlier, the vertex shader needs to know about two vertex attributes (color and position), it needs to set the position of the vertex to the position it's been told to, and it needs to pass the color to the fragment shader.

Let's write this sucker!

1. **Add the vertex shader file to the project.**

   Choose File➪New File. Create a new empty file. Name it Shader.vsh.

2. **Add the shader code.**

   Open the new Shader.vsh file, and add the following code to it:

   ```
   attribute vec4 position;
   attribute vec4 color;

   varying vec4 colorVarying;

   void main()
   {
     gl_Position = position;

     colorVarying = color;
   }
   ```

Here's what this code does:

1. It declares that it's interested in two vertex attributes: the position and the color. It also says that it's going to pass the color information to the fragment shader:

   ```
   attribute vec4 position;
   attribute vec4 color;

   varying vec4 colorVarying;
   ```

2. The code then sets the position of the vertex to the value provided in the position attribute:

   ```
   gl_Position = position;
   ```

3. The shader passes the color attribute to the fragment shader by putting it in the `colorVarying` variable:

   ```
   colorVarying = color;
   ```

Now that that's written, you need to write the fragment shader.

The fragment shader

The fragment shader needs to take the color that was passed down by the vertex shader, in the `colorVarying` variable:

1. **Add the fragment shader file to the project.**

   Choose File➪New File. Create a new empty file. Name it Shader.fsh.

2. **Add the shader code.**

Open the new Shader.fsh file, and add the following code to it:

```
varying lowp vec4 colorVarying;

void main()
{
  // Make the fragment be the color that was
  // passed down by the vertex shader
  // Note that this value will be interpolated,
  // making the entire primitive be smoothly shaded
  gl_FragColor = colorVarying;
}
```

Here's what this code does.

First, it declares that it wants to know the value of the `colorVarying` variable. Remember, this is the variable that was also declared in the vertex shader and was used to pass the color information:

```
varying lowp vec4 colorVarying;
```

After the fragment shader has the color information, it just needs to set the color of the fragment to the color it was told to use:

```
gl_FragColor = colorVarying;
```

Step 2 of the Render Master Plan we discussed in Chapter 22 is complete. OpenGL now knows about the shader!

Now it's time to do something with them.

Tying it all together

We mentioned before that when you combine a vertex shader with a fragment shader, you get a shader program. So, how do you combine the shaders? It's pretty simple: You tell OpenGL to make it for you.

Shader programs are objects, just like buffers. To create a shader program, you generate it, bind it, and then give it the source code to both the vertex shader and the fragment shader. You tell OpenGL to compile both shaders, and then link them together. After you've done that, you have a fully working shader program that you can use to do drawing.

To make this process happen in your code, you need to add the methods that do this process for you. During this process, you need to tell OpenGL to attach the vertex attributes to specific numbers so that you can refer to them later:

1. **Add the list of vertex attribute numbers.**

   Add the following code to OpenGLTrafficView.m, above the @implementation line:

   ```
   enum {
       ATTRIB_VERTEX,
       ATTRIB_COLOR,
       NUM_ATTRIBUTES
   };
   ```

2. **Add the method that compiles shaders to OpenGLTrafficView.**

   Add the following method to OpenGLTrafficView. This code loads the contents of the shader source code and stores it in a variable. It then gives OpenGL the source code and tells it to compile it. If an error exists in compiling the shader, it returns FALSE; otherwise, it returns TRUE:

   ```
   - (BOOL)compileShader:(GLuint *)shader type:(GLenum)
           type file:(NSString *)file
   {
   GLint status;

   const GLchar *source;

   source = (GLchar *)[[NSString
           stringWithContentsOfFile:file
           encoding:NSUTF8StringEncoding error:nil]
           UTF8String];
       if (!source)
       {
   NSLog(@"Failed to load shader");
           return FALSE;
       }

   *shader = glCreateShader(type);

   glShaderSource(*shader, 1, &source, NULL);
       glCompileShader(*shader);

   glGetShaderiv(*shader, GL_COMPILE_STATUS, &status);
       if (status == 0)
       {
   glDeleteShader(*shader);
           return FALSE;
       }

       return TRUE;
   }
   ```

   Here's how this code works.

   First, the code declares a couple of variables it will be using later: an integer, for storing the status of the compilation, and a pointer, which will point to the shader program source code:

```
GLint status;


    const GLchar *source;
```

After that's done, the contents of the shader file are loaded into memory by making an NSData load the contents and then getting a pointer to the raw bytes that it's loaded. If the source code can't be loaded for some reason, the method returns FALSE, indicating that the shader couldn't be built:

```
source = (GLchar *)[[NSString
        stringWithContentsOfFile:file
        encoding:NSUTF8StringEncoding error:nil]
        UTF8String];
    if (!source)
    {
NSLog(@"Failed to load shader");
        return FALSE;
    }
```

After you have the source code, you can make the shader. First, you need to tell OpenGL that you want to create a shader. Tell OpenGL what type of shader it is (fragment or vertex — this was passed to the method as a parameter) and OpenGL returns an object reference. You store this in the shader parameter:

```
*shader = glCreateShader(type);
```

After the shader object has been created, you need to give OpenGL the source code and then tell OpenGL to compile it:

```
glShaderSource(*shader, 1, &source, NULL);
    glCompileShader(*shader);
```

After this has happened, OpenGL should have successfully compiled the source code. You can check to see whether everything went well by asking OpenGL about it. If the compilation didn't work, return FALSE:

```
glGetShaderiv(*shader, GL_COMPILE_STATUS, &status);
if (status == 0)
{
    glDeleteShader(*shader);
    return FALSE;
}
```

3. **Add the code that links the shader program.**

Add the following method to OpenGLTrafficView.m. Linking binds two shaders together to form a shader program, which can be used to render primitives in your scene:

```
- (BOOL)linkProgram:(GLuint)prog
{
    GLint status;
```

```
    glLinkProgram(prog);


    glGetProgramiv(prog, GL_LINK_STATUS, &status);
    if (status == 0)
        return FALSE;

    return TRUE;
}
```

4. **Add the code that prepares the shaders.**

Add the following code to OpenGLTrafficView.m. This code uses the other methods you just wrote to compile and link together the vertex shader and the fragment shader.

First, the code creates an empty shader program. Then, it creates and compiles the vertex shader, followed by the fragment shader. After that's done, the two shaders are attached to the shader program and link them together.

After having done all that, it's then possible to get information about the location of the vertex attribute variables and the uniform variables. This information is used later to store information in the variables, during the rendering process:

```
- (BOOL) prepareShaders {
GLuint vertShader, fragShader;

NSString *vertShaderPathname, *fragShaderPathname;

shaderProgram = glCreateProgram();


vertShaderPathname = [[NSBundle mainBundle]
        pathForResource:@"Shader" ofType:@"vsh"];

if (![self compileShader:&vertShader type:GL_VERTEX_
        SHADER file:vertShaderPathname])
    {
      NSLog(@"Failed to compile vertex shader");
      return FALSE;
    }

fragShaderPathname = [[NSBundle mainBundle]
        pathForResource:@"Shader" ofType:@"fsh"];
    if (![self compileShader:&fragShader type:GL_
        FRAGMENT_SHADER file:fragShaderPathname])
    {
      NSLog(@"Failed to compile fragment shader");
      return FALSE;
    }

glAttachShader(shaderProgram, vertShader);
```

```
    glAttachShader(shaderProgram, fragShader);

    glBindAttribLocation(shaderProgram, ATTRIB_VERTEX,
        "position");
    glBindAttribLocation(shaderProgram, ATTRIB_COLOR,
        "color");

    if (![self linkProgram:shaderProgram])
    {
      NSLog(@"Failed to link program: %d",
          shaderProgram);

      if (vertShader)
      {
        glDeleteShader(vertShader);
        vertShader = 0;
      }
      if (fragShader)
      {
        glDeleteShader(fragShader);
        fragShader = 0;
      }
      if (shaderProgram)
      {
        glDeleteProgram(shaderProgram);
        shaderProgram = 0;
      }

      return FALSE;
    }

    if (vertShader)
      glDeleteShader(vertShader);
    if (fragShader)
      glDeleteShader(fragShader);

    return TRUE;
}
```

That was another huge chunk of code! Here's how it works.

First, the variables that will be used to refer to the vertex shader and fragment shaders are created, as well as the strings that will be used to store the paths to the shader files themselves:

```
    GLuint vertShader, fragShader;

NSString *vertShaderPathname, *fragShaderPathname;
```

With that done, you need to tell OpenGL to create a shader program. After it's created, it won't have any shaders attached to it — you need to do that yourself:

```
shaderProgram = glCreateProgram();
```

To compile the vertex shader, the code first works out the path to the Shader.vsh file that was added to the project. It then calls the compile Shader method to make OpenGL load and prepare the shader. If an error exists, the entire method returns FALSE.

The code then repeats the process to prepare the fragment shader:

```
vertShaderPathname = [[NSBundle mainBundle]
      pathForResource:@"Shader" ofType:@"vsh"];

if (![self compileShader:&vertShader type:GL_VERTEX_
      SHADER file:vertShaderPathname])
{
  NSLog(@"Failed to compile vertex shader");
  return FALSE;
}

fragShaderPathname = [[NSBundle mainBundle]
      pathForResource:@"Shader" ofType:@"fsh"];
if (![self compileShader:&fragShader type:GL_
      FRAGMENT_SHADER file:fragShaderPathname])
{
  NSLog(@"Failed to compile fragment shader");
  return FALSE;
}
```

After the two shaders have been prepared, you can link them together and form a working shader program. To do this, the code attaches both the vertex shader and the fragment shader to the shader program, and then tells OpenGL to link the shaders together.

Before linking, though, the code tells OpenGL to bind the locations of the vertex attribute variables to the numbers that you set up earlier. This makes it possible to work with the attributes later on.

Again, if any problems exist, the method returns FALSE, after deleting the resources that were created:

```
glAttachShader(shaderProgram, vertShader);
glAttachShader(shaderProgram, fragShader);
glBindAttribLocation(shaderProgram, ATTRIB_VERTEX,
        "position");
glBindAttribLocation(shaderProgram, ATTRIB_COLOR,
        "color");

if (![self linkProgram:shaderProgram])

{

  NSLog(@"Failed to link program: %d", shaderProgram);

  if (vertShader)
  {
    glDeleteShader(vertShader);
    vertShader = 0;
```

```
  }
  if (fragShader)
  {
    glDeleteShader(fragShader);
    fragShader = 0;
  }
  if (shaderProgram)
  {
    glDeleteProgram(shaderProgram);
    shaderProgram = 0;
  }

  return FALSE;
}
```

Finally, the shader program has been created, and you don't need the individual shaders themselves anymore. So, we delete them and return TRUE to indicate that the shader program was successfully created:

```
if (vertShader)
    glDeleteShader(vertShader);
  if (fragShader)
    glDeleteShader(fragShader);

return TRUE;
```

5. **Prepare the shaders when setting up OpenGL.**

   Add the following code to the end of the prepareOpenGL method. All this code does is call the prepareShaders method you wrote earlier. If the method returns FALSE, it puts a warning message in the run log:

```
if ([self prepareShaders] == FALSE) {
  NSLog(@"Failed to prepare the shaders!");
}
```

After you're done, your shader object is ready to go. It's time to put it to work!

Drawing the Scene

To draw the scene, you need to do the following things:

1. **Clear the buffer.**

   You want to start the rendering operation with a clean slate and don't want to worry about the contents of the last frame you rendered (because that picture was *so* 30 milliseconds ago).

2. **Tell OpenGL about the size of the viewport.**

   OpenGL needs to know about how big the rendering area is so that it can position the vertices appropriately on the screen.

3. **Give OpenGL your vertex attributes.**

   OpenGL can then give them to the vertex shader.

4. **Tell OpenGL to draw the thing.**

   This causes pixels to be drawn into the render buffer by running all the vertex attributes through the vertex shader and then running all the fragments that this generates through the fragment shader.

5. **Tell Cocoa Touch to present the render buffer.**

   This shows the picture to the user.

The rest of this chapter shows how to draw pixels to the screen, using the shader program you wrote in the previous sections.

Setting up the vertex arrays

To render the scene we want, you need to set up two arrays of vertex attributes: one for the position of the vertices and one for the color.

The vertex positions are set up so that they describe a rectangle that almost fills the entire screen. The color attributes describe a selection of colors, which (when combined with the vertex positions) will make the rectangle multicolored.

Drawing the scene

To do the drawing, replace the contents of the `render:` method in OpenGLTrafficView.m:

```
- (void) render:(CADisplayLink*)sender {

static const GLfloat squareVertices[] = {
    -0.9f, -1.0f, // bottom left corner of the screen
    0.9f, -1.0f,  // bottom right corner of the screen
    -0.9f,  1.0f, // top left corner of the screen
    0.9f, 1.0f, // top right corner of the screen
    };

static const GLfloat squareColorCoords[] = {
    1.0, 0.0, 0.0, // red
    0.0, 1.0, 0.0, // green
    0.0, 0.0, 1.0, // blue
    1.0, 1.1, 0.0, // yellow
};

glBindFramebuffer(GL_FRAMEBUFFER, framebuffer);
```

```
    glViewport(0, 0, self.bounds.size.width, self.bounds.
            size.height);

    glClearColor(0.0, 0.0, 0.0, 1.0);
    glClear(GL_COLOR_BUFFER_BIT);

    glUseProgram(shaderProgram);

    glVertexAttribPointer(ATTRIB_VERTEX, 2, GL_FLOAT, 0, 0,
            squareVertices);
    glEnableVertexAttribArray(ATTRIB_VERTEX);

    glVertexAttribPointer(ATTRIB_COLOR, 3, GL_FLOAT, 0, 0,
            squareColorCoords);
    glEnableVertexAttribArray(ATTRIB_COLOR);

    glDrawArrays(GL_TRIANGLE_STRIP, 0, 4);

    glBindRenderbuffer(GL_RENDERBUFFER, colorRenderBuffer);
    [context presentRenderbuffer:GL_RENDERBUFFER];
}
```

We'll now go through this code and work out what it does.

This code creates two arrays: position information, which describes where
the vertices are on-screen, and color information, which describes the color
of each vertex:

```
static const GLfloat squareVertices[] = {
    -0.9f, -1.0f, // bottom left corner of the screen
    0.9f, -1.0f,  // bottom right corner of the screen
    -0.9f,  1.0f, // top left corner of the screen
    0.9f, 1.0f, // top right corner of the screen
    };

    static const GLfloat squareColorCoords[] = {
    1.0, 0.0, 0.0, // red
    0.0, 1.0, 0.0, // green
    0.0, 0.0, 1.0, // blue
    1.0, 1.1, 0.0, // yellow
    };
```

Just like we did in Chapter 22, the code binds the framebuffer to the context to
start working on it, sets up the viewport, and clears the buffer (this time, to black):

```
glBindFramebuffer(GL_FRAMEBUFFER, framebuffer);

glViewport(0, 0, self.bounds.size.width, self.bounds.size.
        height);

glClearColor(0.0, 0.0, 0.0, 1.0);
glClear(GL_COLOR_BUFFER_BIT);
```

It then tells OpenGL to start using the shader program that we set up earlier. This means that every vertex is processed using the vertex shader you wrote, and every fragment is processed using the fragment shader:

```
glUseProgram(shaderProgram);
```

The code then sends both of the arrays of data to OpenGL. The vertex position data is sent to OpenGL, and you tell OpenGL to use the information for the position vertex attributes. The code then does the same thing with the color information, and it tells OpenGL to use it for the color vertex attributes:

```
glVertexAttribPointer(ATTRIB_VERTEX, 2, GL_FLOAT, 0, 0,
        squareVertices);
glEnableVertexAttribArray(ATTRIB_VERTEX);

glVertexAttribPointer(ATTRIB_COLOR, 3, GL_FLOAT, 0, 0,
        squareColorCoords);
glEnableVertexAttribArray(ATTRIB_COLOR);
```

Finally, we tell OpenGL to draw four vertices. OpenGL then splits the vertex attribute information and passes it to the vertex shader, which positions the vertices on the screen so that the graphics chip can rasterize the triangles. The rasterized fragments are then sent to the fragment shader, which figures out what color to show for each pixel:

```
glDrawArrays(GL_TRIANGLE_STRIP, 0, 4);
```

Finally, the finished picture is presented to the user, just like we did in Chapter 22:

```
glBindRenderbuffer(GL_RENDERBUFFER, colorRenderBuffer);
[context presentRenderbuffer:GL_RENDERBUFFER];
```

And with that method in place, you can compile and run your game. You're done! You now see a multicolored rectangle behind the game, as shown in Figure 23-1. Hooray!

With this, Steps 3 and 4 of the Rendering Master Plan from Chapter 22 are complete. We're now drawing our own pictures!

Chapter 24

Texturing with OpenGL

. . . .

In This Chapter

▶ Exploring textures

▶ Compressing textures to save space

▶ Texturing background images

. . . .

*I*n Chapter 23, we showed you how to set up the OpenGL drawing view to show a rectangle underneath the game view — but the rectangle is multi-colored and looks like it belongs in a disco.

In this chapter, you find out how texturing works in OpenGL and make the OpenGL view draw the road speeding underneath the game. You also explore compressed textures and find out how to write a texture-mapping shader.

Figuring Out How Textures Work

The pixels that are drawn using the code in Chapters 22 and 23 have been using colors that we set up in code. By assigning a color to each of the vertices that are being drawn, OpenGL can figure out what color to pass to the fragment shader. If you need a quick refresher on what a shader is, head back to Chapter 23!

However, using this method to create a complex picture is no fun — imagine the amount of data you'd have to hard code — and it also doesn't make much sense to store the color information in your code. After all, code is for describing behavior, not data. That's what resource files are for!

To solve this problem of storing information, a very clever guy named Ed Catmull figured out a method of storing color information in files and drawing them on rasterized triangles. This method is called *texture mapping*, and it's what we'll use to make the road texture appear on the background rectangle.

Ed Catmull went on to write the rendering code that was used in the production of *Toy Story* and currently works as the president of Disney Animation Studios, so he knows what he's talking about.

Texture mapping works by combining an image (known as the *texture*) and information on where to attach the texture to vertices (known as *texture coordinates*). To do texture mapping, you provide the texture coordinates for each vertex. The vertex shader then passes these coordinates to the fragment shader. Chapter 23 showed how OpenGL interpolates the values of varyings when rasterizing. This also applies to texture coordinates.

The upshot is that the fragment shader receives the precise texture coordinate that it needs to use for the pixel it needs to color. It then takes the texture image, figures out what color the texture is at the texture coordinates it's given, and sets the fragment color to what it finds. When you repeat this process for the entire collection of rasterized fragments, you end up displaying the entire texture on the primitive you told OpenGL to draw!

If you've followed through the development of the *Traffic* game thus far, your game looks something like Figure 24-1: a multicolored rectangle, behind the main game view.

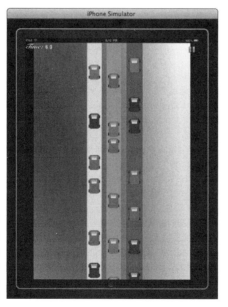

Figure 24-1:
The starting
point for
your game.

By the end of the chapter, your game should look like Figure 24-2. (It looks a lot better when it's moving. Paper technology has not yet advanced enough to let us show you moving pictures.)

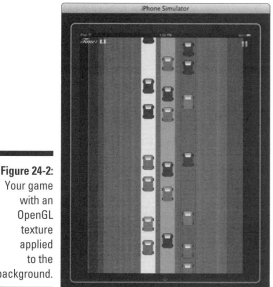

Figure 24-2:
Your game
with an
OpenGL
texture
applied
to the
background.

Compressing Textures

Textures can get pretty big. A true-color image uses three bytes for each pixel (one byte each for red, green, and blue), and more often than not, you'll be using a texture that's 256 pixels square (or larger!)

If you're using a true-color texture that's 512 x 512 pixels in size, the size of the texture will be 768K. That doesn't sound like very much by itself, but if you're writing a complex game, you can very quickly run into a situation where you're using so much texture memory that the graphics card won't be able to hold them all in its internal memory. When that happens, the rendering speed of the graphics card has to slow down dramatically. So, how can you use lots of high-resolution textures while still keeping memory usage down?

The answer is compressed textures. A *compressed texture* is a texture that is crunched down to reduce the amount of size it takes up in memory, much like a JPEG or PNG image. However, when working with graphics hardware, the interesting thing about compressed textures is that the images stay compressed, even when they're uploaded to the graphics chip. This dramatically cuts down on memory usage, allowing you to store even more textures.

iOS devices support a texture compression format called PVRTC. PVRTC is a very efficient format, capable of storing pictures in true color while only taking up two bits per pixel. (That's right, two *bits* per pixel. PVRTC is *crazy.*)

PVRTC stands for PowerVR Texture Compression. PowerVR is the company that builds the graphics chips used in iOS devices.

To work with PVRTC textures, you first need to convert your images from their original format to the PVRTC format. To do this, use a software tool that comes with the iPhone SDK, which is called *texturetool*. The texturetool program reads a picture, compresses it to PVRTC, and saves it to disk. You can then put the compressed texture file in your project and use it later.

To get things going, you first need to compress the background texture:

1. **Prepare the texture file.**

   The texture you'll be using in this chapter is the Tarmac.png file, which is in the texture pack we instructed you to download in Chapter 1.

   Open the Terminal application in the Applications/Utilities folder on your hard drive and copy the Tarmac.png file to your desktop.

2. **Compress the texture.**

   Type the following into the Terminal application:

   ```
   cd ~/Desktop
   /Developer/Platforms/iPhoneOS.platform/Developer/usr/
           bin/texturetool -e PVRTC --bits-per-pixel-2 -o
           Tarmac.pvrtc Tarmac.png
   ```

   These instructions tell your computer to locate the texture file and then compress the texture using the PVRTC format, saving it in the 2-bits-per-pixel mode.

3. **Add the texture to your project.**

   Drag the Tarmac.pvrtc file that appears on your desktop into your project's resources.

With that done, you're now ready to make your application load the texture. Are you excited? We thought so.

Loading Textures

To work with textures, you need to generate a texture object and then bind it to the OpenGL context — it's a similar process to creating buffers or shader program objects. After you have a texture, you need to give OpenGL the texture data itself. Because OpenGL on iOS already knows about the PVRTC format, you can just give it the contents of the texture file.

To draw using the texture, you need to attach the texture to a *texture unit*. Although you can have a lot of textures stored in OpenGL at once, a rendering operation can only deal with a limited subset of them. To select which textures to use when rendering, you assign them to texture units; then, when the fragment shader runs, your code uses the texture unit to get access to the texture image itself.

Before we get to that, though, we need to load the texture into memory:

1. **Add the code that loads and prepares texture files.**

   Add the following code to OpenGLTrafficView.m:

   ```objc
   - (void) loadTexture:(GLuint *)texture
           fromFileNamed:(NSString*)fileName {
     // First, we need to get the full path to the
           texture file.
     NSString* filePath = [[NSBundle mainBundle]
           pathForResource:fileName ofType:@"pvrtc"];

     // Next, load the texture data into an NSData, and
           then get a pointer to
     // the actual bytes.
     NSData* textureData = [NSData dataWithContentsOfFile
           :filePath];
     void* textureBytes = [textureData bytes];

     // We'll make the assumption that the textures are
           512 by 512, with no alpha,
     // and 2 bits per pixel.
     GLenum format = GL_COMPRESSED_RGB_PVRTC_2BPPV1_IMG;

     // The total size, in bytes, is the width multiplied
           by the height, multiplied by the
     // number of bits per pixel (which we then divide by
           8 to get the number of bytes)
     GLsizei size = 512 * 512 * 2 / 8;

     // Next, generate a texture object, and bind it to
           the context.
     // Once that's done, OpenGL knows that we're working
           with it.
     glGenTextures(1, texture);
     glBindTexture(GL_TEXTURE_2D, *texture);

     // Now we do the important step: uploading the
           texture information
     // to OpenGL!
     glCompressedTexImage2D(GL_TEXTURE_2D, 0, format,
           512, 512, 0, size, textureBytes);
   ```

```
    // Finally, we need to tell OpenGL how it should
        scale the texture.
    // It's unlikely that we'll ever see the texture at
        1:1 scale,
    // so OpenGL needs to be able to resize it when
        necessary.
    glTexParameteri(GL_TEXTURE_2D,GL_TEXTURE_MIN_
        FILTER,GL_LINEAR);
    glTexParameteri(GL_TEXTURE_2D,GL_TEXTURE_MAG_
        FILTER,GL_LINEAR);
}
```

Here's what this code does: First, the code works out the path of the texture file and then loads the contents of the file into an NSData object. This gives us the ability to give the information directly to OpenGL:

```
NSString* filePath = [[NSBundle mainBundle]
        pathForResource:fileName ofType:@"pvrtc"];
NSData* textureData = [NSData dataWithContentsOfFile:
        filePath];
void* textureBytes = [textureData bytes];
```

This code makes the assumption that the textures are 512 pixels wide and 512 pixels high, and that each pixel uses 2 bits of information. This lets us figure out the total amount of memory required — by multiplying 512 by 512 by 2, we know how many bits we'll need. To convert that to bytes, just divide by 8 (because you find 8 bits in a byte.) The total amount of memory we need, then, is (512 * 512 * 2) / 8, or 65,536 bytes — 64 kilobytes.

```
GLenum format = GL_COMPRESSED_RGB_PVRTC_2BPPV1_IMG;
GLsizei size = 512 * 512 * 2 / 8;
```

After the texture information is prepared, the code then tells OpenGL to create the texture object and binds it to the OpenGL context, allowing us to start working with it:

```
glGenTextures(1, texture);
glBindTexture(GL_TEXTURE_2D, *texture);
```

After the texture object is bound, we give OpenGL the compressed texture information:

```
glCompressedTexImage2D(GL_TEXTURE_2D, 0, format, 512,
        512, 0, size, textureBytes);
```

The last steps tell OpenGL how to scale the texture up or down on the screen. The texture is 512 x 512, but the size of the background rectangle on the screen is likely to be a different size. This means that OpenGL needs to know how to resize it:

```
glTexParameteri(GL_TEXTURE_2D,GL_TEXTURE_MIN_
        FILTER,GL_LINEAR);
glTexParameteri(GL_TEXTURE_2D,GL_TEXTURE_MAG_
        FILTER,GL_LINEAR);
```

2. Add a texture variable to the OpenGLTrafficView class.

To be able to load and reuse a texture, we need a way of referring to it.

Modify the code in the interface declaration so that it looks like the following code:

```
#import <UIKit/UIKit.h>
#import <OpenGLES/ES2/gl.h>
#import <OpenGLES/ES2/glext.h>
#import <QuartzCore/QuartzCore.h>
#import <CoreGraphics/CoreGraphics.h>

@interface OpenGLTrafficView : UIView {
  EAGLContext* context; // the OpenGL drawing context
        for the game
  GLuint framebuffer; // the frame buffer that we do
        all drawing into
  GLuint colorRenderBuffer; // the render buffer
        that's displayed on screen
  GLuint depthBuffer; // the depth buffer, used for
        internal distance calculations

  GLuint shaderProgram; // the shader program, used
        for positioning and shading the objects

  GLuint backgroundTexture; // the background road
        texture

  CADisplayLink* displayLink;
}

@end
```

3. Load the texture itself when setting up OpenGL.

You have the code that loads the texture and a variable for referring to the texture. The final step is to make your code actually do the loading.

Add the following code to the end of the `prepareOpenGL` method:

```
[self loadTexture:&backgroundTexture
        fromFileNamed:@"Tarmac"];
```

When your program starts up, you'll be loading the texture and storing it on the graphics chip. Next, you need to update the shader program so that it actually uses the texture.

Updating the Shaders

In the code that you wrote in the previous section, the shaders don't make use of the textures that are being loaded. We need to correct this. Remember, to do texture mapping, you need both texture coordinates and a texture itself. The texture coordinates change depending on which vertex you're drawing, but the texture remains the same for the entire drawing operation. Additionally, the texture coordinates need to be passed from the vertex shader to the fragment shader.

This means that the texture coordinates should be vertex attributes, the texture itself should be a uniform (a value that does not change during the drawing operation), and the texture coordinates also need to be passed to the fragment shader using a varying (a value that *does* change during the drawing operation — see Chapter 23 for details on what these are!). You need to update the shaders to make texture-mapping work. First update the vertex shader, and then update the fragment shader:

1. **Update the vertex shader to send texture information to the fragment shader.**

   Replace the contents of Shader.vsh with the following code.

   This new shader sets the position of the vertex based on the `position` attribute, just like it did in Chapter 23, but it also passes the texture coordinate information to the fragment shader using a new varying variable:

   ```
   // Attributes sent to OpenGL.
   attribute vec4 position;
   attribute vec2 texCoord;
   attribute vec4 color;

   // Varyings, which we send to the fragment shader.
   varying lowp vec4 colorVarying;
   varying lowp vec2 texturePosition;

   void main()
   {
     // Make the vertex appear at the position described
     // by the position attribute
     gl_Position = position;

     // Pass the texture coordinates to the fragment
         shader
     texturePosition = texCoord;

     // Pass the color information to the fragment shader
     // (this isn't actually used any more, but it could
     // be handy later.)
     colorVarying = color;
   }
   ```

2. **Update the fragment shader to load the color from the texture.**

   Replace the contents of Shader.fsh with the following code.

This code uses the texture coordinate information that the vertex shader provided and uses it to figure out what color to use based on the texture that the "texture" uniform points to:

```
// Varyings, passed from the vertex shader
varying lowp vec2 texturePosition;
varying lowp vec4 colorVarying;

// The uniform containing the texture unit
uniform sampler2D texture;

void main()
{
    // Take the color of the texture at the given
        texture position
    gl_FragColor = texture2D(texture, texturePosition);
}
```

With these modifications done, the shader is now able to work with texture coordinates and read color information from the texture unit. However, this code added some new variables to the shaders: a new texture coordinate vertex attribute and a uniform, which contains the texture unit that the fragment shader needs to load information from.

To be able to put information into these variables, you have to be able to refer to them. This means that you need to do a little more set up when preparing the shaders: You have to bind the vertex attributes to a number (which you'll use later), and you also need to ask OpenGL for the location of the new uniform that we added to the shader.

To store the location of the "texture" uniform, create an array of numbers that you'll use later when the shader has been linked, and when we need to tell OpenGL to store a value in the uniform.

You also need to add another entry in the list of vertex attributes, which you then bind the attribute to:

1. **Add the uniform location array.**

   Add the following code to the start of OpenGLTrafficView.m. This code creates an array of variables that we use to get access to the shader uniforms:

   ```
   enum {
       UNIFORM_TEXTURE,
       NUM_UNIFORMS
   };
   GLint uniforms[NUM_UNIFORMS];
   ```

2. **Add the new vertex attribute reference number.**

Modify the vertex attribute list at the top of OpenGLTrafficView.m so that it looks like the following code:

```
enum {
   ATTRIB_VERTEX,
   ATTRIB_COLOR,
   ATTRIB_TEXCOORD,
   NUM_ATTRIBUTES
};
```

3. **Bind the `texCoord` attribute to the new attribute reference number.**

   Modify the `prepareShaders` method so that the code that binds the vertex attributes looks like the following code.

   What we're doing here is binding the location of the texture coordinate to the number that we set up in the last step:

```
glBindAttribLocation(shaderProgram, ATTRIB_VERTEX,
        "position");
glBindAttribLocation(shaderProgram, ATTRIB_COLOR,
        "color");
glBindAttribLocation(shaderProgram, ATTRIB_TEXCOORD,
        "texCoord");
```

4. **Store the location of the "texture" uniform.**

   Add the following code to the `prepareShaders` method, just before the `return TRUE;` line. In this code, you're asking OpenGL to tell you how to refer to the "texture" uniform, which lets you store information in it:

```
uniforms[UNIFORM_TEXTURE] = glGetUniformLocation
        (shaderProgram, "texture");
```

With that, the shader is all set up and ready to use the texture. By this point, OpenGL now knows about the `texCoord` vertex attribute, which you'll use to provide the texture coordinates for each vertex, as well as the "texture" uniform, which you'll use to tell the shader about the texture unit you want it to use. The next step is to make the shader actually draw something!

Drawing the Texture

In Chapter 23, we created an array of colors and provided them as vertex attributes to the vertex shader. We're going to update this: We need to provide vertex coordinates to the shader.

We also need to get the texture ready for drawing. To do this, we first need to tell OpenGL about the texture unit we want to use. We're only using one texture at the moment, so we'll use the first texture unit, also known as texture unit 0.

After that's done, we need to bind the background texture to the context. This gets OpenGL ready to start reading texture information and attaches the texture to texture unit 0.

Finally, we need to tell the shader to use texture unit 0. This is done by setting the "texture" uniform to 0 — this value is then used by the fragment shader, where it loads the color information.

The last step is to tell OpenGL to draw the vertices. When it does that, it goes through the processing pipeline and gets the shaders to do the texture mapping!

1. **Add the rendering code.**

   To make this happen, change the contents of the render method so that it looks like the following code.

   This new code stores the texture coordinate information in another array, which is passed to the shader program as a set of vertex attributes. Additionally, the background texture is bound to texture unit 0, and the shader program is told to use texture unit 0 for the texture information.

   ```
   - (void) render:(CADisplayLink*)sender {
     static const GLfloat squareVertices[] = {
           -0.9f, -1.0f, // bottom left corner of the
           screen
         0.9f, -1.0f,  // bottom right corner of the screen
           -0.9f,  1.0f, // top left corner of the screen
         0.9f, 1.0f, // top right corner of the screen
         };

     static const GLfloat squareColorCoords[] = {
         1.0, 0.0, 0.0, // red
         0.0, 1.0, 0.0, // green
         0.0, 0.0, 1.0, // blue
         1.0, 1.1, 0.0, // yellow
     };

     static const GLfloat squareTextureCoords [] = {
         0.0, 0.0, // bottom left of the rectangle
         1.0, 0.0, // bottom right
         0.0, 1.0, // top left
         1.0, 1.0, // top right
     };

     glBindFramebuffer(GL_FRAMEBUFFER, framebuffer);

     glViewport(0, 0, self.bounds.size.width, self.
         bounds.size.height);
   ```

```
glClearColor(0.0, 0.0, 0.0, 1.0);
glClear(GL_COLOR_BUFFER_BIT);

glUseProgram(shaderProgram);

glVertexAttribPointer(ATTRIB_VERTEX, 2, GL_FLOAT, 0,
      0, squareVertices);
glEnableVertexAttribArray(ATTRIB_VERTEX);

glVertexAttribPointer(ATTRIB_COLOR, 3, GL_FLOAT, 0,
      0, squareColorCoords);
glEnableVertexAttribArray(ATTRIB_COLOR);

glVertexAttribPointer(ATTRIB_TEXCOORD, 2, GL_FLOAT,
      0, 0, squareTextureCoords);
glEnableVertexAttribArray(ATTRIB_TEXCOORD);

glUniform1i(uniforms[UNIFORM_TEXTURE], 0);

glEnable(GL_TEXTURE_2D);

glActiveTexture(GL_TEXTURE0);

glBindTexture(GL_TEXTURE_2D, backgroundTexture);

glDrawArrays(GL_TRIANGLE_STRIP, 0, 4);

glDisable(GL_TEXTURE_2D);

glBindRenderbuffer(GL_RENDERBUFFER,
      colorRenderBuffer);
[context presentRenderbuffer:GL_RENDERBUFFER];
}
```

This new code prepares and sends another array of vertex attributes to the vertex shader — in this case, it's the texture coordinate information, which tells OpenGL how each corner of the texture matches the vertex:

```
static const GLfloat squareTextureCoords [] = {
   0.0, 0.0, // bottom left of the rectangle
   1.0, 0.0, // bottom right
   0.0, 1.0, // top left
   1.0, 1.0, // top right
   };
```

It then passes this data to OpenGL:

```
glVertexAttribPointer(ATTRIB_TEXCOORD, 2, GL_FLOAT, 0,
      0, squareTextureCoords);
glEnableVertexAttribArray(ATTRIB_TEXCOORD);
```

It also stores the number 0 into the "texture" uniform, which the shader uses. This is because you are telling OpenGL that the texture you want it to work with exists inside texture unit 0. Finally, the code enables texturing, tells OpenGL that we're working with texture unit 0, and binds the texture to the context:

```
glUniform1i(uniforms[UNIFORM_TEXTURE], 0);
glEnable(GL_TEXTURE_2D);
glActiveTexture(GL_TEXTURE0);
glBindTexture(GL_TEXTURE_2D, backgroundTexture);
```

After drawing, it disables texturing, to keep things simple:

```
glDisable(GL_TEXTURE_2D);
```

After all of this work has been done, the image is ready to be displayed.

2. **Run the game.**

   You can see the road beneath the cars, but it's not moving! You need to fix that, and we show you how, in the next section.

Making the Road Move

To create the illusion of the road speeding underneath the cars, we need to change the position of the road every frame. We *could* move the rectangle itself, but then we'd run into the problem of what to do when the rectangle moved off the screen — we'd need to move it back, but that would be tricky to do seamlessly.

The easier solution is to move the texture itself. By changing the texture coordinate, you change the position of the texture on the screen, which has the same effect as moving the rectangle.

To make this movement, we need to tell the shader how much to move the texture by. This needs to be controlled by the amount of time that's gone by. Fortunately, we have a very simple way of getting access to this information: the CADisplayLink object!

The CADisplayLink class contains a property called timestamp, which contains the time that the last frame was rendered. We can use this to update the texture coordinate positions by moving the vertical component of the coordinate by the amount of time. The end result is that every frame, the position of the texture is moved a little bit more, creating the illusion of constant movement.

To make this happen, we need to add a new variable to the vertex shader, which stores the time. We then provide the timestamp value to the vertex shader every frame. Finally, inside the vertex shader, we make the shader update the texture coordinates based on the time:

1. **Update the vertex shader to add the texture movement ability.**

   Modify the code in Shader.vsh so that it looks like the following code:

   ```
   attribute vec4 position;
   attribute vec2 texCoord;
   attribute vec4 color;

   varying lowp vec4 colorVarying;
   varying lowp vec2 texturePosition;

   uniform highp float time;

   void main()
   {
     gl_Position = position;

     texturePosition = texCoord;

     texturePosition.y += time;

     colorVarying = color;
   }
   ```

   Here's what the new code does.

   It adds a new uniform, which is used to store the time (which drives the position of the texture):

   ```
   uniform highp float time;
   ```

   Secondly, the position of the texture coordinate is updated based on the time value. This is the part of the code that actually moves the texture. Simple, isn't it?

   ```
   texturePosition.y += time;
   ```

2. **Tell the OpenGLTrafficView class about the new uniform.**

   Because we've added a new uniform to the shader program, we need a way to store information in it. We need to store the location of the uniform in the list of uniform locations.

   Modify the list of uniform locations at the top of OpenGLTrafficView.m so that it looks like the following code:

   ```
   enum {
     UNIFORM_TIME,
     UNIFORM_TEXTURE,
     NUM_UNIFORMS
   };
   GLint uniforms[NUM_UNIFORMS];
   ```

After that's done, you need to store the location of the uniform.

Update the code that gets the uniform locations in `prepareShaders` so that it looks like the following code. All we're doing here is storing the location of the new uniform so that we can access it later when rendering:

```
uniforms[UNIFORM_TIME] = glGetUniformLocation
        (shaderProgram, "time");
uniforms[UNIFORM_TEXTURE] = glGetUniformLocation
        (shaderProgram, "texture");
```

3. **Set the value of the time uniform in the render method.**

To make the vertex shader update the position of the texture based on the time, you need to store the time in the uniform you set up.

Add the following lines of code right after where you set the "texture" uniform:

```
glUniform1i(uniforms[UNIFORM_TEXTURE], 0);
glUniform1f(uniforms[UNIFORM_TIME], [displayLink
        timestamp]);
```

Now run the game. Watch the road rushing underneath the cars, and feel the wind in your hair!

Chapter 25

Kicking Up Your Game a Notch

In This Chapter
▶ Accessing an iPod library
▶ Responding to shakes

*I*n this chapter, we show you how to add a couple extra features to your game. These are little extra goodies that can add fun to your game; additionally, it doesn't hurt one bit to find out how to access the iPod and how to deal with people shaking it!

Accessing the iPod Library

Once upon a time (in 2007), there was no such thing as the iPhone. There was just this iPod gadget, which was selling pretty well for Apple. Every iOS device has evolved from the iPod, and consequently, every iOS device is a pretty powerful media player. Your game can access the library of content that the user has stored on her device and can take control of the built-in iPod functionality.

Your app can do a wide variety of things with the user's music collection; it can search for content in the library, pull album artwork and other information, play and pause content, put together playlists, and generally clone almost every aspect of the iPod application. So, how do you work with this library? Time to take a look!

 We give you a quick overview of the iPod library access system, but as always, you could explore more. If you're curious, look in the iOS Software Development Kit (SDK) documentation — check out the *iPod Library Access Programming Guide*, which you can find online at `http://developer.apple.com/iphone/library/documentation/Audio/Conceptual/iPodLibraryAccess_Guide/`.

Media items, media pickers, and music players

Everything inside the user's media library is a media item. A *media item* is a song, audio book, or podcast, and it's how you refer to the specific bits of content that the user loads into his device.

You can access iPod content in a couple ways. The method that we look at in this chapter uses media picker controllers. A *media picker controller* is a view controller that displays the user's library and lets her select media items. You can create a media picker controller and present it to the user, just like any other view controller.

To actually let the user hear something, you need to work with a music player. The *music player* is the object that represents the actual music playback system. By telling the music player to play one or many media items, you make sound come out of the speakers.

Importing the framework

To work with the iPod, your application needs to import another framework: *MediaPlayer.* This framework contains the classes and information your application needs to talk to the iPod.

Import the MediaPlayer framework by right-clicking the Frameworks folder in Xcode and choosing Add➪Existing Frameworks from the menu that appears. (You've added frameworks before — check out Chapters 14, 15, and 18 for examples!)

Adding the user interface

To control the built-in iPod music player, we show you how to let the user pick his soundtrack from the pause screen. To do this, add a button that presents a media picker controller, which lets the user select the music he wants to hear. When the user dismisses the picker, the tracks he's selected start playing.

In general, do four things to enable all this:

1. Add a button to the pause view and attach it to a new IBAction method.

   This method needs to create and display a new MPMediaPickerController.

2. Make the TrafficViewController conform to the MPMediaPicker ControllerDelegate protocol.

   This makes your view controller able to respond to events that come from the media picker controller.

3. Add a method that is called when the user cancels the media picker controller, without doing anything.

   This method needs to get rid of the media picker controller, allowing the user to get back to the game.

4. Add the method that gets called when the user picks a few tracks and taps the Done button.

   This method needs to tell the iPod music player to play the songs that the user's selected; it also needs to make the media picker controller go away so that the user can keep playing.

Time to get started:

1. **Import <MediaPlayer/MediaPlayer.h> at the top of TrafficView Controller.h.**

2. **Update the TrafficViewController class to make the class conform to the MPMediaPickerControllerDelegate protocol, by changing the line in TrafficViewController.h that declares the class so that it looks like the following code (the new code is in bold):**

   ```
   @interface TrafficViewController :
           UIViewController <FBRequestDelegate,
           MPMediaPickerControllerDelegate> {
   ```

3. **Add the following line of code to TrafficViewController.h, just before the @end line to add the new IBAction method:**

   ```
   - (IBAction) displayMediaPicker:(id)sender;
   ```

   This method is called when the user taps the button you add in the following step.

4. **To add the Pick Music button to the pause view:**

   a. *Open TrafficViewController.xib in Interface Builder and then open the pause view.*

   b. *Drag in a new UIButton into the paused view, and label the button Pick Music.*

   c. *Hold down the Control key and drag from the button to the Traffic Controller; select the* `displayMediaPicker:` *action that appears in the list.*

5. **Add the code that displays the media picker to TrafficView Controller.m:**

```
- (IBAction) displayMediaPicker:(id)sender {
  MPMediaPickerController* picker =
        [[MPMediaPickerController alloc] init];
  picker.delegate = self;
  picker.allowsPickingMultipleItems = YES;
  [self presentModalViewController:picker
        animated:YES];
  [picker release];
}
```

This code creates and prepares an MPMediaPickerController and sets its delegate to the current object. This way the Traffic View Controller receives messages from the media picker when interesting things happen, like when the user chooses music or dismisses the picker.

The code then makes the media picker controller appear *modally* — the view controller takes up the entire screen.

The media picker is then released, and you don't need to refer to it later. The media picker is retained by the system when you present it to the user.

6. **Add the code that handles the media picker being canceled to TrafficViewController.h:**

```
- (void) mediaPickerDidCancel:(MPMediaPickerController
        *)mediaPicker {
  [self dismissModalViewControllerAnimated:YES];
}
```

This code runs when the user taps the Cancel button on the media picker. The code gets rid of the media picker, letting the player get back to the game.

7. **Add the code that plays sweet, sweet music for the player, in TrafficViewController.m:**

```
- (void) mediaPicker:(MPMediaPickerController *)
        mediaPicker
  didPickMediaItems:(MPMediaItemCollection *)
        mediaItemCollection {

  MPMusicPlayerController* iPod =
        [MPMusicPlayerController iPodMusicPlayer];
  [iPod setQueueWithItemCollection:mediaItemCollect
        ion];
  [iPod play];

  [self dismissModalViewControllerAnimated:YES];
}
```

This code runs when the user selects a bunch of tracks and taps the Done button. This code makes the music happen by instructing the iPod music player to play the tracks that the picker selected.

With that, you're done! When you pause the game, you can select tracks that you want to hear.

Detecting Shakes

Every iOS device comes equipped with a built-in accelerometer, which your game can work with to make your game react to the user's movement.

"What's an *accelerometer?*" you ask; it's a device that measures force. That's the textbook definition, anyway. So, how is an accelerometer useful for mobile devices? Well, when you think about it, gravity is a force that acts on every object on the planet, pulling things toward the center of the earth. An accelerometer can detect that force and can also detect the direction that the force affects it from.

This means that the accelerometer can figure out which way is up and which way is down. This is used in iOS to allow applications to rotate between portrait and landscape modes — when you turn the device on the side, the accelerometer notices that the direction of gravity has suddenly changed. iOS can then figure out how the device is held and then tell the currently running application to adjust accordingly.

Gravity isn't the only force that acts upon an accelerometer, though. When you pick up your device, you apply a force to it. When you shake the device, you also apply forces to it. When you throw the device out of a window and watch it fall seven stories until it smashes onto the ground, these are also forces. (iOS might have trouble working with the last example, though your device will valiantly record the acceleration until the impact.)

Shake events can be detected when the accelerometer notices that forces move from one extreme to another very quickly. Pick up your iPhone and shake it — keep an eye on how you can feel it moving in your hand and imagine what those forces must feel like inside the device.

Shaking gestures are a lot of fun, and we take a look at them in a bit more detail.

Detecting shake events

Shaking gestures are used a bit less frequently than gravity-based gestures, but they have their place. One use of a shake gesture is in the Cocoa Touch text system. If you open a text-editing program, such as the built-in Notes application, type something, and then shake the device, your iPhone asks whether you want to undo the last thing you did.

Shake gestures are also useful in games. These uses vary depending on the kind of game you make — you might use the shaking gesture to trigger sending your ship into hyperspace in an asteroid-dodging space game, or you might use it to clear the entire screen of rocks.

Some devices are easier to shake than others. The iPhone and iPod touch are pretty small and light, but the iPad is rather large and heavy. Shake gestures are still possible when using the iPad, but they require more effort.

Clearing the screen

For the *Traffic* game, implement some code that makes the game clear the entire board of cars when the user shakes the screen.

This requires doing two things:

- ✔ Detecting that the user has shaken the device
- ✔ Removing all the cars when this happens

To quickly and easily detect a shaking gesture, you can implement the `motionBegan:withEvent:` method in any of your UIView classes. This method is called when the iPhone receives a *motion event,* which right now is a shaking gesture. Later versions of the OS may include different kinds of motion gestures, but for now, there's only one.

In addition to `motionBegan:withEvent:`, there's also `motionCancelled:withEvent:` and `motionEnded:withEvent:`. A motion can be canceled for the same reasons as a touch can be — the application could be interrupted, or the view controller went away. Motions end when, well, the device stops moving. These methods don't get called for every separate shake, but rather they get called when shaking starts and when shaking stops.

`motionCancelled:withEvent:` is spelled with two Ls, not one.

The final thing to be aware of is that motion events are sent only to one object — a view that's displayed onscreen, which is also the first responder. The *first responder* is the view that first receives input events from the user. There's only one first responder at any time, and your view needs to explicitly request to become the first responder.

To do this, you need to do two things: Call the `[self becomeFirst Responder]` method and then implement the canBecomeFirstResponder method, which needs to return YES (to indicate that your view can become the first responder).

You adapt the OpenGLTrafficView to detect this shaking, because it's a nice, large background view that you've already written code for (in Chapters 22, 23, and 24), so you can just add the extra stuff you need.

You need to make the OpenGLTrafficView aware of the TrafficController so it can make the game get rid of all the cars. Next, you need to add the code that responds to a shake gesture, which informs the TrafficController to get rid of all the cars onscreen. Finally, you need to add the method that makes the TrafficController class remove every car from the screen. To add this shaking behavior, follow these steps:

1. **Add the `gameController` instance variable and outlet to the OpenGLTrafficView class by modifying OpenGLTrafficView.h so that that it looks like the following code:**

```
#import <UIKit/UIKit.h>
#import <OpenGLES/ES2/gl.h>
#import <OpenGLES/ES2/glext.h>
#import <QuartzCore/QuartzCore.h>
#import <CoreGraphics/CoreGraphics.h>

@class TrafficController;

@interface OpenGLTrafficView : UIView {
  EAGLContext* context; // the OpenGL drawing context
        for the game
  GLuint framebuffer; // the frame buffer that we do
        all drawing into
  GLuint colorRenderBuffer; // the render buffer
        that's displayed on screen
  GLuint depthBuffer; // the depth buffer, used for
        internal distance calculations

  GLuint shaderProgram; // the shader program, used
        for positioning and shading the objects

  GLuint backgroundTexture;

  CADisplayLink* displayLink;

  TrafficController* gameController;
}

@property (nonatomic, retain) IBOutlet
        TrafficController* gameController;

@end
```

2. Synthesize the `gameController` property by adding the following line of code to OpenGLTrafficView.m, just below the `@implementation` line:

```
@synthesize gameController;
```

3. Open TrafficViewController.xib in Interface Builder and then connect the `gameController` outlet in the OpenGLTrafficView to the Traffic Controller object.

For a refresher on how to connect objects to outlets, visit Chapter 6.

4. Make the OpenGLTrafficView become the first responder by updating the `awakeFromNib` method in OpenGLTrafficView.m so that it looks like the following code:

```
- (void) awakeFromNib {
  [self prepareOpenGL];

  displayLink = [CADisplayLink
      displayLinkWithTarget:self selector:@
      selector(render:)];
  [displayLink addToRunLoop:[NSRunLoop mainRunLoop]
      forMode:NSRunLoopCommonModes];
  [displayLink setFrameInterval:2];

  [self becomeFirstResponder];
}
```

This code makes the class call becomeFirstResponder when it starts; additionally, it overrides the canBecomeFirstResponder method and makes it return YES.

5. Add the following method to OpenGLTrafficView.m:

```
- (BOOL) canBecomeFirstResponder {
  return YES;
}
```

6. Make the class respond to motion events by adding the following method to OpenGLTrafficView.m:

```
- (void) motionBegan:(UIEventSubtype)motion
      withEvent:(UIEvent *)event {
  [gameController removeAllCars];
}
```

This tells the gameController variable to remove all the cars, and the Traffic Controller object sends the removeAllCars message whenever the user shakes the device.

Shaking a simulated iPhone is a little hard, because you can't really shake a picture on your screen. To send a shake gesture to the Simulator, choose Hardware⇨Shake Gesture. If you access the accelerometer force information directly (which you can find out how to do by looking at the documentation for UIAccelerometer), you don't see any changes — the shake gesture calls only the motionBegan method.

To make the TrafficController class remove all cars from the screen:

1. **Add the removeAllCars method declaration to TrafficController.h just before the @end line:**

   ```
   - (void) removeAllCars;
   ```

2. **Add the removeAllCars method to TrafficController.m**

   ```
   - (void) removeAllCars {
     for (Vehicle* v in vehicles) {
       [v removeFromSuperview];
     }

     [vehicles removeAllObjects];
   }
   ```

   This code takes every car currently managed by the Traffic Controller and removes it from the game board. The code then empties the list of cars, which means that they're effectively removed from the game entirely.

With that, you're done. Run the game and shake your iPad. *Presto:* Every car onscreen disappears!

Part V
The Part of Tens

The 5th Wave   By Rich Tennant

In this part . . .

In this final part, we give you some insight into the biggest key differences between building games for iPad versus building them for iPhone and share our marketing tips.

Finally, because everyone needs to stop and play some games sometimes, we share our top ten iPhone and iPad games — don't forget to play other people's games! Here's a breakdown of each chapter:

- ✔ Chapter 26 gives you the top ten key differences between building iPhone and iPad games.

- ✔ Chapter 27 shows you the ten marketing tips for making your game a success in the App Store.

- ✔ Chapter 28 finishes things off with a bang by surveying the top ten (in our opinion) games available for iPhone and iPad.

Chapter 26

Ten Differences between the iPhone and the iPad

*1*f we hadn't already driven the point home in earlier chapters, now's the time to really take the fist of knowledge and drive it firmly into your skull: Here we cover ten key differences between game design for the iPad and game design for the iPhone.

Ready? Don't worry — the fist of knowledge is merciful and kind to those whom it embraces; it's also wrapped in Bubble Wrap.

The iPad Is Social

The iPad is a giant slab and is completely at home resting on a table; it's not pocket-sized, and you can't hold it comfortably in one hand while you play a game on it. Play to the strengths when you design your games.

As a shareable computer, the iPad positively screams for group games where people sit around the thing, poking at it with their grubby paws. Got it? The iPad is like a board game; it's something lots of people can use and enjoy.

The iPhone Is Personal

On the other hand, the iPhone is a single-person device like a book or an old-fashioned handheld game. (Back in your box, Nintendo, nobody loves you now!) Games on the iPhone are either single-player or social via the Internet, Bluetooth, or Wi-Fi — multiple people don't sit around an iPhone poking at it with childlike glee. Instead, someone holds it tightly and becomes engrossed in her own little world while she sits on the bus and fights aliens in the palm of her hand.

The iPad Offers More Direct Control

Because of the huge touch screen and the capability to detect up to 11 individual touch points, the iPad is significantly more suitable for games where the player touches and interacts directly with a variety of things (or multiple players, as the case may be) in the game world.

Play to the strengths and the screen space, and give the user the ability to manipulate stuff directly in your iPad games — people love it.

You Can Play the iPad Really Loud

Just as we suggest playing to the iPad's strengths with your game design and making your games playable by a group of people clustered around a single iPad, play to its audio strengths as well — the iPad has louder speakers, and if multiple people are playing, it's unlikely to be used with headphones.

Your game's sound should be correspondingly designed first and foremost to be played through the built-in speakers and while the device sits in a loud, distraction-filled room. Perfectly tuned sound might be missed in a loud room that's filled with lots of people — remember this.

iPhone Users Often Wear Headphones

Just as the iPad might be the center of attention in a group setting, the iPhone is likely to be used in a situation where the user is wearing headphones — in this case, your sound should be personal, designed not to be annoying, and should take advantage of stereo.

If you let the user listen to his own music while he plays your game, make sure your game's sound effects don't drown out the music (while at the same time making sure that they're discernable from the background noise — both background noise from the user's own music library, and from the real world they're holding their iPhone in).

Games Can't Always Be Easily Scaled from iPad to iPhone

What more can we say? When translating a game from the iPhone to iPad, or from the iPad to iPhone, your first instinct — which for most people is just scaling the whole thing up or down — isn't necessarily the right one.

Even if you've designed the most amazing iPhone game in the world, go back to the prototyping (yes, get out the paper again — see Chapter 1!), to make sure that what you plan to do works on the large screen before you transition the game to the iPad.

Users Expect More from an iPad Game

Because iPad apps have settled on a somewhat higher price point when compared to their iPhone brethren, people often expect (rightly or not) that a game they get on the iPad is bigger or better in some way.

How you approach this is up to you — just remember that an iPad translates to bigger in your users' minds, and your game play needs to take that into account — as well as your graphics; see the OpenGL chapters (see Chapters 22, 23, and 24) for some hints on taking your graphics to the next level).

The iPhone Is Used in High-Distraction Environments

Just as we say in Chapter 1, the iPhone is likely to be used in a very distracting environment, which means your games should be simple to grasp and simple to play, with appealing and well-themed graphics.

When you build a single-player game for the iPad, on the other hand, you can often safely make the assumption that there's less distraction — if she sits to use her iPad, she's likely to be somewhere comfortable instead of standing at a bus stop.

Take advantage of this and tax your player's brain a little more in your single-player iPad games.

Users Spend More Time Playing iPad Games

Just like with brainpower, if your players use their iPad, they probably have a little more time on their hands, too. In addition to taxing their brainpower a little more, you can design your games to take up a little more of their time.

If you're porting a game from iPhone to iPad, you might want to change your game play so that the average play time moves from 30 to 60 seconds, to 3 to 5 minutes — of course, don't do this with arbitrary delays! You have to be clever.

The iPhone Is Highly Portable and Moveable

The iPhone is small and easy to wave around — so although the iPad has most of the same movement sensors as the iPhone, because the iPad is quite a bit bulkier and heavier, your players are less likely to want to wave it around in the air like they just don't care.

If you want to use the accelerometer or the compass, make sure you remember the context and physical characteristics of each device when designing your game play and deciding what to expect of your users.

Chapter 27

Ten Ways to Market Your Game

In This Chapter

▶ Making the most of social media

▶ Giving away your game and getting it reviewed

▶ Marketing via a press kit, App Store reviews, and a Web site

▶ Using push notifications and In App Purchase

▶ Watching your sales and using analytics

*I*f you've followed along so far, you've made a lot of progress in developing the game. Pat yourself on the back, grab a ridiculously colorful drink, and take a seat in a comfortable chair — it's time to think about getting the most out of the wonderful game that you've made.

This chapter covers the final pieces of the iPhone and iPad game development puzzle. Everything in this chapter should be read with the mantra so gleefully espoused by one of your witty authors, Neal, in mind: "It's not over until the last user is dead." We talk about building a community around your game, hooking your game into the pulse of social networks such as Facebook or Twitter, and the potential of additional technologies, such as push notifications and In App Purchase, to further build the community, and therefore sales, of your game.

We also take a step out of the geek world into advertising and media as well as the potential for purchasing advertising for your game, sending press kits to review sites, and making friends who help you to get the word out.

Read on for the top ten ways to get word of your game out to the world and to build a community around the thing you've worked so hard and for so long on.

FriendTube, Tweetfeed, YouFace: Engage with Social Media

As an iOS game developer, one of the easiest and most painless ways you can get your name out there is to join social networking sites like Twitter and Facebook. Take a look at Figure 27-1, where we show a snippet of the Twitter feed of Firemint, the successful developers of *Flight Control* who we mentioned in earlier chapters. What do you see?

You can also turn to video distribution sites, such as Vimeo and YouTube, to share game play videos of your games with the world. Lots of video views often translate to strong sales.

Figure 27-1: Firemint's Twitter feed.

Here's a clue: You see a highly engaged game developer who's honestly and enthusiastically engaging with fans via this social networking site.

Why do we show you this? Because you should do it, too. "Talk to your users and potential users" may sound simple, it may even sound stupid, but it's quite simply the easiest way to generate long-term fans, repeat customers, and users who spread your game far and wide (and generate new sales by recommending it to their friends!)

In short: Engage with your users, talk to them, tell them you'll consider their suggestions and, above all, be chatty and cheerful to them online. Oh, and be present on at the very minimum both Facebook and Twitter.

Give Away Your Game

A wise man (Wil Shipley, founder of Omni Group and Delicious Monster, actually) once said something along the lines of, if anyone asks for a free copy of your software, give it to them.

Use your promo codes. Don't be afraid to give away your game to those who ask for it — you never know who they are, what connections they have, or who they'll tell.

Don't be tempted to think about the times you give the game away as lost sales — they rarely ever are.

Get Your Game Reviewed

Befriending a few iPhone and iPad game review sites prior to the launch of your game is a great way to get extra eyeballs on your game and is an effective way to build community anticipation.

If you send a test build (see Chapter 13 to read how to perform ad hoc builds of your game) exclusively to a site or two, not only will they like you for providing them with a unique piece of content to talk about, but you'll get people reading about your game before it's out (and the anticipation that comes with it).

The top review site is `http://www.toucharcade.com`.

Create a Press Kit

Build a press kit for your game. Always, always, *always* build a press kit!

What's a press kit? Pretty simple — a *press kit* is a collection of the best screenshots and videos from your game, bundled together with a succinct, yet punchy, description of the game with anything you feel represents your game.

Why make one? Journalists and tech reviewers are busy people, and the easier you make it for them to gather the essential facts and media to write about your game with, the more likely they are to do it.

Use Push Notifications

We don't cover using Apple's Push Notification Service in much detail in this book, because it's not a core facet of game development. However, with the knowledge you gain from this book, you know everything you need to on a fundamental level to leverage the power of Push!

How? You can use push notifications to let your players know that new levels are available to download, or to notify them that one of their friends has challenged them or defeated one of their high scores — the possibilities are endless. A push notification is like an SMS text message sent to all individuals with your game installed. And they all end with someone launching your game again, which increases the chances they'll talk about it to their friends. Good stuff!

To find out more about how you can implement push notifications in your game, look up the *Local and Push Notification Programming Guide,* which comes with the developer documentation. You can find it online at

```
http://developer.apple.com/iphone/library/
        documentation/NetworkingInternet/Conceptual/
        RemoteNotificationsPG/Introduction/
        Introduction.html
```

Offer In App Purchase

Push notifications are a good way to inspire your players to purchase things within your game. In App Purchase can be a quick way to give your fans an extra hit of your brilliant game while at the same time generating a nice boost to your wallet.

Want to build some extra levels but don't feel like they quite fit in your shipping game, or feel like the game is already big enough? Add them as an In App Purchase and get some extra dough!

In App Purchase allows you to lock away pieces of your game behind a pay-wall, prompting the user to purchase those pieces using their standard iTunes credentials without leaving the game. It's really very clever!

For more information, look up the *In App Purchase Programming Guide,* which comes with the developer documentation. You can find it online at

```
http://developer.apple.com/iphone/library/documentation/
        NetworkingInternet/Conceptual/StoreKitGuide/
        Introduction/Introduction.html
```

Solicit iTunes App Store Reviews

A lack of reviews altogether can sink a game just as badly as no reviews at all. To avoid a lack of reviews, put a prompt that links to the iTunes App Store in your game, and make it appear only once after your game has been launched three or four times. This way, you can remind people to review your game.

Don't ask for positive reviews because you might incite negative ones — just suggest that they might like to review the game and let others know what they think. This is a foolproof way to get feedback and build a bit of community around your product.

Watch Your Sales Closely

Watching your sales closely may sound simple, but it's something that many people forget to do. If you launch your game at one price point, unless you keep a close eye on your sales, you won't know how effective that price point is. Watching your sales like a hawk lets you rapidly respond to the market, and raise or lower the price as appropriate (or even make the game free for a short time!)

Use Analytics

We don't cover analytics in this book because it's a fairly large amount of work to do, but if you find yourself with a hit on your hands, instrumenting your game to find out how people play it can be a big help. Instrumenting refers to collecting data on how people play and interact with your game for analytics purposes.

Prominent iPhone game developer ngmoco has all their games log player interactions (anonymously) to their server — ngmoco can even change the game play variables without updating its game via Apple. (Remember Sid Meier's rule of halves from Chapter 1? ngmoco can put it into action remotely!)

Getting a clear idea on what your users are doing, and rewarding new behaviors or changing game play to encourage behavior you want to see can make your game feel more alive, not to mention allow it to cater to the gamers' wants more effectively.

Flurry is a popular analytics platform, and you can find more information on it at their website: `http://www.flurry.com/index.html`.

Make Your Web Site Awesome

Making a unique site for your game is crucial. The Web site should ideally be a completely separate site to the rest of your business and should immediately tell visitors

- ✔ Why your game is awesome and how it works
- ✔ Where they can get your game (linking prominently to the iTunes App Store)
- ✔ How much your game costs

Don't harass your visitors by marketing too much at them — if they're on your Web site, they want to know more about your game already. You don't need to convince them of that at this point. Give them the facts.

Chapter 28

Ten Insanely Great Games

*A*s we suggest in Chapter 1, one of the best ways to really figure out how to develop great games for the iPhone and the iPad is to play other people's games. The only problem with this is that although exploring games and playing them is fun, it only shows you what someone else did; however, it doesn't necessarily give you the architectural and game design understanding of *what* they did and *why* they did it that you need to build your insanely great games.

If you've followed along in this book, you know enough to take real advantage of studying other games. By all means, look at these games and use them as jumping-off points to come up with your own unique game ideas. iPhone and iPad games usually have simple mechanics and a strong, well-executed theme. Remember this when you play other games and take notes on how you can improve you own games with this knowledge.

Here are the ten iPad and iPhone games that we like the best. You can find all these for sale in the iTunes App Store.

Canabalt

Canabalt is one of those rare games that can get by with only one user-interaction point. You play this game by tapping anywhere on the screen, which causes the player controller object — a running man, in this case — to jump. You owe it to yourself to play this game — it's an exercise in minimalism and cleverness.

See if you can figure out the plot. Now, go and try your daring escape.

Flight Control

Flight Control is the quintessential line-drawing game for iOS. Prototyped on a weekend by one person, this game is loved by many. *Flight Control* is a masterful example of the ability of an effective theme — in this case, the golden age of flying — to carry a game to the next level.

Pay attention to the music and visual style — it really brings things up a notch from, when you think about it, what is really a basic set of game play features.

Plants vs. Zombies

Much has been written about *Plants vs. Zombies,* one of the most popular Mac and PC games, and accordingly, one of the most popular iPhone and iPad games (when it finally appeared!).

A wicked sense of humor, fantastic art, and a great collection game mechanic with entertaining and impressively visualized plants (plus awesome game play) makes this one a game to ponder deeply.

Ramp Champ

Ramp Champ, a new twist on classic arcade games like Skee-Ball and pinball, could be called *Style over Substance* — if the game play wasn't so much fun, that is!

Check out the clever (not to mention highly effective) use of In App Purchase, collection elements (trophies and objects you can buy), and lavish graphics, sounds, and music (some of which is done by the fabulously talented David Weiner of Atomicon, who supplied the music and sound you can download to build *Traffic* with).

DoodleJump

You've probably already heard of, if not played, *DoodleJump.* We wouldn't do the iPhone gaming world justice if we didn't include it though.

The original and the best sketchbook-themed jumping game, this stylish and funny game deserves your attention because it shows how you can rise to the top of the charts, and people's hearts, by taking a simple concept and running with it. The game even has Christmas and other holiday themes!

Frenzic

Frenzic is a perfectly designed puzzle game, created specifically for the iPhone from the ground up. Simple mechanics (it's just a collection of pie charts) and simple graphics (it's just a few simple colors) — it's a perfect execution of game play, graphics, and audio.

If puzzle games are your thing, check out this one for an example of how to make it addictive and simple.

Pocket God

Is *Pocket God* actually a game? We leave that one up to you!

Giving you full control over a colorful sandbox, with amusing little characters, scary sharks, dinosaurs, and natural events may not sound like a game, but it's one of the most entertaining experiences on an iPhone.

Take a look if you want to build a game that doesn't fit any of the traditional categories, but keeps gamers coming back time and time again. Great use of updates to keep the game fresh and add content, and a clever use of icon changes to keep people launching it over and over again after each update.

Words With Friends

Take a time-tested board game concept, make it highly social, and fit it in with the iPhone usage patterns of regular people, and you have *Words With Friends*. Take out your iPhone at a bus stop, play a word against your girlfriend, and put it back in your pocket — play the game at your pace.

Unique, clean style, and highly social — the very elements of a great game.

Chopper (and Chopper 2)

Interesting, exciting, clean, and clever graphics and helicopters! What more could you want? *Chopper* and its sequel, *Chopper 2,* offer multiple ways of controlling the game, precise and perfect sound effects, and a great mission-based structure that still allows for some free-form game play.

The latest *Chopper 2* even lets you fly your chopper using your iPhone as a remote control for your iPad!

Check this one out for an action game that doesn't feel like an action game!

Tap Tap Radiation

Disney acquired the developer behind *Tap Tap Radiation* for good reason — Tapulous, the developer, is darn clever, as are all of Tapulous's games.

Part game (and a good one at that) and part marketing machine, this iPad rhythm game has you tapping and singing (the singing isn't part of the game, we might add) while you complete successively more difficult challenges based on the rhythm of music. A great example of a game that lets you explore new media (in this, helping you discover new music) while being bright and colorful, and at the core, having really simple and fun game play.

Index

• C •

• 𝒟 •

• E •

& Macs

For Dummies
0-470-58027-1

e For Dummies,
dition
0-470-87870-5

ook For Dummies, 3rd
n
0-470-76918-8

OS X Snow Leopard For
mies
0-470-43543-4

ess

keeping For Dummies
-7645-9848-7

terviews
ummies,
dition
0-470-17748-8

nes For Dummies,
dition
0-470-08037-5

ng an
e Business
ummies,
dition
-470-60210-2

Investing
ummies,
dition
-470-40114-9

ssful
Management
ummies
-470-29034-7

Computer Hardware

BlackBerry
For Dummies,
4th Edition
978-0-470-60700-8

Computers For Seniors
For Dummies,
2nd Edition
978-0-470-53483-0

PCs For Dummies,
Windows
7 Edition
978-0-470-46542-4

Laptops For Dummies,
4th Edition
978-0-470-57829-2

Cooking & Entertaining

Cooking Basics
For Dummies,
3rd Edition
978-0-7645-7206-7

Wine For Dummies,
4th Edition
978-0-470-04579-4

Diet & Nutrition

Dieting For Dummies,
2nd Edition
978-0-7645-4149-0

Nutrition For Dummies,
4th Edition
978-0-471-79868-2

Weight Training
For Dummies,
3rd Edition
978-0-471-76845-6

Digital Photography

Digital SLR Cameras &
Photography For Dummies,
3rd Edition
978-0-470-46606-3

Photoshop Elements 8
For Dummies
978-0-470-52967-6

Gardening

Gardening Basics
For Dummies
978-0-470-03749-2

Organic Gardening
For Dummies,
2nd Edition
978-0-470-43067-5

Green/Sustainable

Raising Chickens
For Dummies
978-0-470-46544-8

Green Cleaning
For Dummies
978-0-470-39106-8

Health

Diabetes For Dummies,
3rd Edition
978-0-470-27086-8

Food Allergies
For Dummies
978-0-470-09584-3

Living Gluten-Free
For Dummies,
2nd Edition
978-0-470-58589-4

Hobbies/General

Chess For Dummies,
2nd Edition
978-0-7645-8404-6

Drawing
Cartoons & Comics
For Dummies
978-0-470-42683-8

Knitting For Dummies,
2nd Edition
978-0-470-28747-7

Organizing
For Dummies
978-0-7645-5300-4

Su Doku For Dummies
978-0-470-01892-7

Home Improvement

Home Maintenance
For Dummies,
2nd Edition
978-0-470-43063-7

Home Theater
For Dummies,
3rd Edition
978-0-470-41189-6

Living the
Country Lifestyle
All-in-One
For Dummies
978-0-470-43061-3

Solar Power Your Home
For Dummies,
2nd Edition
978-0-470-59678-4

Internet

Blogging For Dummies,
3rd Edition
978-0-470-61996-4

eBay For Dummies,
6th Edition
978-0-470-49741-8

Facebook For Dummies,
3rd Edition
978-0-470-87804-0

Web Marketing
For Dummies,
2nd Edition
978-0-470-37181-7

WordPress
For Dummies,
3rd Edition
978-0-470-59274-8

Language & Foreign Language

French For Dummies
978-0-7645-5193-2

Italian Phrases
For Dummies
978-0-7645-7203-6

Spanish For Dummies,
2nd Edition
978-0-470-87855-2

Spanish
For Dummies,
Audio Set
978-0-470-09585-0

Math & Science

Algebra I
For Dummies,
2nd Edition
978-0-470-55964-2

Biology For Dummies,
2nd Edition
978-0-470-59875-7

Calculus For Dummies
978-0-7645-2498-1

Chemistry For Dummies
978-0-7645-5430-8

Microsoft Office

Excel 2010 For Dummies
978-0-470-48953-6

Office 2010 All-in-One
For Dummies
978-0-470-49748-7

Office 2010 For Dummies,
Book + DVD Bundle
978-0-470-62698-6

Word 2010 For Dummies
978-0-470-48772-3

Music

Guitar For Dummies,
2nd Edition
978-0-7645-9904-0

iPod & iTunes For
Dummies, 8th Edition
978-0-470-87871-2

Piano Exercises
For Dummies
978-0-470-38765-8

Parenting & Education

Parenting For Dummies,
2nd Edition
978-0-7645-5418-6

Type 1 Diabetes
For Dummies
978-0-470-17811-9

Pets

Cats For Dummies,
2nd Edition
978-0-7645-5275-5

Dog Training For Dummies,
3rd Edition
978-0-470-60029-0

Puppies For Dummies,
2nd Edition
978-0-470-03717-1

Religion & Inspiration

The Bible For Dummies
978-0-7645-5296-0

Catholicism For Dummies
978-0-7645-5391-2

Women in the Bible
For Dummies
978-0-7645-8475-6

Self-Help & Relationship

Anger Management
For Dummies
978-0-470-03715-7

Overcoming Anxiety
For Dummies,
2nd Edition
978-0-470-57441-6

Sports

Baseball
For Dummies,
3rd Edition
978-0-7645-7537-2

Basketball
For Dummies,
2nd Edition
978-0-7645-5248-9

Golf For Dummies,
3rd Edition
978-0-471-76871-5

Web Development

Web Design
All-in-One
For Dummies
978-0-470-41796-6

Web Sites
Do-It-Yourself
For Dummies,
2nd Edition
978-0-470-56520-9

Windows 7

Windows 7
For Dummies
978-0-470-49743-2

Windows 7
For Dummies,
Book + DVD Bundle
978-0-470-52398-8

Windows 7 All-in-One
For Dummies
978-0-470-48763-1

San Mateo
Public Library